The Literature of the Middle Ages

The
Literature of the
Middle Ages

W. T. H. JACKSON

Columbia University Press

New York

Copyright © 1960 Columbia University Press

ISBN 0-231-02429-0   (cloth)
ISBN 0-231-05935-3   (paper)
Library of Congress Catalog Card Number: 60-13153

Manufactured in the United States of America

For Erika

zwei leben diu enwurden nie
alsus gemischet under ein

Preface

The purpose of this book is explained in the introduction. Like
most authors, I believe it fulfills a need—by providing the information necessary to read medieval literature with pleasure
and understanding. A book organized as this one is must necessarily reflect the personal tastes of its writer, and I must therefore apologize to those who may feel that I have overemphasized
the importance of one work or author and minimized others. I
have concentrated on major works and have not attempted a
history of literature. For reference, however, a chronological
list of works and authors, where known, has been provided. It
does not profess to be complete. The bibliographical material is
substantial and offers the means to study medieval literature in
considerable detail. My debts to previous scholars in the field
are too great to enumerate. I do not stand on the shoulders of
giants but merely hold their hands. The only originality which
this book can claim lies in some of the opinions and evaluations
expressed and in its organization. Many of the opinions I may
well owe to colleagues at Columbia University and elsewhere and
to students in my seminars. To these and especially to Professors
Maurice J. Valency and B. Hunningher, who read some parts of
the book, my sincere thanks. I am grateful also to the libraries
whose facilities I have used, to the Guggenheim Foundation and

the American Council of Learned Societies, whose generosity helped to provide free time for writing, and particularly to the officers and editorial staff of Columbia University Press, who advised without insisting and were virtually always right.

W. T. H. JACKSON

August, 1960

It was the author's intention to revise this work before its paperback publication; we regret that Professor Jackson was unable to undertake this task before his death in 1983. LITERATURE OF THE MIDDLE AGES is being reprinted as it first appeared, in the belief that it remains a valuable guide for students of the period.

Contents

Abbreviations

DVLG   Deutsche Vierteljahrsschrift für Literaturwissenschaft und Geistesgeschichte

EETS   Publications of the Early English Text Society (all series)

PBB   Beiträge zur Geschichte der deutschen Sprache und Literatur (Paul/Braune Beiträge)

PL   Migne, Patrologiae latinae cursus completus

PMLA   Publications of the Modern Language Association of America

SATF   Société des anciens textes français.

Introduction

In popular speech the term "medieval" has a definitely pejorative sense. Any idea which the speaker considers old-fashioned (and hence bad), any method of work or habit of mind of which he disapproves may be dismissed as "medieval." Many writers who ought to know better think that the highest praise they can bestow upon a work written in the Middle Ages is to say that it is "almost modern" in thought and feeling. The popular usage reflects opinions about the period which are unfortunately still too widespread and which prove how thoroughly certain Renaissance humanists did their work. The Middle Ages are still treated as a kind of unfortunate interlude between the calm, clear light of classical antiquity and the scientific reasoning of the modern age.

It would be possible to make a good case for the thesis that the later Roman Empire had more in common with the Middle Ages than it had with Periclean Athens, and it is certainly true that the Middle Ages fade imperceptibly into "modern times" at differing periods in different parts of Europe. There are enormous differences in thought, social organization, and cultural level between the eighth and the twelfth centuries. Nevertheless the term "medieval" is sanctified by usage and there are certain features

which distinguish the period from those which came before and
after it.

One of these features has been perhaps the principal reason
for the sometimes excessive admiration with which various
groups, particularly the Romantics, viewed the Middle Ages.
The apparent unity of Christendom and the deep, simple Christian faith which accompanied it were the objects of uncritical
admiration. The unity was not so complete nor was the faith so
naive or so widespread as has often been supposed, but the
Church and its teachings did form the background of nearly all
activity. Our own age too, often described as frightened and in-
secure, has shown an increasing interest in medieval art, literature, and music.

Unfortunately, it is not easy to pursue this interest, at least
so far as literature is concerned. Medieval works are written
either in Latin or in an early form of one of the modern vernaculars. There are thus difficult linguistic problems to overcome before the reading of medieval literature can begin. To give only
one example, it is necessary to learn Old English to read *Beowulf*. It is doubtful whether any of the other, quite numerous,
works written in the language is of sufficient literary value to
justify learning a new language—but *Beowulf* is. The Old English in which it was written differs considerably from the normal-
ized West Saxon given in primers of the language, and many of
the words in the poem are found only once—in *Beowulf*. The
same might be said of several other languages.

Although English translations of some medieval works exist,
good ones are rare and, whenever possible, it is advisable to read
a work in the modern version of its own language. Translations
are mentioned in the notes to this book whenever they exist.

Similarly there are many obstacles in the way of an English
speaking reader who wishes to know something of medieval literature written in Europe. Chaucer and Dante have been well
treated and Middle English literature has naturally been carefully studied. For this reason the present book will say little on

these subjects. But the situation is quite otherwise with the literature of France and Germany. A concise history of French literature to 1300 is available. For Germany, however, there exist only the few pages in general (and utterly inadequate) histories of German literature and a thorough study of the Old High German period, whose interest is linguistic and cultural rather than literary.

The object of the present book is to attempt to lighten some of the difficulties which lie in the way of the literary study of the Middle Ages. It does not profess to bring the results of new research to the problem, nor does it profess to be a history of medieval European literature. Many literary works are ignored completely, many only mentioned in passing. The later Middle Ages receive very scanty treatment, and the concentration is upon the literature of the High Middle Ages, that is, the twelfth and thirteenth centuries. The reason for this is simple. It was during this period that the works of the greatest literary excellence were written and that literature was most characteristically medieval. Many readers will be surprised at the small representation of English and Italian literature. The same reason is valid. Little of genuine literary merit was written in England or Italy during the High Middle Ages. Dante is an author whom it would be an impertinence to treat in a book of this kind and Chaucer comes too late. For those who wish to study literature further, adequate information is given in the bibliographies. I have chosen to treat literary works by genres rather than by nationality or chronology. Only in this way is it possible to understand the interrelation between them and to understand how literature developed.

The Literature of the Middle Ages

I

The Survival and Influence of the Classics

The Middle Ages extended for a long time. It is necessary to stress this because it is easy to think of it as a period when thinking was static and when literature remained under the same influences. Whether we date their beginnings at the traditional 476 when the Empire of the West dissolved or, with Pirenne, with the beginning of Arab ascendancy in the East, the Middle Ages extend over a much longer period than "modern times," the period from the Renaissance to the present. The state of culture within this period varied enormously, nor was there a steady loss or gain in knowledge. At the beginning of the period the forms of classical education were still preserved in the West.[1] The schools of rhetoric still performed their functions, even though the education they offered was of form rather than substance. The great bulk of the classical authors, Greek and Latin, was still available, but was read less and less, and fewer people could read Greek. The manuscripts perished and the schools eroded under the influence of the new Germanic states, even though much of their influence remained in monastic teaching. Com-

[1] See the books by Laistner, Chadwick, and Sandys in the reading list of background material; also T. Haarhoff, *The Schools of Gaul: A Study of Pagan and Christian Education in the Last Century of the Western Empire* (1920).

pendium knowledge became normal, and only a very limited number of manuscripts was required—or available. The efforts of Charlemagne and his education minister Alcuin restored some of the prestige of learning in secular circles, but much of the gain was lost once more in the chaos which followed the breakup of Charlemagne's empire and the raids of the Norseman. The rise of stronger national governments and the improvement of communications provided the more settled conditions needed for intellectual revival in the eleventh century. Increased contact with areas outside Western Europe, particularly with the Arabs, gave the twelfth century a vastly improved cultural background, a background no longer the exclusive property of the clerics or those clerically educated. The secular courts of the nobility became the centers of literary activity. The newly discovered works of Aristotle gave the impetus to a great revival of ecclesiastical literature in the thirteenth century, at a time when the weakening of the powers of the nobility and their loss of wealth placed literary patronage rather in the hands of the wealthy bourgeois of the cities. The changes in the cultural background within the Middle Ages themselves were therefore considerable. A learned layman of the thirteenth century had immensely more material at his disposal than had been available to Alcuin or Bede. His attitude to literature was different. Nevertheless it is important to realize that certain influences on literary production were always present during the whole period, although in differing degrees and differing ways. Some of these influences we may now discuss.

The image of classical antiquity was always present in the mind of any writer of the Middle Ages. The language which he learned to read was Latin. The books he read were Latin books and their authors had, for the most part, lived in the Roman Empire, which remained the model of a stable political institution. He therefore found himself reading the authors of a civilization which was condemned as pagan by the Church Fathers whose works formed the basis of his morals and religious beliefs. There was thus a dichotomy in his attitude. Classical antiquity was the basis of his culture, but its works had to be read with circumspection, for it was a pagan civilization. The problem was solved in very different ways by different periods and different men. To the earlier generations of medieval writers the danger of a reversion to paganism was very real and the subtle influence of authors such as Ovid and Vergil was felt to be a very present danger to morals and religion. It is to these generations that the famous dream of St. Jerome clearly applies.[2] But to the twelfth-century writer such fears could hardly seem real. The church was established, and paganism, though rife in the world, was personified rather by the Mohammedans than by classical antiquity. The classics could be read like any other works. The only objections came from moralists who attacked the classics, as they attacked contemporary works, on the ground that they corrupted the spirit and led to sin.

Although it is certain that the classical authors formed the basis of all medieval education, we should be very careful in estimating the effects of this education. Mere references to classical authors and even quotations from them do not prove a first-hand acquaintance with the originals. Most reading in schools was done in anthologies, composed of a mixture of well-known classical authors in excerpt and fragments of later Christian writers.[3] The content of these anthologies varied considerably from one century to another and from one institution of learning to another, but from them we can gain some idea of the basic reading of an educated man. Fortunately we have more reliable guides for the twelfth century. Opinions about the validity of

[2] St. Jerome reports that he was transported to Heaven in a dream and that when he was asked what he was, he replied, "Christianus sum." "Non Christianus, sed Ciceronianus" came the reply, and the saint awoke black and blue from the beating he received.

[3] For a list see Manitius, I, 480. Few anthologies have been published and many of the manuscripts described as anthologies or *libri manuales* (e.g., Eva M. Sanford, "Classical Authors in the *Libri Manuales*," *Proceedings of the American Philological Association*, Vol. LV [1924]) are in fact whole works bound together. Relatively few *early* anthologies survive.

pagan literary works as studies for a Christian varied considerably and were discussed in works still extant: Hugh of St. Victor thought them marginal, if not useless; Bernardus Silvestris grants them a much higher place. In the cathedral school of Chartres more attention was paid to the classical authors than was the case anywhere else during our period. The study of the "auctores" to some extent displaced the formal discussions of the opinions of the Fathers upon points of religion and doctrine, and classical authors were regarded as good preparation for the "artes" or branches of philosophy. One of the greatest representatives of that school, John of Salisbury, secretary to Thomas à Becket, has left us in his works good evidence of the classical knowledge available to a learned man of the day.[4] The list of authors quoted and clearly well known is astonishingly large, and a modern classical scholar would probably be surprised at the number of books with which he was acquainted. Vergil, Ovid, Caesar, Quintilian, Statius, Seneca, Juvenal, Persius, for example, are known in their entirety, but the omissions are equally significant. Cicero's orations are hardly represented, Livy's *Histories* are unknown, Horace is represented by the *Satires* and *Epistles* but not the *Odes*. The stress is on the utilitarian rather than on the literary, and works in which style rather than content is important are absent. From the moral works of Cicero much edification could be gained; the *De Officiis,* for example, contained precepts which accorded entirely with Christian ideas of the virtuous life, but the speeches against Catiline and Antony seemed little more than empty words. Similarly the *Odes* of Horace, airy trifles in praise of theoretical sin, had little appeal compared with the popular moralization of the *Satires,* which the Middle Ages took a great deal more seriously than Horace ever did.

It is precisely here that we have to raise a question about the influence of classical antiquity. How did the medieval scholar

---

[4] See the *Policraticus,* ed. C. Webb, 2 vols. (1909). Library lists afford some guidance. See the books by Lehmann, Gottlieb, and Thompson on the medieval library listed in the reading list of background material.

read the classics? He conceived himself as in some ways their heir and continuator. He could read their language easily (although he learned it, as we do, artificially). But he had no power of placing the classics in context. His knowledge of the history of Greece and Rome, when it existed at all, was confused and inaccurate, and he had no way of imagining classical culture.[5] We should not blame him too much. The images of snow-white handsome Greeks and of Roman debauches in motion pictures are still with us. But this lack of historical context meant that he read the classics as he would documents of his own day. He ascribed to the persons who appeared in them the mentality of his contemporaries and he reinterpreted their statements in the light of Christian knowledge. The process was aided by the system of allegorical interpretation of the Bible which was normal procedure in the schools and of which more will be said later. Students trained in this system were accustomed to look for "higher" and "deeper" meanings behind the words which they read, and they therefore found it easy to read new and better meanings into the words of classical authors. Vergil was, of course, a great beneficiary from this process. The Messianic Eclogue early established him as virtually a Christian writer, his description of the Underworld as a person conversant with the secrets of the hereafter. His manuscripts received the same care from the scribes as did those of the sacred writings, and around his name there accumulated a mass of apocryphal material establishing him as the greatest of magicians.[6] His proclamation of the mission of the empire of Augustus was only half understood and his deep feeling for humanity and its tragedy passed almost unnoticed. But he *was* read, his language was echoed by numerous imitators, and occasionally he evoked a not altogether un-

---

[5] A glance at the historians used—Orosius, Fredegarius, Eusebius—will show how impossible a historical viewpoint was. The division of history into empires, the concept of *Heilsgeschichte,* and the Augustinian view in the *City of God* all added to the confusion.

[6] See Comparetti, *Virgilio nel medio evo,* and Spargo, *Virgil the Necromancer.*

worthy imitation. The great popularity of Ovid is also largely to be explained by reinterpretation. His stories of gods and heroes were in any case fascinating, but the idea of *Metamorphoses* accorded exactly with medieval taste. He could be, and was, allegorized and moralized into one of the most popular books of the Middle Ages, the Ovid *moralisé*.[7] These books can hardly be called classical but, again, they ensured that Ovid was read and his style and subject matter passed into the common stock of the writers of literature. Less easy to explain than this interest in the *Metamorphoses* is the enormous popularity of the *Ars Amatoria,* or *Art of Love.* This cynical, ironic study of the whole art of seduction should, by all normal standards, have been condemned outright and excluded from all reading lists. But there is good evidence that it was widely read and for the twelfth century, as we shall see, it established its author as the master lover and teacher of these who would excel in the art. Reinterpretation is again partly responsible for this popularity, but there is little doubt that the secularizing mentality of the twelfth century saw clearly enough what Ovid was doing and read him literally as a master lover, not perceiving, perhaps, the irony of his approach.

One of the basic reasons for reading the classics in the schools was, of course, to learn the Latin language. It was inevitable, therefore, that much of medieval literature should follow the classical forms. Epic is modeled closely upon Vergil, Claudian, and Statius, when written in Latin, and there is a vast amount of descriptive and elegiac poetry modeled upon Ausonius and the late classical authors. Lyric poetry in all periods, but especially in the Carolingian, continues to use the Sapphic and Alcaic ode forms, even though there was no feeling for quantity and the authors merely followed, as did a nineteenth-century schoolboy, the rules for versification given in the schoolbooks. Manuscripts

---

[7] Arnoul of Orléans, *Allegoriae fabularum Ovidii;* John of Garland, *Integumenta Ovidii;* F. Ghisalberti, "*L'Ovidus moralizatus* di Pierre Bersuire," *Studi romanzi,* Vol. XXIII (1933).

of Terence were read but not properly understood, and imitations of his dramas were rare. This imitation of classical forms also affected vernacular writing, but not to the same degree. Much more important for literature generally was the study of rules of writing and of literary commonplaces which is usually described by the rather misleading term "rhetoric."

Until recently the importance of the role of rhetorical studies in the development of medieval literature had received scant recognition from literary historians and not until the appearance of Curtius's book *European Literature and the Latin Middle Ages* in 1948 was its significance fully realized. The study of grammar, one of the three subjects of the *trivium* or elementary course, always involved the study of selected passages of literature and these followed a rhetorical tradition of imitation, which can be traced back to the Greek schools of rhetoric. Originally the intention of rhetorical studies in classical antiquity had been to prepare a man for public life, in politics or in the law. The main stress was upon the accurate presentation of a case, on facts and arguments, and the refutation of the opponent. But the desire to win over an audience led at an early stage to the search for verbal devices to impress the hearer and arouse attention and admiration. The Hellenistic rhetoricians already had an organized system of verbal figures and tropes. These were taken over by the Latin writers and are listed, with examples, in the *Ad Herennium,* the most popular treatise on rhetoric in the Middle Ages, which was universally ascribed to Cicero. Since virtually all education in Rome was education in rhetoric, the influence of the organized system of verbal tricks had an increasing impact upon literature. It is already marked in the work of Ovid and in the writers of the first century A.D., and in the later Empire it becomes the predominating influence. Writers outdo one another in the extravagance of their verbal gymnastics and incomprehensibility becomes the aim of literature—a not unfamiliar phenomenon in a period of decline. Quintilian's great work, the *Institutes of Oratory,* still shows the art at its best, and he was doubtless sincere when he repeated Cato's dictum that the ideal speaker was a good man skilled in speaking. But by his day the opportunities for oratory had been severely restricted. There was little point in training for political controversy when none existed. More and more stress was laid on the formal aspects of rhetoric and, in particular, on such exercises as the panegyric in praise of a ruler, a skill naturally much sought after when rulers were absolute and changed frequently. Here again the stress was on eloquence, language, verbal skill. Thus the oratorical tradition which was passed on to the Middle Ages was one in which the persuasive and argumentative elements of rhetoric had largely disappeared and the stress was on verbal ornament. For medieval writers this was probably a fortunate occurrence. There exist considerable collections of passages which are designed to illustrate not only the formal figures of rhetoric, such as antithesis, prolepsis, hyperbole, litotes, and paranomasia, but also almost every possible type of formal literary description—the perfect female beauty, the chaste matron, the noble king, the lovely city, the delights of spring. Such passages were often learned by heart and influenced both Latin and vernacular writing deeply. Their very existence tended to channel poetic works into particular forms, of which the best-known example is the opening of love poems with a stanza in praise of spring.[8] Needless to say, a skillful poet could and did vary these commonplace descriptions so that they appear fresh and original but lesser men used them *ad nauseam*. So deeply embedded were these literary examples that they became actually set subjects for poetry. Curtius gives to them the name "topos," avoiding the original *loci communes* or commonplaces because of the change in meaning which the term has undergone. These topoi appear over and over again in medieval literature, sometimes alone, constituting a single poem, sometimes in longer works. An obvious example is the topos of the world turned upside down, where everything

---

[8] See Faral, *Arts poétiques,* and Curtius, *European Literature and the Latin Middle Ages.*

follows an order precisely opposed to that of nature, or the topos of the degeneration of the world and the sharp contrast with the golden age which has passed. When these topoi appear, we can expect, generally, a similar treatment in each case. The description of a lady, for example, which occurs over and over again, invariably begins with the top of the lady's head and proceeds downwards. Eyes are discussed, the nose may be praised, but ears are never mentioned (they were hidden under the hair or cap, presumably). Such formal descriptions undoubtedly limited an author's expression, but for the vernaculars striving to become literary languages their usefulness was incalculable. In the twelfth and early thirteenth century they were incorporated in "Arts of Poetry," books formally dedicated to collections of examples illustrating the various types of writing. Examples of such works for vernacular poetry do not appear until the end of the thirteenth century but oral instruction on the same lines was undoubtedly given by and to the professional poets writing in the vernaculars. This "rhetorical training" was probably the greatest single identifiable influence on literature in the Middle Ages, but this does not mean that we can regard medieval literature as a series of topoi nor that we should be content to identify the topoi and regard this as literary criticism. The best writers remodeled them to their will, and in the great works of the period they are subservient to the genius of the writer.

The topoi and their treatment were not the only results of rhetorical training to affect literature. Classical theoreticians had recognized the desirability of using different styles for different types of writing. By the Middle Ages these distinctions of style had been classified in two different ways. The *ornatus facilis* (easy ornament) was a style designed primarily for narrative, and indicated that the ornament would be verbal only. The thought remained relatively simple. *Ornatus difficilis* (complicated ornament) involved a complete change in style. Thoughts were expressed in tropes or elaborate thought metaphors. From this distinction spring many of the stylistic variations found in vernacular writing—for example, the difference between *trobar plan,* or simple poetry, and *trobar clus,* esoteric poetry to be understood only by interpretation—which are found among the troubadours. The distinction continues throughout the Middle Ages and into the Renaissance.

The other rhetorical distinction of style is easier to understand but less significant for literature. It divides style into three groups—*tenuior* (for pleasure), *mediocris* (to teach), and *plenior* (to stir emotion). The meaning is obvious. Little more is indicated than adaptation of style to subject matter, with ornament becoming more complicated in the higher flights of style. Such divisions, however, did ensure that every author was conscious of his obligation to use a style and language appropriate to his work and to impress his audience by his verbal skill. This obligation is reflected in almost all the works of the High Middle Ages, especially in those of the lyric poets. Dante's work *De vulgari eloquentia* (*On the Vernacular*) is in effect an attempt to determine the correct style and language for various types of poetry.[9]

We have seen some of the effects of classical and postclassical rhetorical training on medieval style, and when considering the various genres of literature we shall have occasion to revert to these considerations and study them in greater detail. The great material contribution made by classical literature must now be considered. It is clear that the mythology used by medieval writers was that of the Greek and Latin world. The Northern gods appear only in a few Germanic works. Once the fear of a reversion to paganism had faded, the names of Greek gods and stories about them were used in literature, but never with the freedom or grace of the Renaissance. One reason for this was the lack of any easily accessible organized book of mythology.

[9] Dante is most concerned with the *canzon* (see the chapter on lyric poetry), but his whole case is based on the assumption that some poetic forms are nobler than others and that there is a fixed style for each. See the edition of *De vulgari eloquentia* by A. Marigo (1938).

The stories of Troy and Alexander were known but in garbled forms. The Middle Ages drew frequently, and often without acknowledgment, on the stores of anecdotal material found in such authors as Aulus Gellius and on collections of proverbs and moral sayings. The compiling and summarizing authors of late classical antiquity and the early Middle Ages were enormously influential—Isidore's encyclopedia, the *Origines* or *Etymologiae,* the *Marriage of Mercury and Philology* of Martianus Capella, and the works of Cassiodorus (*On Orthography, Institutes, Variae*). The works of Boethius were probably of greater significance than those of any other classical author except Vergil. Unfortunately the material presented in these late authors was often distorted, often fabulous, and always uncritical. Without them, however, the Middle Ages would have been ignorant indeed.

This is not the place to examine the influence of ancient philosophy on the Middle Ages, but one or two points should be noted. The influence of Plato and Aristotle was due not so much to the direct reading of their works as to the incorporation of much of their thought in Christian doctrine and commentary and in the works of later authors. The researches of Klibansky and others have made it clear that much more was known of Plato than was formerly believed,[10] and we can trace with considerable accuracy the increase in knowledge of Aristotle from the *Lesser Organum* to the whole corpus by the beginning of the thirteenth century. But the writings of Cicero, Boethius, and Porphyry, which were relatively easily accessible throughout the whole period, had made the outlines of their philosophical thinking, although not their disciplined method of reasoning, available to any reader of the Middle Ages in a form easier for him to understand than the original works. Hence such basic Platonic concepts as "ideas," or the division between body, soul, and will, were well known to almost any educated man, and reflections of this are to be found in numerous works of literature.

---

[10] See Klibansky, *Continuity of Platonic Tradition.*

Moreover, they formed part of what, for lack of a better term, we may call the intellectual climate of the day. The presence of Platonic, Neoplatonic, or Aristotelian ideas does not always imply a direct acquaintance with the works of the author in question. Libraries were scarce and manuscripts hard to obtain. Most ideas were probably conveyed orally, particularly to those not specifically trained as schoolmen. It is consequently very difficult to detect specific influences in works of literature, as distinct from those of philosophy and religion, and many works display a mixing and confusion of ideas drawn, quite unconsciously, from various classical sources. In the thirteenth and fourteenth centuries the task is easier than in the eleventh and twelfth, for there was more formal education of laymen and knowledge depended more on written transmission.

Classical culture was the soil from which medieval literature, both Latin and vernacular, grew. Only classical literature could provide the relatively crude and untried languages of Western Europe with a sense of literary form and linguistic discipline. To its rhetorical training the writers of the Middle Ages owed their vocabulary, their ornament, their topics, and their treatment. But it would be ridiculous to regard medieval literature as a mere compost of classical literature. Although many men regarded themselves as the heirs of classical culture and, like Albertus Magnus, made generous admission of their debt, others paid only lip service to it or denied its value while using its material. Moreover the sense of tradition was markedly different in various parts of Europe. In Italy the sense of continuity was never lost. The language and civic organization, in spite of all changes, retained the stamp of Imperial Rome. In France, too, the rhetorical tradition of education was native. The great schools of rhetoric of Southern Gaul passed on their traditions to the monastic schools and ultimately to the education of laymen. In Britain and the Germanic countries it was otherwise. There the Roman tradition was alien, something transplanted, and although there was little difference in the methods of teaching or in the subject matter in the various parts of Northwest Europe, the stress on the verbal and stylistic element, which is always so clear in French literature, is less marked in the Germanic countries. Interests of another sort, in character, religion, and ethics, are usually stronger. As we shall have reason to remark later, there are enormous differences in the treatment of the same theme in the various countries. We may further observe that native elements springing from the Germanic background are much more persistent in the North than in France and show more resistance to classical reshaping. One need only compare the *Chanson de Roland* and the *Nibelungenlied,* both "native" poems, to see how true this is.

Although Christianity had been deeply influenced by the philosophical thinking of Greece and Rome, and indeed owed the shaping of its thought to persons trained in that philosophy, there existed in the minds of most medieval thinkers a strong sense of cleavage between their world and that of classical antiquity. They were reinforced in this belief by many of the most influential of the Christian Fathers, by Tertullian's condemnation of the worldliness of his day, by St. Jerome's profound doubts as to the value of his classical background, and in particular by the writings of St. Augustine, the greatest single influence on the thought of the early Middle Ages.[11] The ascetic nature of early Christianity, an ascetic tradition which remained strong throughout the Middle Ages, rejected the worldly nature of the pagan outlook and insisted on the transitory and unworthy nature of the things of this world. This rejection of pagan values was consonant with the hope of the second coming of Christ and with the view of history which regarded all events as merely preparatory to Christ's kingdom. This view of life as an essential dichotomy between the transient and the permanent, the real and the ideal, the shadow and the substance, affected all medieval literature. It is not necessarily expressed in Christian or even religious terms. It became so much a way of

[11] See E. K. Rand, *Founders of the Middle Ages.*

thinking that it may be traced in types of literature which are purely secular in conception and execution, such as the Provençal love lyric. Medieval satire is largely a comparison between an ideal world and the failure of this world to realize it. Medieval romance, with its idealized setting, records the efforts of various men to attain an ideal, sometimes with success, often with failure. Classical literature knew, of course, the ideal after which men strove, but it is not dependent upon the battle between the real and the ideal, as medieval literature very largely is. This dichotomy is the most marked effect of Christianity on literature in the Middle Ages.

Less widespread, perhaps, but nevertheless of great significance was another aspect of the Christian attempt to explain and systematize human conduct. Classical antiquity had recognized types of individuals in whom one characteristic seemed to predominate—the miser, the spendthrift, the boaster—and had described the types in such works as the *Characters* of Theophrastus. The Greek New Comedy and its Roman successors were largely based on the conception of persons in whom one characteristic was dominant. Aristotle, too, had shown virtues as a mean between two vices and thus by implication had set up a system of division of human characteristics into virtues and vices. Christian writers, however, went much further. Aristotle's main concern was with the effects of social and antisocial conduct. To the Christian writers the question was the effect of conduct upon a man's immortal soul and upon his hopes of salvation. Hence they early began to categorize conduct into virtue and vice, good conduct and sin. The emergence of such strict categories as the seven deadly sins and the seven cardinal virtues was relatively slow and there was never complete agreement among writers, but the *Moralia* of Gregory the Great show that the basic concepts were firmly established by his time.[12]

---

[12] See M. Bloomfield, *Seven Deadly Sins*, and Bernard of Clairvaux, *De gradibus humilitatis*, ed. and trans. G. B. Burch (1940), Latin and English; good introduction.

The sins of pride, envy, anger, moroseness, avarice, gluttony, and lust were regarded as the worst, while the chief virtues were humility, courage, self-restraint, justice, faith, hope, and charity. It is not difficult to see the more obvious results of this categorization upon medieval writing. The whole genre of allegorical literature is largely dependent upon it, and particularly the idea of battle between virtues and vices which found its clearest expression in late classical antiquity in the enormously influential *Psychomachia* of Prudentius. In this poem the whole resources of ancient rhetoric were used to describe the sins and good qualities, and the attributes assigned to them by Prudentius, for example, Pride on her charger, remained attached to them for all subsequent writers and deeply influenced their representation in painting and sculpture. What had originally been abstract qualities became living beings, and the system was extended to include moods and feelings of all kinds. It reaches its finest flower in the *Romance of the Rose*.

The systematization of conduct also affects the behavior and the problems of many of the heroes of the romance. There has been much dispute as to whether a definite system of knightly virtues existed and whether this system was based upon the pseudo-Aristotelian *De vitiis et virtutibus* or upon the *Moralium dogma philosophorum* of Guillaume de Conches.[13] The question is not capable of definite solution and may very probably be irrelevant. The virtues demanded of the knight were essentially those demanded of every Christian, that is, the cardinal virtues, modified, or rather with special emphasis upon those aspects suited to a man of arms. John of Salisbury's definition of the duties of a warrior reflects this accurately enough. "To defend the church, attack unbelief, venerate the priesthood, protect the poor from injury, keep peace in the state, pour out their blood for their brothers." The fundamental problems set

[13] Ed. J. Holmberg (1929). Includes versions in vernaculars. See E. Neumann "Der Streit um das ritterliche Tugendsystem," in *Festschrift für K. Helm* (1951).

to the heroes of the great medieval romances were, as we shall see, concerned with the observance of Christian virtues, particularly *temperantia* or self-restraint, with a context of social convention.

That the heroes of literary works should strive after clearly defined virtues and that their opponents should be affected by equally well-recognized vices is not surprising. What is less often recognized but is of great importance is that the medieval concept of character drawing in literature is based upon these considerations. A modern reader has been brought up to regard "character development" as one of the chief features of any type of narrative literature. The events spring in part from the actions of characters and in their turn shape and develop those characters. The best-known type of writing of this kind is the German "Erziehungsroman." The medieval author did not think of character in these terms. Just as the medical science of his day saw health determined by the lack of or overabundance of certain humors, so character was determined by the presence or absence of virtues or vices and by the combination of them. A man's character in most medieval works of imagination is fixed from beginning to end. He possesses certain virtues and is afflicted by certain vices or, more usually, by one particular vice, such as pride. A frequent problem faced by the hero is the choice between two courses, each of which involves the sacrifice of one virtue or the commission of some sin or social misdemeanor. Events call forth the virtues within him and, in many cases, the vice is purged from him by experience and suffering, but the interest lies in the full realization of the potential character with which he is born and the failure which may result if one particular sin is not conquered. Complex character studies in the modern sense are very rare if not unknown in medieval literature.

Furthermore, medieval society believed firmly in the transmission of qualities by heredity, even though they would not have expressed it in that way. Although any objective examination of their own society would have convinced them that the children of noblemen could be as base as peasants and those of peasants could have the power to rule, literary convention prescribed that a man of noble birth was *ipso facto* a superior being and endowed with the virtues of his social group. The wicked knight is an aberration, a traitor to his class and is vanquished by the good knight because of the evil qualities which make him a recreant. On the rare occasions in which peasants appear in imaginative literature they have the virtues or vices of their class, not those of knights or noblemen. Even when patronage of literature passed into the hands of the bourgeois, the stratification of character according to social status continued. The nobleman of fiction is distinguished from his earlier counterparts only by the fact that his virtues are often so exaggerated as to be ridiculous.[14]

Medieval character study, therefore, may be said to consist largely in describing how far a man keeps within or departs from an ideal norm for the class in which he finds himself, and in determining which qualities, good or bad, make him conform to that norm or diverge from it. The most interesting studies of character are the subtle examinations of a noble character under prescribed sets of difficult circumstances. The romance provides the best examples.

The effect of the Christian categorization of virtues and vices is very clear. We may also note in passing that it led ultimately to the concept of character types which embodied one or more virtues or vices—the greedy friar, the vain squire. In the romances the most obvious example is the figure of the steward, Sir Kay, a man of noble birth who demeans himself by boasting (the sin of *vana gloria*) and hence betrays his birthright and becomes a figure of ridicule.

We have briefly considered the effects of two aspects of the Christian outlook upon literature. We must now turn to the

[14] See Huizinga, *Waning of the Middle Ages*. There are numerous examples in Chaucer, viewed with irony.

source of all Christian thinking, the study of the Bible and of sacred writings. Although Homer has sometimes been called the Bible of the Greeks and the study of his poems formed the basis of Greek education, it would be ridiculous to compare the influence of his works or those of any other author in classical antiquity with that of the Bible in the Middle Ages. This influence is not due merely to the fact that the Bible was a sacred work and that all real wisdom could be found in its pages. It is rather the method of studying it and its verbal content which are important for secular literature. As we have seen, the number of books available to any single reader in the Middle Ages was very small. A large library would contain perhaps six hundred volumes. A person with literary tastes would therefore know a few books extremely well rather than many books superficially, as most modern readers do. Of these he would inevitably know best the Bible and commentaries upon it. The effects of this circumstance upon literature were profound. The language of the Bible and incidents from it, particularly those of the New Testament, are reflected in all literature in varying degrees but most of all in Latin satire and parody. Some examples of this parodistic satire are very well known—the *Evangelium secundum marcas argenti,* usually translated "The Gospel according to St. Silver Mark," is probably the most famous —but what is unfortunately less frequently recognized, in the present lamentable state of Biblical knowledge among laymen, is that almost every line of medieval Latin satire is enriched in meaning by its references to Biblical passages and events. Parody depends upon recognition of what is being parodied or it loses its point. A medieval writer could be sure of such recognition and, even when his writing was not in the full sense parodistic, he could be sure that his implied contrasts between the conduct laid down in sacred writings and the sad state of affairs which he described, often in Biblical terms, would not be lost on his readers. More will be said on this topic later.

Even more important for literature in general was the method by which the Bible was studied. The New Testament was, of course, read as a life of Christ and for the doctrine which could be formulated from his utterances. Harmonies of the Gospels, which reconstructed them into a whole, made their appearance early and were very popular.[15] But this was only the beginning of Biblical study. Certain parts of the Old Testament clearly prophesied the coming of the Messiah, but to the Christian mind the whole of it must be brought into line with this event. The practice therefore began at a very early period of reinterpreting passages in the Old Testament so as to bring them into direct connection with the Christian viewpoint. Thus Abraham, the founder of the Israelites, is the creator of the first, imperfect Kingdom of God. Sarah his wife foreshadows, again imperfectly, the Virgin's bringing forth of a New Kingdom of God, while the incomplete sacrifice of Isaac foreshadows the complete sacrifice of Christ upon the cross. The techniques of allegorization were already at hand in Greek culture. Homer's works had been treated allegorically, partly to explain away the contrasts between his morality and that of later periods. Commentators such as Servius and Macrobius allegorized Vergil and the *Dream of Scipio,* and Philo applied the techniques to the study of the Old Testament. Christian writers were therefore easily able to use these well-tried methods in the study of the Bible and the reading of pagan authors.[16]

As scholarly techniques became more complicated, the system was extended. The literal meaning of the text became secondary to its allegorical meaning, that is, its interpretation in regard to the Christian religion, and its moralized meaning, that is, its interpretation as a guide to human conduct in the Christian

---

[15] One of the best known is that by Tatianus, which has a long manuscript tradition and has numerous vernacular versions. Some parts of the Bible were naturally studied more often and more thoroughly than others.

[16] See Smalley, *Study of the Bible in the Middle Ages,* and Spicq, *Esquisse d'une histoire de l'exégèse latine au moyen-âge;* also A. Nemetz, "Literalness and the Sensus litteralis," *Speculum,* Vol. XXXIV (1959).

sense. Finally it could be used anagogically, that is, as a guide
to actual points of Christian doctrine. This rereading of texts
made it possible to justify the study of pagan works whose
literal meaning was unchristian or indeed anti-Christian. St.
Jerome stated that pagan works should be treated in the manner
prescribed in Deuteronomy for the taking of a foreign wife by
the Israelites, namely, the cutting off of hair and nails so that
beauty should not seduce and should thus be made to serve
God. This and other arguments advanced by him were used
throughout the Middle Ages and even in the Renaissance to
justify the study of pagan authors.[17] By applying the allegorical
method, almost any text could be made to impart Christian
morality, and in such works as the *Gesta Romanorum* or the
Legenda Aurea anecdotes of a highly unedifying nature were
twisted into moral tales. A good example is the story of the
young man whom his father refused to ransom from an enemy
prison and who was released by his captor's daughter on condition that he marry her. On his return the father refused to
recognize the marriage on the grounds that the girl was of bad
character, having deceived her father because of her sensual
passion. The girl replied neatly that she could hardly have any
sensual passion for an emaciated prisoner and that she could
hardly have cheated her father of a ransom which the captive's
father refused to pay. The story was originally one of the stock
pieces argued in the schools of rhetoric and appears in the
collection made by the elder Seneca. However, the "real" interpretation proves to be that the son is the human race, the father
is the world, and the daughter is the divinity of the soul which,
in the shape of Christ, came down to earth to save mankind.[18]
    Such crass reinterpretation is commonest in the collections

[17] See J. de Ghellinck, *Le Mouvement théologique du XIIe siècle*
(1948), and Curtius, *European Literature and the Latin Middle Ages*,
p. 48.
    [18] *Gesta romanorum*, ed. H. Oesterley (1872); trans. C. Swan (1924),
pp. 80 ff.; Sénèque le rhéteur (Seneca the orator), *Controverses et
Suasoires*, ed. H. Bornecque, 2 vols., 2d ed. (1932).

of *exempla,* anecdotes used for the preaching of sermons to the laity. But it was used more subtly, in all types of writing. For the study of vernacular literature we are concerned not so much with the actual allegorization or reinterpretation as with the kind of attitude it produced. The cultured reader expected to have to search for different levels of meaning in a sophisticated work. He could enjoy the literal meaning of, say, an Arthurian romance and be excited by the adventures of knights, the glowing colors of the court, the sorrows of lovers. But he expected more than this. The characters represented something greater than themselves. They were human types in contrast or cooperation, human characteristics in action, good or evil forces in interplay. Although the Christian mythos is always present, it is not always expressed or even consciously felt. Thus the very frequent apparent death of a courtly hero and his rebirth is not necessarily to be interpreted as a conscious parallel to the death and Resurrection. It is felt as one example of the triumph of nobility over death, of good over evil. This feeling for allegorization, for double and triple levels of meaning, is one of the features which distinguish the great works of imagination in the Middle Ages from the mediocre. The idealized world of courtly romance frequently was populated with mere adventurers, medieval cowboys, whose only interest for their audience lay in their shattering of spears and unseating of giant opponents. Only in the hands of the great poets does this world become a reflection of all things human and divine and then only to the perceptive reader who observes, as the medieval audience, at least in part, did, the different levels of understanding. Formal allegory, of course, is clearly intended to be reinterpreted and was popular largely because of the feeling that good literature needs interpretative study.[19]

Before leaving the subject of Biblical literature, mention

[19] I cannot agree with the distinctions made by C. S. Lewis in his *Allegory of Love.* Formal allegory emphasized the medieval interest in qualities rather than people; it reflected the concern with the ideal, as

should be made of the enormous influence of apocryphal writings. Certain works, such as the Gospel of Nicodemus,[20] were regarded as almost as authentic as the books of the Bible as we now know it, and material from them was freely used. In addition to these there were large numbers of works, many of Jewish origin, which provided further legendary material on Biblical figures, for example, on the attempts to revisit paradise made by Adam and his successors, the burial place of Adam, the descent of the wood of the Cross, the journeys of Christ's followers. These works are now so little known—often, indeed, unobtainable—that allusions to them are hard to trace. No doubt the information they contained was usually transmitted orally and in fragmentary form, so that stories often appear in a garbled state or under different forms in different authors. We may also mention the *Vitae* or lives of saints in this connection. Stories accumulated around the names of saints at an early date and were set down in writing. (Some of them are clearly transferred from pagan heroes.) The miracles they performed and the pains they endured for the faith made them one of the most popular forms of narrative entertainment in the Middle Ages and one of the earliest and most enduring subjects for didactic literature and for the emerging drama.

Mysticism is not, of course, a purely Christian attitude, but it is convenient to mention it here. The word has been so often

---

opposed to the real, with the general as opposed to the particular. Furthermore, the characters can be manipulated more easily in an allegorical framework since their conventional aspects are already known to the audience. Such dissimilar works as the *Psychomachia* and the *Roman de la Rose* are alike in this respect. "Nature" within the allegory (and elsewhere) is formalized because it too shows a set situation, a recognizable frame within which humans operate.

[20] The *Descensus Christi* and the *Gesta Pilati* were combined in the *Evangelium Nicodemi,* which became part of the Apocrypha and of which numerous Latin and vernacular versions exist. For influence see P. Wülker, *Das Evangelium Nicodemi in der abendländischen Literatur* (1872).

misused that it may be as well to define what we mean by it. A mystic is one who seeks to draw closer to God or to some intangible spirit rather by emotional, ecstatic experience and even partial or entire identification than by reasonable and logical means.[21] All religious movements necessarily have a mystical element, but it is usually less articulate and therefore less likely to be expressed in writing than the more systematic type of theology. It is also frequently distrusted by the orthodox as too irrational and too individualistic. The twelfth century saw the production of much highly influential mystical writing, of which the works of the Victorines (Hugh and Richard of St. Victor) and of Bernard of Clairvaux are by far the most important. Bernard's sermons on the *Song of Songs,* which interpreted the love song of Solomon as the love between Christ and the church, with great circumstantial detail, showed how human emotions could be turned into religious channels and revealed in writing the close personal relation between the Christian and Christ.[22] The effects of this and similar works were not confined to religious literature. The sublimation of the emotions in a Christian sense could be related also to spiritual love between individuals, and the expressions of love in some courtly lyric, where all pretense at sensual love is professedly abandoned, undoubtedly owe much to the inspiration of mystical literature.

The cult of the Virgin, which grew markedly stronger from the twelfth century on, was also deeply influenced by mystical feelings. Much has been written about the influence of this cult upon the literature of courtly love.[23] Some critics maintain that the characteristics of the pure love of the Christian for Mary

[21] Important books on mysticism are: J. Bernhart, *Die philosophische Mystik des Mittelalters* . . . (1922); C. Butler, *Western Mysticism,* 2nd ed. (1951); J. M. Clark, *The Great German Mystics* . . . (1949); M. Grabmann, *Mittelalterliches Geistesleben,* 3 vols. (1926–56).

[22] Bernard of Clairvaux, *Sermons on the Song of Songs,* trans. T. L. Connolly (1951).

[23] See Kolb, *Begriff der Minne,* and Moret, *Débuts du lyrisme,* in bibliography to Chapter VIII.

were transferred to the pure worship of the poet's lady. The problem is hard to solve, but the evidence seems to point the other way. The language of the courtly love lyric was undoubtedly used to express the deep feelings of the Christian lover of Mary.

The influence of the classics and of Christianity upon the form and content of medieval literature is relatively easy to trace, even though critical opinions may differ as to its extent in individual works or upon individual authors. It was largely transmitted by the written word and through formal education, and such difficulties as we have in discussing it are due chiefly to the loss of materials known to have been available to the Middle Ages and the lack of information about the way they were used and disseminated. Some of these difficulties may well be removed as more works are published and more research done on manuscripts. It is quite otherwise with certain other sources of material and influences on style, whose importance was not as considerable as that of the classics or of Christianity, but which nevertheless contributed greatly to the special character of the great works of medieval literature. The principal sources of this influence were materials from the East, the mythologies of the Germanic and Celtic peoples, and that vague but very important phenomenon known as folklore.

We use the term "Eastern" here in the sense of "coming from Asia Minor and Persia." There were influences of some significance from India, which will be mentioned. Chinese civilization had virtually no impact. The close connection between Greece and the older civilizations of Asia Minor and Egypt had brought stories of Eastern mythology and culture into the main stream of Western culture at a very early date, and modern researchers are by no means so certain of what can be described as "Hellenic" and "classical" and what as "Eastern" as were their predecessors. The influence of Eastern mysticism upon Plato, for example, was profound. The enormous spread of Greek culture after the conquests of Alexander not only brought the Greek language and Greek culture to the East but also infused Hellenistic popular literature with tales of wonder, magic, and romance.[24] It is very hard to disentangle the separate elements in these stories. They were frequently sub-literary, in the sense that they passed from mouth to mouth, and written copies were few. The so-called *Fabulae Milesianae* (Tales from Miletus) are the best-known examples, but the Greek romances of *Daphnis and Chloe, Ethiopica,* and *The Ephesian Tale* are easily available texts which illustrate best the trend of such works.[25] Although our knowledge of this prose fiction is scanty, it must have enjoyed a wide circulation and constituted a considerable body of romantic literature. That the stories were put into Latin and circulated widely throughout the Empire cannot be doubted. Their influence can easily be seen in such Latin works as *Cupid and Psyche*[26] and the *Golden Ass* of Apuleius.[27] Their essentially oral tradition probably helped them to survive the disintegration of classical civilization, since the professional storytellers continued to recite them, changing name and milieu to suit the new audiences. Many of the stories, later used in collections of *exempla,* originated in this way, for example, those in the *Disciplina Clericalis* of Petrus Alfonsi.

There were, however, major works which passed from Hellenistic Greek through Latin to the Western vernacular cultures. By far the most important of these was the romance of Alexander, already constituted in classical antiquity, which made the historical conqueror into a legendary hero and provided him with marvelous adventures more reminiscent of Sinbad the Sailor than of the King of Macedon.[28] This romance, in various forms, passed into Western literature in written form

[24] See M. Hadas, *Hellenistic Culture: Fusion and Diffusion* (1959); G. Jacob, *Der Einfluss des Morgenlandes auf das Abendland vornehmlich während des Mittelalters* (1924); R. Reitzenstein, *Hellenistische Wundererzählungen* (1906).

[25] *Three Greek Romances,* trans. M. Hadas (1953).

[26] The story is in the *Metamorphoses,* English trans. by W. Pater (1951), by E. Carpenter (1923).

[27] Trans. R. Graves (1951).

[28] See the works on the Alexander romances cited in the readings for Chapter V.

in the early Middle Ages, as we shall see, but its oral transmission was probably earlier. The story of Troy was similarly garnished, and late Greek and Byzantine versions very different from that of Homer were accepted as authentic and became widely diffused.[29] There were undoubtedly many others which we have not yet been able to trace.

There is no reason to think that the flow of such material from East to West ever ceased completely throughout the Middle Ages. The idea of complete cultural separation between the Greek East and the Latin West is no longer tenable. Not only was there continuous trade with the empire of Byzantium, even if the scale was small, but the Greek civilization of parts of Italy and Sicily provided a channel through which cultural contacts could be maintained. The stories which attached themselves to the name of Vergil are excellent examples. Many of them, particularly those connected with mechanical marvels, are clearly distorted accounts of the ingenious machines used at Constantinople to impress visitors with the almost supernatural powers of the emperor.[30]

The vigorous Moslem communities in Sicily and Spain provided further opportunities for cultural contact. Once the initial period of conquest was over, the more advanced Arab communities provided the West with a new fund of learning, part of it Greek, part of it Eastern. The extent of the cultural contacts between Spain and Latin Christendom has been much disputed, but it should not be forgotten that there were always Christians living in Arab communities who were at once deeply influenced by the culture of their neighbors and yet felt close ties to their coreligionists in Europe. Nor should the role of the Jewish communities as cultural intermediaries be forgotten. Recent discoveries in the field of early Romance lyric, of

---

[29] The most important are those of Dares Phrygius and Dictys Cretensis. See readings for Chapter V.

[30] See Spargo, *Virgil the Necromancer,* and G. Brett, "The Automata in the Byzantine Throne of Solomon," *Speculum,* Vol. XXIX (1954).

which we shall have more to say later, show how closely the Christian and Arabic cultures were interwoven in Spain. The crusades, of course, brought a new realization of the high state of civilization in the Arab world and a different attitude to Moslem civilization. Philosophical thinking was profoundly influenced by such writers as Avicenna and Averroes, and such works as Wolfram's *Parzival* show the deep penetration of fragments of Eastern knowledge even among those who were not formally concerned with learning.

One story should be mentioned here which was exceedingly popular in the Middle Ages and which, in its transmission and distortion, may well be regarded as typical of the way in which Eastern material passed into Western culture. The story of the Gautama Buddha, his conversion to the ascetic life, and his ministry passed into Arabic literature in the early Middle Ages. Apparently because of a confusion between two Arabic characters, his name was changed from Bosiphata to Yosiphat and passed into the Western languages as Josaphat or Johosiphat. His guide upon the road to asceticism and self-contemplation was Balaam. The milieu of the story remained Eastern, but Balaam was turned into a Christian who converted Josaphat, the son of a great prince whose father desired to shield him from the world.[31] To judge by the number of versions of the story and the number of manuscripts of those versions, the work must have been highly popular and illustrates well the ability of the medieval writer to turn even the most unpromising material to good use.

Any reader who has the slightest acquaintance with the medieval love lyric will not need to be reminded of the controversy over the question of Arabic influence upon the troubadours. The question will be considered fully in the chapters

[31] Important works on Josaphat are: E. W. A. Kuhn, *Barlaam und Joasaph, eine bibliographisch-literargeschichtliche Studie* (1893); St. John Damascene, *Barlaam and Iosaph,* with Eng. trans. by G. R. Woodward and H. Mattingley (1914).

on lyric poetry, but we may note here that many critics believe that Arabic love poetry largely determined the form and principal ideas of the troubadour love lyric and hence to a considerable extent also those of the German *Minnesang* and the love lyrics of the Italian imitators of the troubadours. The idea is not new. It was advanced by Italian writers as early as the sixteenth century. This is one of the few aspects of the problem of the influence of the East upon medieval literature which has been the object of intensive research and where there has been a violent clash of critical opinion.

The influence of Celtic and Northern materials has been studied even more intensely, and correspondingly more heat has been engendered. Since the "rediscovery" of the Middle Ages by the Romantics, several generations of scholars have busied themselves with the study of the origins of national material, often, it must be said with regret, from a narrowly nationalistic viewpoint. The study of historical linguistics in the nineteenth century here exerted a particularly strong influence. The desire to demonstrate that particular characteristics of literature were "Germanic," "Aryan," or "Indo-European" led to attempts at the reconstruction of early works which were often remarkable rather for their perverse ingenuity than for scholarly objectivity. A glance at the histories of medieval literature of the nineteenth century will provide the reader with such detailed descriptions of these early works that he will be surprised to discover (with some difficulty) that not a line of them exists and that they are largely creations of fantasy. It would be ridiculous to deny that there were primitive works of an epic nature which were not written down. They are mentioned, in very general terms, by classical authors, and such works as the *Edda, Beowulf,* and the *Nibelungenlied* presuppose a considerable body of organized mythology and narrative verse. But the evidence is too slight for us to be able to reconstruct the works in detail or to pass judgment on their form or style.

The direct influence of Norse mythology on medieval literature is relatively small.[32] Only works written in Old Norse use it as actual subject matter and even these were written down by Christian writers at a relatively late date. The indirect influence is considerable. *Beowulf* incorporates stories drawn from mythological material, and the feeling of conflict between the pagan powers of evil and the Christian God is still very strong. In spite of its Christian veneer, the *Nibelungenlied* has an essentially pagan morality and the subject matter of the story is drawn to a large extent from Northern mythology, even though much modified. In the literatures of the non-Germanic lands the influence of German mythology or pre-Christian German culture is slight. Germanic figures, such as Dietrich von Bern, may appear, but they are characters from the period of the Germanic migrations of the fifth, sixth, and seventh centuries, not from Germanic prehistory. There is, however, a great deal of evidence of the survival of the principle that loyalty to the chief and to the idea of kingship is the greatest of moral virtues. No one would call this a specifically Germanic trait, but in the literature of Western Europe it undoubtedly takes its origin from the social organization of the new Germanic kingdoms which appeared in Europe in the early Middle Ages. The accepted behavior of the knightly class, its stress on physical courage, ability in combat, and unswerving loyalty, owed a great deal to the morality of this society, but not so much as used to be believed. As we have seen, Christian ethics and the ancient philosophers were also important, even when their influence was not directly felt.

The study of Celtic mythology in connection with the literature of Western Europe is a relatively recent development.[33] The inaccessibility of much of the material and the fact that the languages in which it was written were known to relatively

---

[32] See W. A. Craigie, *The Religion of Ancient Scandinavia* (1914); H. Schneider, *Die Götter der Germanen* (1938).

[33] See the works on the subject in the readings for Chapter V; see also Stith Thompson, *Motiv-Index of Folk-Literature* (1958).

few scholars caused it to be neglected. In spite of some dissent from certain critics, it is now clear that a great deal of the subject matter of the Arthurian romances, the huge cycle of stories which revolve about the idealized court of King Arthur, was derived from Celtic mythology and from historical events among the Celtic inhabitants of Britain. Direct evidence is hard to obtain because many of the Celtic texts are of later date than the Arthurian poems and may even have been influenced by them. It may be said, however, that the connection between the adventures of the heroes of Irish folklore and Welsh history and those of Arthur's knights is too close to be accidental, and the proper names, in spite of their Gallicized forms, can be clearly demonstrated to be Celtic in origin. This is not to say that the French and German authors were conscious of this Celtic heritage or influenced by it. It does not affect the spirit of the poems nor contribute to their ethical and social background. More will be said on this subject when we discuss the Arthurian romance.

In assessing the effects of folklore upon the literature of medieval Europe, we are faced with several problems, by their very nature difficult if not impossible of solution. The term itself is extremely vague. It refers to the mass of sub-literary material which descends from one generation to another by oral transmission, including proverbs, riddles, stories, narrative poems, lyric poems, charms and spells, fairy stories, legends, and the like. Scholarly opinion has shown wide variations in its assessment of the impact of folklore upon literature, and it would not be unjust to say that belief in its importance goes in and out of fashion. The strong feeling of the Renaissance and early eighteenth century that only in classical antiquity was real literary worth to be found left the study of folklore materials to a few cranks and curious amateurs. The later eighteenth century and especially the Romantics reversed this judgment completely. The collecting zeal of such persons as Percy and the brothers Grimm, and the theoretical writings of Herder, convinced most critics that folk poetry and folk tales were the only "genuine" writing. They reflected the spirit of a people and sprang spontaneously from the people's consciousness.[34] Lyric poetry and even long epics grew artlessly from work songs and lays, uncontaminated by formal literature. A great deal of nineteenth-century theory on the rise of national poetry, particularly primitive epic, was based on this idea of spontaneous growth. Largely under the influence of Lachmann, the great classical epics and those of the Middle Ages were divided up into their separate lays and their ultimate composition was seen largely as a matter of chance. For the purposes of these critics, the Middle Ages were regarded as a primitive period. Epic and lyric grew in this spontaneous way. Although not a shred of evidence could at that time be found for the existence in the early Middle Ages of folk lyric in the Romance countries, a whole school of French critics, led by Gaston Paris and Alfred Jeanroy, postulated for the highly complex troubadour love poetry an origin in folk song.[35] Critics in other countries were equally emphatic.

The major mistakes, of course, lay in assuming that the Middle Ages were "primitive" and in ignoring the strong influence of classical and Christian tradition. But the more general error was in the assessment of the nature of folklore and folk poetry itself. More thorough research demonstrated that folk poetry and song is not spontaneous. It is created by artists and becomes popular. True, the artist is often unknown and modification is considerable. It is also true that folk song tends to prefer certain themes (parting, the girl I left behind me, etc.),

[34] See W. Grimm, *Die deutsche Heldensage*, 2d ed. (1867); J. G. Herder, *Stimmen der Völker* (Volkslieder), in *Sämmtliche Werke*, ed. Suphan, Vol. XXV. These men in their turn were much influenced by the publication of Percy's *Reliques* in England.

[35] See G. Paris, *La Poésie au moyen-âge* (1885); A. Jeanroy, *Origines de la poésie lyrique en France*, 3d ed. (1925). Later speculation has naturally been affected by Jungian archetypal theory and anthropological cult considerations.

but it has been possible to show over and over again how an art song of known origin became popular among the people, was modified by succeeding generations, even had its proper names and milieu changed, but still remained fundamentally the same. Theories again changed. The artist was rehabilitated and it was recognized that an epic needed a genius to write it, even if he used materials which were the common property of all men.

Medieval works began to be examined from the point of view of written tradition, and it was soon discovered that most of their material and the influences upon their form and style could be found in written works and that there was no need to postulate a vague element of folk song to explain them. This does not mean, however, that we can eliminate from consideration the whole question of oral transmission and folk tradition. There is not the slightest doubt that all of the great medieval poems derived their material from earlier works composed for listening, not reading, which were subject to continuous modification. These works were largely in the hands of professional singers, many of them skillful poets of great artistic sensibility, who worked out complicated patterns of rhythm and music and who sang them to an audience which, at least in part, must have been able to appreciate their subtleties. The influence of these anonymous writers on literature was enormous. The whole structure of the vernacular epic and romances, for example, is their work. But it should be emphasized that they were artists. The work is not "spontaneous" folk song. There was almost certainly lyric poetry of this type, too. We have no means of determining its origin; texts are scanty in the extreme, but unwritten vernacular lyric poetry did exist before the lyric of the troubadours and *Minnesänger* and contributed to its themes and forms, although not to anything like the extent formerly believed.

Medieval literature, then, like the literature of all periods, was subjected to many influences. We are fortunately able to trace them much more easily than we can, for example, those for Greek literature. The influence of the classics was profound, recognized by the authors themselves, and transmitted through reading and education. It was, however, of a different kind from that which influenced the writers of the Renaissance—more a matter of tradition, less consciously bookish, and not clearly defined as "classical." Christianity too was a conscious element, pervading all writing, secular and religious, with its material and its methods, conditioning not only the ideas used but the whole thinking of medieval writers. The other factors we have discussed contributed material and subject matter, but had far less effect on thinking and treatment. Often their contributions consisted in the provision of stories and forms of whose ultimate origins the writer was quite unaware, in other words, material which was simply part of the author's cultural background. Out of this intermingling of classical civilization and Christianity with the cultures of the Celtic and German West came a new literature, whose effects lasted far beyond the Renaissance and some of whose ideals have become basic in modern literature.

2

The Reasons for Writing Literature

To a modern reader it may seem ridiculous to discuss the reasons for writing literature at all. In an age in which twelve-year-old schoolboys write their memoirs, and the love affairs of disillusioned adolescents become best sellers and make millionaires of their authors, it may well seem that the writing of literature is so normal a function for any literate person that any inquiry should be directed to discovering why literature was not written rather than why it was. No one became rich in the Middle Ages from writing nor, happily, was it possible to present one's works to a large and undiscriminating public and gain easy fame overnight. We shall discuss the questions of the audience for literature and the means of distribution in the next chapter. Here we may ask ourselves simply: what prompted an author to write literature?

The answer varies, of course, from one period of the Middle Ages to another. Before the Carolingian period the main concern of the few literate persons in Western Europe was to conserve what learning they had available. Compiling and copying were their chief activities. Such new literature as was produced was purely imitative in character, continuing with little originality the lyric and short narrative tradition of the later

Roman Empire. Only in the writing of Christian hymns [1] is there evidence of real creative talent. In the vernaculars there is extremely little written material which can be dated before 800. *Beowulf* can almost certainly be ascribed to the eighth century, and reflects, to a considerable degree, the culture of an earlier epoch. Even during and after the Carolingian revival of interest, writing is still largely a matter of practical living, not creative imagination. It is true that there was an improvement in the sense of style and that certain characteristics of later works, such as the praise and almost deification of Charlemagne himself, became significant.[2] Basically, however, writers were still too concerned with imparting a minimum of knowledge to be able to write literature in the true sense. Vernacular works are usually attempts to impart the fundamentals of religion and learning to laymen and hence are largely translations. A few fragments only give us some idea of the great loss of European culture suffered when Charlemagne's son ordered the destruction of the collection of Germanic songs made by his father. These songs and lays were the only true literature of the period. They were written for the entertainment of Germanic courts by professional singers and, like *Beowulf,* show some of the principal reasons for creating literature among the Germanic peoples: the desire to connect the present with a glorious past by recounting the great deeds of the ancestors of the noblemen in the audience, hence the creation of a spirit of tribal solidarity and a feeling of superiority; the desire to please a noble sponsor, especially important for the professional singer. To these reasons may be added another, perhaps not so clearly felt but never-

[1] See Blume and Dreves, *Analecta Hymica,* for texts. For discussion, see Raby, *A History of Christian Latin Poetry,* and the works there cited. It should be noted that the hymns anticipate many of the techniques of the secular lyric, particularly the use of figurative language.

[2] See Curtius, *European Literature,* the chapter on Hero and Sovereign, and the works there cited, esp. P. Lehmann, *Das literarische Bild Karls des Grossen, vornehmlich im lateinischen Schrifttum des Mittelalters* (Sitzungsberichte der bayerischen Akademie der Wissenschaften, phil.-hist. Klasse, 1934, No. 9).

theless present, namely the didactic purpose of instilling and encouraging a moral code based on loyalty and endurance and on accepting the dictates of fate. It need hardly be added that this literature was entertainment and its primary purpose was to appeal to the audience. But the type of work was largely determined by the reasons given above. A strong historical sense is one of the characteristics of the national epic which is the closest successor to these lays of which we have such scanty knowledge.

The Germanic poets were writing largely at the behest of patrons. Christian writers wrote in the service of God. A conscious wish to serve the Lord in the best possible way is undoubtedly responsible for a great deal of medieval writing. Unfortunately much of it can hardly be classed as literature. We have already mentioned compilations and translations. A desire to substitute wholesome Christian works for pagan adventure and frivolous love poetry is stated by several authors to be their purpose in writing. Among them we may mention, briefly at this point, the "anti-Terence" plays of Hroswitha of Gandersheim, the adaptation of the *Chanson de Roland* made in German by Pfaffe Konrad, the *Heliand,* a Saxon life of Christ written in the meter of the Germanic epics, the verse life of St. Alexis, and the various versions of the story of St. Brendan.

These works show the fear which the church had at this period of a relapse into paganism and of the influence of pagan literature upon the minds of the people. The need for a counterblast was a powerful incentive to write, although it must be confessed that the counterblast was usually weaker than the original. The desire to serve God in writing and a plea for his inspiration are frequently expressed in the prologue to poetic works, for example, by Juvencus, Prudentius, Paulinus of Nola, Aldhelm, and many others, but in itself this desire rarely produced great literature. The didactic element was too strongly felt; the author was too restricted in his outlook. Moreover, the work was often undertaken by men whose literary ability was considerably less than their earnest desire to serve. True religious fervor expressed itself better in hymns, sermons, and mystical writings, occasionally in such works as Bernard of Cluny's *De contemptu mundi*. Only Dante succeeded in producing a completely successful sustained work of Christian inspiration.

Much literature has been produced by authors who felt that society needed their help in overcoming its evils. Most satirists are would-be improvers of their social milieu. The more didactic authors of classical antiquity appealed strongly to medieval readers, since they had a purpose, announced or unannounced, to improve morals and lash out at wickedness. They were much imitated by medieval writers, and it is tempting to think of the writers of medieval satire as moral reformers with a serious social purpose. Such a description may apply to some of the ascetic writers, although their objects were more religious than social, but in the majority of cases the works were rather exercises in verbal gymnastics, new treatments of commonplaces, which compared the imperfect present with either an ideal or an idealized past. The earlier Middle Ages regarded society as too stable to be the object of reform. When genuine social comment begins, in the thirteenth century, it seeks rather to recall rulers to a proper sense of duty than to advocate changes, and it still uses the accepted commonplaces and comparisons to do so. The social motivation is never clearly separated from the religious, as may be seen, for example, in *Piers Plowman*. Chaucer's characters in *The Canterbury Tales* provide us incidentally with rich commentary on the social life of his time, but it would be audacious to argue that Chaucer's motivation came primarily from a sense of obligation to society. The brilliantly drawn characters are incidental to the storytelling.

It is, curiously enough, in the less obviously didactic works that the social element is strongest. Although the primary purpose of the courtly romance and the national epic was to entertain, the idealized setting of the former and the historical background of the latter made its authors (and audience) very sensible of conformity to a set of values, often idealized, and of the demands of a particular social milieu. It is doubtful whether any court in Europe was ever conducted on the lines of King Arthur's court (although some history books give that impression), but the influence of the works of chivalry upon actual conduct was undoubtedly profound during the period in which they appeared and even greater in succeeding centuries when they had acquired glamour and respectability. The authors of these works were conscious of their impact and proud of their influence. They believed in the morality which they depicted and in the ethical value of the stories they told.[3]

The same may be said, though in a more limited fashion, of the lyric writers of France and Germany. They too were conscious of the social implications of their ideals, and many of them, as we shall see later, combined the writing of idealized lyric with that of sharply pointed topical satire. We have still to mention, however, the principal reasons for writing, reasons which vary little from one age to another—the urge to express oneself to one's fellows, the desire for patronage (in its crudest form, a livelihood), and the fact that writing was often a fashionable pursuit. On the first of these reasons little need be said. A person with literary talent turned to the types of literary expression most used in his day and, if he had true genius, modified them and reshaped them into greatness. The centuries before the twelfth were not favorable to such men, for the literate were few and the permitted fields of activity small. As always, the flowering of great literary talents needed a suitable social milieu, which the aristocratic society of the twelfth and early thirteenth centuries and, to a lesser extent, the courts of the fourteenth and fifteenth provided.

Patronage implies that the patron has an interest in what he is supporting and usually that he will gain social prestige by

---

[3] It should be noted, however, that Chrétien de Troyes, among others, appears to view many of the features of the Arthurian world with irony. See J. Frappier, *Chrétien de Troyes.* Later writers satirize its more extravagant aspects.

his patronage. The Roman Empire had seen patronage at its best in Maecenas, at its worst in the effects upon literature of unrestrained panegyric of the ruling emperor. Formal encomia of the ruler still continued in the Middle Ages and the image of Charlemagne seen by posterity has undoubtedly been influenced by the rhetorical efforts of writers of his own day. Medieval patronage generally, however, was beneficial. It owed its origin as much to the Germanic tradition of the chief who regarded the minstrel as an honored member of his entourage as it did to the classical heritage.[4] Moreover, the patron himself could be and often was an expert practitioner of the art he patronized. There is not a great deal of evidence in medieval literature of undue deleterious influence of patrons. Flattery there is, and poems written to help a patron politically. A poet who was singing for his supper could hardly avoid taking his patron's side in politics. But breaks between poet and patron are frequent, accompanied by stinging verses from both sides. The great advantage of patronage was that it did produce a class of professional writers who could make a living from literature—a precarious one, indeed, but no more so than that of most of their contemporaries. They were assured of an audience of people who, in varying degrees, could appreciate them, and were able to exercise their literary talents. Not all the writers of the great works of the Middle Ages were professionals in this limited sense, but a great many of them were and we should bear this in mind in considering their works. They were writing for a specific audience, and their forms and subjects were designed to please that audience. Not every troubadour was necessarily enraptured with the lady he celebrated.[5]

[4] See A. Heusler, *Die altgermanische Dichtung*, 2d ed. (1941), pp. 113 ff.

[5] See D. Legge, "The Influence of Patronage on Form in Medieval French Literature," in *Problems of Style and Form in Literature*, ed. P. Böckmann (1959). Note also the remarks of Chrétien in his prologue to *Lancelot*. Heinrich von Veldecke's *Eneit* was actually delayed for years because the incomplete manuscript was "borrowed" by a patron and not returned.

Patronage, as we have said, assumes that the patron regards the thing he patronizes as worth while. It cannot be assumed automatically that any rich man will support poetry or even any art. We all know rich men who do not. The tradition of "largesse" or generosity for its own sake helped the idea of patronage, but there were many noblemen who enjoyed an unenviable reputation as nonsupporters of literature.[6]

Certain courts outdid all others in their generosity but, generally speaking, there was, in the twelfth and subsequent centuries, a widespread interest in the support of literature. The system of education helped a great deal. Even an elementary education in Latin involved the study of verse forms and the writing of practice poems. Moreover, the exercise was regarded as difficult, good training for the mind, a severe discipline. Great stress was laid on verbal skill, and virtuosity in meter and rhyme was much admired. Patrons had a certain satisfaction in knowing that they had at their court a poet who was capable of such achievements. Literature, in short, was fashionable and had a certain esoteric quality which made its writers and their supporters a superior race. We should not forget the strong influence of educated women. They had more leisure for education and to a large extent set the tone in the courts of southern France. Although the more ascetic clerics sometimes classed professional poets with the actors and jugglers they so much detested, their status from the twelfth century on seems to have been fairly well assured, even when they were not of particularly high social station. There were no doubt innumerable aspiring poets who never succeeded in finding a patron, and those who did were always dependent on the whims of their protector, but the fact that a high percentage of the poets whose names we know belonged to the minor nobility (*ministeriales, menestrailles,* hence "minstrel") or to the clerics or clerically

---

[6] Marcabru has some bitter things to say about Aldric of Vilar. Walther von der Vogelweide criticizes Leopold of Austria for his failures as a patron of poetry (32, 7 ff.).

educated men not in full orders shows that the profession was fairly respectable.

A word should be said here, in anticipation of the fuller treatment in Chapter 8 on the subject of the Goliards. One of the most enduring myths of medieval literature is the story of a group of fugitives from strict monastic discipline, unfrocked clerics or wandering students, who roamed Europe and composed on the way happy, carefree love songs or depicted their personal adventures in love-making, dicing, and carousing. That there were wandering students is established by documents and it is equally demonstrable that they frequently made a nuisance of themselves to the authorities.[7] But an occasional poem which mentions drinking and gambling does not provide a link between these students and the often very sophisticated Latin poems which have been ascribed to them. The great mass of the Latin poetry called Goliardic was written by clerically trained professional poets, such as the Archipoeta, or by clerics as an exercise. The love poetry, though often extremely skillful, is far from spontaneous, and the gambling and drinking poems, relatively few in number, are often mock statements of the poet's "sins." Doubtless some of the stray efforts of learned but destitute scholars and of the rag, tag, and bobtail of medieval learning have crept into our anthologies, but to speak of Goliardic poetry as a separate phenomenon is misleading.

We have mentioned the training of poets in the schools and, so far as academic training in the forms of classical Latin verse is concerned, we have little difficulty in understanding how the skills were imparted and the necessary practice obtained. But there is much in a poet's training and in the works themselves which cannot be explained in this way. The rhythmic, rhymed Latin verse in which the most successful medieval Latin shorter poems were written is not part of the classical tradition. Whatever its ultimate origins, it does not emerge as a suitable in-

[7] Helen Waddell documents the unpopularity of the *vagantes* in *The Wandering Scholars.*

strument for secular Latin verse before the eleventh century. During that period, and in particular in the century which followed, a degree of virtuosity in its use was achieved which can be explained only by systematic development and training, in other words, by a school tradition. The writing of rhythmical verses must either have been incorporated into the verse-writing practice which formed part of the study of grammar and rhetoric or, more likely, have constituted a kind of advanced course. We have little or no evidence on the subject. Perhaps one poet studied with another. Although we do possess a few examples of the first efforts at the new rhythmical forms, the number of such works available in writing to a contemporary must have been very small. In the absence of such written material, we must assume a definite system of oral training, for the works are too sophisticated and too polished to be the result of a merely haphazard acquisition of skills.

Even more obscure is the system by which the poets writing in the vernacular were trained. The extent of formal education must have varied enormously, ranging from virtually nil in the case of some of the early Germanic poets to very considerable for such poets as Gottfried von Strassburg and Dante. The degree of education of vernacular poets has, I think, usually been underestimated. Even in the twelfth century many of them were given instruction under the chaplain or as potential clerics. But formal education explains only part of their work, such as classical allusions and rhetorical features. The verse forms, language, and material of the vernacular poems differed in many ways from those written in Latin, but they have their own strongly marked traditions. There can be little doubt that young poets sat at the feet of an acknowledged master and learned from him. The almost sacred nature of the minstrels' art among the Germanic tribes and the extreme complication of form and metaphor indicate a strong oral tradition of teaching, almost an apprenticeship system. We have occasional allusions to deliberate preparation for literary work in authors of the twelfth and thirteenth centuries. Giraut de Bornelh is said to have spent his winters in school and his summers in singing,[8] and Walther von der Vogelweide says that it was in Austria that he learned to sing and compose verses. Walther, furthermore, makes it fairly clear that he studied under Reinmar der Alte. It was no doubt through such associations that the techniques of writing were acquired and ultimately improved. Such schooling would also account to some extent for the stress upon virtuosity in rhyme and meter. It should be added that many nonprofessionals must also have benefited from the instruction, for virtuosity needs an understanding audience to be appreciated and some of the best poetry was written by persons of too high rank to be professionals in any sense.

Any statement about the training of poets is bound to be unsatisfactory. Evidence for it is lacking. But we should not therefore assume that the whole growth of vernacular poetry was unsystematic and spontaneous. All education in the Middle Ages was oral rather than written, and the training of poets probably followed the same pattern. If we assume some such semiformal training of poets, we can more easily explain why some stories receive repeated treatment in medieval literature while others, apparently, to our view, equally available, are ignored. We can also understand more easily why there are varying "versions" of the same story side by side. Modern critics, dependent on written materials, tend to think that the Middle Ages worked in the same way. The medieval poet used rather what he heard than what he read. The versions he heard and (sometimes imperfectly) remembered from his master were the ones he followed.

We have offered some ideas on why literature was written— for the greater glory of God, for social and moral improvement, for patronage, and for a living. But in the end the main reason

[8] According to his *vida* or biography.

was that the author had an urge to write and the ability to put that urge into practice. While culture was confined to a small group of clerically trained men, dedicated by very necessity to religious works, literature could flourish only among the Germanic peoples. There were always a few men who were content to write for their own amusement. Such works as the *Ysengrimus* must have had a very small circulation, for their language is too difficult for anyone but an expert to understand, and then only by reading, not by hearing. The Carolingian period, important as it is for the transmission of culture, was a false dawn for literature. Its products were purely imitative and it lacked the tradition and the courage to strike out in new directions. Those with the urge to write had to wait until increasing security in social life, increasing secularization of outlook, and a feeling that this life was not all vanity made it possible to combine classical learning with the vigor of vernacular material and thus forge a new literature.

3

The Audience for Medieval Literature

Literary historians have paid relatively little attention to the question of the audience for medieval literature, with the result that certain vague ideas are widely prevalent which have little foundation in fact—visions of long-mustachioed Germanic chiefs, their drinking horns full of mead, their helmets all in place, listening enraptured to *Beowulf,* or ladies listening to troubadour songs played on a guitar under their window. The problem is in fact very hard to solve, since most of our evidence can come only from the works of literature themselves and from chance references in other writings.

Let us first consider the facts of written distribution, the audience for the written word. No subject could make us more conscious of the fallacious nature of the term "Middle Ages." At the beginning of our period, literacy was at low ebb. Very few laymen could read at all, and there was grave danger that the classics would vanish completely because of the lack of copies and the lack of interest in preserving them. Only a very few people were both able and willing to devote themselves to reading the classics for pleasure. The Carolingian copyist activity undoubtedly saved many works from extinction and slightly increased their availability, but down to the twelfth century reading a manuscript to oneself must have been an exceptional way of acquiring knowledge once one moved away from the great centers of learning. The medieval library catalogues show how small most libraries must have been.[1] Even if we make generous allowance for manuscripts subsequently lost, few people could have had regular access to copies of the classics and still fewer to written versions of the great works written in the vernacular, such as the *Chanson de Roland,* of which we have only one manuscript antedating the thirteenth century.

Profound changes come at the end of the twelfth century and in the thirteenth. We have fairly numerous references to the commissioning of manuscripts and—the plague of any person who possesses books—to the failure to return manuscripts that were borrowed. The establishment of universities meant that the old haphazard methods of imparting knowledge would have to be abandoned and more reliance placed on the written word. The *stationarii,* bookshops set up in the neighborhood of universities, began to reproduce manuscripts in larger numbers. It would be ridiculous to speak of mass production of manuscripts. It is indeed doubtful whether the Middle Ages ever matched the manuscript reproduction of classical antiquity, if only for the reason that they never had a cheap medium like papyrus to write on. (Paper did not come into common use until the fourteenth century and was still relatively expensive.) Nevertheless, as a glance at any modern manuscript li-

[1] Useful works on this subject are: H. J. Chaytor, *From Script to Print* (1945); E. Faral, *Les Jongleurs en France au Moyen Age* (1910); W. Wattenbach, *Das Schriftwesen im Mittelalter* (1875); Ruth Crosby, "Oral Delivery in the Middle Ages," *Speculum,* Vol. XI (1936); W. Craigie, *The Art of Poetry in Iceland* (1937); R. K. Root, "Publication before Printing," *PMLA,* Vol. XXVIII (1913); J. Schwietering, *Die Demutsformel mittelhochdeutscher Dichter* (Abhandlungen der königlichen Gesellschaft der Wissenschaften zu Göttingen [1921]); Dorothy Whitelock, *The Audience of Beowulf* (1951); H. S. Bennett, "The Author and His Public," in *Essays and Studies by Members of the English Association,* Vol. XXIII (1938); R. Girvan, "The Medieval Poet and his Audience," in *English Studies Today* (1951).

brary catalogue will show, the number of manuscripts produced during the fourteenth and fifteenth centuries was far greater than in the earlier periods.

Sheer numbers, however, do not provide an answer to the question of the degree of written distribution of literature. The manuscripts reproduced in such numbers were standard "educational" texts in law, philosophy, theology, and medicine. The study of classical literature was included in philosophy, but the vernacular works of literature had no place there. Copies of such works were made specially for men wealthy enough to commission them and interested enough to want to possess them. Presumably the author had a written version and copies were made for his patrons. But the small number of manuscripts thus produced could hardly account for the popularity of many authors and the numerous references to them by contemporaries and later authors. It does account, in part at least, for the fact that even authors famous in their own day were completely forgotten three hundred years later and that such fame as they now enjoy is due to the antiquarian interests of eighteenth-century scholars and the industry of nineteenth-century philologists.

The audience for vernacular medieval literature and for the secular literature written in Latin must, therefore, have acquired its knowledge and its tastes in ways other than by reading. In both classical and medieval times the sound of literature was much more important than it is to us. Even when alone, the average classical or medieval reader read his text aloud, as we know from the astonishment of witnesses who saw St. Ambrose reading and heard no sound.[2] Most literature was heard, rather than read, and it is fairly safe to say that most knowledge of vernacular literature was acquired by hearing it recited on numerous occasions. Among the Germanic tribes professional bards sang or chanted traditional poems and made

[2] The incident is recorded by St. Augustine in his *Confessions*, Book VI, chapter 3.

up their own. That they were able to recite very long poems from memory is not as remarkable as some critics appear to think. They were professionals and they began to learn the poems as children. The memory of a modern actor is capable of similar feats.

The vernacular works of the twelfth and later centuries were probably disseminated in a similar way. We know that lyric poetry was often recited not by the author but by professional "jongleurs" who accompanied him and were presumably often paid by him. It was therefore perfectly possible for such poems to become quite widely known in the course of a year or two at the relatively few courts which had an interest in such matters. A few written copies distributed among professional singers would ensure fairly wide dissemination. For such distribution of the longer poems of the twelfth and thirteenth centuries we have little evidence. They were too long to be recited at one sitting and, since they never became "traditional" in the sense that the national epics did, they were less likely to be learned by heart by professionals. Yet they were well known. The probability is that they were recited piecemeal, perhaps by the author, to the court of his patron. Written copies, few in number, then passed from one literary court to another and were recited there. Secular literature in Latin may well have been distributed in the same pattern except that the courts were probably those of bishops rather than secular princes, and the reading of such works by individuals was certainly much more common.

The decline of feudal courts and the rise of a bourgeois audience brought further changes. Recitation of works continued but reading either alone or in smaller groups became more common. The famous story of the making of a manuscript collection of German lyric poetry by the wealthy Manessa family is typical of the interest of the intelligent bourgeois of the fourteenth century in the literature of the past. We owe our knowledge of the literature of the twelfth century principally to this interest. The possession of such manuscripts was no doubt the mark of a cultured man, and there is every reason to assume that the reading, as distinct from the hearing, of vernacular literature was widespread in the fourteenth and fifteenth centuries.

We may now turn to the actual composition of the audience and then study the effects of this audience on literature itself and on the method of approach to literature. We need not spend very long on the Latin prose productions of the early Middle Ages. They were not, in the real sense, literature, but rather compilations intended for the use of scholars. They were practical works and are of importance as channels of transmission of knowledge. Into this category fall the works of Bede, the chronicle histories, the *De rerum naturis* of Hrabanus Maurus (a kind of encyclopedia), and such vernacular work as the translations made by Alfred the Great, the Old High German versions of Tatian and Isidore, and the commentaries on Boethius by Notker Labeo.

More significant are the works already mentioned whose purpose was to offer to a newly Christianized Germanic society an acceptable life of Christ. Such works were the Old Saxon *Heliand* (early ninth century), the translation of Genesis into Old Saxon [3] and Old English, the German versions of such stories as that of Christ and the Woman of Samaria, and the *Evangelienbuch* of Otfried of Weissenburg.[4] It seems at first sight obvious that these works were intended for the use of those who could not read Latin and who were to be instructed in the life of Christ. In the case of the *Heliand,* in particular, the literary histories (with notable exceptions) contain facile statements to the effect that Christ is made to appear as a Germanic chieftain, surrounded by his loyal thanes, the Apostles. According to this view the spiritual side of the life of Christ and

[3] *Heliand und Genesis,* ed. O. Behagel, 6th ed. (1942); modern German trans. by O. Kunze (1925).

[4] *Evangelienbuch,* ed. J. Kelle, 3 vols. (1856–81).

particularly the qualities of mercy and forgiveness of one's enemies are played down. As Schwietering has shown,[5] all these works rest securely on a foundation of the orthodox theology of the time and most of the confusion has arisen because of the inevitable use of the vocabulary associated with the Germanic chiefs and their followers in epic usage. Otfried's work is even more closely associated with the school learning of his day. He deliberately used a verse form associated with Latin hymns, and his poem follows the school tradition of commentary and allegorization. Otfried was determined to demonstrate the ability of the Franks to be learned men and the capability of their language to express learned material adequately. That he was not altogether successful is not surprising. The work was, for its day, a great achievement. But it is clearly aimed, like all similar poems, not at a general lay public, which could not possibly have understood it, but at the small group of people who, although already educated in Latin, spoke German as a native tongue. Furthermore, such works were of great assistance to the large number of students who never read or understood Latin with complete ease and who needed assistance in understanding Latin works. The audience, then, was small and "learned." We must banish the picture of large-scale readings of the *Heliand* to enraptured Germanic chiefs.

The work of Otfried is closely connected with the whole Carolingian tradition, and of this a word must now be said. Few literary historians would dispute the thesis that the Carolingian revival of learning was primarily due to the personal drive of the great emperor himself. Charles was not in fact a learned man, although his contemporary biographies dutifully did their best for his reputation, but he recognized the value of learning, and his choice of Alcuin as director of his educational policy was a wise move. The result of Alcuin's effort was an increase in the number of men well acquainted with the learning available in their time and a broadening of the base of educa-

[5] *Die deutsche Dichtung im Mittelalter*, p. 8.

tion, not a rise in its level, nor any great intellectual achievement by individuals. There is a great mass of literature from the Carolingian period, say from 800 to 900, and almost all of it is insignificant. Respect for the past was high, and knowledge of the classics, late classics, and commentaries quite widespread. The literature produced followed the pattern which might be expected—some good hymns, for here there could be genuine feeling; lyric poetry on stock subjects such as the pleasures of learning; formal laments on the death of great personalities; descriptions in verse of gardens and cities, etc., and, significantly, a considerable amount of eulogy of the emperor himself. The poems show considerable formal skill. They are full of references to and quotations from the classics and of rhetorical artifices. The poets were in fact writing entirely for the other members of their own circle. Of them all only Anghilbert, Theodulph, and Walafrid Strabo can be said to have any poetic gift, and even they are able rather than inspired. The Carolingian period in literature is remarkable for what it preserved rather than for what it achieved. It looked back rather than forward, and few signs of the great works which were to come can be seen in its literary products. Its audience consisted of the learned circle which was created at the court of Charlemagne and in the centers of learning which were connected with it. The audience is still a small and learned circle.

The century which followed the Carolingian period was not favorable to literary production. Not only was it a period of social chaos, with a constant threat of complete collapse in western Europe under the impact of pagan invasion from the north and east, but the reformers of Cluny had brought into learning a more ascetic and less secular attitude. Vernacular literature must have been in existence, and some of the great works of the twelfth century were undoubtedly developing, but we have no written evidence of them. Their audience could only have been the listeners at the fireside of the chief, or the men and women gathered at a corner in the market place. They were essentially popular works, and we know too little of them to say more than that they provided the intermediate stages leading to great works later.

A few Latin works written in this period, which will be discussed in their proper place, are puzzling from the point of view of possible audience. In the tenth century Hroswitha of Gandersheim wrote, among other things, plays on the martyrdom of saints. "Plays" is perhaps the wrong word.[6] Her own explanation is that she saw many people seduced by the pleasant language of Terence into reading his immoral comedies and that she proposed to provide a more wholesome substitute in the same form. Her actual contribution to the history of drama will be discussed later, but we may ask, "Who read these plays?" Were they acted and what are we to understand by "acting"? She must have hoped for a wide audience if the immorality of Terence were not to continue its wicked sway. There is little evidence that she succeeded. Only one complete basic manuscript of her work survives, and she is never mentioned by other authors. One suspects that only a few persons outside her convent ever became acquainted with her plays. She wrote for a definite moral purpose without paying too much attention to the audience for her work or its distribution to that audience. Here, as frequently in the history of medieval Latin literature, it can be said that the author's purpose rather than the taste or anticipated reaction of an audience is the deciding factor. Such is certainly the case with the satiric beast epic *Ysengrimus*.[7] The work, written in a difficult style, is a vicious anticlerical satire, which has been brilliantly worked out both in the delineation of character and by verbal allusion, but only a learned man could have understood it, even if he had the manuscript before him. The audience, therefore, was very limited, and the influence of the work on later literature negligible. Such lit-

---

[6] Hroswitha von Gandersheim, *Werke,* ed. K. Strecker (1930); *Plays,* trans. by C. St. John (1923), by H. J. W. Tillyard (1923).

[7] *Ysengrimus,* ed. E. Voigt (1884).

erary products are the results of a compulsion in the author, not a desire to write for an audience.

Rather different are the circumstances of the production of the Latin epic *Waltharius*.[8] Controversy about the date of this work and its author still rages, but the account given in the records of the Abbey of St. Gallen is interesting, whether it applies to the extant work or a similar one. The Latin poem is described as the attempt of a pupil to render into Latin verse a German poem, the *Waltharilied*, which, as we know from other sources, definitely existed. Almost a century later, says the account, the resulting epic was discovered and revised to remove imperfections of versification. In other words this whole poem, of 1,456 lines, was written as an exercise, with no audience worth speaking of in mind. The *Waltharius* is by no means despicable as an epic, and critics have overemphasized its dependence on such classical models as Vergil and Statius. Perhaps a great deal of its vigor comes from the Germanic original. But the point to be made is that a relatively long poem such as this could have been written purely as an exercise.

Such must have been the circumstances under which much of the Latin literature of the period was produced. Some of the material so written was undoubtedly incorporated into collections, and later became popular. Anonymity is the rule, not the exception, with secular medieval Latin writings, and often the "name" of an author is meaningless or insignificant. One reason for this anonymity is the fact that the author was not thinking of impressing an audience when he wrote.

The twelfth century shows great changes. Latin learning was no longer so exclusively the property of the priest and monk. As we have seen, the number of those trained as clerics (not necessarily priests) increased considerably, and literature ceased to be a mere by-product of school learning, even though its roots remained in the instruction given there. In fact, the study

[8] *Waltharius,* ed. K. Strecker (1951); with German trans. by K. Langosch in *Waltharius, Ruodlieb, Märchenepen* (1956).

of Latin authors often became an end in itself, rather than a method of approach to more serious studies. The result was the formation of an audience for secular poetry, particularly lyric and satire, which was highly sophisticated and capable of appreciating the best efforts of any poet. This audience has often been identified with the *vagantes* or wandering scholars, but they formed at best only a part of it. The officers of the church were probably more secular-minded in the twelfth century than at any other time during the Middle Ages, and their courts welcomed polished performers.

The knowledge that such an audience existed is clearly reflected in the best Latin lyrics and satires of the twelfth century and is an important factor in determining their form and content. The satire is not a serious effort at social castigation but a brilliant verbal treatment of the clichés of unacceptable behavior. The author relies on the ability of his audience to recognize his skills and appreciate them and knows that he can assume a standard of knowledge which makes such appreciation possible. It is not too much to say that in the Latin literature of the twelfth century the best poems are the short poems and they were short because they could be *recited* to an audience capable of grasping their values. The disappearance of this secular-thinking, Latin-trained audience, when the Church became stricter again in the thirteenth century, doomed the Latin lyric to extinction.

We may now turn to the question of the audience for vernacular poetry and its effects on literature. It may be as well to state at once the obvious fact that everyone who was capable of listening constituted an audience for vernacular works. There was probably no period in the Middle Ages when there were not professional storytellers and reciters whose reputation stood little higher than that of the jugglers and tightrope walkers who wandered the roads with them. Their material was traditional and derived from many sources. The audience affected that material only in the sense that it liked some stories and disliked others. No doubt audience reaction of this sort was an important factor in selecting the stories which later became important works of literature, but it is hardly tangible enough to discuss.

We have already mentioned and shall mention again the artistic knowledge of at least some members of the audience for the Germanic epics and the resulting emphasis in those works on the use of elaborate metaphors, of "kennings" or formal word substitutes. The knowledge that the audience expected such elaboration led to its constant and even exaggerated employment and ultimately to its decay as a means of literary expression. The audience itself, however, could not survive the society which formed it. The impact of Christianity upon this audience meant also the introduction of classical literary forms and of classical material. The desire to break with a pagan past and to move with new literary fashions destroyed the audience for the Germanic epic or lay by depriving it of the traditional knowledge which alone could make that epic comprehensible as a literary form. It is thus no accident that we have little or no epic material in its original form from the southern Germanic peoples. *Beowulf* shows the type in a later, Christianized form, and the *Hildebrandslied* is short and lacks the elaboration of language which we know from other works to have been characteristic. In the northern countries, particularly Iceland, the society for which the epics were designed survived much longer, and even the advent of Christianity did not destroy it for a long time. The survival of a comprehending audience meant the survival of the art form and, since there were literate men among that audience, its survival for future generations to read. It is also worth noting that the individual family and its ancestors were of far more significance in the small, isolated communities of Iceland than on the mainland or in France and Germany. Norse literature is an interesting example of the preservation of an older type of literature by the survival of its audience. It is also a warning to literary historians that the survival of a type in a particular area does not prove that it originated there or that it survived in a "purer" form. The loss of the "trained" audience for Germanic material meant that the stories were used in a more popular form. The original adventures were mixed with material of different origin to provide an exciting mixture of the exotic, the marvelous, and the pseudohistorical which would appeal to an audience less interested in form than in matter. Such are the stories of *Herzog Ernst* and *König Rother*,[9] German epics of the twelfth century. And such, no doubt, were the earlier forms, no longer extant, of the works of the Roland cycle and the adventures of Guillaume d'Orange. The taste of the audience which required wonders and adventures left a mark upon the more artistic versions of the later twelfth century, for the later authors were reluctant to remove incidents already hallowed by tradition, even when they accorded ill with new ideas of literary taste or moral purpose.

We may mention one characteristic of these early epics, probably due to the desire of the minstrel to hold the attention of an audience primarily interested in the narration of events, which was destined to exert a significant influence upon the form of the later epic and romance. This is the almost invariable division of a story into two sections, in the first of which the hero seems to have achieved his purpose of winning a wife or battle or both with relative ease, only to be deprived of his gains by a sudden turn of fortune which leaves him in a worse position than at the start. In the second part he (or his successor) must painfully work his way forward again to final success. Exactly how this almost universal type originated cannot, of course, be stated with certainty, but it is not improbable that it springs from circumstances not dissimilar to those under which Scheherazade told the stories of the *Thousand and One Nights*,

[9] *Herzog Ernst*, ed. K. Bartsch (1869); *König Rother*, ed. Th. Frings and J. Kuhnt (1922).

namely, the desire to hold the interest of the audience for a longer period and possibly keep the singer in a warm hall instead of the cold snow for one more night.

Later artists found their material thus divided and retained the form, but used it for vastly different purposes, as we shall have occasion to remark in later chapters. Sometimes, as in the *Nibelungenlied*, it does seem probable that the two halves of the poem came from two different original stories, but this is by no means always so. The desire to retain the attention of the audience was usually the determining factor.

The topic of the audience for the courtly romance and lyric has been much discussed, not always realistically. Certain facts are clear and can be simply restated. The more settled conditions of life in the twelfth century, particularly in southern France, produced, for the first time since the Roman Empire, a relatively leisured, wealthy, and cultivated audience for literature. This class was, of course, the aristocracy of the day, educated by chaplains or clerics but not influenced to any large degree by the stricter moral standards of the church. It was the same class of society which had listened to the cruder epics in the previous century, but certain significant changes were obvious. The levels of formal education, artistic training, and general sophistication had all risen, and the relative importance of cultivated women was far greater.

There has been, even in the works of some competent literary historians, a tendency to idealize this society, as if in some way it were identical with the courts portrayed in the Arthurian romances. This is as nonsensical as the opposite view, which sets down all members of medieval feudal society as little better than the pigs which rooted in their castle yards. It is highly doubtful whether all those who sat in the Athenian theater were capable of appreciating the true greatness of Sophocles or that all Elizabethan groundlings saw in the character of Hamlet the subtle interplay of psychological forces which modern critics profess to find there. Just as Shakespeare's tragedies can be enjoyed on the primitive plane of bloody embroilment, so can the medieval romances be taken as fanciful adventure in a fairy world. No doubt a large proportion of the courtly audience heard them as such and enjoyed them. No doubt too there were unenlightened spirits who grunted to others of like mind that they were heartily sick of this new-fangled type of story, and who preferred less courtliness and more broken heads. What is important is that there were enough people in the audience who could appreciate the artist's use of an idealized world and new standards of knightly conduct to make it possible for him to write. The same is true of the love lyric. Only a highly sophisticated audience could appreciate it and that audience must have been there. It is hard, in my opinion, to exaggerate the importance of the woman patron. The desire to appeal to feminine predilections and tastes is clear both in the lyric and in the romance.

The writers of the courtly romance wished to use the idealized world they created to set before their audience a new standard of values which could act as a model for behavior. A later generation followed their suggestions with a fidelity which seems to us almost comic. But there is nevertheless good evidence that for some artists this audience still fell short of the standard needed. Gottfried von Strassburg, in his prologue to *Tristan,* makes it quite clear that he is writing for a still more select audience, a cherished few who could appreciate the refined idealization and allegorization of the love theme which he was presenting.

In the small groups which formed the audience for courtly poetry, writer and audience were very close. The ideas of the audience could be shaped by the artist, but he in his turn was personally affected by their reaction and bound to follow their needs. His heroes were forced to behave in the pattern with which they were familiar and which they expected. It is clear that the widening of this audience or a lowering of its standards could have a bad effect on literature. And precisely these things happened. Both in France and Germany there was social disturbance. The Albigensian Crusade shattered the culture of southern France, and in Germany there was political and social disruption in the thirteenth century. The refined audience was lost, the material of the stories remained, and inevitably the stress again was placed on the relatively crude aspects of the poems—the wonders of fairyland and the wholesale slaughter of giants by the hero. The subtleties of character and of morals vanished with the audience, never large, which could appreciate them.

It is customary in literary histories to speak of the audience for literature in the fourteenth and fifteenth centuries as predominantly bourgeois. Like most generalizations, this statement needs considerable modification, particularly when the change in audience is offered as an explanation for changes in the character of literature. Any reader of Huizinga's *Waning of the Middle Ages* must be aware of the paradoxical situation in many of the more cultivated courts of western and particularly northwestern Europe. The most exaggerated respect was paid to lineage, aristocratic bearing, courtly manners, and rich clothing by a society whose wealth was dependent less and less on land and more and more on trade and commerce. The new possessors of wealth were much concerned to imitate the ideals of gentility and, as far as possible, to identify themselves with the society they so much admired. The result was that the outward forms of "chivalry," as interpreted from the earlier courtly romances, were practiced more thoroughly than they had ever been in the period of the finest flower of the romance. The treatment of the French king, John II, by his captors at Poitiers is a good example. Extremes in dress, manners, and behavior went hand in hand, and they were practiced by the courts as much as by the bourgeois. The widening of the reading public also contributed to a greater knowledge of aristocratic manners and chivalrous behavior. No doubt the persons on the fringe of aristocracy or even well outside the circle then, as now, followed its activities with more wonder and admiration than its own members did. An element often described as characteristically bourgeois is didacticism. It is true that there seems to be a tendency in bourgeois-dominated societies to feel that literature should, so to speak, pay its way by inculcating moral virtues.[10] Didacticism becomes more obvious in the thirteenth and fourteenth centuries, but it had already been present, if not crudely obvious, in courtly literature, and its increasing importance is due at least in part to the revival of the stricter moral standards within the church and to the influence of scholasticism.

Literature, as usual, reflected these social tendencies in its own way. The story cycles remained the same, although there were changes in emphasis. The Arthurian cycle gradually declined in popularity, although new stories appeared about minor heroes with the characteristics of Arthurian knights. The Alexander romances became much more popular, and Charlemagne and his peers passed definitely from history to legend. The stress in all the stories was upon the superficial aspects of chivalry, its successful fights, its wooing of ladies, its exaggeratedly courteous behavior. The style and language used reflected these tendencies by stress on verbal richness, lush metaphor, and rhetorical devices. Prose versions of the stories began to appear, with similar characteristics.

In lyric poetry the original brilliant impetus of courtly love passed to repetition of well-worn themes. A standard had been established which, it was felt, could not be surpassed but only imitated. New forms, such as the ballade, virelai, rondeau, and estampie, were developed out of the troubadour forms and used to express, often very effectively but in conventional terms, the poet's amours and his feelings towards life. The persons who wrote these works were usually attached to courts, and the audience to which they directed their work was still the aristocratic group capable of patronage. But it was not a small

[10] See A. A. Hentsch, *De la Littérature didactique du moyen âge s'adressant spécialement aux femmes* (1903); G. R. Owst, *Literature and Pulpit in Medieval England* (1933).

group with a special culture. Literature was a fashion and an interest worthy of a gentleman, but little more. In reading the works of an Eustache Deschamps one sometimes has the impression that quantity of output was more important than depth or sincerity.

The striking popularity of allegory during this period is at least in part due to the same cause. Literature was fanciful, a plaything, and remote from existence. Just as the romances of chivalry were related to an earlier, idealized form of feudal society, so allegory could be set in a fairy land of make-believe where characters could be manipulated in accordance with idealized codes of behavior. Such literature, moreover, had the added advantage of being mysterious and requiring skill to be understood. Many tapestries of the later Middle Ages reflect very well the current tendencies in literature.

The foregoing remarks may have given the impression that religion and morals disappeared from the literature of the later Middle Ages. Such an impression would be far from the truth. Many of the works, particularly those written in Germany, are of an almost painful religiosity. Occasionally, and particularly in England where the advent of Arthurian literature was late, true nobility appears in literary works. *Sir Gawain and the Green Knight* is one of the most remarkable of all Arthurian poems, and in Malory's *Morte d'Arthur* the story of the Grail finds one of its finest expressions.

We have discussed the question of the audience for medieval literature wherever it seemed that generalizations could be made and where the audience seems to have been a determining factor in the direction taken by literature. Many problems are not capable of such generalized solutions, and we shall take note of them when a particular branch of literature is discussed, for example, the question of the audience for the sophisticated Germanic epic and, most important, for the gradually developing drama.

4

The Literary Types

Before discussing in detail the most important literary genres of the Middle Ages and the greatest of the works by which they are represented, it will probably be convenient to indicate what those genres are, and to make clear the technical terms used by literary historians in discussing them.[1]

We may mention first those genres which are clearly derived from their counterparts in the literature of classical antiquity. The writing of the Latin epic continued throughout the Middle Ages but never reached the heights of good literature, except possibly in one work, the *Waltharius*. The model was always Vergil, never Homer, whose work was known only through the short poem *Ilias Latina*, which, while pleasant enough, hardly does more than give the story of the *Iliad*. The classical imitators

[1] The following works are of use in the discussion of questions of literary theory and genre division: E. A. Bloom, "The Allegorical Principle," *English Literary History*, Vol. XVIII (1951); H. Kuhn, "Zur Deutung der künstlerischen Form des Mittelalters," *Studium Generale*, Vol. II (1949); H. P. H. Teesing, *Das Problem der Perioden in der Literaturgeschichte* (1949); K. Viëtor, "Probleme der literarischen Gattungsgeschichte," *DVLG*, Vol. IV (1931); M. Wehrli, *Allgemeine Literaturwissenschaft* (1951); R. Wellek and A. Warren, *The Theory of Literature* (1949). There is also much information in P. Zumthor, *Histoire littéraire de la France*, and W. Stammler, *Deutsche Philologie im Aufriss*, under the names of the various genres.

of Vergil, Statius, Valerius Flaccus, and Lucan, also exerted an influence on language which was not confined to Latin epic. More important still were the Christian imitators of Vergil, particularly Prudentius, who adapted the Vergilian verse forms and the rhetoric of Vergil's imitators to Christian purposes. The Latin epic of the Middle Ages is not significant in the history of literature and will not be discussed in detail.

Much more important is the history of satire. Here, for various reasons, Horace, rather than Juvenal, was the model. The satires of Juvenal are hard to comprehend without a detailed understanding of contemporary conditions in Rome, and general moral considerations must be derived from the study of particular instances. Horace states much more clearly the moral faults and human weaknesses which he is satirizing, and for didactic purposes his method was more easily adaptable to medieval requirements. The standards he set were adopted by one medieval satirist after another and became commonplaces. In the less creative periods of medieval literature the dependence is almost complete. The great satirists of the twelfth century, however, went far beyond him. They used the instrument of parody and Biblical reminiscence to chastise faults in an entirely new way. Moreover they used with great effect the new rhythmical and rhymed verse techniques which Horace, of course, did not know. It may be said that the influence of classical antiquity on the best satire is confined to largely incidental resemblances in language and theme.

The vernacular satirists lean heavily upon their Latin predecessors. The same themes are treated, and the language and topoi are much the same. There is no vernacular genre in medieval literature more indebted to its Latin counterpart than satire.

We should distinguish between social satire of the type just described and the moral poems which chastise the sins of the world from a Christian point of view. Although the two types borrowed from each other, their attitudes were fundamentally different. The Christian poems reflect a deep distrust in things secular, a belief that this world is basically unsound and fundamentally incapable of reformation and that the soul can be saved only by strict attention to Christian principles and a virtual denial of the world. Their censure of the moral failings of the world is sincere and bitter, and it is these moralists who came closest to the deep indignation of Juvenal, even though their grounds for indignation and their methods were often different. Their antifeminist attitude, for example, is very close to his. They accuse women of the same crimes but in more general terms and on religious, not social grounds. The social satires on the other hand, although they inevitably reflect Christian morality, are concerned with the criticism of the behavior of man in society and are frequently not meant to be taken seriously.

As we have already seen, the practice of imitating the themes and forms of the classical lyric continued throughout the Middle Ages. Here again one would anticipate that the influence of Horace would be predominant. Such, however, is not the case. The Middle Ages could not be expected to perceive that his amours were largely imaginary and that his praise of wine, though no friend of Horace would question its sincerity, did not necessarily imply a drunken stupor every evening. More modern critics, who have less excuse for ignorance, have found it necessary to apologize for him. Consequently Horace's verse forms were used, but not his themes. Most quantitative lyrics, that is, those written in classical verse forms depending upon syllable length, tend to praise the quiet life, a city or a garden, when they do not take up a religious theme.

Much more important than the imitative quantitative lyric was the rhythmic, rhymed lyric which developed from the forms used in the so-called Ambrosian hymn. The forms were slow in spreading to secular poetry, partly because the classicizing nature of the Carolingian period checked their adoption by learned men, but from the tenth century onward they developed into one of the most flexible and polished means of expression ever used in lyric poetry. They did not suffer from the incubus of a half-understood tradition and they could be read or even sung with feeling, since the rhythms they employed were perceived by writer and listener alike. A wealth of occasional verse, love poetry, satire, parody, drinking songs, and elegies appeared, mainly in the twelfth and thirteenth centuries, most of it anonymous but revealing a verbal skill and ability to handle the most varied verse forms which have rarely been matched in any period. It should be stated quite firmly here that, contrary to an impression still widespread, these poems are not "vulgar" or beneath the classical level. Rhythmic verse was the natural form of expression in medieval Latin, which had no feeling for quantity. The authors of the rhythmic poems were educated men who could and often did write in the classical meters. They were, however, wise enough to realize the immense superiority of rhythmic verse for expressing their thoughts, and to its composition they devoted their best efforts. The Latin they use is, in fact, so simple, clear, and free of "medievalisms" that only an attempt at imitation will reveal the skill necessary to produce the seemingly effortless rhyme schemes and polished verse patterns. It may be truly said that in its lyric and occasional verse the literature of the Latin Middle Ages reaches its highest level of technical accomplishment.

Although the Christian hymn is not usually considered part of the literature of classical antiquity, it was nevertheless a fully developed genre by the fourth century after Christ. The best hymns written before the collapse of classical civilization used the well-known quantitative meters, particularly the Sapphic. The hymns of short lines with some rhyme or assonance, usually called Ambrosian, were clearly popular productions, and it is still not completely clear how far they were intended to depend on syllable length and how far on stress accent. More will be said on this subject in the chapter on lyric verse. However this may be, the use of a rhythmic rhymed verse form developed from them and, as might be expected, some of the deepest lyric expression of the Middle Ages is to be found in these hymns. Although many of them have been popularly ascribed to particular authors, the bulk remain anonymous and are even hard to date. Their allusive language and use of figures had great influence on secular lyric, both Latin and vernacular.

In describing the forms derived from classical antiquity, we should not forget the humble fable. Even if, as one scholar remarked, the fables of Aesop were not written by Aesop but by another man with the same name, (surely an all-time low in learned quibbling), the Middle Ages persisted in regarding them as Aesop's fables. The original Greek form was not known but Phaedrus' adaptation was, and even more popular were the versions which went under the name of "Romulus." Their frequent appearance in manuscripts is proof of their popularity and wide influence.

The drama had already gone far along the road to extinction in classical times. The classical comedies of Plautus and Terence made little appeal to Roman audiences; the efforts at tragedy made even less. Seneca's works, so influential in the time of the Renaissance, were cabinet dramas designed at best for recitation. The mime, in itself no despicable art form, degenerated into mere spectacle in the later Empire and caused such Christian writers as Tertullian to class the drama with gladiatorial contests as a demoralizing amusement for the masses. Although the actual theaters continued to stand for centuries, Isidore's descriptions of "comedia" and "tragoedia" make it quite clear that all conception of the true nature of classical drama had passed away by the seventh century. Terence, however, was easily accessible in manuscript; Plautus was also accessible to a lesser extent. Terence was apparently much read and occasionally imitated but, it would seem, in the belief that his dramas were a type of declamation, where two persons alternately read the various roles. Classical drama had little effect until the Renaissance. The loss of the classical plays, however, did not mean the loss of a sense of drama. There can be little doubt that informal acting of improvised, and even traditional, scenes continued among groups of professional entertainers. It would be hard to produce written evidence for a continuous tradition from the ancient Roman mime to the medieval strolling player, but the likelihood is strong that such a tradition existed. It would be equally hard to demonstrate by documents the modern circus tradition known to exist in many families. The spring and winter festivals in all countries gave scope for lively dramatic performances of a traditional nature, and these affected the first of the forms we are to discuss which was clearly not derived from classical antiquity, namely, the drama of the church.

Since the monumental researches of Karl Young it is assumed by almost everyone that modern drama derives from certain extra-liturgical features of church services at feasts, particularly Easter and Christmas, which gradually assumed a dramatic form. There is good evidence for this view, as we shall see in the chapter on drama, but not all features of later medieval drama can be explained by it. Why should comic scenes be introduced into a serious Easter play? What led to the enormous extension of the scope of the dramas? How "dramatic" were the church plays in fact? Influences other than those within the church itself must be postulated to explain these developments. By the end of the Middle Ages there was an enormous complex of dramatic biblical presentations in which actors took part, but they contained little which can be called true drama. For the best medieval comedy we must look elsewhere, to the group of writers in Arras, who clearly had little connection with the developing church drama but who had a strong sense of theater and dramatic possibilities. In spite of the efforts of this small group, it must be said that the greatest writers found their mode of expression not in the drama but in the romance.

The word "romance" has been so much abused that it must first be made clear how the term will be employed. In speaking of the literature of classical antiquity the term is usually used of prose tales of fiction embodying romantic and unreal adventures. Only a few of these have survived. English writers usually use the term to describe the body of works in prose or, more usually, in verse, which present fictional themes, such as those of the Arthurian knights, the Trojan cycle, and some English traditional material, such as Sir Bevis of Hamptoun or Havelock the Dane, in an idealized setting. Although the verse forms of the romance have much in common with epic poetry, they are distinguished from it by the fact that their themes were regarded by the author as either nonhistorical or so remote as to be capable of fictional treatment.

It should be noted, however, that French and, particularly, German terminology does not follow the same pattern. The French term "roman" is often used in a much wider sense than the English "romance" to designate a larger body of fictional work and, in more modern literature, it includes the novel. Care is necessary in interpreting the word, especially in works not dealing specifically with medieval literature. Many features of the *chansons de geste* would appear to identify them with the romance, but French critics invariably keep them in a separate class because their material, in spite of considerable distortion and the importation of numerous themes from folklore and legend, remains basically historical. The term "epopée" is occasionally used for narrative poetry, including the *chansons de geste*.

Although some German writers use the term *Roman* in the sense, more or less, of the English "romance," most literary histories employ an altogether different terminology. The division is made between "courtly epic" [*höfisches Epos*] and "popular epic" [*Volksepos*]. The former is applied to long poems using the fictional or remotely historical material of the Arthurian cycle or the stories of Troy, Alexander, or Rome, and takes its name from the fact that the German writers were of noble birth, wrote for a courtly audience, and derived their material directly from French, that is, fashionable, sources. The works of Hartmann von Aue, Gottfried von Strassburg, and Wolfram von Eschenbach fall into this category. The *Volksepos* on the other hand draws upon Germanic material, historical, quasi-historical, or legendary. It employs Germanic, not French, verse forms, and it appealed to a more popular audience. The distinction between the two types is not so clear as the two terms would imply, but it is unlikely to disappear from works written in German.

We should also note that "romance" is sometimes used of a short narrative poem with lyric elements found in Provençal and French literature and, of course, as an adjective in the sense of "coming from a country whose language is of Latin derivation." It is characteristic of the confusion surrounding the whole question that the best known of all the works with "romance" in its title, namely, the *Roman de la Rose,* should be an elaborate allegory whose resemblance to the normal romance lies only in the fact that its story is the fictional pursuit of an ideal goal and that its background is that found in the courtly romances.

The romance, then, was essentially a work of fiction, felt to be such by both its author and its audience. We shall discuss in a separate chapter the themes it chose and its methods of treating them. The knowledge that he was writing fiction enabled the author to treat his material with considerable freedom, changing incidents to suit his purpose and delineating character according to his own point of view. It also enabled him to spend considerable time on lengthy descriptions both of incident and material (castles, clothing, treasures) and to make great use of magic, supernatural happenings, and wonders beyond the normal experience of his audience. As the romance developed, a conventional idealized world in which it was set developed with it, so that the audience had the same frame of reference as readers of western cowboy tales, spy stories, and other modern fictional reading develop—a frame of reference of which they have no direct experience and which bears little resemblance to the actual society which it purports to portray (for example, life at the court of Charlemagne or in Troy) but which nevertheless is accepted by them as normal for stories of this kind.

The great writers of romance also set up within this idealized world an idealized code of behavior. Details must be reserved for a later chapter, but we may note here that this code was not so rigid as some critics would have us believe. It is not likely that the romances reflect a real-life code of ethics, but the fact that they were writing fiction made it possible for the great writers of romance to set before their readers standards of conduct which could and did act as a model for noble behavior. It is this feature of the genre which constitutes its greatest and most enduring quality, that out of a mass of legend, fairy story, crude adventure, and distorted chronicle history it forged an idealized society of such grace and beauty, of such nobility set in the glowing colors of an imagined earthly paradise, that it became an inspiration not only to the finest spirits of its own age but also for the centuries which were to follow.

We have seen that the romance was regarded as a fictional genre. It was otherwise with the *chanson de geste* and the national epic in Germany, Spain, and the northern countries. Although we can do little but make informed guesses about the early stages of the works now extant, there is definite evidence of actual events in the history of each country on which the works were founded. The historical incident, curiously enough, was very often a defeat rather than a victory—the death of Roland, Count of Brittany, in a minor skirmish with the Basques, the destruction of the Burgundian tribe by Attila the Hun—and it is almost impossible to escape the conclusion that the original forms of these poems may have been in the nature of apologies for these defeats or at least attempts to ennoble them. Even modern documented history is not without examples of the same tendency to convert retreats into glorious victories.

But though the incidents were much modified and distorted,

and additional material from legendary and unhistorical sources was introduced, the authors remained conscious that they were writing of the history of their people, and that their characters were not creations of the imagination but personages who had shaped the destiny of later generations who were their descendants. Such a feeling imposed restrictions upon the author which were not felt by the writer of the romance. He had to preserve what he considered to be the traditional morality of the ancestors of his nation, he could idealize them only as representatives of that morality, and he could place them only against a background historically conceived. This does not mean that the background was in fact historical. Medieval writers did not have at their disposal any means of determining what the background of their ancestors was. But they preserved the forms, attitudes, and characters of their original material to a far greater extent than did the writers of the romance, and tradition was so strong that there is often an observable clash between the features preserved and those added by the author from his own experience. The superficial courtliness and Christianity of the *Nibelungenlied,* for example, are utterly out of harmony with the basic morality of the poem.

The later development of a country necessarily had its effect upon these historical works, particularly if, as in the *Chanson de Roland,* it was possible to view that development as a direct continuation of the historical events described in the poem. Charlemagne was a consciously Christian king, and it is not remarkable that, under the impact of the Crusades, he should be viewed essentially as a monarch working in the service of Christianity. The poem simply intensifies and develops a historical event. More interesting is the fact that he becomes entirely a French king ruling subject races elsewhere. Here the subsequent political developments and the fact that the poem arose on French territory have imparted to it a new element, unhistorical in fact but highly typical of the nationalistic tendencies of the epic. In verse forms, language, and spirit the epics (including the *chansons de geste*) reflected their connection with national feelings and history. But as they became more sophisticated, the sense of history diminished. The mere fact of their being written down tended to make them appear more like works of literature than historical documents. Moreover, they were inevitably influenced by the romance. The result was an increasing tendency to disregard the historical aspects or at least to make more use of pseudohistory. The fantastic plays a larger role. Charlemagne in particular is provided with a totally unhistorical childhood deriving directly from folklore and popular fiction. Trivial incidents are distorted beyond recognition and made the basis for striking adventures. By the later Middle Ages there was little difference between the romance and the successors of the national epic.

We need do no more than mention that there were in the Middle Ages other, shorter forms of narrative poetry. They exist in all languages and from the twelfth century on are very numerous. Most important are the *lais* and *fabliaux*,[2] poems of varying length with subjects from very diverse sources. There are also collections of poems with didactic purposes, as well as those on such stock subjects as debates between water and wine, summer and winter, and the body and soul. Except where they impinge on other genres, these poems will not be discussed.

We may also briefly dismiss most medieval prose writings. Such prose as exists before the twelfth century cannot truly be called literature. It is utilitarian, though it provided literature with much of its material. From the twelfth century on the Latin prose *exempla*[3] become very important. They are prose

[2] J. Bédier, *Les Fabliaux*, 4th ed. (1925); A. De Montaiglon and G. Raynaud, *Recueil général des fabliaux des XIIIe et XIVe siècles*, 6 vols. (1872–90); E. Faral, "Le Fabliau latin au moyen-âge," *Romania*, Vol. L (1924); P. Nykrog, *Les Fabliaux* (1957); B. Woledge, *Bibliographie des romans et nouvelles en prose français antérieurs à 1500* (1954).

[3] For editions, etc., see J.-Th. Welther, *L'Exemplum dans la littérature réligieuse et didactique au moyen-âge* (1927); J. A. Mosher, *The Exemplum in the Early Religious and Didactic Literature of England* (1911).

tales from varied sources collected with the ostensible purpose of providing moral tales for sermons. Some of them would hardly seem to be edifying, but ingenuity and allegorization could often make them so. They are often neatly written, and it could easily be argued that every prose story written since can be traced back in basic form to a story in these collections. The Franciscans, in their earnest desire to bring the Word of God to the laity, were the great systematic collectors of *exempla,* and it is to the thirteenth and fourteenth centuries that we owe such collections as those of Etienne de Bourbon, Roger of Hovedon, Jacques de Vitry, and the *Speculum Laicorum.*

The *exempla* provided the material for literature, but were hardly a literary form in themselves. The same may be said of such collections as the *Gesta Romanorum,* tales from history with morals, only remotely connected with the Romans, the *Legenda Aurea,* the *Dialogus Miraculorum* of Caesar of Heisterbach, and above all of the *Vitae,* the lives of the saints. Throughout the Middle Ages this hagiographic literature was of great importance to cleric and layman alike. Its purpose was, of course, to tell the wonders wrought by the saints and thus demonstrate the power of the God whom they served. The incidents in the lives of the major saints early developed into a kind of canon, but it should not be forgotten that in the Middle Ages canonization was not the formal process which it has since become. There were innumerable local saints, of great prestige in their own area and often recognized by the local bishop or even "officially" canonized by the civil administration, who were virtually unknown elsewhere and who never received official canonization. The stories which clustered about their names were not infrequently folk tales, suitably altered to fit the new circumstances.

Both in the lives of the saints and in the stories of the miracles of the Virgin the Middle Ages were able to find entertainment coupled with edification. It is no accident that so many of the incidents are wonders and miracles, for these made most impression on the people and were most susceptible of literary treatment. It goes without saying that the saints' lives were frequently put into verse, both Latin and vernacular, and later provided subjects for drama. It may be added that both the educated and uneducated lay public was far more familiar with these stories than a modern audience would be and that references to incidents in their lives could be understood without footnotes.

Prose in the vernacular, other than translations of moral and some philosophical works, can hardly be said to exist before the thirteenth century. Its use as a literary medium was slow in developing, and it is not too outrageous to say that from the purely literary point of view all prose written before the later Middle Ages could be ignored. The best vernacular prose style was written by the mystics, principally German, of the thirteenth and fourteenth centuries. They developed new possibilities of expression for the language and made clear the potentialities of prose works written in the vernacular. Their intention was, however, to justify in theology their position as mystics and to bring others to a like faith. The literary aspect was secondary.

We have remarked on the mass of romantic tales which must have been current throughout the European Middle Ages. Some appear in Latin works such as the *Courtly Trifles* of Walter Map.[4] It was not until the thirteenth and fourteenth centuries, however, that collections of such stories begin to appear in vernacular writing. Among them we may mention the stories of Pfaffe Amis,[5] an earlier Till Eulenspiegel, and the numerous fabliaux. The verse romances began to be put into prose form, often very voluminous, in the thirteenth century. The earliest form of the Grail story in prose, the *Joseph, Merlin, Perceval,*

[4] Walter Map, *De nugis curialium,* ed. M. R. James (Anecdota Oxoniensia, Medieval and Modern Series, Vol. XIV [1914]), trans. by F. Tupper and M. R. Ogle (1924), by M. R. James and others (1923).

[5] Der Stricker, *Pfaff Amis,* ed. H. Lambel, in *Erzählungen und Schwänke des 13. Jahrhunderts,* 2d ed. (1883), modern German version by K. Pannier (1878).

may antedate 1210. Other prose versions of the Grail story followed, and the adventures of Tristan also were gathered into prose form. During the two centuries that followed almost all the great cycles of romance and *chanson de geste* were reduced to prose form in France and Germany and, later, English versions of them appeared. As might be expected the same occurred with the specifically German works, the stories of Siegfried and Dietrich von Bern. In Scandinavia there was also much adaptation of French and German material, but the native sagas, written in prose, continued to flourish and assumed their definitive form in the thirteenth century.

Two important genres are still to be discussed, the vernacular lyric and the beast epic (which was sometimes a beast novel). The vernacular lyric is second only to the romance in its importance in medieval literature. Of its origins and the wide differences of opinion concerning them we shall speak in the appropriate place. The twelfth century witnessed the development in Southern France of a school of lyric poetry of striking homogeneity in form and content. The attention of the principal writers was concentrated on the production of the *canzon,* a formal poem of idealized love, written in an increasingly rigid and complicated strophic form. Stress was on virtuosity of rhyme and meter and on variations of imagery within a prescribed pattern. Minor genres were also practiced, but in them too the formal element predominated. The poets who wrote these love poems were in the best sense professional writers. The fact that they were imitated by a certain number of noble amateurs does not invalidate this conclusion. Many of them also practiced non-lyric genres, such as the *tenson* and *sirventes,* which allowed strikingly free comment on the contemporary scene and which did not spare even the greatest figures of the day. At its best this troubadour lyric is among the greatest lyric poetry of all time, polished, deeply felt, and of great formal beauty. At its worst it is a banal collection of outworn commonplaces, where obscurity has to take the place of originality in an effort to hold the reader's attention. It should not be forgotten that this poetry was intended to be sung and that the author was also the composer of the melody. Recent scholarship has made great strides in reconstructing from the medieval notation, which is found with some songs in some manuscripts, the melodies to which the lyrics should be sung. But the amount of information given by medieval notation is much less than that provided by the modern five-line staff. Time intervals in particular are hard to judge and anyone who has heard various modern interpretations of the same melody will agree that we are still far from knowing exactly how the songs were rendered.

It is customary to say that we cannot really judge medieval lyric poetry because of our ignorance of the music. Some critics go so far as to argue that the music was the most important part of the song and that the lyric itself was little more than a framework for the singing of a melody. This viewpoint is ridiculous. The amount of care spent on rhyme and versification and the cultivation of verbal imagery argues against it. No doubt the medieval audience, educated in a tradition which linked lyric poetry to song, derived great pleasure from the perfect combination of words and melody. Our own tradition is different, since we read poetry silently and evoke rhythmic effects only by the imagination. Whether the effects are the same as those produced on a medieval audience by the same poem is a question that can never be answered, but at least we can say that the best of these poems, read in our fashion, still rank as great works of art. The situation is not, after all, very different from that of the Greek and Latin lyric, where we cannot hope to appreciate the subtle rhythmic and melodic effects which were undoubtedly part of the pleasure of the contemporary audience. Nor would the discovery of an accurate method of reconstructing the melodies be of great help. Musical idiom has changed so much that the modern ear, while intrigued by the novelty of medieval melodies and songs, soon finds them unsatisfying and monotonous. Music is far from being a universal language, as anyone who has ever listened to Eastern music will admit. It is best to discuss the medieval lyric as poetry, and this will be done in this book.

The forms and themes of the Provençal lyric were adopted in northern France, Germany, and Italy, but it is incorrect to argue, as some critics have done, that the lyric poetry of these countries is a mere imitation or offshoot of the Provençal. New attitudes are easily observed in the northern French lyric, and the German *Minnesänger* are indebted to the Provençal only in the most general way. There is virtually no direct imitation of southern French authors and the themes, while generally similar, are treated utterly differently, with far more attention to content and far less to virtuosity in verse form.

The forms developed by the troubadours continued to be used in the thirteenth century but new forms of lyric poetry, many perhaps derived from popular types, also became widespread. The concentration on the idealized love theme was modified, although its conventions persisted. Much more occasional poetry was written. But the tendency to rely more and more on the rhetorical type of treatment, derived from the arts of poetry, led to the production of masses of commonplace lyric with only an occasional touch of real inspiration. The lyric poetry of the fourteenth century in France and Germany is often pleasant but rarely moving.

In Italy it was otherwise. The Provençal troubadours of the early thirteenth century visited Italy and were welcomed at the courts there, particularly in Montferrat. Their forms and themes were much admired and imitated, some of the Italian poets even writing in Provençal. A study of Dante's theoretical work *De Vulgari Eloquentia* (On the vernacular) makes clear the relative popularity and authority of the poets so far as their Italian audience was concerned. Fortunately the Italian writers did not content themselves with mere imitation. The early fourteenth century saw the development of the "dolce stil novo," which imparted to the lyric forms a content which comes close to metaphysical poetry. Its authors were often deliberately obscure and always esoteric, but from their concern with form and spirit developed the sonnet and the lyric poetry of the Renaissance.

We have already noted that fables modeled on those of Aesop continued to be popular in the Middle Ages. They were, however, almost entirely in Latin, and vernacular versions of them do not appear until the late Middle Ages. Much more popular, and appearing relatively early in vernacular works as well as in Latin versions, were stories centering about the rivalry between the fox and the wolf. Although it is possible to see resemblances between these stories and the incidents in Aesop's fables, it is unlikely that the two are intimately connected. It is clear that the basic incidents of the rivalry must have been established at a period considerably earlier than the first written version, which is the extremely sophisticated Latin hexameter poem *Ysengrimus,* ascribed to Master Nivardus of Ghent. Although later versions of the story accumulate new incidents and produce a long "epic," the core of the story remains remarkably consistent. Perhaps even more remarkable is the fact that the early versions of the story are without exception products of the area of the lower Rhine, of Flanders, northern France, and northern Germany. Even when the material had become widely known and very popular in the late Middle Ages the majority of the versions was produced in this same area of Europe.[6]

The beast epic shares with the fable the conventions of its type: animals speak to one another and to humans, and they have a culture which is similar to that of the society of their author and therefore varies to some extent from one period to another. The animals each personify a basic human type— vanity, pride, cunning, or stupidity—but it would be doing the beast epic less than justice to consider it a mere moral tale with animals representing people. Although there is almost always

[6] For editions, works, etc., see readings for Chapter X.

a satiric intention, the animals do have a character of their own, and the interest of the reader is held far more by the comic-heroic struggle between the stupid wolf Isengrim and his rival Renard than by any parallel with human society. This is the great virtue of the beast epic. Unlike the fable, it has an interest which does not depend on a didactic comparison between the conduct of animals and that of men.

In this chapter we have sketched the most important types of medieval literature. No mention has been made of philosophy and theology, nor of purely learned writings. History and chronicle writing have also been ignored, although they often provided the material for literature. In the following chapters an attempt will be made to discuss the development and literary value of the most important literary genres of the Middle Ages: the romance, the *chanson de geste,* the national epic, the Latin and vernacular lyric, including short occasional poems, satirical and minor narrative poetry, the beast epic, and the drama. Only major works will be discussed in any detail; many of the minor works, which are often inaccessible, will not even be mentioned. They may be found in the literary histories. The major works themselves can be understood only by reading them, preferably in the original. The following chapters merely profess to give some help in understanding them.

5

The Romance

As the romance developed during the late twelfth and particularly the thirteenth century, it tended more and more to be classified into cycles associated with a person or event. Of these cycles the most important were those of classical antiquity, often called *matière de Rome,* of which the principal constituents were the stories of Troy and of Alexander the Great, and the Arthurian cycle, the *matière de Bretagne.* The third cycle, the *matière de France,* concerned with Charlemagne and his peers, Guillaume d'Orange, and other French heroes, we shall discuss in the chapter on the *chansons de geste.* Although there were works in French, German, English, and other languages associated with the cycles of Troy and Alexander, the Arthurian cycle provided in all countries the material for the romances of the greatest literary value and also a chivalric background which deeply influenced the treatment of all the other cycles of romance. We shall therefore discuss in some detail the development of the Arthurian romances and particularly the works of Chrétien de Troyes and Thomas of Britain and of the German authors who adapted and imitated them.

It is doubtful whether the person who gave his name to the cycle was in fact a king at all. His name is mentioned in a Welsh poem *Gododdin* of about 600 as a famous warrior, but it is in the *Historia Brittonum* of the pseudo-Nennius that we first hear of his deeds. He is described as *dux* (duke or leader) and, although the twelve victories ascribed to him are probably fictitious or at best distorted history, he clearly was a man of reputation. He appears in various Welsh works, with more and more elements of fantasy, culminating about 1100 in the prose work *Kulhwch and Olwen.* In this work a large number of the elements of later Arthurian romance are already present and many of the knights most prominent at the court of Arthur are named—Kei, Bedwyr, and Gwalchmei (or Gawan). But there is already evidence—for example, the name Gwalchmei, an adaptation of French Gauvin—that the Celtic works were in their turn being influenced by a continental tradition of Arthurian legend which was being brought back to Britain by Breton *conteurs.* Even more significant is the evidence that Celtic folklore and Irish saga had already lent new elements to the story of Arthur.

We possess two major sources of knowledge of Irish folklore and saga, the *Book of the Dun Cow,* copied about 1100, and the *Book of Leinster,* about fifty years younger. There are three major cycles, one of mythology and the deeds of Irish gods, another, the Ulster Cycle, composed of stories telling the exploits of chiefs, particularly Cuchulainn, who were descended from gods, stories in which the gods themselves appear, and the third, the Finn cycle, telling of the deeds of Finn, with considerably less admixture of the supernatural. The hard work of many scholars has shown beyond reasonable doubt that the characteristics and deeds of many of the heroes of these cycles, particularly Bran, Finn, and Cuchulainn, were transferred to Arthur and his followers and became incorporated in the Arthurian legend.

The same may be said of many of the folklore motifs found in the later Arthurian stories. It is not difficult to find in any folklore such motifs as the lonely voyage, the isles of the blessed, the beheading test, the young man born of a *fée,* whose origin is disguised. Such a motif as the marriage of a widow to her husband's slayer, found, for example, in *Yvain,* is clearly derived from the practice of the slaying of the mate of a fertility goddess and his replacement by a new mate. In themselves these motifs could have entered Arthurian literature from any of numerous sources. But when the motifs are connected with names which can be clearly connected to early Celtic forms, and when specific details of original Celtic stories are preserved through numerous redactions in different languages, the Celtic origin of the material can hardly be denied.[1]

The question of the transmission of these Celtic stories of Arthur to the French authors who wrote down the earliest versions of the Arthurian romances has been the subject of a considerable amount of acrimonious debate. There are two main possibilities. The Anglo-Normans living on the borders of Wales could have heard the stories and transmitted them to the French. The evidence for this is not very strong. We would expect at least a mention of Anglo-Norman writers and singers of Arthurian stories, whereas we have in fact the reverse—a statement that the Arthurian tales were told by Bretons. There is a good deal of evidence for this second possibility, that the Celtic stories of Arthur reached the French through Brittany. The considerable emigration of Celtic-speaking peoples from Wales and Cornwall to the continent in the sixth and seventh centuries must have meant the importation in some form of Celtic stories of Arthur. The Bretons early became bilingual and took their stories to the courts of France and Norman England. William of Malmesbury in the *Gesta Regum Britanniae* (1125) specifically refers to Arthurian tales told by Bretons, and Geoffrey of Monmouth adds his testimony that the stories were told from memory "as if written down." We know the name of one conteur, Bleheris. The forms of names also suggest that

[1] For detailed studies and references to historical material and Celtic analogues, see the appropriate chapters in Loomis, *Arthurian Literature.*

they had passed through a Breton stage before appearing in French, although the Breton conteurs who visited the British Isles often inserted new place-name details from their own travels, and even influenced the Celtic versions developed in Wales.

The theory of Breton transmission is to my mind the more satisfactory, although we may note in passing that clarification of the problem is not made any easier by the use of the words "Britannia," "Bretagne," etc. for both Britain and Brittany, and of "Britones" for the people of both countries.

We have mentioned that the Welsh work *Kulhwch and Olwen* presents many of the features of the developed Arthurian romance. Almost contemporary with it is another work, one of the most important documents in Arthurian scholarship, the *Historia Regum Britanniae* of Geoffrey of Monmouth, written in 1136. About one fifth of this work is devoted to the story of Arthur and his court, and Arthur is described as a conquering king, ruling large territories and holding a splendid court composed of great ladies and knights who were patterns of chivalry. It is virtually impossible to decide how much of this material was taken over by Geoffrey from his predecessors. We have seen that Arthur already enjoyed a high reputation, but here he is at the center of a chivalric court of great renown. In my opinion there is a deliberate attempt in Geoffrey's work to create a figure in British history which would rival that of Charlemagne in France. Several of the later "biographies" of Charlemagne contain references to an unhistorical conquest of England, and local patriotism may have been responsible for Geoffrey's reply. He had a figure already made famous by the conteurs and sufficiently remote historically to make fiction possible.

Whatever Geoffrey's intent, his work was highly influential in spreading the fame of Arthur. We know of a copy at the abbey of Bec in 1139. Other evidence shows that Arthurian characters were known in Italy by the early twelfth century.[2] But what is most important is that Arthur's court was becoming the milieu in which all romances of chivalry were set, and it is to this phenomenon that we must now turn our attention.

No reader of the Arthurian romances can fail to be impressed by the extraordinary variations in the character of King Arthur himself. In those few romances, such as *La Mort d'Artu,* in which Arthur is a central character, and in the great assembly of Arthurian legends made by Malory, we find the original Celtic elements of the great king who will come again to rule his people after sojourn in the Isle of Avalon, but whose glorious reign ends tragically in the death of almost all his knights, in his own mortal wound at the hands of Modred (his own son born in incest), and in his separation from his queen Guinevere and her lover Lancelot. Here Arthur is a noble if tragic figure. But in the great romances of Chrétien, Wolfram, Gottfried, Hartmann, and Thomas of Britain it is quite otherwise. In these romances Arthur is at best a background figure whose court sets the tone for courtly behavior. At worst he is a tired, middle-aged cuckold and coward who cannot defend his own wife from abduction nor prevent her from being the mistress of one of his knights.

In my opinion there is little point in trying to explain these variations by appealing to different types of source material, although I agree fully that the sources of the various extant stories probably differed widely. The earlier works clearly made Arthur into a great king, strong and generous. Wace in his *Brut* (1155) made him the king at whose court the Round Table was set. His court became a chivalric ideal and no knight could count himself perfect unless he were part of this court and gained its approval. Reception as a member of the Round

---

[2] The most important piece of evidence is the appearance of named Arthurian figures on the archivolt of the Modena cathedral. Unfortunately, exact dating of the archivolt is impossible. For a summary of the contending viewpoints, see R. S. Loomis and Laura H. Loomis, *Arthurian Legends in Medieval Art.*

Table made a hero into a perfect knight and once this fact became established as a literary convention every hero, whether originally connected with Arthur or not, was made to establish his credentials by moving in the Arthurian circle.

The stories about these heroes, however, though frequently drawn from the same mythological and folk material as that which provided Arthur with his adventures, were not directly concerned with him and, since they had another hero, they naturally played down the importance of the character of Arthur himself while maintaining the accounts of the splendor of his court. This is the situation in *Erec,* in *Yvain,* and in several of the versions of the *Tristan* story. In the Perceval stories and in the tales of Lancelot the character of the king is still further degraded. Here he is a coward, refusing to fight for his wife or losing her to his friend. Here surely we have examples of a story of the seduction of a queen by her lover or her abduction by force which was attached to Arthur's name *because* he was so famous. In other words, after the establishment of the famed Arthur and his court, he was bound to suffer the penalties of that fame as well as its advantages.

The process would be less surprising if it did not occur with other major figures. Charlemagne becomes little more than a buffoon in the *Pèlerinage,* and even in the *Chanson de Roland* he is more dignified than decisive until after the death of Roland. Similarly Siegfried, the hero of the *Nibelungenlied,* is a poor second to Dietrich von Bern and other heroes of later poems.

Whatever indignities the figure of the king himself may suffer, there is never a loss of prestige in the Arthurian court. It is not always situated in the same place—Camelot, probably a confusion of Avalon and Caerleon, Cestre (the modern Chester), Dinasdaron (probably Dinasbran in North Wales)—but its characteristics are always the same: great splendor, perpetual search for noble deeds, a highly civilized code of behavior, and great stress on the influence of ladies. A standard opening for Arthurian adventures was the practice of King Arthur not to sit down to his dinner on the Feast of Pentecost until an adventure had been started.

Although the authors of Arthurian romances frequently refer to Breton versions of the tales as the authentic ones, they also complain about *conteurs* and others who have confused the stories and told them incorrectly. In fact, of course, their motive in making these statements had nothing to do with a desire for purity of transmission or historical accuracy but was merely a kind of advertisement for their own version. There is no evidence that the writers of the great epics were interested in the historical Arthur or in the origins of the stories they retold. The great merit of the Arthurian cycle lay, for them, in its remoteness and susceptibility to fictional treatment. They took the story of a particular hero and put it in an Arthurian setting. Its connection with the Arthurian cycle may or may not have been established before the writing of the versions we now possess. In most cases it probably was. In order to magnify the virtues of the current hero he was brought into contact with men of already established reputation, of whom the chief was Gawain. Although the only important romance in which Gawain is the chief hero is late (the fourteenth-century *Sir Gawain and the Green Knight*), it is clear that he had a high reputation in the twelfth century.[3] The characters of *Erec* and *Yvain,* who have major works in French and German devoted to them, appear only in very minor roles in other Arthurian romances. Lancelot, the greatest of all the knights in the twelfth century, can be clearly traced back to Irish and Welsh characters of mythology, and becomes a figure second only to Arthur in general importance and with several works devoted to him. But even in his case authors found it necessary to make comparisons with Gawain in order to establish his priority.

[3] *Die Krone,* a thirteenth-century German epic by Heinrich von dem Türlin (ed. G. H. F. Scholl, 1852), makes Gawain a Grail hero by having him ask the correct question *immediately* and thus release the victims in a castle of the dead. The story is little more than a string of fantastic adventures.

Perceval is usually associated with the story of the Holy Grail, and his career differs from that of most knights in moving on a more religious level. The comparison with Gawain, however, is even more direct than usual, for both Chrétien and Wolfram von Eschenbach described Gawain's adventures at great length in works of which Perceval is the hero, in order, presumably, to point the contrast between two types of knightly conduct. The character of Sir Galahad in Malory's work is similarly exalted by comparison with that of Lancelot and Perceval.

The writer of Arthurian romance had then a clearly visualized "Arthurian world" in his mind and a mass of largely unwritten material on which to draw for his characters. It is small wonder that there are discrepancies between various works as to incidents in the careers of various characters. Some of these are due to the use of varying source material, some to carelessness and poor memory (failings which critics, for some reason, tend to ignore), some to failure to understand a source, particularly when it was in a foreign language. Often, however, the writer changed his material deliberately. He wished to show his character in a different light from that in his source. He had his own ideas of how a man should behave and what direction human endeavor should take. He might even have a stronger or weaker sense of literary form. Much has been made of the respect of medieval authors for "authority," of their reluctance to change or omit incidents in their sources. What is often forgotten is that the medieval writer had very different ideas of what was important from those held by a modern critic. Digressions, to us irrelevant, were to him pleasing variations. The character of his hero was not necessarily marred by behavior in these digressions which did not accord with the high standard set for him in the main adventure. Lancelot, for example, wanders from one mistress to another, although he is supposed to be a model of faithful, if adulterous love. It is true that we have here tales about Lancelot derived from various sources, but we should not blame the apparent inconsistency upon slavish reliance on source material. The medieval author and reader were not worried by the inconsistency of behavior in what, to them, were separate adventures. The important thing was that the hero should behave as a gallant knight in each of them.

We shall examine in some detail the relationships between French and German versions of some of the greatest Arthurian romances: the *Yvain* of Chrétien de Troyes and the *Iwein* of Hartmann von Aue, Chrétien's *Li Contes del Graal* and the *Parzival* of Wolfram von Eschenbach, the *Tristan et Yseult* of Thomas of Britain and that of Gottfried von Strassburg. Before doing so, however, it will be well to say a few words on the question of the moral and social background of the romances and, in particular, about "courtly love."

It can hardly be doubted that the knights of the Round Table were expected to behave in a way far more noble, more generous, and more cultured than the living knights of their day. Their behavior was in fact to be an example which could be imitated but never attained. Some of its characteristics were highly fanciful and would surely have provoked laughter rather than admiration had they been carried out by real persons. There has been a great deal of dispute as to whether an actual code of courtly behavior, of knightly virtues, existed and, if so, of what elements it was composed and what their origin was.

If we study the romances (as distinct from lyric poetry), we find that the knight should obey certain rules. He should be at all times physically brave, ready to undertake even the most hazardous adventure at any odds if asked to do so by his liege lord, his lady, or any person too weak to defend himself—or, more often, herself. This insistence on physical courage will surprise no one, and since each hero is, for the purposes of his own story, well-nigh invincible, it does not put too much strain either on him or the credulity of his readers. In medieval society a man's very existence depended on his physical prowess, and therefore admiration of it is natural.

The interesting element is the use of physical prowess to protect the weak. This was not normal in a society which had, until just before the time the great romances were written, been very definitely favorable only to the conqueror. There can be little doubt that we see here the operation of Christian concepts of *fortitudo* as a virtue, not mere physical strength but bravery in the cause of the Lord. This idea of the Christian knight was well expressed in the mid twelfth century by John of Salisbury, in the passage already quoted.[4] It had been further strengthened by the Crusades. We may say, therefore, that the ideal virtue of bravery in the romances is a heightened and imaginative conception of what was, in medieval society, the best type of courage. The fact that the heroes of the romances fight three giants at once does not alter this. Impossible odds merely heighten the effect.

Generosity was also a principal virtue. The giving of gifts was a mark of the great man in primitive society. It is one of the characteristics of the Homeric chiefs; it is found in the Germanic epics. There is every reason to believe that it actually was a normal practice in medieval society and that the first meetings and partings of noblemen were accompanied by gift giving. The custom had for a writer the great advantage of enabling him to describe the gifts and thus insert passages of description which could give his readers at least a vicarious pleasure. Again, the characteristic of generosity corresponded to the Christian virtue of *largitas,* the obligation of the person well endowed with the goods of this world to share them with the poor. In a society as stratified as that of the Middle Ages, where the orders of society were viewed as determined by God, generosity on the part of the rich was the only way in which even a modicum of redistribution of wealth could be attained. In the romances, however, the generosity rarely extends to the poor, who were unexciting literary material. The literary reason for the practice of generosity is the opportunity it affords for

[4] See p. 15.

description. The quality does not motivate the actions of the characters in romance.

The loyalty of the knight to his liege lord was of course a basic tenet of feudal society, as was the corresponding obligation of the lord to protect his vassal. Although loyalty can hardly be called an exclusive prerogative of the Germanic peoples, it is probably fair to say that this particular relationship, known in Middle High German as *triuwe,* does derive from Germanic tribal custom. It is a powerful motivating force in the Germanic epics and is equally important, in a different way, in the romances. For loyalty to the liege lord is often set in deliberate opposition to the love of the knight for his lady, the liege lord's wife. Although the basic story was often a primitive motif of an uncle-nephew conflict for the same woman, the interest for a medieval audience lay in the rival claims of two virtues and two loyalties—to the lord and to the lady. It is largely so in the Lancelot and in the Tristan stories. Where loyalty is not an occasion for conflict it is usually a relatively unimportant virtue. Although the narrative motivation for many of the adventures of Arthur's knights is loyalty to him and to the fellowship of the Round Table, the true motivation is usually sheer love of adventure. The course of the action is not affected by the quality of loyalty.

The concept of honor plays a very important role in the behavior of the knights of Arthurian romance and must be discussed in some detail. We must be very careful to distinguish between various aspects of the idea of honor. To the Middle Ages there were two different aspects—the opinion held by other people, or one's reputation, and the correspondence with ethical standards. The two did not necessarily agree. It was often very important for a knight to save a lady's honor, that is, her reputation, by keeping her love affair with him a secret, even though her honor, in the sense in which we usually understand the term, was already forfeit by the fact that she had committed adultery and deceived her husband. One of the most common ethical problems posed to the knights of romance was a conflict between two kinds of honor—between the necessity to bear himself as a true knight and win all battles and the necessity to maintain a disguise as a less worthy person, between the desire to serve a lady as her true lover and the desire to seek for adventures. The classic case is the hesitation of Sir Lancelot to ride in a cart (the vehicle of peasants and condemned criminals) in order to rescue Guinevere. His standing as a knight demanded that he should reject the unworthy vehicle; his desire to be the perfect servant of his lady demanded that he should use it. His slight hesitation was observed by Guinevere and interpreted as a sign of imperfect dedication.

It will be observed that honor was very often a question of external appearances, of how one appeared, rather than one of conformity to a real code of ethics. This is particularly true of relations with women, as we shall see. There is, however, no subject which is more variously treated by different authors. To some the question of honor is entirely a question of conformity with the externals of a code, very much like the ludicrous "honor" which caused duels to be fought over the cut of a man's cravat. To others honor is a matter of deep personal concern unaffected by the question of reputation. The treatment depends, as one might expect, on the seriousness of the author's purpose.

We have spoken of bravery, generosity, loyalty, and honor. One great virtue affected all of these, that of moderation. Known in Latin as *temperantia,* it is called in Provençal *mezura,* in French *mésure,* in German *maze.* It is not temperance in the sense of self-restraint but rather in that of balancing the various virtues to produce a character which will be at all times stable. The connection between this and the Greek ideals expressed in the proverb μηδὲν ἄγαν (nothing too much), the Aristotelian mean, Stoicism, and the Christian ideas of self-restraint is very clear, but we should beware of seeing here the influence of any particular philosophical system. The desire for self-restraint is probably a social phenomenon, springing from Christian ethics, which attempted to modify some of the coarser aspects of medieval behavior. The poets' use of it in literature, however, is highly formalized. We have already seen how two different concepts of honor could lead to a conflict of ideals. Similar conflicts were posed by authors whose ideal was the attainment of balance or moderation. The two stories of *Erec* and *Yvain* are excellent and complementary examples. In the former the hero, after winning Enid as his bride, devotes himself to her service so thoroughly that his love degenerates into uxoriousness. Only after experiencing deep tragedy and near-death does he reestablish the true balance between love of his wife and the duty of a knight to seek for adventure. In *Yvain* the imbalance is reversed. After winning his wife the knight obtains her permission to go on adventures for a year and a day. He forgets the date in his enthusiasm, is rejected by his wife, and wins her back only after despair has led to madness, and good deeds in defense of women have established his right to forgiveness. Medieval authors are much concerned with this "balance" (probably the best translation of *mesura*), and the desire to demonstrate how it should be attained is partly instrumental in determining the form of many of the romances.

It is clear from this list of virtues that there was, in the mind of medieval writers, a concept of an ideal knight. Yet this ideal never appears throughout any of the romances. Only Sir Galahad in Malory is perfect, and here the Christian element is so strong and the emphasis on the attainment of the Grail so pronounced that we cannot regard this example as typical. Moreover, by Malory's time the whole picture of the Arthurian world had been completely modified. In the great age of the romance the interest usually lies in the failure of a particular knight to be perfect and in the struggle he makes to attain perfection. Only in the stories where illicit love is the major theme (the Lancelot-Tristan group) is the end of the story failure, death, or unfulfilled longing.

The obvious presence of specific ideals and virtues in the

romances has led many critics to postulate the existence of an
actual courtly code of behavior possessing almost the validity
of a philosophical system. The best-known of these attempts
is that of Gustav Ehrismann, who sought to show that the ancient
philosophical concepts *summum bonum* [highest good], *honestum* [honorable life], and *utile* [material goods] had been
changed under Christian influence to life in God, honorable
life in this world, and materialism, and that the object of the
courtly code was to attain the first through reconciliation with
the other two. Curtius reveals the defects in Ehrismann's system by showing that the philosophical works which he claims
as its basis could never have served this purpose. The existence
of such a system is open to very serious question, and it may be
said that if it existed at all it certainly affected only a few of
the writers of medieval works.[5]

The questions of conduct in the romances can be more easily
explained by considering a combination of the social status of
the knight, rising gradually from a mere horse soldier to a person with moral obligations, the effects of Christianity and the
Crusades (with their special orders of knighthood) upon this
status, the civilization of courts under the influence of increased
social stability and luxury, the widespread knowledge of the
basic Christian virtues and the ideals demanded by them, and
the increasing insistence upon good upbringing and gentlemanly
conduct. It cannot be too strongly emphasized that there is not
a completely uniform standard of behavior in "courtly literature." There are considerable discrepancies between the various
standards of conduct even in contemporary works in the same
country, still more when these works are written in different
languages. Nor is the standard the same in the different genres.
As we shall see, the romance has different standards from those

[5] Discussion in Curtius, *European Literature*, Excursus XVIII; E. Neumann, "Der Streit um das ritterliche Tugendsystem," in *Festschrift für
Karl Helm* (1951); F. W. Wentzlaff-Eggebert, "Ritterliche Lebenslehre
und antike Ethik," *DVGG*, Vol. XXIII (1949).

of the lyric. The most we can say is that in the romance certain ideals were exalted and certain moral problems were treated in the same way.

There can be little doubt that one of the principal "civilizing" influences upon the medieval court was the increasing power of women. Their great importance in the cultural life of the twelfth century is fortunately not a matter of guesswork. We know the names of several ladies, of whom the most famous is Eleanor of Aquitaine, who acted as patrons of literature. We have already mentioned that the women at noble courts probably had the opportunity to become better educated than the men. It is also highly likely that their social status gained considerably by the long absence of husbands and brothers on Crusades, so that the lady became for long periods the representative of a noble family whose favor was to be sought by those desiring patronage. There can be little doubt that authors were affected by the necessity of appealing to a feminine audience, and that such literary phenomena as descriptions of dress, of magic gardens, and of lands of fantasy were given a certain impetus by the knowledge that works were destined for a patroness.

The principal feature of medieval works, however, which marks feminine influence is that called "courtly love." No literary term has been more abused and misunderstood than this one. We should note first of all that it is not a medieval term. It was, so far as I know, first used by Gaston Paris in the mid-nineteenth century. Secondly, we should avoid the common error which postulates a certain type of love valid for all kinds of "courtly" literature—romance, lyric, *lai,* occasional poetry. In point of fact the treatment of love varies widely according to the genre, and even within the genre in the case of lyric poetry. Thirdly, we should attempt to separate the literary conventions of particular genres from the social conventions of the medieval courts.

One aspect of the treatment of love in literature can be stated at once. Women, or at least women of a certain social status, were treated in an idealized fashion. This is true both of the romance and the lyric and is the more remarkable because of the lack of any literary or indeed social antecedents. Respectable women do not appear in the love poetry of classical antiquity. When the ladies are not merely imaginary, they are courtesans or slave girls. The Lesbia of Catullus is an exception in that she belonged to a noble family, but respectable she can hardly be called. Love poetry is sensual and conventional, and only rarely is there any emphasis on tenderness and spiritual affection. In the early Middle Ages the literary treatment of love and of women in general understandably declined still further. They were the daughters of Eve, the ensnarers of men, sensual temptresses. The influence of asceticism and the Church Fathers was everywhere evident. Antifeminine satire was widespread, nor did it cease with the advent of the courtly attitude in vernacular literature. Much Latin lyric poetry reflects the classical tradition of playfulness and sensuality; only rarely does it show the effects of the idealization of women found in vernacular poetry. Even during and after the period in which "courtly love" was a popular theme, there was much poetry in all languages which continued the stock complaints against the greed, sensuality, and sinfulness of women.

Narrative works written before the twelfth century show little evidence of the coming movement. In the *Chanson de Roland,* for example, women play a completely subordinate role and have no influence upon the conduct of their men or the action of the story.

Numerous attempts have been made to explain the relatively sudden change in attitude. Parallels have been cited from Arabic literature, and there is no doubt that Eastern poetry does offer works in which women are idealized and in which language is used very similar to that of the troubadours. We shall have more to say on this subject in connection with lyric poetry. The increasing significance of the cult of the Virgin has also been noted, together with the mystical concepts of the Church as the Bride of Christ. These ideas may have affected the language used but are hardly likely to have led to the secular movement towards idealization.

There is little doubt in my mind that the idea of "knightly service" to the lady originates in the social factors mentioned earlier. The lady is the patroness, the poet her liege man or servant. She is thus able to dictate her wishes, to demand obedience. She determines what is good and bad; she educates man to bring him to, or near, her level; she brings out the noblest qualities in him; she raises him to heights of valor and nobility otherwise unattainable. But she is a hard and exacting taskmistress. Her social position renders her difficult of attainment. Proof must be given of the knight's worthiness and he must be content with little reward.

These are the qualities which seem to me to spring more or less directly from social factors. It has been argued by many critics that only married women could move freely in medieval courtly society and that love must therefore necessarily be adulterous. In support of this they cite the well-known work on love by Andreas Capellanus. In fact, however, adulterous love is exceptional in the romances. Erec and Yvain both are interested only in their wives. Parzival is a glorious example of the true love possible between married persons. The Lancelot-Tristan group stresses an adulterous relation, partly because of the original source material, partly because of the intention of the poets to discuss the power of love. There is a good deal of evidence of disapproval of the Tristan story on the grounds that it glorifies an immoral relationship. Chrétien de Troyes himself attacks the popularity of it in the introduction to his non-Arthurian romance *Cligès*. The true fact is that, in the romances, the stress is on *service* to a lady and its implications, not on love as passion. Again with the exception of the Lancelot-Tristan group, the interest lies in the knight's duty rather than in his relations with the opposite sex.

In the work already mentioned, Andreas Capellanus, who

was probably a chaplain to the court of France at the same period as Chrétien was writing his romances, sets out the rules for love-making at court. Interpretations of his work differ considerably, and it is probably advisable to give an outline of the work. It is written in Latin and hence must be considered a learned or would-be learned work. Its title is, in the various manuscripts, *De Amore* (On love) or *De Arte honesti amandi* (How to love like a gentleman). "The Art of Courtly Love," used as a title by the best-known translation, prejudices consideration from the start. The first two books give advice to a certain Walter on how to be a successful lover. The definition of love given at the beginning is a standard one and is actually close to the definition of concupiscence given by the Fathers. It certainly has little to do with idealized or spiritualized love. The bulk of the first book is devoted to dialogues between a man and a woman of each of three classes, the upper nobility, the lower nobility, and the bourgeois. Other classes are expressly excluded from anything but brief mention. The dialogues show the man pleading for the lady's love, usually with indeterminate results, and in many cases trying to level out problems created by social inequality. Except in the eighth dialogue, between two members of the higher nobility, the whole stress is on these social differences. In the eighth dialogue the man, changing within the text from a married nobleman to an unmarried bishop, presents to the lady, who is successively maiden, widowed, and married, the arguments that have been used again and again as descriptions of courtly love: that love cannot exist between the members of a married couple, that service has the right to reward, that love dignifies a woman. He also raises the question of *amor purus* [love short of physical intercourse] and *amor mixtus* [love of body and spirit combined]. The lady, showing more sense than many contemporary and later writers, rejects *amor purus* as impossible.

In these dialogues Andreas is clearly using stock arguments heard in the love rituals played at court, putting them into a pseudo-learned form. The whole book has no consistent presentation or rationale, and contradictions are numerous. The second book continues the description of how the love game should be played with "judgments" given by Marie de Champagne and rules about love-making. These two books are an amusing social document and probably represent well the kind of pastime in which a small sophisticated circle of women indulged, but we should be very careful not to exaggerate their importance for literature. Medieval marriages among the nobility were political. Small wonder, then, that sophisticated ladies should imagine ideal love affairs as outside the circle of marriage. Probably some of them practiced what they preached. Others, equally numerous, probably practiced without preaching. We must not assume, however, that in literature courtly love had to be adulterous when so many of the romances tell us precisely the contrary. What we do learn from Andreas is the social condition which produced the idea, common to romance and vernacular lyric alike, that the courtly lady was regarded as a superior being, beautiful and desirable but, even more, inspiring and difficult of attainment, whose favor had to be sought and earned.

Andreas further complicates the issue by making his third book a recantation, saying that the first two merely told Walter what not to do, and then parading all the standard antifeminist arguments of the ascetic and satiric misogynists. One can only say that one is reminded of the effects of banning a book in Boston. Nevertheless, some critics contend that only the third book represents Andreas's true point of view. I personally believe that the third book is a face-saver for a man who was, at least in name, a cleric, but the matter is unimportant. The first two books, however intended, give us a good description of the way in which the game of love had to be played to please the ladies of the court.[6]

[6] Andreas Capellanus, *De amore libri tres,* ed. E. Trojel (1892), trans. J. J. Parry (1941), as *The Art of Courtly Love.* There are numerous

The social background, then, ensured that the lady be served and worshiped in literature. In the romance, with very few exceptions, the worship does not go beyond the externals of service and certain conventional manifestations, such as exaltation to great deeds and madness at the loss of love. Little attempt is made to analyze the nature of love, nor is it ever "platonic" in the sense that only spiritual union is sought. The goal of the lovers in the romances is to win their lady fully, in spite of her caprices and strict demands. Only in the lyric, and then not universally, can a case be made for "spiritual" love where the physical side is deliberately rejected.

Although the romances do not show evidence of a spiritualized love, it cannot be denied that they all recognized love between man and woman as a great power, working upon man for good or evil. The degree to which this power is emphasized and the role which it plays vary with each romance and author. It is most significant in the Lancelot-Tristan group, least important in the Grail stories. Ancient philosophy had already seen that love could be a force for evil ("Venus petulantiae") where it drove men to destruction in search of sensual pleasure and a force for good ("Venus legitima") [7] where it led to spiritual exaltation. The former is implicit in the episode with Dido in Vergil's *Aeneid* and in Horace's description of Cleopatra. Love as a creative force is envisioned in Plato's *Symposium,* and in Neoplatonic philosophy it is idealized in the *Cupid and Psyche* story. To the Christian Fathers love inevitably was divided into love of the flesh and love of the spirit. *Charitas* is the all-embracing love which is the greatest of virtues. The writers of romance naturally differed widely in their knowledge of the theoretical and philosophical contributions made to the study

medieval vernacular translations. See also D. W. Robertson, "The Subject of the *De Amore* of Andreas Capellanus," *Modern Philology*, Vol. L (1953); W. T. H. Jackson, "The *De amore* of Andreas Capellanus and the Practice of Love at Court," *Romanic Review*, Vol. XLIX (1958).

[7] See Robertson, "The Subject of the *De Amore*," and the literature there quoted.

of love, but all of them show awareness of the distinction between destructive love and ennobling love. The way in which
the story of Aeneas is changed both in the anonymous French
version and, even more, in the German version of Heinrich von
Veldecke demonstrates this very well. The Dido episode is made
to appear as the effort of demonic power to destroy Aeneas, and
the episode of the marriage to Lavinia, the daughter of Latinus,
which in Vergil is a mere political match, is turned into a full-
scale love affair in which Aeneas is made to win his lady by
knightly service and to be inspired by her to victory over Turnus,
his rival for her hand. It is love of a destructive kind, the love
between Lancelot and Guinevere, which shatters the Arthurian
world in the later versions of the story, and even in the romances
where that love is idealized the destructive element is always
present.

Noble, idealized love on the contrary is the great constructive
force and can be brought into harmony with the other courtly
virtues to produce the ideal balance. This "hohe Minne," as
the German poets called it, made men like gods. In the *Parzival*
of Wolfram von Eschenbach, unlike the other Grail stories, it
merges with love of God as the ultimate in earthly aspiration.

The ethical and social background of the romances is highly
important for their understanding. It should never be forgotten,
however, that they were intended primarily for entertainment.
They contained strange adventures because an audience likes
action, love affairs because their patrons were largely women,
topoi of ideal landscapes and fairy palaces because people then,
as now, had no objection to escaping from the drabness of the
everyday world. The really great writers went further, but they
used and improved all these conventions. Let us now see how
they are used in some of the greatest of Arthurian romances,
the stories of Yvain, Tristan, and Perceval.

The two versions of the Yvain story which we shall discuss
are those by Chrétien de Troyes and Hartmann von Aue.
Chrétien, possibly the "Christianus, canon St. Loup" mentioned

in a document of 1173, was almost certainly born in Troyes and was active at the French court. He had as patrons Marie, Countess of Champagne, and Philippe, Count of Flanders. At the beginning of his work *Cligès,* he lists the following works already produced: a redaction of the *Ars Amatoria* (and perhaps also the *Remedia Amoris* of Ovid); a version of the Philomena episode from Ovid's *Metamorphoses;* a poem on Pelops, also from Ovid; a poem on King Mark and Iseut la Blonde, perhaps a version of the Tristan story; and *Erec,* the earliest extant Arthurian romance. *Cligès,* a romance combining Byzantine romance and Breton conte, was followed by the *Chevalier de la Charette,* a version of the Lancelot story, written at the request of Marie de Champagne, but left unfinished by Chrétien and completed by Godefroy de Lagny. This work must have been written after 1164, when Marie became countess. *Yvain le Chevalier au Lion* was probably the next work. After a non-Arthurian poem, *Guillaume d'Angleterre,* comes *Li Contes del Graal,* an unfinished version of the Perceval story. Many critics and particularly French critics assign to Chrétien the merit of having created Arthurian romance.[8] While conceding that he drew upon various sources, Celtic, classical, and Eastern, they contend that he was the first writer to combine them into romances and that the Arthurian world is virtually his own creation. While no one would deny the great importance of his work, this claim seems exaggerated. The evidence for the existence of longer works before his time is too strong. There is no doubt, however, that the versions he produced became very popular and exerted a profound influence on all subsequent Arthurian writing. All of his romances are written in rhyming octosyllabic couplets.

In order to discuss *Yvain* satisfactorily, it will be necessary to summarize the story. King Arthur was holding court at Whitsuntide in Carduel (Carlisle) and after a banquet, while

---

[8] An extreme presentation of this point of view is to be found in S. Hofer, *Chretien de Troyes, Leben und Werke* (1954).

the king and queen had withdrawn, Calogrenant begins to tell the story of a disgrace he had suffered seven years before. Guinevere joins the group, but the story is broken off by an exchange of insults between Keu and Calogrenant. After peace is restored Calogrenant tells how he had ridden to the forest of Broceliande and there had been entertained at a small fortress by a *vavasour,* or minor nobleman, and his fair daughter. The next day he met a Giant Herdsman guarding savage bulls and by him was directed to a fountain where he could obtain an adventure. Adventure he certainly found, for when he poured water from a golden basin upon an emerald block a great storm arose. When the air cleared, birds flocked to the trees near the fountain and a black knight, Esclados li Ros, appeared, accused Calogrenant of intruding on his domains, and struck him to earth. Calogrenant returned discomfited. Arthur hears the story from Guinevere and swears he will reach the fountain by the Eve of St. John and spend the night there. Yvain, however, slips away, determined to avenge his cousin. He goes through the same adventures as Calogrenant but mortally wounds the knight of the fountain, pursues him to his castle, and is trapped between two portcullises. The knight, really a king, dies, and Yvain can see from his prison both the dead man on his bier and his beautiful widow, Laudine, with whom he promptly falls in love. He is discovered by the lady's maid and *confidante* Lunete, to whom he has fortunately been courteous at Arthur's court some time before at a time when her own conduct had antagonized all the other knights. She gives him a ring to make him invisible and thus preserves him from the vengeance of the dead king's knights. Meanwhile she smooths the path for Yvain to her lady and finally brings about their marriage. When Arthur's court arrives at the fountain Yvain entertains them and Lunete accepts Gawain as her lover, an incident of which nothing more is said in the romance. So ends the first part of the story.

Gawain persuades Yvain to seek adventure with him and he

obtains Laudine's permission to go, provided that he returns within a year. She gives him a ring to protect him from loss of blood. In his enthusiasm for tournaments, Yvain does not remember his promise until a maiden messenger from his wife appears at the court in Chester, rebukes him, and snatches away the ring. His remorse drives him mad, and he wanders hopelessly, finding refuge in a hermit's cave. Here he is found by a lady and her two maids. The lady returns to her castle and, after Yvain has been restored to sanity by a magic ointment, he is brought to this castle and rearmed. He rewards his benefactress by defeating her enemy Count Alier but refuses to stay longer, much to her disgust.

After leaving the castle Yvain rescues a lion from the attacks of a snake, and henceforth the animal follows him faithfully, keeping watch over him and even attempting to commit suicide with the knight's sword when Yvain falls to the ground in a swoon on returning to the fountain. In the chapel near the fountain Yvain finds Lunete imprisoned on charges that she had been instrumental in promoting the marriage of her mistress to Yvain. She is charged by Laudine's seneschal and his two brothers. Yvain promises to act as her champion at her trial the next day. He spends the intervening night at a neighboring castle and early the next morning kills a giant, Harpin, with the aid of his lion. He arrives in the nick of time to challenge the accusers of Lunete. They protest against possible intervention by the lion, which is ordered by Yvain not to interfere. When the battle is going against his master, however, he attacks and gravely wounds the seneschal. The three enemies are forced to admit defeat and are burnt at the pyre intended for Lunete. Without being recognized by Laudine, Yvain brings about a reconciliation between her and Lunete.

Yvain is now sought out by a messenger from another lady, the daughter of the Sire de la Noire Espine, to sustain her claim to part of the estates of her dead father of which she had been deprived by her older sister. Yvain agrees without knowing that the other sister has secured the services of Gawain to defend her cause. On the way he enters the castle of Evil Adventure, ignoring warnings of the fate which awaited him within. There he finds a large number of damsels working at embroidery. One of them tells him that the King of the Isle des Pucelles who came to the castle long ago had been forced by its two half-demonic owners to purchase his life by agreeing to send an annual tribute of thirty maidens. Many knights had died trying to rescue them. Yvain is hospitably entertained by the noble-man, his wife, and his daughter whom he finds in the castle, but is forced the next morning to fight the two demonic brothers. With the help of the lion, who has been kept away from the combat on the demand of the two brothers but releases himself to help his master, he kills one and forces the other to yield. Refusing the noble's offer of marriage to his daughter, he picks up the younger sister whose rights he is to defend and goes to the place appointed for the combat. Again Yvain arrives in the nick of time, armed so as to be unrecognizable, and fights with the equally unrecognizable Gawain. They struggle without any advantage on either side until nightfall, when they make them-selves known to one another and each thereupon cedes victory to the other. King Arthur then decides the case on its merits, awarding her just share to the younger sister.

The lion, firmly locked up during the contest with Gawain, now rejoins his master and the two, accompanied by Gawain, go back to the fountain. Lunete is asked by her mistress for advice in finding a defender for the fountain. After carefully ex-tracting an oath from Laudine that she will not vent her dis-pleasure on her for any advice of which she does not approve, she recommends the Knight with the Lion. Laudine agrees, Lunete fetches Yvain, Laudine, bound by her oath, is forced to accept him, and they are reconciled.

There was a historical Yvain—Owain ap Uryen, whose father was a king of Rheged, in the north of England or southern Scot-land in the later sixth century. He has nothing to do with the hero of the romance, although Professor Loomis finds motifs such as his father's love for a water-fay reflected in the story. There is a Welsh prose tale *Owain* of the thirteenth century which has many features in common with *Yvain,* and the two may well have had a common source.

Before examining the structure of the romance and Chrétien's treatment, let us note some of the features which are typical of Arthurian romance in general. The time is Whitsuntide, Pentecost, the beginning of the adventure season, the place, Arthur's court. The stage is set by the recounting of a previous adventure. Here surely we see the traces of a long-established epic tradition, the harking back to an old adventure to introduce a new one. Chrétien's setting became almost obligatory in later romances. It will be noted that Arthur's role is confined almost entirely to giving authenticity and the prestige of his name to the action and particularly in scenes involving judgment. He is no warrior but of such fame that decisive actions such as the union of Yvain and Laudine and the judicial combat between Gawain and Yvain are made to take place in his presence. Only a long previous tradition could have brought his reputation to this point.

The reputation of Sir Kay is also well established. He had originally been an honorable knight and appears as such occasionally in Celtic stories and, in part, in Malory. Generally, however, he is a bad-tempered, discourteous boaster, given to undertaking tasks beyond his powers and suffering discomfiture in attempting to execute them. He is jealous of the attainments of other knights and insults them, and often their ladies, with or without cause. Kay is traditionally the seneschal of Arthur, the person who manages his household, and it is clear that his character has been affected by the bad repute of all seneschals in romance. (Note that the unjust accuser of Lunete is also a seneschal.) It is difficult to escape the conclusion that seneschals, who would be in direct charge of minstrels and strolling players in a medieval castle, suffered from the fact that they often had poor personal relations with them, and the minstrels replied with the only means at their disposal. Kay is really an extension into the romance of the boasting soldier, loudmouthed and ultimately ludicrous. He is frequently used as a foil to the courtly Gawain, who uses polite methods to succeed where Kay has failed.

We may note in passing that Calogrenant is probably Cai le grenant, Kay the Grumbler, and that in the opening scene Kay is really quarreling with himself. It not infrequently happens that a character develops a new name and that subsequent authors, failing to recognize the identity, use both in the same story as different characters.

The appearance of Gawain in *Yvain* also follows a set pattern. He becomes the lover of Lunete as a parallel to Yvain's marriage to Laudine, a role which he fills in many romances and which probably makes him the "knight with most ladies" in Arthurian literature. As the knight adventurer par excellence he is instrumental in persuading Yvain to leave his lady to go on a quest in search of adventure. The final test which Yvain has to endure is the indecisive combat with Gawain, again the ultimate test of a knight's prowess. It is clear that here, as with Arthur, we have to do with a fully established tradition which makes Gawain the perfect hero for purposes of comparison. He is cast in the same role, although with considerably more artistic effect, in Wolfram's *Parzival*.

It could probably be proved that, in one or the other of the Arthurian romances, Gawain has every adventure, except the Grail experience, ascribed to the other knights of the Round Table, which brings us to another important characteristic of the romances, namely the use of the same incident, in slightly varied form or with a change of locale or names, in many different narratives. The episode of the *vavasour*, the Giant Herdsman, and the Knight of the Fountain, is a good case in point. Close parallels of all or part of the episode are to be found in *Owain, Sir Gawain and the Green Knight*, the Irish *Briciu's*

Feast, the *lai La Mule sans frein,* and *Kulhwch and Olwen.* The only part of the story significant for the plot of *Yvain* is the episode of the Knight of the Fountain. The other elements are merely incidental but have been incorporated presumably because they were already attached to the main incident in an earlier version. Much of the apparently irrelevant incident in Arthurian romance can be explained only in this fashion.

Generally speaking, however, Chrétien is less guilty than the majority of writers of introducing incident and adventure without motivation and thus producing that chaotic formlessness which is all too characteristic of later romances. It is clear that he has selected incidents from various sources with a definite purpose in mind. The central incident is, of course, the defense of the fountain. In origin this surely represents the widespread myth of the goddess (or her mortal representative) at a sacred shrine, with a kingly mate whose purpose it was to defend the shrine and who was automatically replaced as mate by any challenger who could defeat him. The myth accounts for the basic and, to Chrétien as to us, rather unpleasantly sudden acceptance by the widow of her husband's murderer. But there the importance of the mythological element ends. The author was at some pains to reshape the whole story for a new purpose, namely, to set against each other two of the duties of a knight, his service to his lady and his duty to use his physical prowess in the service of the unfortunate. The first part of the story is concentrated on the winning of the lady. It retains in substance the elements of the defeat of the old king—the magic properties of the fountain, the shrine (now described as a chapel), and the residence of the king and his lady. But the details of the combat are modified to bring it within the experience of a courtly audience, and the winning of the lady is more prolonged. The widespread motif of a ring of invisibility is introduced to explain the interval which Chrétien felt had to elapse before the union of Yvain and Laudine could take place. Yvain is made to fall in love with Laudine's beauty,

to desire her as an honorable knight should, not to take possession of her by right of conquest. The assistance of the intermediary Lunete, again rationalized by her previous good treatment at the hands of Yvain and her explanation to her mistress,
that the logical defender of the fountain is the victor, reflects a
further attempt to modify the crudities of Laudine's sudden
marriage to her husband's killer. We never have the impression
that Laudine really loved Yvain. She is won over to accept him.
The hollowness of Lunete's argument is shown by the fact that
the fountain is left undefended during Yvain's long absence.

So far Yvain's duty and his love have moved together. Erec's
wooing of Enid shows a similar unity. But now the problem must
be introduced—the conflict of values which reverses the results of the first part of the story. Yvain's overlong absence
brings rejection and mental, moral, and spiritual collapse, or
to use Aristotle's term, a peripety. From the high point at the
end of the first part, the apparent achievement of all goals, the
hero is flung down to a low point of demoralization. We shall see
that the great romances (not the poorly constructed ones)
follow this pattern frequently. *Erec* certainly follows it; so do
Tristan (the marriage to Mark after the union of the lovers)
and *Parzival* (the denunciation by Kundrie after the acceptance
of Parzival at Arthur's court). There can be little doubt that
the intention was at least partly didactic—the uncertainty of
human existence, pride before a fall—but it was also conditioned
by a framework already demonstrable in such early Germanic
epics as *König Rother, Salmon and Marcolf,* and *Herzog Ernst,*
namely the use of two stories in one. In the first part the hero
apparently achieves his aim, usually the winning of his lady,
only to be thwarted by a sudden twist of fortune. The *Chanson
de Roland* similarly has two parts, no doubt under the influence
of the same fashion, and the *Nibelungenlied* and *Gudrun* follow
the same pattern of apparent end and new beginning.

Chrétien uses the established framework skillfully. Yvain's
whole attitude must be modified under the influence of sorrow.

He must be taught humility. It is no accident that his adventures
in the second part are almost all concerned with the rescue of
women from injustice. Chrétien has carefully assembled tales
from the common stock which stress this feature. The rescuing
culminates with an actual judicial combat before Arthur's court
with the best knight of that court. (The Round Table itself is
not mentioned in *Yvain.*) As usual in the romances, it is possible to indicate a precise point at which recovery begins. Here
it is the smearing of the magic ointment which cures Yvain of
his madness (a female sorceress, undoubtedly a manifestation of
Morgain la Fée is responsible) and brings about a rebirth. In
Erec it is the apparent death of the hero, in *Parzival,* the learning of humility from Trevrezent. Some critics have seen here
definite religious symbolism, but this is unlikely. The idea of
rebirth may perhaps reflect a Christian viewpoint, but it is too
common to be set down as conscious symbolism.

The whole construction of *Yvain,* then, is consciously determined by two factors—a tradition of a dipartite structure in
the works of the *conteurs,* and the posing of a moral problem
of conflicting duties which is solved by demoralization, recovery,
suffering, and attainment of balance. It will be noted that
Chrétien's treatment is entirely concerned with the problem of
Yvain. Although Laudine is the beloved and is responsible for
Yvain's actions, her personality is shadowy and her character is
not examined. The usual lip service is paid to her beauty and
charms, but the writer is concerned much more with Yvain's mental conflict than with Laudine's welfare. The knight must justify
his place at Arthur's court by conforming to its code. Such
feminine interest as there is in the poem is concentrated on the
personality of Lunete, the first of a great line of sprightly *con-
fidantes* in French literature. Untrammeled by the necessity of
being perfect, she is able to behave in very warm and human
fashion, and her conversations with her mistress show a neat
sense of opportunism and *savoir faire.*

The fact that we can perceive in *Yvain* the definite posing of a social-moral problem and its solution should not lead us into the error of regarding the work as didactic. We have already pointed out how strong was the dualistic conception of life in the Middle Ages. The contrast between the real and the ideal was always implicit in medieval writing, and Chrétien is no exception. He shows us an ideal world in which the problem he poses finds ultimately an ideal solution. But many of his readers had more interest in the external features of that world, in its castles, its fair ladies, its gardens and fairyland atmosphere, its high adventure, and the trappings of a chivalry on a higher level than their own, than in the problems posed. Chrétien himself is far from insisting too strongly to his listeners on the moral implications of his works. To him compliance with the social rules for his ideal society was more important than the moral feelings of the hero, although in fact the forms were the outward expression of an inner moral code. It is in this respect that he differs most markedly from his German follower Hartmann von Aue.

Hartmann was probably a *ministerialis* or landless nobleman dependent on the support of a patron. That he had such a patron we know from his deeply moving lament at the loss of his lord and his vow to go on a crusade, probably that of 1189, but further details are lacking. Hartmann was born about 1160–65, most probably near the little town of Eglisau in Switzerland. He received a clerical education, possibly at nearby Reichenau. His first work, c. 1185, was the *Büchlein,* a theoretical treatment of love in verse. A relatively free adaptation of Chrétien's *Erec* followed, in which Hartmann revealed his concern with the theoretical social and moral problems raised. After this came two non-Arthurian works, the *Gregorius,* a treatment of the legend of the noble sinner whose repentance of his sin of unknowing incest with his mother was so sincere and his penitence so strict that he was chosen pope, and *Der arme Heinrich* (Poor Henry), a German popular tale of the salvation of a nobleman stricken with leprosy because of his pride and the salvation he attained by humility at seeing the readiness of a peasant's daughter to sacrifice herself for him. Apart from some lyric poetry, his last work, written about 1200, was a version of Chrétien's *Yvain*.

Hartmann's version of *Erec* shows clearly how different his viewpoint was from that of Chrétien. The questions of *zuht* (education and behavior) and *maze* (balance) are stressed much more than in the French poem, and the reader's attention is called to them by passages of comment on the conduct of the characters. Hartmann is much less interested in the externals of the Arthurian world than is Chrétien and lacks the French poet's ability to make them alive. His accounts of courtly life and adventure have little of Chrétien's brilliance. He believes, in *Erek,* at least, in a code of behavior which can regulate life in a strict ethical pattern, and this pattern, though it pays lip service to Christianity, is based not so much on religion as on social education. In other words, it is secular but nevertheless firmly based on moral values and capable of producing an ideal character. Hartmann uses *Erek* expressly as a vehicle for his ideas.

The two intermediate poems show a reversal of this attitude. Many critics believe, probably rightly, that the change was caused by the emotional crisis brought on by the death of his lord. In *Gregorius* and *Der arme Heinrich* the insufficiency of a worldly code is made very clear. Hartmann sees the necessity of humility before a higher power. His *Iwein* marks a return to Arthurian literature, but with a somewhat modified viewpoint. His youthful belief in the efficacy of the courtly code had been modified. He could view the work of Chrétien in more detached fashion and perhaps was closer to him in thinking of the romance as primarily entertaining and only secondarily edifying. However this may be, his version of the *Yvain* is much closer to its original than *Erek* had been. There is relatively little change of incident, and it is clear that Hartmann is much less personally involved than he had been with the earlier poem.

The formal quality of the work gains much from this objectivity. The organization is better, the versification smoother. Nevertheless, a comparison of the lengths of the two poems shows how much Hartmann added—8,166 lines against 6,818. Hartmann expands individual incidents, and his descriptions are often longer, but a great deal of the additional material comes from moralistic comment. Chrétien's lively dialogue passages are often actually abbreviated.

Many critics have called attention to two of Hartmann's characteristics as a writer. The first is his tendency to alter any incident which he believes demonstrates conduct on the part of the hero which is unworthy of a real knight. A good example is the pursuit of the wounded Knight of the Fountain. Chrétien enjoys this pursuit and shows Yvain trying hard to get in one more good slash at his wounded foe. Hartmann modifies the incident, removing all details which might seem uncourtly. The sense of moral rectitude was strong in him.

The second characteristic was remarked on even in his own day, namely, the clarity of his style. That he is clear and precise is true. The often turgid passages of early German writers are lacking, and he reproduces beautifully in German the language of Chrétien. It must be confessed, however, that compared with Wolfram and Gottfried he is unexciting. His rhyming couplets often seem to jog along somewhat wearily and, in spite of his undoubtedly more sensitive perception of courtly values and the true meaning of knighthood, we would have to grant supremacy to Chrétien had Hartmann been his only imitator in German.

The Yvain story enjoyed relatively little popularity after the Hartmann version. Apart from the Welsh *Owain* already mentioned, no full-length work was devoted to Yvain. As we have seen, however, many of his adventures reappear in works devoted to other heroes. The absence of other works proves perhaps more conclusively than anything else the fact that Chrétien had selected and organized material for a very specific purpose out of the mass available to him. The stories were already there, but to Chrétien we must concede the credit of organization.

The story of the quest of the Holy Grail is a very different matter. Superficially the situation seems much the same as that of *Yvain*. The first extant poetical work on the subject is a poem by Chrétien, this time incomplete, which is imitated by a German poet shortly afterwards. The resemblance, however, ends there. Chrétien's work is a relatively weak effort which neglects the great moral and religious possibilities of the theme. The *Parzival* of Wolfram von Eschenbach is one of the greatest poems in world literature. Furthermore, Wolfram drew upon sources unknown to or ignored by Chrétien. It is clear that the story of the Grail was at once more widespread and of wider ramifications than the Yvain story. Let us attempt to clarify the origins of the story and its entrance into the Arthurian tradition. First note Professor Loomis's completely accurate statement on the subject: "There is no one authentic Grail legend but a multitude of Grail legends, each a medley of incoherent motifs." [9]

Not only is there a massive inconsistency in the stories of the Grail; there is not even agreement on what the Grail itself was. The word itself seems to mean "large receptacle" or "dish," but not "cup" or "chalice." There is good evidence to connect the Grail with Celtic legends of a magic dish which provided guests with all the food and drink they wished and which was also connected with a figure (Bran), who had been wounded in battle and whose wound had brought infertility to everything in his domains. It is clear that the Grail is connected remotely with the ancient belief of the fertility king who can provide everything unless his own procreative powers are lost. If this happens he must be cured by magic means or perhaps reborn (replaced) by a younger relative.

Many features of this story are apparent in varying degrees and with astonishing variations in detail in the different Grail

[9] *Arthurian Tradition*, p. 372.

romances. The "horn of plenty" motif is almost always present. The wounded king, often a fisher and always living near water, is the keeper of the Grail. He is released from his misery by a younger person, usually by the asking of a question. In this story there can be, of course, no question of Christianity or Christian symbolism. It is a pagan cult and the material Celtic in origin, as is shown by the names and localization of the incidents. Chrétien, and therefore his sources, and several of the Welsh stories do not attempt to connect the Grail with Christian ritual. Its ceremonies are described but not explained. Clearly the Grail was something desirable: it is the object of a quest; the possession of it grants the possessor happiness and unusual power. But it has nothing to do with Christianity nor, in my opinion, is there sufficient evidence to connect it with a liturgy or specific rite of any religion or cult, although innumerable efforts have been made to do so.

Nevertheless, the people who heard or read the Grail legend were Christians. It was hard for them to conceive of a vessel's possessing such powers as the Grail demonstrated without its being somehow connected with Christian tradition. We therefore find that many authors specifically introduce a Christian element into the Grail story. This is true, as we shall see, of the reworking of Chrétien's poem by Wolfram von Eschenbach. Other authors went further still. About 1200, that is, after Chrétien's poem had been written but almost certainly earlier than Wolfram's, Robert de Boron wrote a long verse *Roman de l'Estoire dou St. Graal,* in which he is clearly combining a number of stories which had already become current and which connected the Grail with a Christian tradition. The most sacred vessel in the Christian tradition was, of course, the chalice used at the Last Supper, and there was a considerable body of legend, some of it in the *Evangelium Nicodemi,* which told of the possession of this vessel by Joseph of Arimathea, of his imprisonment and magical release, and of his journey to the West. Later legend added to this his arrival in England and his death at Glastonbury, a legend which the abbey naturally encouraged. Even here, however, there was confusion, for in some legends the vessel was not the chalice but the bowl which caught the blood which flowed from the side of Christ when it was pierced by the lance of the centurion, traditionally called Longinus. The lance, too, became a sacred relic, and parts of it were "discovered" in various places.

It is hardly surprising that a cleric, seeing the great popularity of the original, pagan, Grail story, should attempt to incorporate it into a body of Christian legend, and it is very clear from Robert de Boron's treatment that this was precisely his intention. Unfortunately we have only 4,000 lines of his poem (sometimes, incidentally, called *Joseph*), but from a prose version, bearing his name but not written by him, called *Joseph, Merlin, Perceval* (or *Didot Perceval*) we can form a good idea of the remainder of the work. Many of the features of the original pagan story are obvious, for example, the fertility power of the chalice, the fact that its keeper is called Bron (sometimes rationalized into Hebron, the keeper of the Ark in Numbers, 3:27) and the naming of "the Rich Fisher." An artificial incident is introduced to account for the name "Graal." Most prominent, however, is the detailed description of Christian symbolism connected with the cult of the Grail given in the middle of the poem as it now survives.

The author obviously was at some pains to Christianize the Grail. He succeeded. Most subsequent romances follow his lead and make the Grail the symbol of the highest spiritual experience a Christian knight can have on this earth. It becomes not only the object of a quest by all knights who are true Christians but virtually a means of detecting who is the best of all knights. As literary fashion turned away from the secularized courtly world of the late twelfth century, the knight in literature too ceased to regard acceptance by Arthur's court as his highest reward and adventure for his lady as the greatest achievement. Something higher was required, and it was found in the search for the spiritual exaltation of the Grail. The knight had become, as can be seen in the figure of Galahad, almost a military ascetic, the ideal of the *miles Christianus,* seeking his reward not from his lady but from God. The Grail story represents the highest spiritual aspirations of medieval chivalry, but curiously enough it was at the very beginning of this use of the Grail story that it found its most remarkable expression.

The Grail story of Chrétien de Troyes is incomplete, as we have seen, and it will therefore be better to summarize here the version of Wolfram von Eschenbach and to indicate the very important respects in which it differs from the unfinished poem of Chrétien de Troyes.

Wolfram was born about 1170 of a family of *ministeriales,* almost certainly in the East Franconian village known as Wolfram's Eschenbach, near Ansbach. We have no documents which refer to him, but the numerous personal references in his works make it clear that he moved frequently to the courts of various patrons, among them the famous Hermann von Thüringen. He was proud of his rank and takes great pains to deny that he belongs to the class of literary nobles. He stresses rather that his main interest is the discharge of his duties as warrior and knight. We can readily believe that he did not receive the formal education of his great contemporaries, Hartmann von Aue and Gottfried von Strassburg, but it would be ridiculous to take his statement that he was unable to read at its face value. He denies that he is learned, he demands freedom in treating his sources, but no work of medieval literature contains more evidence of extraordinary, if unsystematic, learning. He clearly had read (and listened) widely, and takes a delight in parading his knowledge and mystifying his readers. It is a great pity that we cannot hear his laughter at the efforts of some scholars to produce neat and orderly "systems" from his work. His sense of humor and his grotesque and deliberate distortions of words and stories have given unending occupation to many whose own sense of the comic is not equal to their learning. He did not escape censure for his "wild" stories and lack of organization even in his own day. The well-known "literary criticism" passage in the *Tristan* of Gottfried von Strassburg, although it does not refer to him by name, clearly shows Gottfried's disapproval of his antics.[10] For all his sense of humor, no poet was more deeply sensible of his moral obligations as a writer or more deeply religious in the fullest and truest sense. This is apparent not only in *Parzival* but also in his incomplete poem *Willehalm* (about 1215), a version of the *chanson de geste* of Guillaume d'Orange, and in the fragment *Titurel,* a romance of the earlier keepers of the Grail (second decade of the thirteenth century). Wolfram died about 1220.

Wolfram's Grail story is extremely complicated and full of minor incidents. In the following summary we shall confine ourselves to the essentials. The poem opens with an account of the adventures of Gahmuret, Parzival's father, a member of the house of Anjou and descended, ultimately, from a fay. He is shown as seeking service with the world's greatest rulers, and chooses not the Christian emperor but a Muslim king. He rescues a heathen Indian Queen, Belakane, from her enemies, marries her, but only according to the heathen fashion, and before the birth of their child, leaves her to return to Europe. In a great tourney in Spain he wins his Christian bride, Herzeloyde. Again he leaves on an adventure before the birth of their child and is killed by treachery in the East.

It is clear that we have in this prologue an attempt to establish one side of Parzival's character by reference to his father. He is deliberately attached to a family of which the most famous representative in Europe was Richard Coeur de Lion, the model of the active, adventurous king. Both of Gahmuret's adventures are concerned with the winning of ladies, Belakane

[10] Gottfried alludes to the "findaere wilder maere, der maere wildenaere," (tellers of wild tales and distorters of the story). See the whole passage in *Tristan und Isolde,* ed. F. Ranke, vv. 4665 ff.

in a serious fight, Herzeloyde in a tourney. He is a man of wide sympathies, unprejudiced enough to recognize in Belakane a womanhood as perfect as that of a Christian lady and to take service with the heathen whose chivalry equaled that of Christian knights. His weakness lies in his lack of identification with Christianity in its higher aspects. He is not merely a knight limited to the Arthurian courtly concepts but he is below the great figures of the Grail company because of his lack of religious purpose. Love is for him still on a lower level. From him Parzival inherits his strength, his beauty, his knightliness.

It should be noted that the brief account given by Chrétien of Perceval's father differs widely from that given by Wolfram. Chrétien himself does not name him, but says he was indeed wounded in battle but lived for many years, long enough to see Perceval's older brother knighted and killed, whereupon he died of grief. His wound had rendered him incapable of defending his lands, and he lived in a manor in a waste forest, where Perceval was brought up. Chrétien's account seems to draw on sources, particularly the Celtic stories of Bran, which Wolfram used in describing Anfortas. Wolfram's fuller explanation and the identification with the House of Anjou are clearly designed to illuminate one aspect of Parzival's character and, of course, to provide for the introduction of the character Feirefiz, of who more will be said later.

In Book III Wolfram begins the story of Parzival, and his narrative now follows more closely that of Chrétien. Parzival, as yet unnamed by the author and not knowing his own name, is brought up in the wilderness by his mother in a deliberate attempt to prevent his hearing of knighthood and thus exposing himself to the fate of his father. His chief passion is hunting with the crossbow and short hunting javelin, but he has deep sympathy with nature. His religious education is entirely informal, consisting of answers by his mother to the question "What is God?" We can only assume his baptism. There is no mention of Christianity. One day he meets knights riding through the wood in shining armor and naively connects them with the beings of light, the angels, of whom his mother has spoken. After hearing what they really are, his innate love of chivalry drives him to demand that he too seek Arthur's court. His mother reluctantly agrees, but dresses him like a fool and mounts him poorly in the hope that ridicule will cause him to return. When he never even looks back on leaving, she collapses and dies without his being aware of it.

Before leaving, the boy had received some advice on courtly behavior from his mother which included the admonition to kiss all ladies and take from them a love token. Upon finding a lady, Jeschute, asleep in a pavilion, Parzival follows this advice all too literally, kisses the lady roughly, snatches a ring and a pin, stuffs himself with the food at her bedside, and departs. Her lover, Orilus, returning shortly, not unnaturally refuses to believe her explanation of the footprints and disorder and swears she shall not change her clothes nor shall her horse be fed until he has punished the man. Parzival thus commits his second unconscious crime.

Riding further, he meets Sigune, holding in her lap the body of her lover Schionatulander, whose death she has caused by her insistence on his fighting for her love. From her Parzival first learns his name and thus becomes a definite person. He reaches the vicinity of Arthur's court and is sent by Ither, a Red Knight whom he meets, to fetch a challenger to revenge the deliberate insult Ither has put upon Guinevere. Although his strange appearance evokes laughter, two persons, the maid Cunneware and the squire Antanor, break vows they had sworn to maintain until they saw the best knight in the world and are roughly punished by Kay for doing so. Again Parzival is the unwitting cause of suffering.

Parzival interprets Arthur's statement that he must win the Red Knight's armor as permission to take it. He goes out, demands the armor and, when Ither pushes him off, kills Ither with his peasant's spear in unknightly fashion.

Now wearing over his fool's dress the armor he has stripped from the corpse, he arrives at the castle of the knight Gurnemanz who, attracted by his beauty and strength, teaches him the externals of knighthood and chivalry and the forms of religion. He is now capable of acting like a knight, but not of understanding chivalry; he follows the rules, but has no concept of their true spirit. Only in the next episode, the rescuing of Condwiramurs (Wolfram changes Chrétien's Blancheflor to the much more graphic "Conduire à amour") does he attain fully one of the goals of Arthurian romance, the winning of the love of a pure lady. He sleeps in her beleaguered castle and she comes to him in the night to plead for his help. Wolfram insists on the innocence of the encounter, whereas Chrétien more than implies a sensual love scene. He rescues her and wins her for his bride. Even so, it is three nights before the marriage is consummated. In the French version marriage is not mentioned.

Parzival has reached the goal of the knights of romance. His position is that of Erec or Yvain at the end of the first part of their story. But unlike theirs, his further career is not concerned with a departure from the social and moral world of Arthur and a subsequent restoration to that world. He has to embark now on a search for a goal higher than that envisaged by Hartmann for his heroes. Whether Chrétien conceived of the quest of the Grail in these terms is made hard to decide by the incomplete state of his work, but there is no doubt of Wolfram's intention. Parzival will not rejoin his wife until their love can be put on a plane altogether higher than that of courtly *Minne,* until it is part indeed of Christian *charitas.*

The reason Parzival gives for leaving his bride is that he wishes to find out what has happened to his mother. Towards evening, at the edge of a lake with no crossing in sight, he is directed to a castle by a man fishing. He is well received and the fisher proves to be the lord of the castle, Anfortas. Parzival is presented with a sword, and sees the great suffering of Anfortas and, without understanding it, the bringing in of a bleeding spear and the procession of the Holy Grail. Gurnemanz has told him that asking questions is unknightly. He therefore restrains his curiosity and asks no questions about his host's wound, a fact that is to cost him dear. On the following day he finds the castle deserted and leaves. The drawbridge flies up behind him and a squire shouts insults, leaving Parzival hurt and puzzled. He has no idea of the significance of the events of the previous night. Although he has seen the power of the Grail to provide food and drink, it seems to him magic. Nor does Wolfram at this point explain its significance to the reader.

The next series of events is connected with earlier ones. Parzival again meets Sigune, learns from her his relation to the Fisher King and receives her curse for not having asked the question. Troubled by her statement, he meets Orilus and Jeschute and, by defeating Orilus, establishes Jeschute's innocence. He has put right one of his mistakes, one which can be corrected by the Arthurian type of knighthood.

Now, in Book VI, he returns to Arthur's court. Outside in the snow he is held in a trance by three drops of blood upon the snow which remind him of the beauty of Condwiramurs. After he has, almost unconsciously, unhorsed two knights, one of them Sir Kay (who is thus punished for his earlier brutality), Gawain covers the drops and leads him to the court. His prowess is recognized; he is about to become a member of the Round Table, when the hideous hag Cundrie appears, denounces his heartlessness in not inquiring about the misery of Anfortas, and declares that the Round Table is dishonored by his presence. The assembly is further disturbed by a call to rescue the ladies imprisoned in the Castle of Wonders and by a challenge to Gawain by Kingrimursel, who accuses him of the murder of his brother. The whole court is thus shattered and does not meet again until Book XIV, when all the adventures have been completed.

It will be noted that both in Wolfram's and Chrétien's ver-

sion we have a peripety such as was observed in *Yvain* and
Erec. The hero has apparently reached the goal he set himself,
namely, acceptance at Arthur's court. The attainment of this
goal, however, means nothing because it is not the purpose for
which his fate has destined him. Although Parzival has at this
time no conception of the true significance of the Grail and no
inkling of the existence of a Grail company, he is nevertheless
fated to become its protector and the leader of its order. The
peripety is thus very different from that in the other romances
mentioned, for there is no question for Parzival of a return to
the same society. He has to rise higher.

The difference between the career of Parzival and that of
the "normal" Arthurian knight is emphasized by the introduction of a new story which parallels his, namely, the adventures
of Gawain. These adventures, which occupy the whole of Books
VII, VIII, and X through XIII, are concerned with events which
reflect the normal occupation of the knight of Arthur's court.
He takes part in a tournament at the castle of Lypant, called
Bearosche (Chrétien says Tintagucl), where he acts as champion of a little girl, Obilot, goes on to enjoy the sensual love of
Antikone, sister of King Vergulaht of Ascalun (in Chrétien
King of Cavalon) and daughter of the man Kingrisin whom
he was alleged to have killed. The scene in which Gawain defends himself with a door bolt and chessboard against certain
inhabitants of the castle who are enraged at the favor he has
found with their mistress is comic and, like many other features of the Gawain episode, is almost satiric in its treatment
of standard Arthurian procedure.

The core of the Gawain theme is his meeting with Orgeluse.
It leads to a confused patchwork of events which are very
similar in the works of Chrétien and Wolfram. Orgeluse herself is the type of the scornful lady, clearly associated with
Liban of Irish myth. She leads Gawain from one adventure to
another (he is, of course, madly in love with her) and ultimately to the Castle of Wonders, erected, according to Wol-

fram, by the magician Klingsor. Here he is made to spend an extremely uncomfortable night, attacked by mysterious forces and a very tangible lion, but he survives and rescues the ladies imprisoned in the castle, among them his own grandmother, mother, and sister, in the best courtly fashion. The parallel between the Grail castle and the Castle of Wonders is obvious, and Wolfram misses no opportunity to make a mock of the latter and to make it clear to the reader that he is merely recounting standard adventures in which he does not believe. Chrétien, on the other hand, makes no such disparaging remarks.

Gawain, after crossing, at the behest of Orgeluse, the perilous ford near the castle, meets the accepted lover of his sister and, strangely enough, is challenged by him. They agree to fight before Arthur's court. Chrétien's narrative breaks off at this point. Wolfram makes his Gawain go on to Arthur's court, fight a losing battle with the unrecognized Parzival (who thus establishes his superiority even in the "lower" Arthurian world), and finally win Orgeluse as wife. It is interesting that Wolfram makes this same Orgeluse the mistress of Anfortas and the person whose love had caused his wound and suffering. She is thus the symbol of his fall from the Grail level to the level of courtly love. Nevertheless she is not in *Parzival,* as she is in Chrétien's poem, a conventional figure of unmotivated spitefulness. Wolfram takes care to explain her conduct, through her conversations with Gawain, as due to her experiences and disappointments in love. The scene at Arthur's court is almost a triumph of Hymen, with Gawain and his sister finding their mates, and the general rejoicing increased by the rescue of Gawain's mother, King Arthur's sister. Nevertheless the Gawain action is clearly designed as a contrast to Parzival's adventures and, although Chrétien must also have intended this contrast, for otherwise the insertion of the Gawain action would have no sense, Wolfram makes the difference in level and depth of experience more pronounced. The love ideal of the courtly code is stressed at the expense of the other features so prominent in Hartmann von Aue, and the contrast is naturally stronger between the two German poets than between the two different works of Chrétien, for, as we have seen, the social and adventurous element is always strong in the French poet, while the German stresses the morality of the courtly world. Wolfram's picture of the Arthurian milieu is probably more vivid than that of either Chrétien or Hartmann, but it is impossible to escape the conclusion that one reason for this was his deliberate humorous exaggeration. Certainly it is true that Wolfram did not take seriously a great many of the social features of the courtly code. For him morality was something more lofty.

In the "Gawain" books Parzival is mentioned just often enough to remind the reader that he is wandering still in search of the Grail Castle. Only once during the account of Gawain's exploits does he appear at length, in Book IX. Nothing could demonstrate more clearly the different objectives of Wolfram and Chrétien than the events of this book. The incident in Chrétien is relatively briefly described (296 lines). Perceval, after five years of wandering, comes upon a party of penitents. By them he is rebuked for riding fully armed on Good Friday and is directed to a hermit's chapel, where he finds the hermit, a priest, and a cleric about to celebrate mass. He is told to confess his sins and admits his abandonment of God and his concern at his failure to ask the question which would have released the Fisher King from his suffering. The hermit proves to be his maternal uncle and reveals that it was the Fisher King's father who had been served with the Grail and that he had been kept alive for fifteen years by it alone. The hermit then gives Perceval some religious instruction and keeps him in the cell fasting until Easter.

The incongruity of this scene has frequently been pointed out. Why is the Grail thus suddenly connected with religion? Why should the salvation of the Grail company depend on such a silly question as "Who is served with the Grail?" Unlike

Wolfram, Chrétien does not make it clear that the feast in the Grail castle, in which Perceval had taken part, was actually provided by the Grail, nor does he appear to differentiate clearly between the Fisher King and his father. The scene in the hermit's cave is formally religious; a priest is present. We can only deduce that Chrétien for some reason wished to couple his previously unreligious Grail story to the Christian view of it which, as we have seen, was gaining currency. The attempt is clumsy and, like the rest of *Li Contes del Graal,* shows that the French poet, either through carelessness or inability, was not master of his material and had not decided what purpose or direction his story should take. Since he did not finish the poem himself, we cannot decide what he would ultimately have done with the idea of Perceval, the Grail King. We can only say that there is little indication of the existence of a Grail society or of a higher moral purpose such as exists in *Parzival.*

Wolfram's treatment of the scene in the hermit's cave is utterly different. It is much longer (2,097 lines) and, although it contains many obscurities, may be accurately described as the key to the understanding of Wolfram's work. In outline it follows the story of Chrétien, but there are many highly significant additions and alterations. Frau Aventiure is called upon to tell of Parzival's wanderings—for he has been seeking the Grail Castle by the "Arthurian" process of adventure. He encounters Sigune for the third time, but now she is in a small cell, fed by Cundrie through the agency of the Grail. Parzival at first does not recognize her, and reproaches her for wearing a ring as love token. He is abashed when he sees who she is, and from her is directed towards Monsalvaesche, where she *believes* the Grail Castle to be. Sigune's introduction is significant. From the weeping mistress she has turned into the penitent, who says that "before God he was my husband"—courtly love has turned to sanctified marriage. Her calm acceptance of her fate contrasts sharply with Parzival's complaint that his suffering is unbearable and undeserved. The transition to the group of penitents who reproach Parzival for his armed state and to the hermit is natural and made more so by the statement that he is now letting his horse wander where it will, that is, that he is subconsciously submitting himself to fate. Parzival had met and defeated a knight of the Grail company and taken his horse, so that this animal might well make its way to the Grail Castle if left alone. Wolfram prepares us for the revelations about the Grail which Parzival is about to receive by telling of his "sources"—the elusive Kyot of Provence, that will-o'-the-wisp of Wolfram scholarship, who found his material in the mysterious East, in books written by one Flegetanis, a heathen, who in his turn had it from—the stars. This beautiful parody of authors who insist on their sources as the only correct ones has produced upon their modern successors much the effect that Wolfram calculated that it would. The "Kyot believers" are still on the trail of Wolfram's creation. We need not waste time on a subject on which too much ink has already been spilled. Wolfram undoubtedly had other sources of information than his main one, Chrétien, but he supplied much from his own fertile imagination. One suspects that Kyot is that imagination.[11]

Parzival's approach to the hermit is direct. He needs advice and confesses his misery. He confesses that he hates God and that he has sinned. The place is the same as that in which Orilus had sworn his oath to go to Arthur's court after his defeat by Parzival—again a return—but now it is bitterly cold; there is snow and misery. The whole scene is one of wretchedness—poor shelter, poor food, cold weather. But when Parzival takes off his armor, he can warm himself, and as he confesses to the hermit, Trevrezent—there is no priest present—he gradually casts off his hatred for God and perceives that his way back to the Grail does not lie in the pride of conquest and adventure,

---

[11] Almost every study of Parzival discusses the Kyot question. Efforts have been made to identify him with other known persons, e.g., Guillaume of Tudela. For the theory connecting Kyot with the Catharists, see the articles by E. Zeydel in *Neophilologus,* Vols. XXXIV (1950), XXXVI (1952), and XXXVII (1953).

in "forcing" God to reward him for his knightly services, but in humility, in dependence on God's wisdom. Only through ultimately attaining love in its full form, *charitas,* not *Minne,* can the Grail be attained. The courtly code is not enough. Trevrezent makes this abundantly clear by his description of his own career. He too had sought fame in the world, just as Gahmuret had done, and in doing so had been responsible for the sin his brother Anfortas had committed, the pursuit of earthly sensual love, which had led to his wound and misery and to his becoming unfit for the kingship of the Grail company. For this fault Trevrezent does penance as a hermit, and he is ready to take upon himself the sin of Parzival too. There is no point in the elaborate discussions which have taken place as to the theological aspects of a lay hermit absolving a penitent. Trevrezent is not giving absolution; he is freeing Parzival from the sins he has committed—the selfishness which caused the death of his mother and the sorrow of Gurnemanz, the murder of Ither, the failure to sympathize with Anfortas, all of whom are related to him—which have divided him from his family. Thus Sigune's curse is removed, and he is near to absolving himself from that of Cundrie. This is not Christian absolution. Wolfram at no time shows himself bound to or even interested in the dogmas or formalities of Christianity which, it should be remembered, were by no means so well defined or so well known to laymen as they became after the Counter Reformation.

The complicated explanation given by Trevrezent of the origin of the Grail—its being guarded first by the angels who were neutral in the conflict between Satan and God and later, after their banishment, by a chosen family—is too involved a problem to be discussed here. It is an example of Wolfram's insertion of pieces of half-digested knowledge, but its artistic purpose is clear—to give hope to Parzival that he too, who has been estranged from God, can yet attain the Grail.

The whole scene reveals to Parzival the full implications of the Grail. It is not merely a mysterious happening, nor is it merely something desirable which he had spoiled for himself by failing to ask a question. The stone which he had seen brought past him by Repanse de Schoye is indeed possessed of strange powers, not only of producing food and drink, but of choosing men and exalting them. It is the center of a society and it is a symbol of all that is highest in human attainment. In fact, it comes close to realizing Heaven on earth. But it is only for the chosen and those who have proved themselves worthy. Its power it obtains from the wafer brought from Heaven by a dove every Good Friday, and it is therefore directly connected with Christianity and the Holy Ghost. However, Wolfram, apparently deliberately, rejects obvious Eucharistic symbolism. What the stone of the Grail was has been hotly disputed, even more the meaning of the expression *Lapsis exillis* engraved upon it. The stone may be due to nothing more than a misunderstanding of Chrétien's text, but more likely it is a confused memory of something from the numerous lapidaries of the Middle Ages. What is most important is its function, its ability to create a new type of society in which knighthood and religion are fused into perfect harmony for the service of God.[12]

We have spent a long time in the discussion of Parzival's scene with Trevrezent and shall have a little more to add later. We must now briefly describe the remainder of Parzival's career. As already noted, we hear little of him during the description of the adventures of Gawain. Not until he fights his incognito duel does he reappear in person. He helps to bring about the happy reunion of Arthur, his sister, Gawain, and Arthur's sister

[12] For lapidaries, see L. Baisier, *Le Lapidaire chrétien* . . . (1936) and Joan Evans, *English Medieval Lapidaries,* EETS (1933). There is a possible connection with the stone which Alexander received at the gates of Paradise. For references see the article by O. Springer in Loomis, ed., *Arthurian Literature.* A devastating critique of the fantastic "explanation" of Mergell is given by H. J. Weigand, in "Wolfram's Grail and the Neutral Angels," *Germanic Review,* Vol. XXIX (1954).

(Gawain's mother), Angive. The joy at the court at this triumph of love has little meaning for him, however, for he passed through this experience at his first meeting with Condwiramurs. His yearning for her, made more intense by the joy around him, is of a very different order, not courtly *Minne* but sanctified Christian love. Parzival leaves Arthur's court in sorrow to continue his search for the Grail, with which his happiness and his love for Condwiramurs is, in his mind and in the author's intention, inextricably bound. There follows the inevitable meeting with a knight of equal caliber, but this time, instead of Gawain, Parzival meets his own half brother, Feirefiz, son of Gahmuret and Belakane, a heathen, who is in search of love and adventure. Parzival's sword is shattered, he is defeated; but Feirefiz throws away his own sword and tells his name, usually a sign of defeat. Recognition follows. Wolfram has thus shown a heathen to be a superior knight to a Christian, both in strength and in courtesy, and he carries this to its logical conclusion by having Parzival take Feirefiz back to Arthur's court where he is accepted as a member of the Round Table. Knighthood is thus shown as transcending the boundaries of race and religion. The events of the earlier books are now reversed. Cundrie again appears, removes her curse on Parzival, and tells him that he is called to be Grail King. He may take one knight with him to the Grail Castle and chooses Feirefiz. The asking of the fateful question "Uncle, what ails you?" is now a matter of form. Anfortas is cured and Parzival becomes king.

Meanwhile Condwiramurs has been summoned, and on the very spot where he had gazed stricken at the blood spots in the snow he meets her and the two children, Loherangrin and Karduz, whom he has never seen. Another episode is rounded off when they find Sigune dead, kneeling over the coffin of Schionatulander. Only one thing remains to be done. Feirefiz, as a heathen, cannot see the Grail. He is so attracted by the Grailbearer, Repanse de Schoye, however, that he asks to be baptized, marries her, and returns with her to the East to spread Christianity and to become the father of Prester John.

Since Chrétien's Grail story is incomplete, it is unfair to make comparisons of quality of structure. Nevertheless, certain points are beyond dispute. Chrétien obviously did not care particularly for the Grail story. In his hands it remains formless and, although he clearly intended a contrast between the characters and conceptions of knighthood of Gawain and Perceval, the contrast is never clearly worked out in the extant version. Nor did Chrétien succeed in making the religious element an integral part of his theme. The formal instruction given to Perceval by the hermit and the priest and the connection between the Grail and the holy vessels of Christianity never go beyond the outward forms. The Grail is mysterious, and Chrétien was clearly influenced by the growing popularity of the Christian interpretation, but it has little effect either on Perceval's conduct or on the disparate elements of the story. It is impossible to decide from the extant version how Chrétien intended to join Perceval with the Grail, or whether he envisaged a Grail society of Christian knighthood to contrast with the society of the Round Table.[13]

In Wolfram's poem, in spite of its linguistic obscurities and the author's tendency to jump from one line of thought to another, the grand purpose is very clear and the structure of the poem follows a brilliantly conceived and generally well-executed pattern. For Wolfram there are two societies, the first that of secular knighthood, with a code of honor, effective in its way, for governing the relations between men and even more between men and women. It is a shallow society, devoted, in spite of its high-sounding search for *aventiure,* to the pursuit of love.

[13] An attempt has been made to show that Chrétien's poem is an elaborate allegory of the Christian church, with the details of the Grail ceremony equated with Christian ritual: U. T. Holmes and M. Amelia Klenke, *Chrétien, Troyes, and the Grail* (1959). I can find no basis for this interpretation.

It is colorful, noble, impressive, dignified, and joyous, and for the great majority of people the ultimate in nobility which they can attain. Gawain is its noblest representative, and his quests and successes represent its highest achievement. It is in fact the world that Chrétien had portrayed so well in *Yvain,* but Wolfram deliberately plays down the moral aspects which Hartmann had stressed in his version. To Parzival such a world is insufficient. He has to rise above it. For Wolfram was a deeply religious man. He felt that there were certain virtues which the courtly code conspicuously lacked and which for the true Christian were of the greatest importance. Of these the most important were humility and love.

If we examine the career of Parzival from this point of view, we shall see how carefully Wolfram organized his material. As a child he is sorry for the birds he kills with his bow; his tears cause his mother to abandon her attempt to catch all the birds near their home and stop them from singing. Here he is showing that pity which is inborn in him. Yet after his first encounter with knighthood in the persons of the knights in the forest this inborn pity is suppressed. His unfeeling abandonment of his mother is the first evidence of this lack of human kindness; [14] it is followed by the crude treatment of Jeschute, the butchering of Ither merely to seize his armor, the utter failure to appreciate the tragedy of Signune, and the omission of the simple question which could have cured his uncle Anfortas. Parzival had pity, but he has stifled it. We should note carefully what causes him to stifle it—the half-understood or misunderstood principles of knighthood. He understands only the forms of the instruction he receives from his mother, from Gurnemanz, and from Arthur. They too are at fault, for the instruction they give assumes a knowledge of the spirit behind the forms, and this Parzival does not possess.

[14] In Wolfram's poem, Parzival does not look back and does not see his mother collapse. Chrétien's Perceval is aware of her collapse but not of her death.

It is impossible to ignore the fact that each of his instructors gives advice only from his or her own point of view, and that the forms they impart suppress genuine humanity. Parzival himself is, of course, to blame. Ignorance is not a valid excuse for the hurts he inflicts, but the system itself stands indicted as insufficient to guide human conduct if not supported by common humanity and Christian principles. Parzival's rejection from the Round Table is caused by the slight on his honor cast by Cundrie. He could have been accepted with all his faults if she had not appeared.

The sins Parzival commits are all the stupid blunders which can be found in many folk tales—the so-called *Dümmling* motif. In Chrétien's version they are not much more than stupid blunders and preserve an element of the comic. In Wolfram too they are described with some humor, but their consequences are serious. All of them have to be rectified, and the method of rectification shows how far Parzival has progressed. The Jeschute wrong can be put right by "Arthurian" methods. But the others require a deeper realization of sin. This is summed up in the scene with the hermit, Trevrezent. The consciousness of insufficiency has brought on a feeling of doubt not only of himself but of God's ability to help him. This feeling Wolfram calls *zwivel,* doubt as to God's ability to save. The word occurs in the first line of the poem and runs through it like a theme.

In his obsession with the courtly world, Parzival has cared little for God or for his fellow men. He has become the victim of pride, a belief that he is himself sufficient or that he has his gifts from God as a right. His failures have led him to anger with God for not giving him the Grail and ultimately to morbid despair. He is not yet completely lost, for he is conscious of the gulf between God and himself (symbolized by his ignorance of the fact that it is Good Friday), but he does not realize how to bridge it. On the day of Christ's greatest humility in sacrifice, in the bare and bitter hermit's cell, he comes to the realization that the way to salvation lies through humility, and reliance on God's wisdom. When he has come to this realization, his path goes upwards. Salvation does not come at once, but the way gradually clears and he makes atonement for his sins. The ultimate achievement is Christian love—love for his fellows, for God, and for the world. His reunion with his wife is also part of this love—it is far above courtly *Minne*. Once he has achieved this state of love, the problems which had beset him become merely formal. The seach for the Grail castle is no longer a search—he is taken there; the question to his uncle is a mere formality. Signe no longer needs his sympathy, for she, the patient sufferer, is reunited with Schionatulander in death.

Forms play little part in Wolfram's conception of religion. The sudden baptism of Feirefiz, which takes place without any previous instruction in Christianity, merely symbolizes his acceptance into Christian society. He is already a Christian in character and nobility. Only the formal act of acceptance is necessary. Nevertheless, Christianity is essential for the highest fulfillment of man's life and for his salvation. A heathen can, in Wolfram's view, be every bit as beautiful (Belakane), every bit as brave and noble (Feirefiz), as a Christian, but he cannot attain salvation, or the Grail, without baptism.

For Wolfram the cooperation of a man with his fellows is of the utmost importance. The Grail for him is not merely an individual experience, an object of a quest which one man can attain. It is something which holds together a superior group of men, sets them higher goals, and makes them dream larger visions. No doubt Wolfram had the Knights Templars in mind, but he is thinking in more general terms. Even more important than general society is the family. All of Parzival's sins are committed against the family as well as against the individual. The complex of relationships in the poem is immensely involved, but clearly Wolfram intended to show that it was by his mother that Parzival was connected to the Grail, by his father to the Arthurian world. His rejection by the family means rejection from the Grail, and it is as family representative, not priest, that Trevrezent takes away his sins. The bonds of the family are close (again, see the relation between Parzival and Feirefiz) and its continuation vital. Parzival has sons to carry on his work and the Feirefiz family spreads Christianity in the East.

This insistence on the family makes nonsense of the attempts to link Wolfram with the Catharist heresy, widespread in southern France at the time and undoubtedly known in Germany too. The Cathars, like the Gnostics, believed in two separate powers of good and evil and that flesh itself contained sparks of good which could be liberated only by its dissolution. Thus the continuation of the flesh was undesirable, and strict adherents of the creed (*perfecti*) ate no flesh and did not marry. Such a viewpoint is so utterly opposed to Wolfram's conceptions that attempts to find in the Trevrezent scene similarities with Catharist ritual are pointless. As we have said, Wolfram was not particularly interested in forms.

Many critics have seen in Wolfram's poem an early example of one of the most popular of German literary forms, the *Erziehungsroman,* the novel of the education and development of a young man from ignorance to maturity. Such a reading is only in a very limited sense valid. It is true that Parzival is "educated" in the sense that he receives instructions, makes mistakes, and has to rectify them. But this is true of almost any novel with a central character. Parzival is not being educated to fit himself to the world, but is being prepared for an ideal goal. Nor is there any question of "character development" here. Parzival does not "learn from his mistakes." They are committed because he is not using properly the gifts God has given him. The actual education for knighthood is completed in little time. The difficulty is the realization of his position towards God. The required humility comes finally from an inner realization and only to a very limited degree from consciousness of failure. As we have said already, the Middle Ages did not conceive of character as "developing" but rather as being composed of good and bad qualities inborn. In the triumph of the good or evil characteristics and their expression in action lay the interest of the story. Parzival sins in ignorance and as a result of half-understood education which suppresses some of his virtues. His triumph is the result not of development but of the purging of his pride by suffering.

It is easy to see in *Parzival* a parable of the human pilgrimage. For Parzival in his home in the wastes is very like the picture of primeval innocence. The outside world breaks in, and he falls. He sins and is in despair and, by achieving humility, rises ultimately to love and an earthly paradise. But *Parzival* is not *Everyman*. Its hero is not an average but an exceptional person, whose duty on earth calls for a man above ordinary men. He is destined for and achieves a role on earth which gives more than normal happiness. He is not a lily-white Sir Galahad, achieving the Grail through purity, but one who attains it through suffering and prowess. His experience of the Grail is not a transitory ecstasy. It is a vision of his duty to society and to God. In him is exemplified the best of which the human being is capable. As we have seen, Parzival could not achieve the Grail until he had achieved humility and love. To him, as to all Christians, the promise was there; he could see it but could not grasp it or, indeed, its significance until he had passed through the fire.

We have mentioned only a few aspects of this remarkable poem. Much more could be written about the opposing symbolism of black and white which runs through it, about its handling of such themes as the love and properties of precious stones, about its brilliant ironical humor, and the proud personality of its author, introduced in numerous digressions. Even the versification, with its swift changes of rhythm, reflects Wolfram's brilliant, unorthodox, and mercurial personality. In *Parzival* the Arthurian romance finds its most momentous, if least typical expression.

No story of the Middle Ages, however well told by a medieval author, has so captured the imagination of later generations as that of Tristan and Isolde. Even such a great work as the *Divina Commedia* cannot be said to have left such a heritage for succeeding generations. The reasons are not far to seek. The enormous importance of romantic love in post-medieval literature, an importance so great that scarcely any work of imaginative literature ignores the subject completely, made these two figures into a symbol of that love which disdains all obstacles in attaining its ends, which suffers and ultimately perishes because of its incompatibility with the commonplace and unimaginative world in which it finds itself, and which is such a law unto itself that it breaks all canons of social behavior and accepted morality in achieving its ends. It is not too much to say that even the debased concepts of romantic love found in cheap novels and films, by which "love" can be made an excuse for the most outrageous conduct, can be derived, though remotely, from the Tristan story. Works on this theme by Thomas Mann and Jean Cocteau in recent years bear witness to its continuing power to evoke great artistic achievement.

In view of this remarkable and continuing influence it is strange that the manifestations of the story in the Middle Ages should be so little known, for, with all due respect to later treatments of the theme, it should be stated at once that it is extremely doubtful whether any of them even approach the artistic worth of the great medieval poems on the subject. But as so often happens, the barriers of language and unfamiliarity have prevented modern readers from enjoying the older versions. The difficulties have been increased by a peculiar accident. Not one of the great poems on Tristan and Isolde has come down to us complete. The version probably best known to modern readers, that of Bédier, is a compilation from various sources, not a complete work. The only complete medieval versions are late and of inferior quality.

The Tristan story is usually regarded as Arthurian romance,

but such a classification is only partly accurate. The milieu is Arthurian, and in some versions, though not in the poems to be discussed, Arthur, his knights, and his court are introduced, but the story is in reality independent and became attached to the Arthurian cycle because it was told by the same Breton conteurs who popularized Arthurian material in France. The standards of behavior, the idea of service to the lady, the power of love, the topography are those of Arthurian romance, and Tristan is, in every respect, a peer of the knights of the Round Table. In later versions of the Arthurian cycle, he is in fact a member of that group.

We have seen that many of the names in Arthurian romance can be traced to Celtic origins, and Tristan is no exception. We know of a Pictish king, Drust, who reigned about 780 and whose name appears in Welsh as Tristan. Contact between Wales and Brittany brought his name to the continent, but it is highly unlikely that the historical king had any connection with the hero of the poem. There is abundant evidence of the widespread popularity of the Tristan story from the beginning of the twelfth century. Bernard de Ventadour mentions Tristan and Isolde as the type of unhappy love about the middle of the century; one of the *lais* of Marie de France, *La Chevrefeuille,* is actually an incident from the Tristan story; and Chrétien lists a version among his own works, as we have seen. It is clear, therefore, that the main outlines of the story were laid down before the writing of the extant versions of the legend. Furthermore, there is strong evidence of its influence on other Arthurian material, particularly on the story of Lancelot, to which it bears many similarities. The characterization of Arthur in his relations to Queen Guinevere and Lancelot was much influenced by the character of King Mark in relation to Tristan and Isolde, and numerous incidents in the Lancelot story are taken directly either from a version of the Tristan legend or from intermediate source material.

In spite of the early establishment and popularity of the

story of Tristan, we shall not be surprised to note that differing
versions incorporate varying incidents. The very popularity of
the material ensured that it would attract to itself many of the
floating tales which, as we have seen, could be told of almost
any knight of reputation. Nevertheless, the basic story shows
remarkable unity. It has been the subject of one of the most
scholarly and thorough investigations of sources ever made,
that of Gertrude Schoepperle,[15] and the Celtic sources of many
of its motifs, as well as numerous analogues in mythology and
folklore, have been clearly established. What is most remarkable, however, is the way in which these stories have been made
to serve such vastly different purposes by the authors who
treated the theme. For there is no doubt that as works of literature the Tristan stories hold one great interest for the modern
reader—their treatment of the theme of love, and its effect on
the human being and on society.

There can be little doubt of the existence of some sort of
French "Estoire" of the Tristan story about the middle of the
twelfth century. We have no direct evidence of its contents, but
the German work of Eilhart von Oberge, written at the court
of Henry the Lion in Brunswick *ca.* 1170–80, is undoubtedly
dependent upon it and may be taken as evidence of its general
content. The fragments of Eilhart's poem still extant show Tristan as a powerful, not altogether "courtly" knight. Little is
said of his youth, but we are told the story of his slaying of
the giant Morholt, uncle of Isolde, for his uncle Mark, thus
delivering Mark from paying tribute to Ireland, of his uncle's
attempts to avoid marriage and thus make Tristan his heir, of
the incident of the hair brought by the swallow and Mark's
resolution to marry only the lady whose hair this is. Tristan
goes to Ireland, kills the dragon, and thus obtains the right to
marry Isolde. She discovers by a notch in his sword that he is
her uncle's killer, but forgives him and agrees to marry Mark.

[15] Gertrude Schoepperle, *Tristan and Isolt. A Study of the Sources of
the Romance* (1913).

On the way they both accidentally drink the love potion prepared for the bridal pair. It binds them so closely for four years that, if they do not see one another for a week, they must die. The rest of the poem is concerned with a string of incidents in which Tristan goes through various adventures to meet Isolde and also marries Isolde of the White Hands in an attempt to forget Isolde the Fair. The poem ends with the wounding of Tristan, his sending for the first Isolde, and their death. Love in this poem is a destructive passion which can be explained only by magic—the love potion. Eilhart comes close to apologizing for his hero's stupidity, and after the four years are over the lovers, banned from court, are glad to hasten back and part. The series of "meetings" in the second part is simply adventure in the cruder tradition and does not demonstrate the power of love. Eilhart's principal concern is to show a model knight as victim of dangerous love. He has no interest in analyzing the passion. A large number of later versions follow his lead in stressing, sometimes cynically, the duplicity of Tristan and Isolde and their success in cheating the feeble Mark. The king himself in Eilhart's version is a strong figure, terrible in his wrath and prepared to inflict horrible punishments in revenge. Had these characteristics persisted in all the versions of the Tristan story it is unlikely that its impact would have been very great.

We have seen that Eilhart took his material from a nonextant "Estoire." Fragments of a French version by Béroul seem to have drawn on the same sources. There must, however, have been another version of the story in which the interest lay not in romantic adventure and amorous deceit but in the triumph of love. It is upon these versions that the authors to be discussed here, Thomas of Britain and Gottfried von Strassburg, must have drawn.

Of Thomas we know virtually nothing. He must have been a poet at the English court of Henry II, and his treatment of the Tristan theme reflects the courtly society which gathered around

Henry's queen, Eleanor of Aquitaine. Only the second half of his poem, written about 1170, has been preserved, so that only a few lines overlap with Gottfried's work and direct comparison of the two is impossible. Fortunately there exists a prose redaction of Thomas's work by a Norwegian monk, Brother Robert, which enables us to follow at least the story of the lost part. It is clear, however, that the Old Norse version omits a great deal of explanation and comment which form an important part of the Anglo-Norman poem.

Thomas's work was written under the same influences as those which affected Chrétien de Troyes. He is concerned to make his characters behave in courtly fashion, to remove the crudities of the earlier versions. Hence he motivates the actions of the two lovers more carefully, makes them behave in accordance with the courtly precepts of service and reward, and particularly changes the character of King Mark from that of a revengeful outraged husband to a man equally in love with Isolde (he too partakes of the love potion) and hence bitterly jealous of his wife. The love between Tristan and Isolde (by Thomas called Yseult and by Gottfried, Isot) is like that between Lancelot and Guinevere. It is admittedly adulterous, but so powerful that no one doubts its validity. The adventures of the two lovers only serve to prove and strengthen that love, and it grows stronger until the very end, being finally consummated in death. The love, however, remains on a normal, human plane. It is not the "spiritual" love of the troubadours and *Minnesänger,* which rejected sensuality, but love adventure, such as we noted in Gawain's part of the Grail romances. It differs from the loves of Erec and Ivain in not ending in marriage (hence its rejection by Chrétien), but it conforms very closely with the fashionable belief in the power of love which we observed in our reading of the *De Amore* of Andreas Capellanus. In other words, Thomas's version of the Tristan story is a courtly romance of adventure in which the emphasis is on the power of love and its attainment. The love adventures must accord with the finer graces of courtly society and the characters must be governed by correct social behavior. Morality is a secondary consideration with Thomas. The emphasis, for example, is not on Mark the cuckold but on Mark the jealous lover. Thomas writes that his work is destined "for all who love." We can well believe him, for his work is a polished, interesting and, it must be admitted, rather shallow love story. "Love conquers all" is a very apt motto.

Thomas's achievement was nevertheless considerable. Out of a series of often crude and fantastic adventures he has forged a consistent romance, with well-motivated characters and a convincing milieu. Gottfried von Strassburg, in his prologue, leaves no doubt as to his dependence on Thomas, and pays high tribute to the "authenticity" of his work. It is interesting that he mentions its "Breton" sources as a proof of this authenticity and tells of others "who have not told the tale correctly." There is no doubt that for Gottfried the reshaping of the tale within a courtly milieu was of the utmost importance and that it is the versions similar to those of Eilhart, unpolished stories of amorous adventure, that he is rejecting. Gottfried follows the version of Thomas very closely, and it will be convenient to summarize the story here.

Tristan's birth and upbringing are described. His father, Rivalin, is seriously wounded in a tournament at King Mark's court. The king's sister, Blancheflur, whom he loves, hurries to his tent. Both believe that he will die, and Blancheflur spends the night with her lover. Tristan is thus conceived under the shadow of death—a reflection of the inaccurate connection of his name with the French word "triste." Rivalin recovers, but is soon afterwards killed in an adventure, and Blancheflur dies of grief. The child Tristan, driven from his lands, is brought up by the faithful steward Rual as his own son. He distinguishes himself in every way, particularly in such intellectual pursuits as music and foreign languages.

One day merchants visit the land, Tristan goes on board

their ship to play chess with them, and is kidnaped. A storm caused the merchants to believe that they have sinned and they put the youth ashore near the territories of King Mark. He joins a party of huntsmen and, by his skill in the arts and ceremonies of hunting, causes them to take him to Mark's court. Mark is impressed by his learning and later learns from Rual that he is his own nephew. Tristan goes back to Brittany to recover his patrimony, but hands it over to the faithful Rual and returns to Mark.

The real action now begins. King Mark is forced to send tribute to the king of Ireland unless he can find a champion to defeat the giant Morholt. Tristan undertakes the task and kills his opponent, leaving a fragment of his sword in his skull, but not before he has received a wound from Morholt's poisoned sword which can be cured only by the latter's sister Isolde (the mother of the heroine). Since he cannot go to Ireland, Tristan lies sick of the fearful wound, whose horrible stench keeps away all but his most faithful friends. Finally he puts to sea in a small ship and then in a tiny boat, taking only his harp. He is blown by the winds to Ireland. He goes to court as the minstrel Tantris and is cured of his wound in exchange for teaching his musical and social skills to the younger Isolde. He later makes an excuse for leaving the court and returns to Mark, where he is honored and promised accession to the kingdom. The jealousy of the nobles at this step causes them to urge Mark to marry the beautiful princess of Ireland and to send Tristan as his emissary. (The motif of the hair brought by the swallow is absent.) Mark reluctantly agrees.

Tristan takes some companions with him, but goes alone to the court. On the way he kills a dragon which is devastating the land and for whose conqueror Isolde has been promised as bride. He cuts out the tongue and puts it inside his clothes. The poison from it causes him to swoon. In this state he is found by the two Isoldes, who take him to court and cure him. While he is sitting in a bath, the younger Isolde examines his sword, sees the notch and, by fitting in the piece found in her uncle's skull, detects Tristan as the killer. She is prevented by her attendant Brangaene and her mother from killing him with his own sword, partly because he is to be her champion against the deceiving steward, who has found the dead dragon, cut off its head, and now claims Isolde as reward. Tristan produces the tongue, the steward sees himself beaten, and Tristan can now formally claim Isolde's hand for King Mark.

The queen entrusts to Brangaene a love potion to be given to the married pair on the bridal night. On the voyage the potion is accidentally drunk by Tristan and Isolde and they yield to their love.

Isolde nevertheless marries King Mark. The attendant Brangaene, bitterly accusing herself for her carelessness in allowing the love potion to fall into the hands of the lovers, agrees to take Isolde's place in the bridal bed. Far from being grateful, Isolde is afraid that she may betray her and attempts to have her murdered by huntsmen. They are moved by Brangaene's behavior and spare her, which is fortunate, for Isolde has already regretted her action. Brangaene returns to court and assists the lovers in a series of attempts to deceive Mark. Tristan's absence from his room is noted by the steward Marjodo and suspicion is aroused. A rendezvous in a garden, arranged by floating chips down a stream which flows through Isolde's room, is discovered by the dwarf Melot, who stations Mark and himself in a tree. Fortunately the lovers see their shadows and are forewarned.

Discovery comes, however, as Tristan, who has been bled, leaps from his own bed to Isolde's over a floor deliberately strewn with flour to trap him and, by opening the wound, puts bloodstains on his own bed and Isolde's.

Isolde is condemned to death by burning but succeeds in warning Tristan, who has escaped, that she is to undergo the ordeal by hot iron on the sea shore, and that he should appear there as a pilgrim and carry her from the boat. He does this and falls with her deliberately, so that she is able to swear that she has lain with no one but her husband and the pilgrim they have just seen. Although she thus escapes the fire, both she and Tristan are banished and spend a long time in the woods together. Mark, on a hunt, observes them sleeping and sees a sword between them. He forgives them and they return to court.

The harmony is of short duration. Suspicion soon leads to Tristan's permanent banishment. He finds refuge with Kaëdin at Arundel and is offered the hand of Kaëdin's sister, Isolde of the White Hands. The name confuses him; he believes he may yet find good fortune in love. At this point Gottfried's poem breaks off, but Thomas tells how Tristan married Isolde of the White Hands, but could not consummate the marriage. When Kaëdin hears this and expostulates, Tristan takes him to Mark's court to show him the reason—the beauty of Isolde the Fair. Kaëdin agrees with him, a rendezvous is arranged for Tristan with Isolde and for Kaëdin with Brangaene, who is furious at being "given" to Tristan's friend and threatens to tell all to Mark. Instead she accuses the steward of undue attention. Tristan adopts other disguises—a madman and a beggar —to approach Isolde, but finally he is wounded in the service of Kaëdin and only Isolde the Fair can cure him. Tristan lies on a cliff, while Isolde of the White Hands watches for the ship which will have a white sail if Isolde the Fair is aboard. She falsely reports a black sail, and Tristan dies just as Isolde arrives. She falls dead upon his body. Mark comes too late to tell them of his forgiveness. They are buried side by side in a chapel, and an intertwining vine and rose grow from their graves.

The story in outline is the same for both poets, and a careful and detailed comparison of the works of Thomas and Gottfried has revealed how close the correspondence is. However, the resemblance in story outline does not prevent major differences in intent and treatment. When Gottfried does depart from Thomas, the changes are deliberate and of major significance, but even when details are virtually identical they are given a completely different meaning by the German poet.

Let us say at once that much of the incident is of the common stuff of Arthurian romance and Celtic mythology—the *imran* or lonely voyage, the tribute motif, the fight on the island, the nobleman disguised as minstrel, the recognition by a fragment of metal, the substituted bride, the shadows in the garden, the floating chips, the white and black sails can all be paralleled in folklore and in other well-known stories. We need not concern ourselves with the details. It is much more important to examine Gottfried's treatment of the love theme and the ways in which he expresses this theme to his readers.

As usual with medieval authors, we know virtually nothing about the man Gottfried von Strassburg. He gives his name and that of his (unidentified) patron Dietrich in an acrostic at the beginning of his poem, but further information can be deduced only from the fact that the manuscripts never describe him as "Herr" and hence he could not have been a noble. The word "Meister" attached to his name is usually interpreted as meaning that he was a bourgeois from Strassburg, but it is not impossible that it is a translation of the Latin "dominus" and that Gottfried was a man of clerical education. His work certainly bears out such an interpretation, for it reveals him not only as a master of the knowledge of his time but as systematically trained in theology and the classics. Unlike Wolfram, he is very conscious of the form in which his work is to appear; he remains close to his "authority," Thomas of Britain, in outline, using the *excursus* or digression for the purposes of explanation and exposition. His French is accurate, his language clear and stylish, and he shows the marked influence of rhetorical training which one would expect from the schoolman, especially in his use of antitheses and elaborate figures. Recent research has also sought to show the influence of number symbolism on the construction of his work, without, in my opinion, producing any conclusive results.

The obvious stylistic excellence of Gottfried's poem long had a curious effect on criticism, particularly in Germany. He was felt to be a polished, almost Frenchified follower of Chrétien de Troyes, an excellent technician indeed and an entertaining writer, but in depth and moral strength one hardly to be compared with Wolfram von Eschenbach. His subject too was assumed to be merely "courtly love," and the critics saw little difference in his treatment from that of other authors. Recent criticism, led in particular by Schwietering and Ranke, has revised this judgment completely. Gottfried has now been shown to be a thinker at least as profound as Wolfram and certainly more systematic, whose boldness of conception and execution in the treatment of the theme of love makes such generalizations as "courtly love" untenable.

Any study of Gottfried's poem must begin with his own prologue, for he here makes it perfectly clear what he is about to do. In spite of his salutation of Thomas of Britain as the best source and his own authority, he reveals that his own poem will be something quite different. Instead of writing "for lovers," he announces that his work is destined for *edle herzen,* "lofty spirits," persons not of the common run of mankind. Such persons, he says, recognize that love is not a mere amusement, a joy in pursuit and yielding, but a state in which sorrow and joy are inextricably mingled, in which yearning is fulfillment and fulfillment renewed sorrow, and for which death is merely the prelude to renewed life. Love is thus not a social grace or a reward for service, or even a blessed and sanctified earthly union, but an inward experience transcending time and place and, indeed, all earthly considerations. Its affinities with religious mysticism are clear. The yearning for the beloved is for a union of soul, expressed by union of the body, but much deeper than any such union. Gottfried boldly uses the language and concepts of religious mysticism, particularly those of Bernard of Clairvaux in his sermons on the Song of Solomon, to describe this type of love which is only for the elite.

It is hardly an exaggeration to say that Gottfried is proclaiming a religion of love. His exposition naturally uses the forms and devices of the religious mystics. His lovers are exemplary figures such as are found in legends or saints' lives. They suffer and die for their love. Although the milieu in which they move is that of the Arthurian romance, and their own conscious actions are often motivated by the principles of that world, they are actually on a completely different level of conduct. Those about them naturally judge their conduct by normal courtly standards, as we can see from the reactions of Brangaene and King Mark to their situation. In fact, however, their conduct is determined by quite different considerations. There is no question of Tristan's "serving" Isolde and winning her love as a "reward for service." The steward who cuts off the dragon's head does this—a parody of the "service-reward" theme.

The growth of love between Tristan and Isolde is subtly delineated. Tristan as Tantris first meets her as a tutor. It is through music that he first makes himself known.[16] No medieval audience could have failed to see the parallel between this situation and that of the most famous of medieval lovers, Abélard and Héloise. Thus the attraction begins. Tristan gives the excuse that he is already married in order to escape from the court, a detail not found in Thomas's version. Even more significant is the scene in which Isolde finds the notch in the blade. Desperately she tries to convince herself that it is her duty to avenge her uncle by killing Tristan. Her mother's statement that she has taken Tantris under her protection and Tristan's appeals to honor do not affect her. She simply cannot bring herself to strike, and finally throws the sword down, weeping.

[16] W. Mohr, "Tristan und Isolde als Künstlerroman," *Euphorion*, Vol. LIII (1959) suggests that Tristan is to be viewed as a professional singer and that much of the poem has a consciously artistic background. I would go further and say that Gottfried is exalting the position of the artist as against the knight. Esthetic considerations are very imporant in the love relationship, for the arousing of love is accomplished by the awakening of the senses through music and the other arts.

Under such circumstances Tristan's revelation of his mission becomes much more significant. From an ineligible minstrel, he has become a nobleman. His killing of the dragon has given him the right to Isolde's hand. No wonder that she weeps on leaving Ireland and scorns Tristan's sympathetic gestures with a rebuff that he is merely the ship's captain. In Gottfried's version Isolde is deeply in love with Tristan before the drinking of the love potion. It is harder to decide whether Tristan is in love with her, and this in itself is significant. The initiative and the interest center on the feelings of the woman. We do not have here the mere acceptance of a man's love but active desire. The strength of love's bond is seen in the feminine, not the masculine, partner.

The drinking of the love potion thus becomes a symbol. It is brought in as wine, and Isolde is reluctant to drink it. Brangaene on discovering what has happened, throws the flask overboard, for there can be no question of King Mark's participating in the same ritual act. Brangaene's language on this occasion is significant. She says the drink will be the death of both of them, and indeed it will, but in a sense which Brangaene cannot comprehend.

Gottfried, unlike Thomas, is at great pains to show the conflict in the hearts of both his hero and heroine between their love, as yet not fully understood, and their sense of honor. There is no quick yielding to sensual passion. Each tries hard to fight, and they are brought together only when Brangaene sees how acute is their suffering and explains to them what has happened. Love then becomes the healer of the sorrow, but mere physical union is not enough. Fulfillment, as we have said, brings new sorrow. In the "sermon" on love which he inserts at this point, Gottfried carefully distinguishes between the higher love and the low "counterfeit" which can be bought for money and which is, though he does not say so, the love of the normal court.

To a modern reader, the fact that Isolde lives a normal married life with King Mark is somewhat repulsive. Gottfried's treatment of the situation shows, however, that he viewed it differently. In describing the scene in which Brangaene is replaced in his bed by Isolde, the author remarks that "to him one was as another, in both he found both gold and brass." The implication is clear. Isolde's love was utterly untouched by Mark's embraces, for he loved her on a merely sensual plane.

It is in the scene in the *Minnegrotte* or "Shrine of Love" that Gottfried reveals to the full his new religion of love. The introduction of the shrine is entirely his own invention. All other versions of the Tristan story treat the life in the woods as banishment. Thomas of Britain is no exception. The lovers endure their life there and are not consoled by their enjoyment of each other's company. Only the assumption that their life there is a banishment from court which they both detest makes their forgiveness and return plausible. Although Thomas had already introduced the grotto and described it as a place of pagan love, he gives it no special significance. It is quite otherwise in Gottfried's version. He also describes the cave as designed for love by the pagans, thus connecting it with classical antiquity, but the connection is strengthened by the allusions to the classical stories they tell and the description of the surroundings, which uses all the rhetorical topoi of the earthly paradise. The shrine is of perfect beauty, utterly isolated. The lovers are completely alone. Even the faithful Brangaene has been left at court. For only lovers of the higher order can live in this grotto, and only those who fulfill in the highest degree the requirements of mystic love can sleep in the crystalline bed in its midst.

This crystalline bed, as has been pointed out, is the bed of Solomon, the bed of mystic union, but here it is a symbol not of the religious union of the soul and God but of the union of perfect love. The rest of the shrine is explained in the same symbolic terms that are used to explain allegorically the form of the church—its smooth surfaces are the simplicity of true love, its height the exaltation of love, light reaches it through windows composed of the virtues. Most important is the fact that the door to the inner shrine can be opened only by a key of the soft metal, tin. No gold will open it, nor will strength. Only those destined to enter will be allowed to do so. The parallel with that of the elect entering Heaven is obvious. That this shrine exists in the heart is made clear by Gottfried's personal remark: "I too have known this shrine since my eleventh year and I have never been to Cornwall." Significantly, however, he says that though he has approached the crystal bed, he has never lain in it.

To any medieval reader the description of the "Shrine of Love" could only recall religious allegory—the *Song of Songs,* the numerous allegorical explanations of Solomon's Temple, the Book of Revelation.[17] Only by using such terms could Gottfried explain his mystical conception of love. He was proclaiming something beyond the sensual. But sensual love was essential to it; it symbolized the union, even as it to some extent debased it. The love of Tristan and Isolde became deadly and destructive when it was translated into sensual terms. Only when the sensual was completely overcome, as it was not in the *Minne-grotte,* could true mystical union be achieved. That union would be a union in physical extinction.

The exposition of love as a mystical force was undoubtedly Gottfried's main purpose. There are, however, other aspects of his poem which should not be ignored. One of the most important of these is its intellectualism, a definite and intentional shift of emphasis from the physical aspects of knightly prowess to those of the mind and spirit. Here again Gottfried demonstrates how far one can depart from one's original even while

---

[17] The allegorization of the church building did not always follow the same system. The best-known medieval works are those of Guilelmus Durandus, *Rationale divinorum officiorum,* and Honorius Augustodunensis, who in their turn draw on Isidore. For other information, see the reading list of background material.

following his story closely, for Thomas of Britain is concerned
to make Tristan an ideal Arthurian knight. The German poet,
on the other hand, takes great pains to stress the training Tristan
received in languages and literature, shows his appeal to Isolde
as being connected with music, and puts into his hero's mouth
soliloquies of self-examination. The physical encounters of Tristan are played down. The defeat of Morholt causes Tristan no
jubilation, and such episodes as the killing of the dragon are
treated without particular enthusiasm. Most significant, however, is the omission, stated by the author to be deliberate, of
the description of Tristan's induction into knighthood, the so-
called *swertleite*. The explanation offered by earlier critics that
Gottfried was a bourgeois and did not know the ceremony will
not do. Even if Gottfried had no personal experience of such
matters, there were plenty of books to guide him. For the ceremony he substitutes a long piece of criticism on the principal
poets of his day, praising Hartmann von Aue and Walther von
der Vogelweide among others and criticizing, though not by
name, Wolfram von Eschenbach as a creator of wild stories.
The digression has, of course, no connection with the story of
Tristan. Its introduction at the point where a knightly ceremony
should conventionally be described can only mean that Gottfried
set little store by the descriptions of ceremonies so dear to the
writers of romance or by the ceremonies themselves.[18] He is
thinking in terms of literature, not social life, of reflection rather
than action. The conventions of Arthurian romance provide only
the milieu for his work—and the lower level of culture and love
above which his own characters must rise. Brangaene and
Kaëdin, admirable characters though they are, are as much
foils to Isolde and Tristan as Gawain is to Parzival.[19]

[18] There is a marked contrast with Wolfram, who loved ceremonies
and constantly insists that the duties of knighthood, not authorship, are
his first concern.
[19] The following works may be mentioned in connection with the incidents and characters named: G. Meissburger, *Tristan und Isold mit den
weissen Händen* (1954); J. J. Meyer, *Isoldes Gottesurteil in seiner eroti-*

As might be expected, characterization in Gottfried's poem is far more detailed and psychologically accurate than in any other medieval poem. Love does not mean the same thing to the two lovers. Isolde is throughout the dominating personality. Her love awakens earlier; it is more fiercely possessive, more ruthless but, curiously enough, more ready to make sacrifices. She refuses to listen to the sweet music played by the bell of Peticriu, a little dog won for her by Tristan, because Tristan cannot hear it too. Yet Tristan is so unsure that he actually marries the second Isolde, confused by the names, but somehow hoping to find a second happiness. It is in Isolde, the eternal feminine, that love is most clearly expressed. It is she who pronounces the words that show their union, even as they part: "For you and I are always but one thing with no distinction."

The characterization of King Mark is also interesting. He is neither the outraged and cruel husband of the earlier versions nor the jealous lover of Thomas's account, but a person incapable of loving in the true sense. Isolde never shows remorse over her treatment of him. Tristan is concerned about his own failure to keep faith as a messenger of his uncle, the king, in other words, about his failure in a feudal duty, but not about his violation of his uncle's marriage. Mark was incapable of the love which Isolde needed, and his failure makes him, as De Boor says, a sinner against the code of Gottfried's love. Nevertheless, he is sympathetically drawn. His forbearance and kindness, his reluctance to take action without full evidence, are admirable.

Gottfried has frequently been accused of being an immoral poet. It is alleged that he preached a love based upon adultery, that he ennobled a low intrigue and encouraged defiance of Christian principles. In particular his comment at the end of the scene in which Isolde swears her false oath and thus holds

schen Bedeutung (1914); W. T. H. Jackson, "The Role of Brangaene in Gottfried's *Tristan*," *Germanic Review*, Vol. XXVIII (1953).

the hot iron without a mark that "Christ will blow with any wind" has been quoted against him. It is true that Gottfried says little of Christianity and that his poem does defy Christian morality. It could even be alleged, though wrongly, that his use of the language and symbolism of mystical Christianity approaches blasphemy. In fact, however, no poet could be less justly charged. His statement about the oath is the reflection of an intelligent man on such barbarous methods of arriving at "truth." His concept of love stands far above that of the writers of romance who pay lip service to Christianity, but show their heroes and heroines breaking all its principles merely for pleasure. It is on this last term that we must insist. For Gottfried, love was not merely pleasure. It was a spiritual experience, at its greatest, the noblest possible experience. Love itself had become a religion.

Even without the mystical interpretation of the love experience, Gottfried's poem would be a superb romance. Its glorious language, masterly description of incident, subtle penetration and exposition of character, use of reflective dialogue, and many passages of lyrical beauty mark it as the greatest stylistic achievement of the German Middle Ages. The brilliant use of figures, the polished phraseology, the interweaving of rapidly shifting sense and sound are the complete answer to those who believe the Middle Ages to have had no sense of style or feeling for the grace of language.

Later writers said that death interrupted Gottfried's work, and they are probably right. Modern critics who believe that he could not see his way to a conclusion or who believe the poem was intended to end with the return from the Grotto are underestimating both the author and medieval respect for the integrity of a story.[20] The attempts to continue his work made

---

[20] B. Mergell, in his *Tristan und Isolde* (1949), is led by his theories about the structure of the poem to believe that it was intended to end with the departure of Tristan from court. Few critics would support this view.

by Heinrich von Freyberg and Ulrich von Türheim prove only
one thing—that most of his contemporaries understood him
even less than we do. His poem was intended indeed for a select
circle of noble hearts. One wonders how many he found, for
no other version of the Tristan story rises to his level. His
continuators proceed in the method of Eilhart, by merely
stringing together one crude adventure after another. Gottfried
remains unchallenged as the greatest of the singers of the
religion of love.

The works of Arthurian romance which we have considered
will bear comparison with the greatest of world literature. In
varying forms and with different emphasis they incorporate the
striving for an ideal without which imaginative literature must,
whatever the naturalists may say, perish utterly. In these works
the Christian desire for a higher life is combined with the best
aims of secular knighthood. The remoteness of the Arthurian
milieu made the idealization of these strivings a literary possibility. Unfortunately the Arthurian milieu was itself no guaran-
tee of great or even idealized literature. Few later works even
approach the artistic standard of the works of Chrétien de
Troyes and only one, *Gawain and the Green Knight,* shows
the moral question and seriousness of purpose of the great
German authors. Its poetic localization, its careful study of
the question of the conflict between personal glory, selfish
enjoyment, and genuine honor, are to be ranked with the highest
achievements on the Arthurian theme.

Too often, however, the Arthurian milieu was used merely
as a background for a loosely connected series of adventures,
undistinguished alike in style and morality. It is small wonder
that by the fourteenth century the popularity of the Arthurian
cycle had declined and that authors of romances were reshaping
other themes.

We can discuss these other themes only briefly. None of
them produced works which can be justly compared with the
great Arthurian works. (The works of the Charlemagne cycle

will be considered in the next chapter.) The two important groups both derive from the material of classical antiquity— the stories of Alexander and of Troy. They have much in common. Each derives its material not from famous literary works of classical antiquity on the same subject, but from minor literary sources of uncertain authorship and date. The material was in both cycles reworked with a chivalric Christian emphasis and the introduction of a considerable amount of new incident.

The *Iliad* of Homer was unknown to the Middle Ages, except by name and through a short résumé in hexameters made in the first century B.C. The story of Troy was known chiefly through two late classical works, the *De excidio Troiae* of Dares Phrygius and the *Ephemeris belli Troiani* of Dictys Cretensis. The names of the authors are, of course, without significance. Even the dates are uncertain, but both are products of late classical antiquity.

The first of these was written from the Trojan point of view, the second from the Greek, and both were long regarded as "historical," in contrast to the fables and fictions of Homer. Neither of these works, both in prose, has any particular literary distinction. That of Dictys is probably better written and certainly covers more ground, but that of Dares was infinitely more popular. The reason for this has nothing to do with literature. Vergil had attempted to create a respectable ancestry for his people by using an apparently quite obscure story that Aeneas had come west after escaping from Troy and had settled in Latium. The Romans had thus in some sort avenged the capture of Troy by their subsequent defeats of the Greeks and the conquest of the Eastern Mediterranean. They were also able to claim an ancestry of considerable antiquity. The example set by Vergil for Augustus was taken up with enthusiasm by historians writing for later kings, and we find mention of such interesting personages as Franco, the Trojan ancestor of the Frankish kings, and Brut, the original Trojan Briton. It is hardly surprising, therefore, that authors should favor the "Trojan" account of the war.[21]

Even in these versions from classical antiquity some changes of emphasis had been effected which were of great importance for the Middle Ages. The wrath of Achilles, the death of Patroclus, and the tragedy of Priam become relatively minor incidents. The story of the origins of the war is told in some detail, and there is a significant increase in stress on the feminine element. It is the refusal of the Greeks to agree to a peace which Achilles has arranged so that he may marry Polyxena, daughter of Priam, which leads to Achilles' withdrawal from combat. There are secret meetings and assignations, and Achilles is finally killed when attempting to meet Polyxena. These elements were seized upon by the romantic writers of the Hellenistic period and made an even greater appeal to the writers of medieval romance. In these Latin accounts, too, we find brief mention of Troilus and the daughter of the seer Chryses, variously named Briseida and Creseida.

The first versions of the Troy story to appear in the Middle Ages were those in Latin hexameters by Joseph of Exeter (twelfth century) and the *De Excidio Troiae* of Simon or Chèvre d'Or, but the best and most influential work was that of Benoit de Ste. Maure. This long romance—it consists of 30,000 octosyllabic lines—was written about the middle of the twelfth century. It sets the story of Troy into the frame of chivalric romance, with individual combats in knightly fashion, motivation by a code of chivalry, and love as a powerful force. This latter is especially prominent in the story of Troilus and Briseida. Benoit seems to have expanded the story, a mere sketch in his sources, into a long incident of passionate love between the Trojan warrior Troilus and the Greek hostage Briseida. Their parting when Briseida is returned to her father is tenderly described, but the courtly attentions of the hero

[21] See the references in Maria Klippel, *Die Darstellung der fränkischen Trojanersage* (1936).

Diomedes are too much for her faithfulness, and Troilus is later killed, despairing of his love. This incident was probably of more significance for subsequent literature than all the rest of Benoit's poem. Chaucer treated it with pleasant cynicism in *Troilus and Chryseide,* Boccaccio with a more romantic touch in *Filostrato,* and Shakespeare made it the subject of a play.

Benoit also fixed for the Middle Ages and largely for the Renaissance the characters of many of the principal figures of the Trojan War. Achilles, although still an outstanding warrior, loses much of his heroic character; Odysseus is cunning rather than clever; even Aeneas—red-haired now, a bad sign—is depicted as a traitor to Troy rather than the founder of the Roman Empire. Hector, as might be inferred from the *Iliad,* becomes the noblest of them all. Benoit had numerous imitators. German authors wrote rather long-winded and ineffective accounts of the war, such as the *Trojanerkrieg* of Herbort von Fritzlar. Of the German versions the *Eneide* of Heinrich von Veldecke alone has real literary distinction. The poem is dominated by an effective treatment of two types of love, destructive with Dido, ennobling with Lavinia. He is much more interested in the problem of love than in heroism or in larger moral problems. There was a French play about "Troie la Grant" (1450) and there were English accounts—the *Seege and Batayle of Troye*—but it cannot be said that any of them was a great contribution to literature. The great theme produced no such masterpieces as did the Arthurian cycle.

Nor were the works devoted to the story of Alexander much better. Here again the source material came from highly romanticized accounts of Alexander's life—the *Iter Alexandri ad Paradisum* (fourth century), the apocryphal letters of Alexander to his mother, the *Epitome,* made in the ninth century, of Julius Valerius' fourth-century translation of the pseudo-Callisthenes Alexander romance, and the accounts of Curtius. These stories incorporated material from many Greek and Eastern tales and had little to do with the historical fact. The exotic elements, however, constituted their major appeal. The translation of Archpresbyter Leo (tenth century), called *Historia de Preliis,* made Byzantine sources known in the West. Of the first romance version, that of Alberic of Briançon, only 105 lines survive, but from the German version of the work by Pfaffe Lamprecht it appears that Alexander was made into a chivalric hero. The German version is highly moral in tone, and depicts the weakness of a brilliant and heroic being whose power is not founded upon a secure Christian faith.

Numerous other versions of the Alexander story followed. Each added more and more apocrypha in the inevitable process of cyclization. Some of the authors are known, but they are unimportant. The cycle, developed about 1170–1200, is far from a perfect unity, and new stories such as the *Voeux du Paon* by Jacques de Longuyon and its continuation, the *Restor du Paon* by Brisebarre, were still being added in the fourteenth century. We may note two features. The romances were written in a twelve-syllable line which hence became known as the alexandrine, and the later versions introduced the widespread concept of the nine worthies, three Jewish (David, Joshua, Judas Maccabaeus), three classical (Hector, Alexander, Caesar) and three Christian (Charlemagne, Arthur, Geoffroi de Bouillon).

There were, of course, many other romances, but they are of limited interest at best. The Arthurian cycle alone produced literature of true greatness. The reasons by now have become clear. The indeterminate nature of its historical background made it possible for writers to develop their own ideas of chivalry and to build upon them an ideal world which incorporated the best and highest of human aspirations of the day. The stories of Troy and Alexander, inspiring though they were, left too little freedom to the author. They encouraged the tendency to biographical treatment—childhood, youth, adventure—or to loose accretions of fantastic deeds. It is easy to remark that the romances treated Alexander and Achilles as medieval heroes, but this is true only to a limited degree. Historical characters were hard to turn into a medieval ideal, and none of the attempts is fully successful.

Great works are written by great authors. No doubt a magnificent poem on Alexander could have been written had the subject attracted a Chrétien or a Wolfram. But it is significant that it was the Arthurian material which did attract them, and it is to the Arthurian cycle that we must turn to find medieval romance in its highest form.

6

The Chanson de Geste

In devoting a separate chapter to the *chanson de geste,* we are following a literary tradition rather than a true genre division. It would be perfectly legitimate to regard the *chansons* as romances or, again, as national epics, but most critics, following the lead of the French, have preferred to keep in a separate classification those poems which have as their subject the deeds and adventures of personages connected, however remotely, with the court of Charlemagne and his successors or with the characters of local French heroes. The cycles of the *chansons de geste* are very numerous and, for any but specialist readers, many of them must remain no more than titles. Two or three of the works, however, are among the greatest achievements in medieval literature and it is to the study of these that this chapter will principally be devoted.

Theories about the development of the genre are almost as numerous as the critics who write about them, and it is very unsafe to read any one book on the subject. The absence of written evidence has led, as usual, to the assumption of intermediate stages of oral and written (but not extant) works. The following facts are as indisputable as anything in the study of medieval literature can be. There is almost always a historical core for the story, an event of often quite minor historical significance. The names attached to this event may or may not be the same in the *chanson de geste* and in the historical sources. The historical event may then be changed in several ways—to make it fit a conventional pattern, to make it accord with changed social or religious conditions, to incorporate motifs imported from sources such as folklore or other well-known poems. Local influences—for example, the popularity of a particular hero or saint—may also modify the original story considerably. (The hagiographic modifications of the story of Guillaume d'Orange, or St. William, are a good example of this.)

Whether transmission was oral or written, certain features common to all early medieval poetry inevitably played a large role in the development of the genre. The tendency to exalt the personality of a great ruler led to the ascription to Charlemagne, for example, of numerous deeds, such as a visit to the Holy Land, which were considered highly desirable, and upon this frail foundation a whole series of adventures was constructed. Coupled with this type of invention was the importation into the poems of elements of wonder and magic, of divine intervention and supernatural interference, which were popular with contemporary audiences. It is neither possible nor profitable to attempt to determine the sources of such importations.

There can be little doubt that there existed at one time numerous versions of the same story and that a few of these actually reached the stage of a written form. Our evidence for such written works, however, is so fragmentary that "reconstructions" of such early stages and hypothetical "stages" of the development of such a poem as the *Chanson de Roland* can at best be said to pay tribute to the ingenuity of the critics who manufacture them. Secular writers no doubt stressed the elements of wonder and adventure, clerics the moral and religious lessons which could be drawn. A tiny fragment of four lines (*Chanson de St. Faron*), quoted by Hildegard (*ca.* 870) in his *Vita Faronis,* seems to point to the existence of some kind of heroic lay, but whether in Latin or the vernacular is not clear. More important is the "Hague Fragment," a Latin poem written down in the early eleventh century, which tells of the adventures of certain heroes who later appear in the *chanson de geste* cycles. Such poems could be nothing more than scholarly exercises, and prove very little about transmission. One thing is certain. Whatever intermediate stages there may have been, it was not until a person of genius took the material and made of it a great poem that the *chanson de geste* was really born. He may have had a poem on Roland as his original, but the enormous popularity of the work we now know as the *Chanson de Roland* and the fact that it determined the form which was taken by all other *chansons de geste* shows that the competition from other works was negligible.

The *Chanson de Roland* has come down to us in a rather strange fashion. Of various manuscripts containing the poem, the most reliable are the Oxford (Digby) version of about 1170, written in Anglo-Norman and the Venice version, written in a kind of Italianate French, of the fourteenth century. Experts believe the original version to have been written in a Norman-Francian dialect, but as usual there is no unanimity on the subject and even less on the date of composition. Such internal evidence as exists, for example, the mention of the piece of the lance of Longinus in Charlemagne's sword, which can be connected with the "discovery" of the lance in Antioch in the year 1098, can be interpreted in various ways. The well-known incident, reported by William of Malmesbury, of the singing of the deeds of Roland by the minstrel Taillefer at the Battle of Hastings in 1066, may or may not refer to this poem. Very probably it does not, for the whole spirit of the *Chanson de Roland* appears to reflect the attitude of the First Crusade and this perhaps is the strongest argument for placing the composition slightly after 1100. A certain Turoldus is named at the end of the poem as having written it—but he may be merely the scribe. Whoever the author was, he had some knowledge of the Latin classics and of the rhetorical rules of composition of his time.

The life of Charlemagne written by Einhard about 835 refers to an incident which took place when the emperor was returning from his campaign in Spain. The rearguard of his army was attacked by mountain tribes (Basques) in the Pyrenees, and severe losses were inflicted. Among the dead was "Hruolandus," the count of Brittany. This is the historical fact—a defeat without vengeance by mountaineers, not Moslems. Legend was soon at work on the incident and localized it at Roncevaux. It is impossible to escape the feeling that here, as in the cases of Arthur and the *Nibelungenlied,* we are dealing with the justification of a historical defeat and its transformation into ultimate victory. It may be true, as Bédier argues, that the poem grew into its present form as a result of the influence of the devotees of St. James on their way to his shrine at Compostella and that the strong Christian element is to be traced to the work of the clerics who worked over the original material and made of it something close to a legend. But there are too many examples of popular rehabilitation of defeats to allow us to ignore the possibility of poetical attempts to remove the one loss which Charlemagne suffered.

The war in Spain is almost over, and the country lies at the feet of Charlemagne and his conquering army. Only Saragossa still holds out and there Marsile, the Moslem king, takes counsel on the best way to avoid total defeat. Blancandrin advises that he make a complete submission to the emperor, swear to become a Christian, accept Spain as a fief from Charlemagne's hands, even give noble hostages—and then wait for Charlemagne to depart. The proposal is accepted. The envoys sent to the emperor find him seated, a figure of awesome majesty among his nobles. The peace proposals arouse the hostility of Roland, greatest of Charlemagne's warriors, but his desire to settle the issue by battle alone is all too clearly motivated by his love of glory and his arrogant temper. His step-father, Ganelon, advises negotiation, but is furious when, on Roland's proposal, he is designated to act as envoy to the Moslems. Although the treachery of the Moslems makes the mission dangerous, it is hard to see why Ganelon is so furious. The story seems to assume previous bad blood between the two. On the way to the Moslem camp Ganelon hatches the plot to destroy Roland: he will persuade Charlemagne to put him in charge of the rearguard, which the Moslems will then attack with overwhelming force.

The first encounter between Marsile and Ganelon is inauspicious, for Charlemagne's demand for surrender is delivered in very plain words and weapons are almost drawn. Blancandrin smooths over the incident, and the compact for Roland's destruction is made. Ganelon returns to his emperor with a huge baggage train of presents, his mission apparently successful.

Charlemagne is disturbed during the night by strange dreams, in all of which he suffers some physical injury, but he is unable to interpret them. The army, with great rejoicing, prepares for the homeward march, and now Ganelon springs his trap. Roland is furious that he has been proposed to command the rear, and his emperor is deeply disturbed, but neither can in honor refuse to act. The army sets out, its long length winding through the dark defiles of the Pyrenees. The pagans, knowing that Roland has only twenty thousand men in the rearguard, rejoice as they prepare to attack with overwhelming numbers. Oliver is the first to see their approach and calls upon Roland to sound his horn, but the pride which had caused the quarrel with Ganelon prevents him from doing so and Oliver's wise counsel is in vain. To the cry of "Montjoie" the Christians attack and the pagans fall by thousands and hundreds of thousands. But the innumerable single combats gradually thin the ranks of the Christian warriors. One by one they fall and finally Roland decides to blow his horn, too late to summon help but perhaps in time for vengeance. Oliver, wounded and bitter, points out how many brave men would still be alive if he had blown it earlier. Roland, unwounded but weary, blows with such force that his temples burst. Far off the horn is heard by the emperor, and all Ganelon's efforts to explain it away are vain. The army turns to the rescue with Ganelon a prisoner. The pagans, seeing the few Christians left alive, redouble their efforts. Oliver and Bishop Turpin are mortally wounded. Oliver, in blindness and weakness brought on by his wounds, strikes Roland on the helmet. Roland's tenderness and the subsequent reconciliation show the better side of his character. Oliver slips from his horse and dies; Turpin, true to his priestly office, blesses the dead whom Roland arranges around him and uses his last remaining strength to bring water and consolation to the dying. Roland again sounds his horn, expending his last strength. His attempts to break his sword Durendal are vain, but with a last smashing blow with his horn he kills a pagan who attempts to steal it. With a final prayer he raises to Heaven his gauntlet, the pledge of allegiance. Gabriel takes it, and Roland's soul is conducted to Heaven by angels.

Charlemagne arrives and drives the pagans into the Ebro. The sun stands still for him as it had done once for Joshua to allow him to complete the Lord's work. Marsile, gravely wounded, flees to Saragossa. Charlemagne sorrows deeply for Roland and his men, but he is warned by the angel Gabriel in a dream that a great battle is impending, and other visions follow which seem to indicate mortal danger.

The reason soon becomes clear. Marsile had long ago sent messengers to Baligant, the most powerful of Moslem emirs, asking for help against Charlemagne. This help, a mighty Moslem host, is just disembarking when the news of the great battle is received. The wretched Marsile dares once again to hope. Meanwhile Charlemagne has returned to the scene of battle and, in terrible grief, ordered the burial of the dead. Over Roland he pronounces a funeral oration which tells of his own deep sorrow. But the Moslems approach and the battle array must be formed. It is described in detail, and then comes the list of pagans. Battle is joined. Again there is a long series of single combats, culminating in the meeting of Baligant and Charlemagne. The emperor receives a frightful wound in the head, but the voice of the angel Gabriel again reassures him. He cuts his opponent down with one stroke. The battle is won, Saragossa falls, and the army returns to France and their capital Aix.

Here Ganelon must be tried. His defense is simple: he has committed no treason, for the tragedy was due to a private quarrel between him and Roland. The assembled nobles, to the emperor's horror, are inclined to agree with him. Only Thierry, a man of no great strength, is prepared to support in combat his statement that Ganelon is a traitor. Against him comes Pinabel, a mighty warrior. But God aids the right and Thierry is victorious. The men who stood as pledges for Ganelon are hanged, and he himself is torn to pieces by horses. Thus traitors perish. Charlemagne has ended one incident, but his duties as the greatest of Christian princes leave him no rest. The poem ends with a summons from Gabriel to new wars for his God.

The *Chanson de Roland* is not a subtle poem. Stylistically it is simple, achieving its effects by such relatively unsophisticated devices as repetition, recurring topoi of description, and powerful epithets. It rarely uses long sentences, and these usually correspond in length to one or two of its octosyllabic lines. The division into *laisses,* or poetical paragraphs, also gives an effect of somewhat primitive simplicity. Yet this very simplicity contributes greatly to the fact that the *Roland* has a good claim for consideration as the most successful epic in the West European vernaculars. Like all the genuine—as opposed to artificial, imitative—epics, it delights in action and broad description and yet concentrates essentially upon one fatal action and its consequences. Just as the *Iliad* represented a mighty struggle of two peoples, yet focused the reader's attention upon the disastrous consequences of the wrath of Achilles, so the *Chanson de Roland,* in showing the ultimate defeat of the forces of the heathen by the power of Christ, makes the struggle easier to grasp by concentrating the reader's attention on the Christian hero, Roland, whose unchristian pride gives a temporary advantage to his adversaries. Roland's heroism and fighting qualities are not sufficient to win victory for his cause. Indeed, until the final scenes in the Pass of Roncevaux, Roland, like Achilles, is far from an ideal hero. He has the outward attributes of heroism, but they are largely nullified by his pride. Whoever invented the figure of Oliver (a name symbolic of wisdom) to set beside him performed a literary masterstroke. For Oliver is far closer to the Christian ideal than Roland. He has all Roland's qualities and, in addition, prudence, humility, and deep wisdom. Yet as an epic hero he would have failed. It is the superhuman, even the bad, qualities of Roland which make him interesting. The author perceived that in epics, as in Heaven, there is more joy over one sinner who repenteth than over ninety and nine just men. Roland's defiance and his final realization of his faults grip the reader's interest and at the same time represent the path of the Christian man who sins, repents, and does penance for his sin.[1]

The *Chanson de Roland* is a Christian epic. It shows Christianity as a militant force, forever struggling against the powers of evil. There is little compromise with the representatives of these powers. The best that can be said—and it is said rarely—of a Moslem is that he might have been a good knight had he been a Christian, but most of the warriors in the pagan host are villains of the deepest dye. We are still far from the tolerance of Wolfram von Eschenbach. But if it is primarily a Christian epic, it is a social epic too. The loyalties of the vassal to his master are the strongest ties that can bind men and the word of the emperor is law. He minces no words in bidding even the

[1] The theological aspect of Roland's death is worth noting. He dies a martyr, in fullness of grace, and his soul goes immediately to Heaven.

closest of his advisers to hold their tongues and give their advice only when asked. The poem clearly reflects the social conditions of a relatively primitive aristocratic society, where personal relationships between nobles constitute both the ethical and legal foundation of society and the mainspring of the action. Ethical principles and abstractions have not been developed to anything like the extent to which they are found in the Arthurian romances already discussed. In so far as they appear at all, they are standard Christian virtues and vices. The result of this, from the literary point of view, is a much greater concentration of interest on character and clash of personality than is possible in the romances and, for most readers, a more direct personal involvement in the vicissitudes to which the heroes are subjected. The memorable episodes of the poem are those in which the heroes rise to superhuman levels of endeavor or triumph over sufferings—Roland's despair as he winds his horn and the struggle of the mortally wounded Bishop Turpin to comfort the dying.

The epic tradition has raised the historical figures to heroic stature. They are viewed as the inhabitants of a greater past, from which the lesser contemporaries of the writer have descended, and they are historical in the sense that they are connected by ties of family and nationality with the audience. Here again they differ from the characters of romance, whose world was conceived as an idealized fiction. About the figure of the Emperor Charlemagne there plays another light. Even in his lifetime his character was being idealized, partly out of genuine admiration for his qualities as a Christian ruler, partly as a result of the tendency to formal panegyric which was part of rhetorical training. The biography by Einhard already mentioned increased this tendency by its efforts to make Charlemagne appear as a worthy successor of the greatest Roman emperors. Legends rapidly gathered about his name—he conquered Britain and made a pilgrimage to the Holy Land and in particular became the chosen instrument of God upon earth.

The character of Charlemagne in the *Chanson de Roland* shows all these influences at work. The author clearly intends to show the emperor in a favorable light, as the dominating character, the figure on whose behalf all heroic deeds are performed. His appearance is majestic, his manner stern and dignified, his power undoubted. Yet there are some curious discrepancies. It would be possible to argue that it is Charlemagne's weakness as a ruler which is responsible for the tragedy of Roland and the defeat of the Christians. It is impossible to avoid the conclusion that Charles was lacking in the accurate judgment of men, which should be the first attribute of a great ruler. Could he not see through the cunning of Ganelon? Did he not realize the depth of the personal enmity between him and Roland? The answer to such questions probably lies in the rigidity of the epic convention. Even the emperor was bound by it and, as we have pointed out already, the medieval writer had little interest in a consequential development of character. The emperor is great, he personifies the perfect Christian ruler, but he does not control the action. The result is that, in spite of formal eulogy, he often appears weak and vacillating. King Arthur suffered in the same way.

The second part of the epic shows Charlemagne in a different light. He emerges as the central figure of the story. Roland, Oliver, Turpin are all dead; the Moslems have a new and more powerful leader. There is now a direct conflict between the forces of Christendom and those of the heathen. Inevitably Charlemagne becomes a more formalized personage, the head of a Christian army, and the culmination of the struggle in personal combat between him and Baligant and the direct intervention of the powers of Heaven in the struggle become inevitable. Charlemagne thus becomes the central figure of the epic, and both the work and the character suffer in the process. The effect is mechanical and, to a modern reader, unsatisfying. It may be doubted whether contemporaries had the same reservations. They would also understand more easily than we can the difficulty of condemning the traitor Ganelon and the limits of Charlemagne's power. Ganelon's peers see his actions as a personal feud between him and Roland, not as treachery to the state, and the emperor, for all his position and feudal supremacy, cannot have him punished until Heaven itself has delivered judgment in a trial by combat.

We have noted that the *Chanson de Roland* has an ethical basis in actual feudal and personal relationships between nobles, however idealized that relationship may be. This factual state of affairs—it is not "realism" in the literary sense of the term—is reflected in the details of combat and life. There are no elaborate codes, no principles, no artificialities. The absence of such codes of behavior is probably the most obvious difference between the *Chanson de Roland* and the Arthurian romances, and nowhere is this difference more obvious than in the treatment of women. Roland and Oliver are both engaged. They express regret at the fact that they will never again see their ladies. But their life is not affected by them, nor is there any suggestion in the poem of service to a lady or of the idealization of women. The world of Roland is a man's world, where action is motivated principally by notions of personal honor, of glory in this world and reward in the world to come, and by a desire to serve France.

This latter aspect is worthy of some attention. Charlemagne was, of course, a German-speaking emperor. His territories included much that is now German, and his favorite residence was in Aachen. In the *Chanson de Roland,* however, he is a ruler who has conquered many lands and who is the most powerful ruler in Christendom, but whose loyalties and the seat of whose power remain essentially French. French nobles constitute the flower of his army and occupy the place of honor in his battle line. They fight for Christ and for the Christian religion, but it is Charlemagne (not the pope) whom they regard as the head of Christendom, and it is more than incidental that in fighting for Christ they are fighting also for France and for the extension of its power.

It is in this respect that the influence of the popular songs about Charlemagne upon the *Chanson de Roland* can be most clearly seen. Only such popular songs could have turned Charlemagne into a French national hero, for the more formal learned Latin works viewed him as the ruler of a united Christendom. The popular tradition ensured that the *Chanson de Roland* should be a French national epic, even though the figure of Charlemagne and the work in general owe much to the tradition of his clerically trained admirers and recorders and to the efforts of several generations of clerical reshaping of the original story.

How strong this clerical tradition was appears most clearly in the German version of the *Chanson de Roland*. The *Rolandslied,* written by a priest called Konrad at the court of Henry the Proud and his successor, Henry the Lion, was probably completed by 1139. It is based upon the *Chanson de Roland* (already mentioned in the *Kaiserchronik,* written at the same court) or, rather, upon a Latin translation of it, but its spirit is very different. It is hardly surprising that the French national element has been suppressed, but this has been done not in the interests of German nationalism but in order to make the whole poem into a purely Christian work. Charlemagne is now devoted entirely to the interests of Christianity and to the defeat of paganism. He is a ruler who is made deliberately reminiscent of the Old Testament kings, fighting the battles of the Lord. His paladins have lost their personal weaknesses. Roland's anger and pride are no longer important. He is a Christian soldier, fully conscious of his role as the exterminator of evil. His death, like those of Oliver and Turpin, is that of a martyr; his loyalty to Charlemagne is merely the reflection of a higher loyalty to God. The love for "sweet France" is replaced by a yearning for another, better world and all the struggles are for the conversion of the heathen or his extermination, not for conquest.

As might be expected, the contrast between Christian and heathen is even sharper than in the French version. The Moslems are destined for Hell and are treated as the representatives of the powers of darkness. They are all black, the Christians all white, and the whole epic is viewed as an incident in the eternal struggle between good and evil. It may be added that Ganelon is viewed not as a personal enemy of Roland but as a wicked man who betrays the Christian cause.

It is almost unnecessary to add that the result of these changes is a much inferior poem. All interest in character has disappeared, and every action is entirely predictable. The language too is bald, the style unadorned. The chief interest of the work lies in its demonstration of the greater qualities of its French original and in its reflection of a strong ecclesiastical tradition in the story of Charlemagne.

The influence and popularity of the *Chanson de Roland* were enormous and called forth numerous reworkings and imitations of the poem—a rhymed *Chanson de Roncevaux* at the end of the twelfth century, a Latin *Carmen de proditione Guenonis* about the middle of the thirteenth, and adaptations in Old Norse (in the *Karlamagnussaga*) and Middle English. The *Chronicle of Turpin* ("Pseudo-Turpin"), purporting to be written by the archbishop who fought at Roncevaux, contains a long section on Roland, recounting numerous adventures of his childhood and early youth, particularly his combat with the giant Ferracutus. None of these works is of any great literary value.

The growth of the legend of Charlemagne—and it is a legend in the strict sense, for the emperor assumes a stature very close to that of a saint—produced a large number of poems which centered upon his fame, some of them directly concerned with his own exploits and even his (quite unhistorical) childhood, some with the exploits of heroes who fought for him, for example, Ogier of Denmark. Many of these are known to us by name only, others in late reworkings. Like King Arthur, Charlemagne was unable to escape the penalty of success. Not only is he sometimes subordinated to another hero but he may even, as in the *Pèlerinage de Charlemagne* (a pilgrimage to Jerusalem), be made into a figure of fun. Still worse was the fate of his successor, Louis the Pious. He is shown almost invariably as a weak and even treacherous king. He appears so in the epic cycle which in literary significance most closely approaches the *Chanson de Roland,* namely, the cycle of Narbonne, the adventures of Guillaume d'Orange. The works which compose this cycle are of different dates, but the central story emerges fairly clearly. Guillaume's youth and his faithful service to the feeble Louis are described in what is generally thought to be the best poem of the cycle, the *Couronnement de Louis.* Here, as in the *Nibelungenlied,* we see a brave warrior showing complete fidelity to his overlord because he bears the title and majesty of kingship, not because he is a noble king. It is in this poem that Guillaume loses part of his nose in battle and earns the name "Guillaume a curt nez"—William Shortnose. In the *Charroi de Nîmes* some of the material of the *Couronnement* is repeated, but here Guillaume, after rejecting a fief which would have been confiscated from an innocent person, undertakes to win one for himself in Orange, in southern France. The title refers to the actual ruse (using carts and entering the town as merchants) by which Nîmes was captured. The *Prise d'Orange* is a bride quest. Orable is the beautiful wife of the Moslem king, Tiebaut of Orange, and Guillaume, fired by tales of her beauty, follows the customary practice in epics of trying to reach her in disguise. He is recognized, caught, and imprisoned. Orable, of course, is already in love with him, and helps him until the arrival of a rescuing army. She is converted and becomes the faithful and courageous wife Guibourg of the oldest of the poems, the *Chançun de Willame.* This Anglo-Norman poem, and the *Bataille d'Aliscans* both recount substantially the same story—the tragic death in battle of Vivien, Guillaume's nephew, the defeat of Guillaume's relieving army, the high courage of Guibourg in defeat and her efforts to help raise more troops, and the eventual destruction of the Saracens. Guillaume is already an old man in these last poems. In the *Moniage de Guillaume* he is a monk but has not forgotten his prowess. Although he is humble enough when thieves waylay him, their attempts to deprive him of his breeches go too far, and he lays about him with a will.

The Guillaume cycle has no single poem which compares with the *Chanson de Roland*. The individual parts are very uneven and of very different dates. The actions and events cannot be made into a unified whole. Each knows of parts of the whole story which came before or after it, but the allusions are frequently not to the extant versions. Yet generally the *Guillaume* cycle is probably very typical of the cyclic *chansons de geste*. Adventure and action are the principal ingredients, loyalty, pride, and family ties the principal motivating forces. Two other features are worth noting—the often Gargantuan humor, and one of the few portraits in the *chansons de geste* of a truly noble woman, Guibourg. This portrait may well have caused Wolfram von Eschenbach to decide to adapt the story into German under the title *Willehalm,* a task he did not complete.

There are many other cycles of *chansons de geste,* but none of them contains any truly great poetry. In spite of the vast bulk which was produced, only one great poem, and that probably the earliest, emerged. The *Chanson de Roland* succeeds because it imparts to the original adventure story a sense of high purpose, of sin and redemption, of nobility in extreme peril. Furthermore, it has a degree of artistic unity which the other works never attained. The *chanson de geste* as a literary genre must stand or fall with the *Chanson de Roland*.

7

The Germanic Epic

The *chansons de geste* are, in a very real sense, French national epics. The *Chanson de Roland,* in particular, can be understood only if the strong patriotic tradition infused by vernacular oral tradition is fully appreciated. Yet the Germanic epics are national—even supranational—in a different sense. Not only is their material specifically Germanic, but the art conventions upon which their original style is formed were developed, so far as can be determined, by poets unaffected by classical rhetoric. The metrical forms and poetic ornament are highly complex and are the result of generations of professional development. To describe them as "primitive" or "barbaric" is nonsensical, but they are characteristic of a society which was itself untouched by either classical civilization or urban living. It is possible to see traces of Vergil in *Beowulf,* and the *Nibelungenlied,* in its extant form, has been largely reshaped to conform to the conventions of the romance, but such changes affect only the externals. The Germanic epics remain essentially the products of a separate civilization and a separate artistic convention.

There has been no lack of research on the origins of the Germanic epic. Since the rediscovery of the *Nibelungenlied* in the eighteenth century generations of scholars, principally German, have labored to uncover the details of epic transmission, to establish the texts of epics that are extant, and to speculate about the form and content of works to which references can be found or which may be presumed from later tradition. The early nineteenth century remained in the shadow of the mighty Lachmann, who applied to the *Nibelungenlied* the theories of the formation of epics which split the *Iliad* and *Odyssey* into different lays and which made the author into little more than a compiler. The theory had unfortunate results, since it concentrated scholarly interest on hypothetical "pre-epic" lays (of which none were extant) rather than on the study of the actual texts. It led, furthermore, to the assumption that the Scandinavian works, in which a more primitive society was reflected, must necessarily be the origin of those written in Germany.

More careful study of the texts during the second half of the nineteenth century revealed that the few neglected voices which had spoken against Lachmann's theories had, nevertheless, been right. There were indeed short lays, of which the one extant example is the *Hildebrandslied,* but in style and treatment they differed so much from the extant epics that it was clear that mere assemblies of the one could not have produced the other. The Scandinavian *Edda* songs too, however closely their content might approximate certain parts of extant epics, were clearly of a different genre. The epic was reestablished as a definite art form which, as W. P. Ker wrote, "could not be made by a process of cobbling." [1]

Before considering specific works of the Germanic tradition, it will be worth while to note some characteristics which are common to them all. As we have stated, the stories are from Germanic history and legend, often inextricably confused. Historical personages appear frequently—Attila, Theodoric, Ottokar. The historical events mentioned can frequently be determined and were clearly felt by the author to be part of the past of his own people. Yet the history has been raised, as always in the epic, to a larger grandeur, to superhuman size.

[1] In *Epic and Romance* (1897).

Folklore and fairy tale motifs are interwoven with the history, motifs which are often similar to those found in the romances— the rescue of the weak king by the great hero, the hero's boyhood spent unknown and deprived of parents, the combat between relations unaware of one another's identity, the fight with the monster or dragon, the tests of manliness to win a bride. Yet it may be said that even here there is evidence of selection. The great strength of family ties is reflected in the popularity of motifs involving revenge for, or combats between, relations. The hero far from his country, exiled or fighting for another, often weaker king, also recur frequently.

Only in the *Eddas* is there direct reference to Northern mythology, but its traces are easy to observe in *Beowulf* and the German epics. The grim figures of evil there encountered reflect the gloomy giants and ferocious beasts whose ultimate triumph is known to Northern gods and heroes alike. Death is inevitable and fate unrelenting. The part of a brave man is to struggle with evil and fate, even though he knows that in the end he must be conquered. Beowulf and Hagen of the *Nibelungenlied* have this sense in common, however much they may differ otherwise, a sense of the inevitability of doom and a determination to meet it with laughter and to fight to the end. The sense of impending doom hangs over all Germanic epics, and the struggle against fate is, in them, more important than the struggle between good and evil. The overlay of Christianity obscures this fact more in *Beowulf* than in the *Nibelungenlied,* but in both the real interest, both for contemporaries and for the modern reader, lies in the determination of the individual hero to vindicate himself in the face of insuperable odds. When Beowulf fights his last fight, old and battle-worn, when Gunnar plays the harp with his toes in the pit of the serpents, when Hagen flings the chaplain into the waves, they are all demonstrating the highest quality of a true hero—the ability to laugh fate to scorn.

The ethic of the Germanic epic rests upon the individual

greatness of the hero—to fight bravely and to die without complaint. There is no elaborate social and ethical code which governs a selected body of men, as it does the knights of Arthur's court. Yet the code governing individual relationships was strict. There must be unquestioning loyalty to his ruler on the part of the liege man, even if such loyalty involves conduct towards others which would otherwise be mean and treacherous. The often quoted words of Tacitus, that the chief considers it disgraceful to leave the field without victory, the liege man to leave the field without his chief, are reflected in the epics. This loyalty overrides even considerations of family, otherwise the strongest influence on conduct. But if the liege man owes loyalty to his chief, he may also demand in return favors, gifts, and continuous protection. A chief who fails to show generosity and hospitality disgraces himself and is unworthy of his station. The epics delight in the enumeration of a king's possessions, the gifts he gives, and the celebrations he holds, for such descriptions do honor not only to him but to his descendants. No doubt the hearers enjoyed the vicarious excitement of such enumeration, but its artistic purpose is to honor the chiefs and show their greatness.

After loyalty to the chief comes loyalty to the family, to those allied by blood. Much of the action of the epics is brought about by attempts at revenge and by perpetuation of feuds. No doubt this reflects an actual state of affairs in society. Later Christian society found such blood feuds repugnant, and the action of stories is sometimes changed to eliminate them. Nevertheless, it is the relationships between individuals, and particularly between members of the family, which determine the action. There is no attempt, as there is in the great romances, to trace the workings of the Christian God upon human affairs nor to explain the relationship between the individual and his God. In this respect too the essentially factual, realistic nature of the Germanic epics appears.

The *Nibelungenlied* and later Germanic epics were written

in various types of rhymed verse, and their style and language were much influenced by contemporary romances. Hence they are, in this respect, not characteristic of the earlier Germanic works. The style of the Scandinavian *Edda* songs, of *Beowulf,* of the *Hildebrandslied,* and of numerous smaller works is characterized by the use of alliterative verse and often by a system of periphrastic epithets (*kennings*) to describe frequently occurring phenomena. The use of such formal epithets is common in all epic poetry, and every reader of the poems of Homer will remember "gray-eyed Athena" and the "wine-dark sea" (if these are the correct translations). The Germanic epithet system, however, is more complicated. It forbids the use of the actual noun in the periphrasis and insists on a double word which is a complete circumlocution. The result is a swelling stream of description which can be understood only by the initiated, and the perfect use of which marked the great artist. It is very doubtful whether a modern reader can realize the full impact of this essentially metaphorical type of narrative upon a contemporary audience. The popularity of such metaphoric narration meant that passages of description in the narrative were frequent, imparting both atmosphere and epic fullness to the story. Dialogue is also frequent, and motivation, historical background, and characterization are more usually effected by these means than by intrusion of the author's own description.

The meter used in *Beowulf* and the Scandinavian poems is also highly complex and only an outline of its form can be given here. There was no rhyme in the modern sense, nor was the number of syllables in any line fixed. Each line contained four main stresses, two in each half line, and the first sound of the word bearing the third main stress had to alliterate with at least one other initial sound of a stress-bearing word in the first half line. It was possible to have three or, exceptionally, four such alliterating sounds in each line. Occasionally there were two alliterating pairs. The number of unstressed syllables was quite indefinite, and the method of their inclusion in the rhythmic pattern has been the subject of much dispute. Complicated rules also governed the priority of words in carrying main stresses; nouns were regarded as more significant than verbs and were given the main stress whenever possible. In its most simple form an alliterative line appeared as follows

brút in búre   bárn unwáhsan

The three *b's* alliterate; the main stress is on *barn;* there is a regular alternation of stressed and unstressed syllables. But, as can be seen from the examples below, such lines are the exception.

hína míti   Théotríhhe || enti sínero   dégano fílu

In this line there is a long anacrusis in each half line. Two main stresses come in succession in the first half.

spénis mich mit dínem wórtun || wíli mih dinu speru wérpan

Here *wortun* definitely alliterates with *wili.* It is more difficult to decide whether there is double alliteration (*s*penis-*s*pero) or whether a stress falls on *werpan.* In the latter event, the first half line is hard to scan. The *Hildebrandslied* presents more scansion problems than most works written in alliterative verse, but even in *Beowulf* and Old Norse poems there are many irregular lines.

Numerous theories have been advanced to account for the form of the meter, of which only two need be mentioned here, those of Sievers and Heusler.[2] The two theories are rather complementary than contradictory. Sievers saw five main rhythmic patterns in use and believed that each half line conformed to one of these patterns: A:/x/x; B:x/x/; C:x//x D//\x and E/\x/. By far the greater part of the lines fall into the first three categories. This theory explains nothing, but merely argues that the rhythmic patterns were conscious. Heusler believes that each line had a fixed length of musical time—two full beats

---

[2] E. Sievers, *Altgermanische Metrik* (1893); A. Heusler, *Deutsche Versgeschichte,* 3 vols. (1922–29). O. Paul, in his *Deutsche Metrik,* 3d ed. (1950)—a simple handbook—summarizes Heusler's theories.

—and, using his own symbols, would appear as: x́x x́x||x́x x́x where x = ¼ beat. Some syllables, however, could be counted as ½ beat or ⅛ or even $\frac{1}{16}$, and thus Heusler could "explain" lines where unstressed syllables were numerous by designating them thus x́◡◡x́x||x́xx◡◡ where ◡ represents ⅛ beat. Unstressed syllables before the main stress were regarded as anacrusis and did not affect the pattern. It will be noted that Heusler regarded a falling (trochaic) rhythm as basic in all Germanic verse.

That the lines had, for listener and author alike, a basic rhythmic and musical beat pattern is highly likely. The poems were very probably recited or chanted to a rhythmical accompaniment and it is clear from the complexity of the schemes used that virtuosity in meter was appreciated. It should never be forgotten that the Germanic epic was essentially an oral form. Those who composed it could not write; those who could write usually despised it. This fact accounts for many discrepancies between various versions of the same story. The written forms we possess were those which a person who could write chanced to hear as local variants. The task of comparison, never easy, is made doubly difficult by this fragmentary and haphazard tradition. Source-hunting is a dangerous amusement under these circumstances; for every version we possess, fifty must be lost.

We may now turn to certain specific works which can be regarded as characteristic of the Germanic epic—the *Edda* songs and Scandinavian sagas, the *Hildebrandslied, Beowulf,* and the *Nibelungenlied.* These works present a problem in sequence. Some of the *Edda* songs are undoubtedly the oldest, but were written down only in the thirteenth century. The *Hildebrandslied,* which is only a short fragment of 69 lines, represents the Germanic lay, but the manuscript fragment in which it appears was written about 830, later than *Beowulf.* The *Nibelungenlied* shows Germanic material deeply affected by the courtly tradition, yet it was written down before the extant version of the

Edda. It will probably be best to treat the *Hildebrandslied* first, then *Beowulf,* and follow with the *Edda* and the *Nibelungenlied.*

We owe our knowledge of the *Hildebrandslied* to a lucky accident. A manuscript containing substantial portions of it was used as the flyleaf for a manuscript of a *Liber sapientiae* found at Kassel. The sixty-nine lines which survive have been the subject of unending discussion and speculation, so much so that it sometimes appears that no German scholar can regard himself as established until he has written at least one article on the subject. Study of the poem is complicated by several factors. It is incomplete, but probably was not much longer than the extant fragment. Worse still, it is written in a strange mixture of dialects, part High German, part Low German, with even a few Old English forms, indicating that it is a reworking. Linguistic specialists have advanced almost as many theories as there are lines in the poem to explain this, ranging from a simple "High German version of a Low German original" to "A Low German version of a Bavarian original written by a Frankish scribe for an Anglo-Saxon patron." Baesecke believes it to be basically Langobardic, which is convenient, since we know very little of their language. The original poem is certainly much older than the present confused version and, in spite of the efforts of scribes and critics, it remains a magnificent fragment. Needless to say, the regularity of the alliterative meter is much affected by the confusion of dialects and versions.[3]

The theme is a very well-known one—the meeting on the field of battle of a father and a son whom he has left at home as an infant. Hildebrand is the best warrior of Theodoric the Ostrogoth, who, contrary to historical fact, is always represented in Germanic heroic legend as having fled from Italy to Attila the Hun in order to escape Ottokar. Hildebrand has left wife and child at home to follow his lord. Now, as Attila's greatest warrior, he finds himself opposed in single combat to the

---

[3] The often fantastic ideas about the dialect of the *Hildebrandslied* are listed in W. Braune, *Althochdeutsches Lesebuch,* 11th ed. (1949), pp. 156 ff.

young Hadubrand, the chosen champion of the opposing forces. In accordance with custom he asks the name of his opponent, who reveals that he believes his father to be dead. Hildebrand is now faced with a dilemma. He cannot refuse to fight, for he would thus bring disgrace upon his own side. He can only attempt to conciliate his opponent, exchange gifts with him, and part honorably. The younger man sees this as a trick and even an admission of weakness. He insults his opponent, and the fight begins. Here the poem breaks off, but the tragic end is known to us from other sources. The son has the father at a disadvantage but, hearing his battle cry "Hildebrand," drops his defenses and is killed. Later versions attempted to avoid the tragedy by effecting a reconciliation.[4]

In spite of its brevity the poem depicts with great power the essential tragedy of the situation. The exile of Hildebrand and his parting from his son have been the result of loyalty to his lord. His sacrifice of family to a higher loyalty has brought him fame as a warrior, but now fate determines that his loyalty shall be tested even more severely. He is now called upon to decide whether he shall kill his own son or be killed by him. To refuse to fight the chosen champion of the opposition is unthinkable. His attempt at conciliation is pathetic, for he is clutching at straws. He can only behave as the code dictates, fight for his chief and kill or be killed.

The *Hildebrandslied* is almost a summary of the essential conflicts of the Germanic epic—of blood relationship and loyalty to the chief, of man with fate. The high proportion of dialogue heightens the tragedy—and the personal involvement of the reader. The economy of narration is remarkable. The poet has chosen the critical moment, immediately before battle. He merely mentions that each is the champion of his side, combines the background of the story with the son's pride in his

---

[4] A comparison of the various versions of the story is given in H. Meyer-Frank, "Die Hildebrandssaga und ihre Verwandtschaft," *PBB*, Vol. LXIX (1947), and H. Rosenfeld, "Das Hildebrandslied: die indogermanischen Vater-Sohn-Kampf-Dichtungen und das Problem ihre Verwandtschaft," *DVLG*, Vol. XXVI (1952).

father and with the father's agony of discovery. The whole trag-edy of the Germanic hero is summed up in Hildebrand's cry:

For sixty summers and winters have I wandered far from my land, ever was I numbered among the fighting men, yet never at any fortress did death come to me. And now my own child is to hew me with his sword or cut me down with his blade. Or I must be his death.

The story proceeds inexorably, without comment or pause and breaks off amid the clash of shields.

There is material for a full epic in the *Hildebrandslied,* but it is not a summary of a longer poem. It combines the tenseness of a well-written short story with the catharsis of tragedy, and its starkness and taut style make it one of the greatest short poems in European literature. It is not, as has so often been stated, the lone survivor of a widespread, primitive literature of popular lays, but a well-composed poem of great literary value. No doubt there were others—but they were not mere epi-sodes which could be strung together into an epic.

Beowulf is an altogether different matter. Here we have a full-scale epic of 3,182 lines, clearly divided into specific sec-tions. Our knowledge of the poem rests upon one manuscript, British Museum, Cotton Vitellius A XV, written in the tenth century. The language indicates that the extant work is a re-working of an earlier version, and research has now made it clear that the poem was written under Christian influences, probably in the first half of the eighth century. The poet seems also to have had some acquaintance with Vergil. In essentials, however, the poem is a Germanic epic, whose metrical and stylistic conventions, as well as its materials, reflect the tastes of a pre-Christian era. *Beowulf* is the story of a man. It is selec-tive in the sense that it concentrates on the points in the hero's career which best illustrate his great qualities, but all the action springs from his exploits, and the generalized struggle between good and evil which the poem depicts is secondary to the struggle between the hero and forces who oppose him.

The story opens with the customary connection of the story with the heroic past. A Danish chief, Scyld, is such a great warrior that his descendants are called Scyldings. He is succeeded, after a long and glorious reign, by Beowulf (not the hero), and he in his turn by three sons, one of whom, Hrothgar, builds a mighty hall to show his wealth and feast his friends. His joy is short-lived. An evil monster of the brood of Cain, living on the wastes outside civilization, sweeps down upon his hall, carries off thirty men to his lair, and thereafter so terrorizes the king's domains that the hall is abandoned. No one is safe and no one can resist him. Worldly splendor is brought down and prayers to pagan idols are useless—Hrothgar's men do not know the true Christian god.

This horrible situation lasts twelve years until Beowulf, a thane of Hygelac, the king of the Geats, hears of it and determines to challenge the monster. With fourteen men he sets sail for the kingdom of Hrothgar. In one of the finest passages in the poem the sea journey and landing are described. They illuminate brilliantly the significance of the sea in the lives of the Germanic peoples and the constant watch necessary against the unknown. Beowulf identifies himself to a coast warden, states his purpose, and is allowed to go to the hall. There he is met by Wulfgar, a herald of Hrothgar, and tells him that he wishes to aid the king in his trouble. Wulfgar reports favorably and Hrothgar, who has heard of Beowulf, guesses his purpose and welcomes him.

Beowulf now tells of some of his own exploits; Hrothgar in turn mentions how he has helped Ecgtheow, Beowulf's father, in his youth and then tells again of Grendel's ravages. During the feast which follows Unferth, one of the court, taunts Beowulf about his alleged failure in a swimming contest but the hero replies that in fact he had a five-day contest with whales and emerged victorious. (The whole incident seems to be an example of the ceremonial boasting at feasts which is well attested elsewhere.) The king and his queen remain gracious in spite of the quarrel with Unferth, and general harmony prevails. Beowulf and his men are left in the hall, and the hero makes it clear that he will fight unarmed, trusting in God.

Only Beowulf remains awake and sees Grendel approach. He bursts down the door, devours one of the men, and then attacks Beowulf himself. A furious fight shakes the hall, but in the end the hero wrenches off one of the monster's arms. Grendel flees screaming to die in his remote lair. Only the arm remains to testify to his defeat, but the following day the warriors are able to trace the monster to his lair by the trail of blood and to see the blood-stained mere. There is much rejoicing, and the minstrel composes in Beowulf's honor a lay about another dragon slayer, Sigmund. Hrothgar calls Beowulf his son and loads him with gifts at a feast in the newly furbished hall. A long lay on the death of King Finn provides an interlude, and the description of a fine gold circlet given to Beowulf provides an opportunity to look forward to the last fight of Hygelac of the Geats. The warriors retire to rest, but on a note of foreboding, for the poet says that one is doomed.

Grendel's mother broods over the loss of her son. The poet once again emphasizes the descent of Grendel and similar monsters from Cain, the outcast murderer of his brother. Grendel's mother sets out for the hall and makes off with Aeschere, a close friend of the king. The next morning Beowulf, who has slept elsewhere, asks whether the night has been peaceful. Hrothgar tells him of the events and relates stories he has heard of two monsters who live in a dreadful mere. Beowulf undertakes to track down and kill Grendel's mother. Hrothgar and his men accompany Beowulf to the mere, which is populated by various monsters, one of which they kill. Beowulf puts on his arms (of which a detailed description is given) and takes a remarkable sword, Hrunting, lent by Unferth. After urging Hrothgar to keep his promise to protect his followers, Beowulf plunges into the lake. It is almost a day's journey to the bottom. There Grendel's mother seizes him and although his armor protects him, he finds it difficult to attack, especially since other sea-monsters help his opponent. She drags him into a large hall where there is no water. A mighty stroke with his sword merely glances off the monster. Beowulf then determines to rely on his own unaided strength, but he slips and only his corselet saves him from the monster's dagger. Fortunately he sees an ancient sword made by giants, and with this is able to cut Grendel's mother down. The mere is purified, a new light shines in the hall. The hero can now see Grendel's body. He cuts off the head and takes back the hilt of the sword he has used, for the monster's blood has dissolved the blade. He rises through the waters and finds on the bank only his own followers. The others, seeing the mere stained with blood, had given him up for lost. They receive him with joy and relief and take back the monster's head in triumph. Beowulf tells Hrothgar the story of his victory. The king praises him, reaffirms his promises, and does not fail to point a moral by contrasting Beowulf with Here-mod, King of the Danes, whose prosperity led him to neglect his duty as ruler and particularly the obligation to be lavish in gift giving.

On the following day Beowulf and his men set out for home. There are speeches, and the king gives rich gifts and praises Beowulf's services in cementing friendship between the Geats and Danes. They sail past the coast warden, who is rewarded for his courtesy by the gift of a sword. On their arrival, the treasures are carried up to Hygelac's palace. There are several digressions at this point; an account of Modthryth, the wife of Offa, at first vengeful, later a good queen, is apparently introduced to set off the virtues of Hygd, wife of Hygelac. Another story about a lady, this time Freawaru, daughter of Hygelac, occurs to Beowulf as he is telling the story of his reception at the king's hall. It concerns the futile attempts to bring about peace between the Danes and the Heathobards by betrothing Freawaru to Ingeld, their king's son. After this tale, Beowulf finishes his account of his adventures and hands over presents to the king. Hygelac gives him rich rewards in turn.

Many years pass. Both Hygelac and his son perish, and Beowulf rules the kingdom for fifty years. Then a slave, fleeing his master, stumbles into a cave where a dragon guards a great treasure hoard. He seizes a jeweled cup to buy his master's favor and makes off with it. The dragon discovers the theft and lays waste Beowulf's land in revenge. The king knows he must defeat the dragon, but feels too that it will mean his death. He has a special shield of iron made to protect him against fire. The author demonstrates his disdain of battle by mentioning again his fights with Grendel and, incidentally, his noble conduct when Hygelac and his son were killed. He makes a farewell speech to his men, again recalling events of his youth. Then, wearing armor, he challenges the dragon which comes out. Beowulf's heavy sword cut fails to stop it. The sword fails him, and so do his companions, except Wiglaf. This young warrior seizes his sword (whose history is related), tells his companions what he thinks of their cowardice, and goes to the king's aid. Again Beowulf strikes, his sword breaks in the monster's head, and he is severely wounded in the neck. Wiglaf weakens the dragon with a sword blow, enabling Beowulf to cut it to pieces. The wound is poisoned and mortal. Beowulf asks to see the treasure he has won. Regretting that he has no son, he gives his armor to Wiglaf and dies. Wiglaf again reproaches the remaining warriors with cowardice. A messenger is sent to Beowulf's stronghold with the news. He speculates on events to come as a result of things past. People come out to view the treasure and lament over their king. Amid gloomy prognostications about the future they raise a tomb in his memory and burn his body on a great pyre.

This story, exciting though it is, can give little idea of the great qualities of the poem. Much of its effect depends upon the use of a rich tapestry of language which raises each event to a level above the ordinary. Probably only a contemporary fully trained in their use could appreciate fully the aesthetic impact of the numerous *kennings*. To us they add a sense of archaic grandeur, of conscious artistry, of remoteness and mystery. The same may be said of the numerous descriptions—of the mere, of gifts, of special swords. Each of these objects described was a thing of wonder.

For this reason we should be wary of placing too much stress, as some writers have done, on the Christian elements in the poem.[5] Although Beowulf frequently mentions and calls upon the great Lord of Heaven and Earth, and although the poet inserts references to Cain as the father of evil spirits and desert places, it cannot be said that such formal acknowledgments constitute a Christian atmosphere. The audience of Beowulf was Christian in the sense that it was formally converted, and believed in the superiority of a Christian God and in his power to resist evil. Their culture, however, was not Christian, nor was their literary tradition. Their virtues were not yet the Christian ones, nor were their deeper beliefs, those they derived from their family and folk traditions, Christian. *Beowulf,* with all its lip service to Christianity, remains a Germanic epic, with the pagan attitudes which the term implies.

It is clear that we have here certain familiar themes: the hero as dragon slayer; the double task of the hero, in which the second has many features of the first but is harder to perform; the rescue of the honorable but weak king by the hero; the discomfiture of the boaster; the loyal retainer who alone has courage to support the hero. Such themes are so common as to provide no indications as to the origin of the material. The specifically Germanic traits must be sought elsewhere, or in characteristic modifications of these themes. The monsters which Beowulf fights are not in any way similar to the routine dragons of, say, the story of Tristan.[6] They are creatures of hell, personified evil, not accurately described, whose very indefiniteness makes them more formidable. Normal weapons are unavailing

[5] The references are very largely to the Old Testament and the Apocrypha.

[6] See the amusing and penetrating essay by J. R. R. Tolkien, *Beowulf: the Monsters and the Critics* (1936).

against them. They can be overcome only with bare hands, that is by the hero's unaided strength, by special weapons which fortune places at his disposal, or at the cost of the hero's life. Much attention is devoted to the description of their haunts, places of gloom near lonely meres, and such descriptions reflect the pre-Christian mythology which endowed lonely places with fearsome guardian spirits. No doubt the concept of Grendel and his mother was influenced by the Christian legend of the devil and the devil's dam. Certainly the tradition of Cain as the progenitor of evil creatures who inhabit deserts is known. But fundamentally they are creatures of northern conception, the evil forces of nature against which man must be forever struggling.

Although the setting of the poem was in the past, so far as its audience was concerned, it was a past which they felt themselves to be connected. Actual historical events are mentioned, such as the defeat in 521 of "Chochilaicus" (= Hugilaikaz = Hygelac), described by Gregory of Tours in the *History of the Franks,*[7] and probably the story reflected glory upon the alleged descendants of its characters. For contemporary audiences there was no such air of remoteness and idealism about *Beowulf* as there was for audiences of the Arthurian romances. His world differed relatively little from the one in which they lived, and his character was not so idealized as to be unattainable. A young hero felt he could emulate Beowulf; an old one regretted that he had never had the opportunity.

The surroundings, too, in which the hero lived were easily grasped by the imagination of contemporary audiences. The stout hall, the ale benches, the storytelling about the fire, the wariness when strange ships came into a harbor, the obligations of royal hospitality, all these were familiar things, even if in the epic they were a little larger than life. The singer in the hall who tells of the exploits might as easily have been singing the song of Beowulf himself.

[7] Additional names in *Liber historiae Francorum.* For details see R. W. Chambers, *Beowulf: an Introduction to the Study of the Poem* (1959).

We have already noted that the character of Beowulf and his individual struggles provide the unifying theme of the poem. Yet its construction is otherwise admirable. It would appear at first to the modern reader that there are too many digressions, too many stories of persons who have too little connection with the main action. The same can be said of any epic poem. But Beowulf is much more natural than would appear at first sight. It should never be forgotten that such poems as Beowulf were intended for listening, not reading. The discursive episodes in which, for example, the stories of Siegmund or of Freawaru are told relieved tension of the main action, acted as parallels, supplied, very often, a little flattery to a chief if he claimed relationship, and served to keep the story in suspense for a longer time. As we have already observed, the audience of the poem *Beowulf* was much like the audience *in Beowulf*. It expected minstrels to tell stories.

The story falls into three main divisions, though there are really only two. The fights with Grendel and Grendel's mother are simply one rising action in which the hero demonstrates increasing powers. They show the Germanic hero at his best and at the height of his ability. He expects success and attains it. His actions bring peace to the land and are but little marred by the jealousies of Unferth and the weakness of the mass of men. The section begins with a hall abandoned and men in terror. It ends with a hall rebuilt and men at peace. Typically also it begins and ends so far as Beowulf is concerned, with a sea voyage, the hero's entry in the world of combat and his homecoming. Throughout the story there is a deliberate contrast between the secure islands of peace and civilization and the wilderness of war and horror.

The civilization of Iceland in the High Middle Ages provides a curious example of an incapsulated culture, where isolation ensured the survival of literary forms and records of a much earlier culture. Iceland was colonized in the ninth century by opponents of Harald Fair Hair, king of Norway, and remained pagan for a considerable time after the rest of Scandinavia had been converted to Christianity. The deliberate separation from the motherland meant that pagan literature and art forms were consciously cultivated and that they survived even the ultimate conversion of the island's population. We are fortunate in possessing a considerable body of this literature. The Codex Regius in Copenhagen, written probably about 1270, contains twenty-nine songs of varying date, which are collectively designated as the *Older Edda,* so as to distinguish them from the younger, prose *Edda* of Snorri Sturluson. The first part of the collection contains stories of the Nordic gods, the second part tales of Nordic heroes. The verse is strophic, its lines always of the alliterative type already discussed, although of differing lengths. The material of the mythological songs is, of course, very old, but it is doubtful whether any of the songs themselves antedate the eighth century.[8] The oldest are probably the "Song of Thrym" and "Song of Hymir," brief, dramatic, and simple poems. Others already show an indifference to the power of the gods which could only belong to a generation whose belief in them was waning. The latest poems were clearly written little earlier than the manuscript itself. They are antiquarian in spirit, hardly more than collections of sayings and precepts. The best of the adventures are told in a style very similar to that of the *Song of Hildebrand,* terse and consisting largely of dialogue. Many of them are comic, even burlesque in character, but others, such as the "Death of Baldur," are purely mythological nature myths. These mythological poems, a few of which, incidentally, are found in other manuscripts, are of little significance for the heroic epic. Much more important are the songs of heroes in the second part.

The songs are concerned almost but not quite exclusively with characters whom we meet again in the *Nibelungenlied* and with their ancestors. (The most important exceptions are the "Songs of Helgi.") They have, of course, been reshaped; names

[8] A summary of the latest views on dating is given in S. Einarsson, *History of Icelandic Literature* (1957), pp. 15 ff.

have been changed; a strong mythological element appears in some of them, but the basic material remains a story from the time of the great Germanic migrations. It was the story of the destruction of the Burgundian kingdom by Attila the Hun, an actual historical event of the fifth century, and of the revenge of a German princess for her brothers. (There was a widespread story that Attila had been murdered by his German wife, but she was called neither Gudrun nor Kriemhild but Hildiko, and she was not a Burgundian.) This story, originally, of course, Frankish or West German, clearly moved up into Scandinavia, where it became popular and was told in many varying forms, some of which are found in the *Edda*. The story is told again in the *Younger Edda* already mentioned, which was basically a textbook for skalds or minstrels, and also in the *Volsungasaga,* a prose work which we possess in a manuscript of the late fourteenth century. Another story, also German in origin, is connected with this series of episodes. It is the history of Sigurd, the German Siegfried, the dragon slayer. The *Edda* songs which tell these stories are brief; the same story is told in two or even three different versions, and a large lacuna of eight sheets in the middle of the most important, the long version of the story of Siegfried, makes comparison difficult. All of the songs have a prose introduction and often interspersed passages of connecting prose to render the story intelligible. The style of the different versions varies as much as their date. "Gudrun's Complaint" is a monologue, a lament for the death of her husband Siegfried. "Gudrun's Incitement" is clearly a later piece, in which Gudrun is made to marry a third time and again is called upon to avenge a relative, this time her daughter Swanhild. Such a piece owes its existence only to the popularity of the Gudrun stories. The exact determination of the dates and places of origin of the various songs related to the Nibelungen cycle is a matter for specialist literature and has not yet been performed satisfactorily. Generally we may say that the songs show that there was a widely known version of the whole story

in Iceland and western Scandinavia by the beginning of the
eleventh century, and that it was at this period that most of the
fuller Nordic versions of the story were written. Into the Siegfried story were incorporated many mythological elements and
common motifs, such as the rescue of the enchanted maiden
Brünhilde from the circle of fire, the ability of Siegfried to
understand the speech of birds, the sword which alone could
slay a dragon.[9]

This story, in spite of variations in detail, was the current
version in the Nordic lands. It differs in many respects from the
German version contained in the *Nibelungenlied* and clearly
represents not only a form which has developed in a different
region, but also one which is not at all influenced by the growing feudal and courtly civilization of more southerly nations.
Action remains the principal interest; revenge and personal
honor are the principal motivating forces. Cruelty, harshness,
violence, all touched with magic, attract the reader's interest
with a kind of fascinating horror; tenderness and mercy are rarely
to be found. There is nobility, greatness in defeat, and sometimes pathos, but the *Edda* songs are gloomy and dark with
foreboding. Their style is dark too—stripped to bare essentials,
implying much more than is said, often assuming previous
knowledge in the reader. Dialogue is the principal form, and
ample and effective use is made of stock epithet. Powerful
though this style is, it does not make for clarity, and the thread
of action is frequently hard to follow. There can be little doubt
that the *Edda* songs we possess are essentially typical of variations on a well-known theme, sung to an audience to whom

---

[9] It is motifs such as this which led many critics to think of the whole
story as mythological in origin. As Heusler points out in *Nibelungensaga
und Nibelungenlied,* it is important to distinguish between the poem—a
work of art—and the ultimate—and for literature irrelevant—origins of
the motifs and characters. Whether Siegfried was originally a sun-god, a
spring-god, or any such figure has no significance for the understanding
of the poem.

the story was already well known and which was probably at least as interested in the way the story was told as in the story itself. We should therefore beware of laying too much stress upon the details of the *Edda* versions in relating them to the German. What we possess is doubtless representative in general of the Scandinavian versions, but details may well be individual inventions.

The following is a brief summary of the story of Sigurd, Brünhilde, and Gudrun made up from the various songs. It is given here for purposes of comparison with the *Nibelungenlied,* for the relationship is probably the best documented and most studied in medieval European literature. The account is based on the *Volsungasaga* already mentioned, but the same story with some variations can be compiled from the *Edda* songs and the explanatory prose accompanying them.

Sigurd the Volsung is the son of Sigmund and Hjothis. After his father's death his mother has been captured while he is yet unborn, and he has been deprived of his rights as a king and a free man. He has then been brought up by the dwarf Regin, a cunning but knowledgeable person, who teaches him the trade of smith. Regin wishes to use Sigurd for his own ends, namely, to win a treasure of gold from his brother Fafnir. The gold has an interesting history. The gods Odin, Loki, and Hönir have killed and skinned an otter. On seeking quarters for the night at the house of Hreidmar they show their spoil and find that they have killed one of their host's sons, who frequently took the shape of an otter. The father requires as blood money as much gold as will cover the otter's skin, and Loki obtains it by catching Andwari, a dwarf who has a ring for making gold and who sometimes takes the shape of a pike. Only by forcing Andwari to give up all the gold and his ring can the skin be covered. Andwari curses the treasure. The effects of the curse are soon evident. Fafnir, one of Hreidmar's sons, stabs his sleeping father and deprives his brother Regin (Sigurd's tutor) of his share. To guard the treasure he assumes the form of a dragon. Regin wishes Sigurd to kill Fafnir and get him the treasure.

The only sword which can stand up to Sigurd's blows proves to be one forged from the pieces of the sword of Sigmund, shattered on Odin's spear. With this sword Fafnir is killed and the treasure obtained. Regin asks for the roasted heart of Fafnir. Sigurd touches it while hot and putting the blood to his tongue learns the speech of birds and that Regin intends to kill him. He anticipates this by killing Regin. Sigurd recovers his kingdom. The *Volsungasaga* and the *Edda* song of Sigrdrufa tell of his seeing the flames upon a hill and of his awakening a Valkyrie, Sigrdrufa (Brünhilde), who had been put to sleep by Odin. She teaches him much secret wisdom and exacts a pledge of love from him. Other sources do not mention this episode.[10]

Sigurd comes to the court of Gjuki, falls in love with Gudrun, and forms a blood brotherhood with Gunnar and Hogni, her brothers. He agrees to woo Brünhilde by passing through the circle of flames. This he does, and they sleep with a sword between them. Sigurd has kept his oath to win Gunnar his bride and not to touch her. He marries Gudrun. (His forgetting of Brünhilde is explained in the *Volsungasaga* by his being given a draught of forgetfulness by Gudrun's mother.)

Later a quarrel arises between the two queens over precedence in bathing in a stream. Brünhilde claims her husband is the braver because he rode through the fire. Gudrun proves that it was really Sigurd. Brünhilde, shattered, demands revenge for her honor. Gunnar fails to persuade Hogni to kill Sigurd

---

[10] The poetic *Edda* gives a fragmentary account, with contradictions at certain points where the songs disagree. The prose *Edda* and the *Volsungasaga* are closer to each other but by no means in complete agreement. The *Thidrekssaga* probably incorporates German material, perhaps taken from the *Nibelungenlied* itself. Many problems are caused by the fact that Brünhilde, the mortal daughter of Büthli, is confused with a Valkyrie, the daughter of Odin.

because they are blood brothers, but Gunthorn performs the deed while Sigurd sleeps and is himself killed. Brünhilde commits suicide in the flames of her house.

Gudrun sorrows deeply over Sigurd, but is at last persuaded by her brothers to marry Atli (Attila), king of the Huns, for political reasons. Atli is treacherous and invites the brothers, after some time, to visit Gudrun, in order that he may destroy them. Gudrun tries to warn them by sending a ring wrapped in wolf's hair. They note the warning, but resolve to go. A great battle ensues, in which the brothers are captured. Gunnar refuses to tell where he has hidden the gold (taken from Sigurd) until he has seen the heart of his brother Hogni. Attempts to deceive him with the heart of a slave fail, because it trembles so much. When his brother's heart is shown to him, he knows the secret is safe, and goes to his death in the snake pit without speaking. Gudrun prepares a horrible revenge. She serves to Atli on his return the flesh of her two sons by him, during the night stabs him to death as he lies in a drunken sleep, and herself perishes in the flames of her palace. The curse placed on the gold by Andwari has worked itself out.

We have seen how this dark tale of revenge appears in the *Edda* songs, the later prose *Edda,* and the *Volsungasaga,* also in prose. The latter two obviously derive their material largely from the older *Edda.* The *Thidrekssaga,* written probably in the twelfth century, also contains the story of Siegfried and Gudrun. Although Scandinavian, it clearly draws on German material, actually naming German "sources," and there has consequently been an as yet unresolved dispute as to whether the compiler knew the *Nibelungenlied* or an earlier version of it. The story itself records the exploits of Dietrich von Bern (Verona), or Theodoric the Ostrogoth, who is shown as one of Atli's warriors, even though he was not born until 455, two years after Attila's death. Dietrich became the center around which heroic legends collected. We shall have reason to mention him again.

Beside the *Edda* songs and the stories of the Nibelungen,

there were numerous Icelandic sagas telling of the exploits of heroes. They are written in a more popular, less artistic style than the Skaldic songs and clearly depend largely on family traditions. Action and adventure are their principal constituents, and usually they are in prose.

The stories of German heroes and of the fall of the Burgundians originated, as we have seen, in Germany, yet there is no trace of a written work on the subject until the appearance of the *Nibelungenlied*. That there was a strong oral tradition is undeniable, and in Germany, as in Scandinavia, there must at some time have been a fusion of two stories, that of Siegfried and Brünhilde and that of the revenge for the death of her relatives by Gudrun. The extant version, however, shows very marked differences from the Scandinavian version just discussed and consequently its growth and sources have been the subject of much speculation. Before discussing the various theories, it will be well to say a little about the text.

The *Nibelungenlied*, written probably about 1203 in Austria, has survived in thirty-four manuscripts, complete or fragmentary, ranging in date from the thirteenth to the sixteenth century. The large number of manuscripts testifies to the popularity of the work, but adds greatly to the difficulties of study because of considerable variations in the length of the text. There are three main groups, represented by the Hohenems-Munich (A), the St. Gallen (B), and the Hohenems-Lassberg (C). All date from the thirteenth century, but C is the oldest. In spite of this, C is a version clearly distinguishable from the others, for it represents an attempt to polish up the text, to make the story smoother and more realistic, and to improve the meter. Some strophes present in other manuscripts are omitted, and new ones are inserted, based on material drawn from the *Klage* or complaint, a poem of more than 4,000 lines found after the poem in all but one of the complete manuscripts. This complaint, which tells of the burial of the numerous dead in Attila's palace, also gives a summary of their exploits. Modern texts, regarding C as a later variant, are usually based upon texts of the A/B group.[11]

The first printing of parts of the *Nibelungenlied,* in 1757, was drawn from an incomplete manuscript. The first complete edition, printed in 1782, which drew from Frederick the Great the comment that the poem was not worth a "shot of powder," was based on this manuscript and the one now called A. Lachmann, perceiving that A was the shortest of the versions with which he was acquainted, assumed that it must, in accordance with his theories of epic accretion, be the earliest, and in preparing his edition used it virtually exclusively.

The truth is a lesson for all persons with dogmatically held theories. The A manuscript is in fact a poorly written and careless version of the B group and is short merely because of this carelessness. All modern editions are based on B, it being assumed that the "original" was copied as follows:

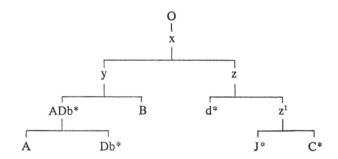

Asterisks indicate a group of manuscripts represented by the individual manuscripts whose letters are shown. A = Hohenems/Munich (late thirteenth century); B = St. Gallen (mid-thirteenth); C = Hohenems/Donaueschingen (early thirteenth); D = Prünn/Munich (early fourteenth); J = Berlin (*ca.* 1323); b = Hundeshagen (early fifteenth); d = Ambraser (1504–15). There are thirty-four complete or fragmentary

---

[11] There is a separate edition of C edited by F. Zarncke.

manuscripts extant. This scheme, evolved by Braune, is given to acquaint the reader with the common method of representing manuscript derivation, since the *Nibelungenlied* is, of the works discussed in this book, probably most suitable for illustration. O represents the lost original, the letters x, y, z lost copies which are postulated as the sources of extant manuscripts (archetypes). The group ADb is a postulated original for the group of extant manuscripts which are clearly closely related. Such originals are often designated by Greek letters. Extant manuscripts are indicated by capital letters early in the alphabet or, in the case of minor manuscripts or early printed versions, by lower case letters early in the alphabet. Sometimes the letter used corresponds to the initial of the particular library in which it was found, but this method can lead to confusion. The above stemma or scheme of manuscript tradition indicates only those manuscripts which show important differences, such as omission or addition of long passages, as compared with other manuscripts, or variations of the narrative.[12]

Close study of the texts in the last half of the nineteenth century revealed that the manuscripts of the B group were most carefully written and probably approximated most closely to the original. But what was this original? Its connection with the Scandinavian stories was readily apparent, and it was for some time assumed that the material had come from Scandinavia. More careful study showed, however, that the material had developed independently in Germany with but slight Scandinavian influence. It was clear that the *Nibelungenlied* combined several separate stories. Furthermore, there was a complete change in the story of Kriemhilde's revenge. Instead of avenging her brothers by killing her husband, she avenged her (first) husband by killing her brothers. For this variation

---

[12] Bartsch's manuscript stemma postulates two groups of mixed manuscripts (D, N, S, b and H, O, I, K, Q, L, d, h). Braune assigns them to the A /B or C tradition.

no Norse original exists. Researchers, still under Lachmann's influence, postulated various "lost" heroic songs in which this variation appeared. Finally Andreas Heusler, himself influenced by W. P. Ker, produced the theory, now generally held, of a few early songs whose authors deliberately brought about changes in the original material, which are to be regarded as the only true precursors of the *Nibelungenlied*. Artistic creation rather than accidental accretion was again regarded as the means by which an epic came into being.

Heusler's theory is best understood by means of the following scheme:

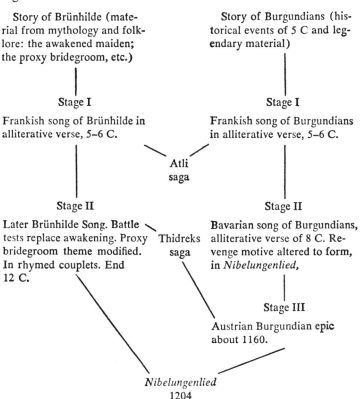

Story of Brünhilde (material from mythology and folklore: the awakened maiden; the proxy bridegroom, etc.)

Story of Burgundians (historical events of 5 C and legendary material)

Stage I

Frankish song of Brünhilde in alliterative verse, 5–6 C.

Stage I

Frankish song of Burgundians in alliterative verse, 5–6 C.

Atli saga

Stage II

Later Brünhilde Song. Battle tests replace awakening. Proxy bridegroom theme modified. In rhymed couplets. End 12 C.

Thidreks saga

Stage II

Bavarian song of Burgundians, alliterative verse of 8 C. Revenge motive altered to form, in *Nibelungenlied,*

Stage III

Austrian Burgundian epic about 1160.

Nibelungenlied
1204

Of this theory it may be said that the first stage for each story is virtually certain, for it is hardly questionable that a short song, similar in essentials to the *Edda* songs, must have existed in the sixth century, especially in the case of the (historical) defeat of the Burgundians by Attila the Hun. It is also certain that at some period a radical modification took place in the Burgundian story, probably under the influence of an East-Gothic story which sought to rehabilitate the character of Attila and make him a king worthy of the services of the hero Dietrich. The greed for gold which motivates his actions in the Scandinavian versions is transferred to Kriemhilde, the Gudrun of the *Edda* songs. More dubious are the "epic" stages postulated as the immediate precursors of the extant *Nibelungenlied*. There is no mention anywhere in literature of such epics, and their existence has been disputed by such writers as Panzer. Heusler believed that the *Thidrekssaga* had influenced the development of the *Nibelungenlied;* others deny this. Panzer believes that there was considerable French influence on the final version and that even Russian stories cannot be excluded. Perhaps the most difficult feature of Heusler's theory is that the author of the *Nibelungenlied* was the first to combine the two stories into a German epic. The combination had already been made in Scandinavia, and it hardly seems likely that there was no German warrant for such a combination before 1203. Perhaps the decision to make the love affair between Siegfried and Kriemhilde the central feature of the poem determined the far-reaching changes in the second part.

The problem is, of course, insoluble. The two parts of the *Nibelungenlied* are very different in style and even vocabulary, and may very easily have been drawn from different sources, but the number of varying versions of the stories available in Germany and Austria was undoubtedly very large, and the artist who wrote our present version must, consciously or unconsciously, have been influenced by many of them. There is, for instance, evidence in the poem that he knew of a previous meeting between Siegfried and Brünhilde, but it is not part of his story; the Nibelungen treasure is often discussed, but its origin is not mentioned, nor is it the real motivating force upon Kriemhilde's actions. Like all medieval authors, the writer of the *Nibelungenlied* used what material he liked and was generally unconcerned about consistency.

Let us now turn to the poem itself. The *Nibelungenlied* is between 11,000 and 12,000 lines long; the length varies according to the version used by different editors. It is definitely an Austrian work, probably written in Passau, for the author reveals a very detailed acquaintance with the topography of the Danube region, so detailed indeed that the journey of the Burgundians to Attila's court can easily be followed on a map. The author uses a peculiar strophe, of which the only other examples are found in the lyrics of Austrian poets, although variations are found in other epics. This strophe has four lines, with masculine rhymes a a, b b, often with internal rhyme, of which the principle appears to be that each half line shall have four stresses. In fact, only the eighth half line shows these stresses in full. The first half lines often put one of the stresses on a syllable which in speech would be unstressed; the second half lines in the first, second, and third line replace one stress by a pause. There is no definite alternation of stressed and unstressed syllables. It is probably more accurate to say that each half line has two full beats of musical time and two main stresses. The efforts of the poet to adapt older material to his new strophe are sometimes painfully obvious, and there is a not inconsiderable amount of metrical stuffing.[13]

The story of the *Nibelungenlied* opens with a general introduction—a call to listen to a heroic story and an enumeration of the Burgundians. Kriemhilde, sister of Gunther, king of

---

[13] The *Nibelungenstrophe* is unusual. Its use by Der von Kurenberg in his lyrics and, in a modified form, by Walther von der Vogelweide has led to surmises that each of them was the author of the *Nibelungenlied*. Such suggestions can hardly be taken seriously.

the Burgundians, dreams of a falcon which she has tamed and how it is killed before her eyes by two eagles. Her mother, Ute, interprets the dream; she will marry a noble husband, but will soon lose him. In the second *Aventiure* Siegfried is introduced. There is no story of his upbringing and youthful deeds such as we find in the *Edda*. His father, a king in the Netherlands with his court at Xanten, is still alive and Siegfried is educated and trained as a knight, with the ceremonies appropriate to his taking of knighthood fully described. This is the first of many instances in which the author is at some pains to impart a courtly veneer to his poem. The hero then sets out to win himself a bride. He follows a well-established precedent in setting out with few attendants to win a lady whose beauty is known to him only by reputation. Arriving at Worms, he is greeted with appropriate ceremonies, and Hagen, Gunther's chief vassal, called in to determine who the unknown warrior is, recognizes him and recounts in detail how he gained the Nibelungen treasure. The story has some resemblances to the story in the *Edda,* but is generally different. Siegfried had been asked to apportion a treasure between two brothers, receiving as reward the sword Baldung; they had quarreled with his verdict and attacked him. He killed them and many of their followers, forced a dwarf, Alberich, who had been in their service, to guard the treasure for him, and stole from Alberich the cloak of invisibility. The gold had originally belonged to Nibelung, the father of the dead brothers. The name "Nibelung" seems to pass to the person who holds the treasure. Hagen also sketches the story of the killing of the dragon, merely stating that by bathing in its blood Siegfried had become invulnerable. There is no connection between dragon and treasure, and the invulnerability has no counterpart in Norse literature. Clearly German and Norse are here separate traditions. Somewhat surprisingly, Siegfried challenges Gunther to a duel for their two kingdoms, possibly to demonstrate that he is the equal of Gunther in rank. The situation is smoothed over and, at Hagen's insistence, Siegfried stays at the court in Worms, without, as yet, revealing his true purpose.

Siegfried helps Gunther win a war against the Saxons, again a common motif in romances, but unknown to the Norse story. On his return he sees Kriemhilde for the first time as she is going to church, and the author is afforded another opportunity of describing ceremonies. Before he can win her, however, he has to agree to help her brother win as bride the queen in Island, who can be won only by defeating her in three contests. The party sets out on the long journey. Brünhilde clearly believes that Siegfried has come to win her. He says that he is merely a bondsman, a declaration which has consequences later. By using his cloak of invisibility Siegfried performs for Gunther the three tasks—a spearcast, a stone cast, and a leap—better than Brünhilde can, and wins him the bride. The whole procedure has slightly comic overtones and is clearly dependent on the fairy tale motifs of the three tasks, the performer, and the helper. It has no counterpart in the Norse versions. A brief episode follows in which Siegfried, returning for his men and treasure, is unrecognized and hard put to defend himself. The expedition returns home with full courtly ceremonial, and the two queens meet. Siegfried's bridal night is happy, but the unfortunate Gunther is tied up by his powerful wife and ignominiously hung upon a nail on the wall. Siegfried again rescues him the following night by breaking down Brünhilde's resistance and leaving her to Gunther. He takes away, however, her ring and belt, and later reveals to Kriemhilde how he has obtained them.

Some years of peace follow, with each king in his own lands, but Brünhilde, apparently suspicious or jealous of Siegfried, complains that, as a bondsman, he should appear at Gunther's court to do service. When this device fails, she says she wishes to see Kriemhilde. The invitation can hardly be refused. The queens, talking about their husbands, quarrel about their respective ranks. Kriemhilde says that her husband, in spite of his own declaration, is the equal of Gunther. Sharp words follow, and the following day Kriemhilde demonstrates superiority by sweeping into church before Brünhilde (an interesting courtly variant of the washing in the river of the Norse tradition). Outside, they quarrel again, and Kriemhilde publicly calls Brünhilde Siegfried's concubine and produces ring and belt to prove it.

Brünhilde calls for vengeance. Gunther, weak as ever, is satisfied with Siegfried's explanation, but not so Hagen. He plots to kill Siegfried. Gunther, at first opposed, is gradually won over. A hunt is proposed, and Hagen cunningly arranges to have Kriemhilde sew a cross on Siegfried's shirt at the one place where a leaf had prevented the dragon's blood from making him invulnerable. He explains that he wishes to protect this place for Siegfried. During the hunt Hagen leads Siegfried to quench his thirst at a spring, removes his weapons, and hurls a javelin between his shoulders. Siegfried hurls at him his shield—his only weapon—and dies reproaching Hagen, his supposed friend. The scene is one of the most pathetic in literature and superbly portrayed. Kriemhilde's first intimation of her husband's death is the bleeding body placed outside her door. Although the murderer's identity is no secret, she elects, in spite of this, to stay at her brother's court. Of Brünhilde we hear little more. She is still alive when they leave for Attila's court.

Kriemhilde makes large presents from the treasure which Siegfried had won, and Hagen, after counseling a reconciliation for this purpose, in spite of the protests of Giselher, her brother, takes it away, lest she use it to buy revenge. The treasure is sunk in the Rhine. In the twentieth *Aventiure* comes a turning point. Etzel, king of the Huns, has lost his first wife, Helche, and seeks another. He is advised by his princes to seek the hand of Kriemhilde, and sends Rüdiger, an old friend of Hagen's, to the court at Worms. Appropriate ceremonial descriptions follow. Only Hagen is against the proposed marriage, since he sees its dangers. Nevertheless it is agreed upon, and Kriemhilde departs. Her journey is minutely described—a good example of epic extension.

After seven years of marriage she bears a son, Ortlieb, and prevails upon her husband to invite her relations in Worms to visit her. He gladly agrees, and she urges the messengers to make sure that Hagen is not left behind. The invitation is well received by all but Hagen, who sees the reason for it and advises its rejection. When the decision is made to go, he accepts it and accompanies the small army which Gunther takes with him. His actions from now on are those of a man defying fate. He attempts to force two mermaids in the Danube into predicting the future by stealing their clothes. He elicits only false information. When they have their clothes back, the mermaids tell him that only the chaplain will return to the Rhine alive, a fact which Hagen tests by hurling him into the water after they have crossed. The chaplain reaches the opposite bank, even though he cannot swim. Hagen also slays the ferryman whose boat he uses to take the army across the river, and has a hard fight later with his avengers. The journey is interrupted by an idyllic episode when the army is entertained by Rüdiger at Bechelare, probably a reminiscence of the entertainment of Friedrich Barbarossa near Pressburg in 1189. The incident is another example of reworking in a courtly sense, and even contains a betrothal—Gunther's youngest brother, Giselher, who is always presented as an ideal young warrior, is betrothed to Rüdiger's daughter.[14]

From now on the scene darkens. Dietrich von Bern warns the Burgundians that Kriemhilde still weeps for Siegfried, but in spite of this they enter the castle. Hagen and the minstrel Volker deliberately incite Kriemhilde, for example, by producing Sieg-

---

[14] The love idyll is possibly intended as a contrast with the harsh outcome of the originally tender love story of Siegfried and Kriemhilde. Many critics overemphasize the role of Rüdiger. Although his anguish at having to decide between friendship and loyalty moves the reader deeply, he is not a leading figure.

fried's sword, and she makes various attempts to egg on the Huns to attack. The combined efforts of Etzel and Dietrich keep the peace, however, even at a tournament when one of the Huns is deliberately run through. It is not until Kriemhilde bribes one of the Hun chiefs with promises of a huge fief that the attack begins. During a feast some Burgundians sleeping apart in a hall are attacked and all killed except Danewart, who brings the word into the feast hall. Hagen's first act is to cut down Ortlieb, Etzel's and Kriemhilde's son, thus placing himself beyond the pale. Dietrich takes Kriemhilde and Etzel from the hall with his own men.

The Burgundians are victorious, and subsequent attempts to attack them, described at length, all fail, although their numbers are considerably lessened. Even the burning of the hall, an old motif, fails to drive them out. Rüdiger is now faced with a painful choice: shall he help his liege lord, Etzel, or his future son-in-law, Giselher? As usual in the Germanic epic, loyalty proves stronger, and he goes to destruction with his men. The news is incredible to Dietrich von Bern. He sends Hildebrand and his men to confirm it. Their wrath cannot be restrained and, in spite of Dietrich's orders to refrain from battle, they attack. At the end only Gunther and Hagen survive of all the Burgundians, and of Dietrich's men only Hildebrand. Dietrich asks for the surrender of the Burgundians, promising them safe-conduct. Hagen refuses, and is wounded, bound, and handed over to Kriemhilde with a plea for mercy. Gunther's turn comes next. Kriemhilde goes to Hagen and asks for the treasure. He refuses to reveal its hiding place while Gunther is still alive. She has Gunther's head cut off and brought to Hagen. He repeats his refusal, knowing that his secret is now safe. Kriemhilde, in fury, snatches Siegfried's sword from him and cuts off his head, whereupon the old Hildebrand, horrified that such a warrior should die at the hands of a woman, cuts her down in turn. Only Etzel and Dietrich are left alive to mourn.[15]

---

[15] It has been pointed out by Heusler, De Boor, and others that there are two traditions attached to Attila. The northern-western shows him

Such is the tale of the Nibelungen. In essence it is a dark tale of revenge whose morality is still that of the Germanic songs from which it drew most of its material. Yet the author may well have been attempting to tell a story of a different sort. He was clearly much interested in the courtly literature of his time, and a great deal of evidence has been produced to show that he copied many of the scenes not found in the Scandinavian versions from French romances and *chansons de geste*. Some of these parallels are very general and should be viewed with caution; others show a convincing amount of detailed resemblance.[16] Whatever his sources, the author was trying to make his epic courtly, and in externals he to some extent succeeds. His descriptions of ceremonial, of arrival and departure, of tournament and battle, of manners and customs, all show a desire to impart a courtly atmosphere. The length of the work, indeed, its expansion to epic proportions, is very largely due to the insertion of descriptive matter and extra scenes in the courtly style. Nor can it be denied that the incidents of the story could easily occur in an Arthurian epic; tales of killing and revenge are not uncommon there. His heroes are shown as Christian knights, with appropriate Christian ceremonial. But there is no deep Christian influence on the work, no contrast between Christian good and pagan evil, nor indeed any sense of a better world to come. The author was unable to escape from the basic concepts of the old tale he was telling, and it is for this reason that Hagen emerges as the central figure of the *Nibelungenlied*.

In the Scandinavian versions Hogni, Gunnar's brother, is a subsidiary figure. He does not kill Sigurd, and he dies before Gunther. The Latin epic *Waltharius* shows us the other tradition,

---

as a bloodthirsty tyrant, the eastern-Gothic as a gentle, almost weak king, the friend of Dietrich. See H. De Boor, *Das Attilabild in Geschichte, Legende und heroischer Dichtung* (1932).

[16] F. Panzer, in *Das Nibelungenlied*, adduces a great deal of evidence for French influence from such works as *Orson de Beauvais* and *Doon de la Roche* (see pp. 344 ff.) and from *Daurel e Beton* (see pp. 355 ff.). He also regards the Slavic bride-quest stories as important (see pp. 322 ff.).

for there Gunther is a weakling and treacherous, and forces Hagano to fight his friend Waltharius in order to save him. In other words, Hagano is forced to the choice of loyalty to king rather than loyalty to friend. This loyalty is the driving force behind all of Hagen's conduct in the *Nibelungenlied,* but it is loyalty to an idea rather than to a person. Hagen is introduced as a dark, hard, rather sinister warrior. He contrasts sharply with the young, bright hero Siegfried. Whether consciously or not, the author has softened Siegfried's character so that he appears as a young idealistic lover rather than a Germanic hero. His prowess as a warrior is undimmed, and Hagen knows that he cannot beat him in a fair fight. Yet he is prepared to demean himself in Gunther's service, to deceive Brünhilde, even to pose as a bondsman in order to win Kriemhilde. Their love affair is clearly an attempt to depict an idealistic courtly relationship by someone whose ideas of courtly love were vague and gained at third hand. Siegfried is always noble, and most noble in his death scene, but he is truculent only at his first appearance, when he offers to fight Gunther for the possession of his lands.

Hagen accepts Siegfried on a calculation of his usefulness. He is a good man to have as an ally. One suspects that Hagen's friendship with him rests on the same basis. All Hagen's actions throughout the epic are motivated by one thought—what is best for the kingdom. He allows no other consideration to affect his judgment, neither friendship nor pity nor, and this is most extraordinary, his personal glory and reputation. Gunther is prepared to accept Siegfried's explanation of the quarrel between Brünhilde and Kriemhilde, and to allow the incident to be forgotten. Hagen sees the matter differently. Gunther's personal feelings are of no significance, for it is not he but the honor of the kingdom which has been offended, and Hagen immediately plots an act of treachery which is worthy of the lowest criminal. He uses Kriemhilde's innocence to find out where Siegfried is vulnerable; he uses Siegfried's trustfulness to gain a position where he can be killed. His behavior could, of course, have no place in a courtly epic, except as the behavior of one destined to perish justly at the hands of a real knight. It is condemned implicitly by the author in the speech, probably the best in the poem, which he puts in the mouth of the dying Siegfried. Yet by Hagen's standards and by the standards of the code of Germanic ethics the murder is justified.

At the end of the first part of the poem Hagen has become its central figure, but he is not a sympathetic character. He has destroyed a love idyll to save the honor of a king who has no honor. He even takes away by force the gold which is Kriemhilde's by right. In all these things he has little support from Gunther and active opposition from Kriemhilde's other brothers, especially the young and idealistic Giselher. Kriemhilde's second marriage seems to him dangerous, for she is gaining power for revenge. When the invitation to Etzel's court arrives, he is not afraid of accusations of cowardice in advocating its rejection. Thereafter his whole conduct is that of a doomed man, and in his actions he becomes, if not sympathetic, then at least admirable. His defiance of fate, even when it involves unnecessary acts of brutality, such as the killing of Etzel's son, has the quality of the hero. Moreover, these actions are completely consequential, for Hagen's belief meant that if his king could not be rescued then he must perish with honor, killing as many enemies as possible, even though those enemies were persons such as Rüdiger with whom he had close personal ties. It is fitting that Hagen should be the person who refuses to reveal the hiding place of the treasure—a purely symbolic act, since Kriemhilde did not need the gold and the Burgundians could not profit from it.

Hagen's character holds the work together. His determination to defend the kingdom at all costs is its central theme. But the kingdom was doomed, as Siegfried was doomed, by the curse upon the Nibelungen treasure, and it is this sense of doom which fascinates the reader. All the ceremonial, the tournaments, the great fights are hollow sham, for we can feel the march to inevitable destruction. Personal character has no influence on fate. One can only die with glory and not with shame. Even to contemporaries this viewpoint must have seemed outmoded, for both the ethics of Christianity and the code of behavior exemplified in the courtly romances taught another point of view. The knight need not yield to fate if he ordered his life properly. Kindness and humility could properly be allied to bravery. This the author of the *Nibelungenlied* either did not know or else could not work into his intractable Germanic material.

The portrait of Kriemhilde also illustrates his difficulty. In the first part she is conceived as a gentle girl, deeply in love with Siegfried, who has wooed her in a manner which, if not exactly courtly, is clearly intended by the author as an approximation. The transition from this picture of innocence to the she-devil of the final scenes is hard for a modern reader to grasp, and the characterization rests, of course, upon the original sources rather than upon logical development. It is made the more difficult by her insistence upon regaining the Nibelungen treasure rather than upon revenge for Siegfried's death. We are again faced with the typical situation in medieval literature that logical development of character was not a primary consideration, for the pity we feel for Kriemhilde is largely nullified by her behavior in the second part of the poem.

The character of Gunther also exemplifies a typical figure which has already been noted—the weak king whose personal attributes and behavior are less important than the position which he occupies. Gunther is a king only because he occupies the throne. He is incapable of decision, as he shows in his handling of the quarrel between Kriemhilde and Brünhilde; he is feeble and ridiculous in his relations with his queen; and in the end he must be sacrificed as a person so that the institution he represents may be upheld in honor. A man such as Hagen could not have respected him as a person. There is a remarkable resemblance between the Arthur of many of the romances, the Louis of the Guillaume d'Orange cycle, and Gunther, king of the Burgundians. We have already noted the contrast between the Siegfried of the *Nibelungenlied* and his counterparts in the Scandinavian versions. We should also remark upon a literary device which the author of the poem uses with great skill. Siegfried is not completely guiltless in the series of events which bring about the tragedy. In his overpowering of Brünhilde he cannot resist taking the ring and belt and, later, telling his wife of the incident. He has broken his trust and must take the consequences. Kriemhilde, too, uses this weapon won by unfair means to crush Brünhilde in a female quarrel over precedence. In this, as in her innocent betrayal of the vulnerable spot, she contributes to the tragedy.

The structure of the poem suffers to some extent from the necessary remodeling of material, from the deliberate insertion of long, sometimes irrelevant, episodes to give epic fullness, and from the author's desire for courtly overlay. The first half, particularly, gives the impression of gaps unfilled and of piecing together. In spite of this the poem has a magnificent sweep to its conclusion and shows great skill in using, for example, the long march, to carry the reader to the inevitable end.

The decision to write a narrative poem in strophes also had an unfortunate effect on structure and style. It is clear that the author had to fill in the spare, terse description of his originals in order to fill out a strophe. He often does this by comment on preceding action which has, for us, a pleasing archaic effect but is of dubious poetic value. Although the author employs some terms taken from the courtly romances, his language generally contrasts with theirs. It is more primitive, much more simple, lacking in abstractions, and gains its effects by the use of quick, episodic drawing of pictures, by brief snatches of dialogue rather than by a smooth narrative flow.

The Germanic national epic finds its greatest expression in

the *Nibelungenlied.* In spite of his desire to appear courtly, the author felt rather than knew where the power of the story lay. In centralizing the action about the figure of Hagen he was able to depict, realistically and with great literary skill, those elements which were the most powerful motivating forces in Germanic literature—the power of fate and loyalty to the chief. In his loyalty Hagen is inflexible, and in his challenge to fate he epitomizes those attributes which, for the audience of the *Nibelungenlied,* constituted true greatness in a hero.

The influence of the *Nibelungenlied* on subsequent Germanic epics was considerable. We possess no other work of the same period which can be compared with it, but a study of *Gudrun,* a work which exists only in a manuscript of the sixteenth century in a form clearly much changed from the original, shows how deep the influence was. The material is obviously derived from various sources, but the basic story is a Viking tale of a bride stolen by a rejected love and of a desperate but inconclusive battle at the Wulpenstrand. The main story has the usual double form of a bride won, lost, and won again, but it is preceded by a long prologue recounting the history of the bride's father and mother in similar fashion. In the *Gudrun* we can see what happened when a composite work was attempted by an author less skilled than the writer of the *Nibelungenlied.* The composition is loose; the action drags; the characters are, with a few exceptions, unconvincing. The author's attempt to imitate and even improve the *Nibelungenstrophe* also falls short of success.

In the *Gudrun,* as well as in other epics, the increasing influence of Christianity is clear. It affects the morals and characterization, and sits uneasily upon the basic Northern story. The result is a loss of energy, of the often brutal but literarily very successful strength of the Germanic epic. *Gudrun,* in short, like all late imitations, falls neatly between two stools.

There were obviously many Germanic epics which have disappeared; there exist many others in late reworkings which demonstrate, as do the later courtly works, the faults of prolixity, of excess incident, of lack of a clearly conceived social and moral milieu. Dietrich in them, as indeed in the *Nibelungenlied,* is the ideal German hero. The eclipse of Siegfried, already fore-shadowed in the *Nibelungenlied,* becomes complete. In the *Rosengarten* he is saved from total defeat by Dietrich only by the intervention of Kriemhilde. It is interesting to note here the same processes at work that we found in the courtly epic—the change in popularity, the replacement of one hero by another, and the defeat of the earlier champion by the later, which confers increase of stature upon his successor. The Germanic stories too were turned into prose form for later generations of readers.

The Germanic epic never attained—in written form—the literary stature of the great Arthurian romances. The *Nibelungenlied* is a magnificent poem, but it was written at a time when the values which it represented were already historical. It succeeds best when the author can project himself into the past and can forget his attempts to compromise with the new and fashionable courtly literature. For the writers of romance it was easy to realize the humanistic and Christian values of the late twelfth century, for the world they wrote of was ideal and had, for them, no historical significance. The Germanic epic does not and cannot loose itself from its historical and cultural background. Its greatness consists in the stark portrayal of that background, and in making it, as the author of the *Nibelungenlied* did, a scene for the interplay of forces which, like those in Greek tragedy, are the universal forces which control man's fate and his relations with his fellow men.

8

The Medieval Lyric

The study of lyric poetry is in all literatures very largely a study of form. Language, rhythm, meter, the intangibles of style are necessarily of greater importance in short poems than in long narrative works. The study of form in medieval poetry is of even greater significance because, during the period of its finest flowering, there existed a conventional restriction of subject as well as a limited audience which could appreciate the subtleties of meter and language in which the poets delighted. The result of this insistence on form has led many distinguished modern critics to denounce the medieval lyric as monotonous, too insistent on its formal virtuosity, too inhibited by conventions. Other critics—particularly, but by no means exclusively musicologists—have insisted that the true greatness of the vernacular lyric lay not in its words but in its music. Some even insist that the words are a mere framework for the melody, that the metrical construction of the lines were dependent on musical modes. Such opinions cannot, in my opinion, be substantiated. The great medieval lyric poets were as capable of joining depth of sentiment with fine form as the lyric poets of any other age. The mediocre poets, as usual, ground out mechanical reproductions. The subtle changes of rhythm within the lines of verse of the great troubadours and *Minnesänger* would be hard to reconcile with the idea of words which acted only as a framework for music. These men were poets first and musicians second.

It is hardly necessary to state that the romantic conception of the troubadour as a wandering musician singing under a lady's window, accompanying himself on something resembling a guitar, is as wide of the mark as is the persistent notion that medieval Latin lyric is the product of a happy, carefree group of wandering scholars, who brought into European literature the ideas of Spring and Nature. Medieval lyric, whether Latin or vernacular, is almost always closely tied with the rhetorical tradition discussed earlier in this book. The great poets use this tradition so skillfully that they transform it into artlessness. But the tradition is always there.

Before discussing the tangled evidence of origin and influence, it will be well to sketch the general pattern of the medieval lyric. The Latin lyric of the Carolingian period is largely imitative and is of interest only in demonstrating the persistence of the rhetorical tradition and of the predominance of certain themes and topics. We shall discuss it only in its relation to the medieval Latin rhythmical lyric which flourished principally from the tenth through the twelfth century and which found its finest expression in satire and formal love lyric. New strophic forms based on rhythmical (as distinct from quantitative) lines were developed, and rhyme schemes of great virtuosity were employed. This lyric was the product of educated scholars. It virtually ceased when the vernaculars became sufficiently developed to be capable of the same fine shades of expression.

There can be little doubt that the medieval Latin lyric influenced the great development of vernacular lyric during the twelfth and thirteenth centuries. How great this influence was is difficult to determine, for of the early stages of the vernacular lyric we know very little. It appears first, in forms already well developed, in southern France. During the twelfth century a limited number of types reached their full development: the formal love lyric (*canzon,* of which there were certain sub-types), the debate poem (*tenzon, partimen*), the poem of social or political comment (*sirventès*), the dawn song (*alba,* a lament on the parting of lovers at dawn), the *pastorela* (in which a knight woos a rustic maiden), the *planh* (or lament), the *chanson de croisade* (or crusading song). There were numerous minor genres. The most important of all these and the one recognized as the supreme achievement of a lyric poet was the *canzon.* Virtually all poets practice it, whereas the other genres are represented in the work of relatively few.

These same genres were imitated in northern France, in Italy, and in Germany, but the poets in these lands should not be regarded as mere imitators. They used many of the formal developments of meter and rhyme, but the attitude, especially in Germany, is fundamentally different, and new genres differing markedly from those in Provençal literature are introduced. German literature in particular developed the gnomic poem of advice and practical wisdom, as well as the poem of political comment. The love poem was extended to include other persons than the nobility and was used ironically for the purpose of satirizing the peasant. In Italy the love poem continued to dominate the lyric, but new forms were developed, of which the sonnet was the most significant.

The Middle Ages possessed a rich heritage of lyric poetry from classical antiquity. It is doubtful whether they knew the works of Catullus, and the elegiac poets Tibullus and Propertius seem to have been little read. The *Odes* of Horace were available in numerous manuscripts but were not as popular as his *Epistles* and *Satires.* Better known were those poets of a later period, such as Ausonius, Apollinaris Sidonius, and Fulgentius, who used the meters and language of great classical poets but whose work tended to be formal description of landscape or city, occasional epigrammatic poetry on the events of everyday life, or sententious advice on the way life should be conducted. These poets often demonstrated an interest in curiosities of form which are not uncommon in medieval lyric poets—palindromes, figure poems, number symbolism. Christian ascetics shied away from pagan love lyric, written as it was for courtesans and slave girls. Its conventions appear relatively rarely in the medieval lyric. A great deal of influence has been ascribed to the works of Ovid, and direct connections have been sought between, for example, the love scene between Paris and Oenone in the *Heroides* and similar descriptions in medieval Latin and vernacular poetry. Although the works of Ovid were widely read and there is no doubt that the influence of his language and usage was considerable, it is extremely doubtful whether any such direct connection exists, particularly for vernacular poetry. The resemblance is due rather to the formal teaching of the use of figures and ornament derived from classical models. It should be especially noted that there is very little in the poetry of classical antiquity to suggest the ennobling power of love which is such an important feature of the vernacular love lyric. The influence of classical literature on medieval poetry is confined to language and style, except where a poem was a professed exercise in imitation.

The Christian hymn was of great significance as a bridge from classical literature to medieval lyric, and one which has, perhaps, been underestimated. Of the very earliest Christian hymns we know little or nothing. It has often been stated that they used the popular type of iambic or trochaic meter, which is known from fragments of soldiers' songs quoted by historians, and that they were based on the ictus or stress accent and not upon length of syllable, as are the classical Roman meters which are imitated from the Greek. The supposition is not unlikely, but it cannot be proved. Written hymns go back to the third century and fall into two classes. The "learned" hymns, best exemplified, perhaps, by the collections *Peristephanon* and *Cathemeron* of Prudentius (fourth century), used the quantitative meters of classical lyric poetry, particularly the Sapphic strophe in which long and short syllables were arranged in the following pattern:

In these hymns were introduced features of great importance for sacred and secular poetry—sustained metaphor, symbolism of features of Christianity such as the wood of the Cross, the blood of Christ, the crown of the martyrs, the flower of life which springs from Christ's death. The hymns cannot be properly appreciated without interpretation of this symbolism. The tradition of imagery and interpretation became an integral part of the writing of hymns, as may be seen from the famous hymn *Vexilla regis prodeunt* (The banners of the King go forward), in which every word has at least two meanings and the traditional associations of color are carefully utilized.

The expression of love in terms at once symbolistic and mystic had a profound effect on both the language and the style of vernacular love poetry. The allusive use of language, and in particular the filling out of meaning by implied reference to Christian concepts and especially to the Bible, was widespread in Latin poetry, even when the material itself was entirely secular. We shall shortly note some examples.

There is considerably less evidence for the direct effect of the hymns in praise of the Virgin upon secular poetry. It is true that they often employ language very similar to that of the poems of courtly love, but this is probably due to the fact that they both drew upon the same linguistic sources. Since the works of mystic adoration of the Virgin appeared only when the Provençal troubadours were already writing, it is equally possible to argue that they drew their inspiration from the secular love poetry. It is highly probable that both were influenced by the growth of mysticism as a spiritual force, a mysticism best illustrated by the interpretation of the *Song of Songs* of Bernard of Clairvaux. He discusses the love poem as an allegory of the love of the human soul for Christ, turning each of the terms of sensual description and affection into a spiritual meaning. In the same way the secular poets could sublimate physical admiration into spiritual adoration. The reading of Christian literature and the hearing of hymns created an intellectual climate of spiritual interpretation, and the vocabulary and style were provided by the combination of rhetorical ornament and Biblical metaphor which the hymns traditionally used. It should be noted that it is very difficult to date most hymns and, for this reason, hard to determine exactly the extent of their influence upon secular poetry.

Side by side with the learned hymn there existed a form, originally much simpler, about which there has been a great deal of controversy. The so-called Ambrosian hymns date from the fourth century or a little later. They are written in short lines, four lines to the strophe, and from the beginning show evidence of rhyme. The meter has been variously described. Some critics insist that it is a perfectly normal four-foot iambic line in the quantitative sense, that is, that it follows the classical rules of patterning long and short syllables. Others insist that the basic pattern is not quantity but stress. The fact appears to be that it is both. Word stress had always been stronger in Latin than in Greek, and there is some evidence that even the classical Latin poets took note of it when writing purely quantitative verse. In late classical times authors appear to have attempted always to make the long syllables in quantitative feet correspond with the word stress. In the iambic line whose feet are theoretically each of two syllables ‿ — (although substitution of a long syllable for the short is allowed in certain feet in the line), the effect would be to make a fairly regular alternation of stressed and unstressed feet and thus produce the effect of rhythmical verse. As time passed the speakers of the Romance languages lost all feeling for quantity; only the number of syllables in a line and perhaps the presence of stresses at the caesura and the end of a line could be appreciated. The line thus developed into one based upon stressed and unstressed syllables.

It is very hard to say how far this development was influenced by "popular" poetry in the countries in which Latin poetry was written. It is certain that the Germanic peoples thought of the poetic line in terms of stress. Of "popular" poetry in the Romance countries we know very little. Mere theorizing about the existence of folk lyric (and there has been a great deal of theorizing) is not a substitute for texts, and of these very few exist. We shall shortly discuss their significance. The fact remains that medieval Latin rhythmic poetry based on word stress is not a popular but a learned phenomenon. It developed in the schools, and it is entirely unlikely that its forms were influenced by a "folk lyric" whose very existence is in doubt. The reading of poetry in which stress and quantity were combined by scholars who had no feeling for quantity would be sufficient to explain the emergence of rhythmic Latin poetry.[1]

The problem of the use of rhyme is, if possible, even more complicated. There is some slight evidence that classical authors occasionally used rhyme as an ornament, both in prose and verse. It could be used to mark a colon or interval in rhetoric. Latin, with its numerous case endings, lends itself to grammatical rhyme. It is thus perfectly possible that a feature originally used rarely for ornament became more and more common. Certainly the phenomenon did not appear suddenly. The early hymns show occasional rhyme but not in a regular pattern. There appear to be no rules for rhyming, and words some-

[1] Good books on the transition from Latin to Romance verse are: W. Beare, *Latin Verse and European Song* (1957); M. Burger, *Recherches sur la structure et l'origine des vers romans* (1957). See also G. Lote, *Histoire du vers français,* Vols. I and II (1949, 1951).

times merely assonate or end with the same vowel. Once the feature had been established it became more and more subject to rule. It appears regularly in the strophe; it follows different patterns. Once it became necessary in rhythmic poetry, it was felt that mere assonance or even rhyming a final vowel was insufficient. A full syllable or two syllables had to rhyme. By the twelfth century perfection had been reached, and the rhyming skill of the great medieval Latin lyricists has never been surpassed. They attempt curious rhyme patterns, succession rhyme with particular vowels, and other products of the virtuoso.

Some critics have not been satisfied with this spontaneous development. They have sought other sources. Rhyme forms are found in the poetry of the Semitic peoples, and the great medieval Latin scholar Wilhelm Meyer sought to demonstrate that the early contacts of the Western Church with the hymns of the East had introduced rhyme into Latin poetry.[2] The theory, incapable of proof or disproof, seems unnecessary, as do other theories which seek to derive rhyme from popular poetry.

Whatever may have been the origin of rhyme, it is clear that by the eighth century rhyming Latin couplets were an established verse form, and by the ninth century they were being imitated by vernacular writers, such as Otfried in Germany, and by the tenth by anonymous French writers. The Carolingian "renaissance," in its attempts to classicize and imitate the quantitative meters of Rome, actually set back the development of rhythmic verse, but its development of rhetorical techniques and recovery of linguistic standards was of great value to subsequent writers. Although much of the lyric written by Anghilbert, Theodolphus, and Moduinus was utterly uninspired, it provided excellent discipline in formal description of natural phenomena, in panegyric, in the neat han-

---

[2] See his *Fragmenta Burana* (Festschrift zur Feier des hundertfünfzigjährigen Bestehen der königlichen Gesellschaft der Wissenschaften zu Göttingen, phil.-hist. Klasse [1901],) pp. 145 ff.

dling of set themes such as disputes between body and soul, sun and wind, and beer and wine. These writers had in their turn learned their craft from such Anglo-Saxon authors as Aldhelm and Bede, who stood directly in the classical tradition preserved in Ireland.

The authors of the Carolingian period introduced no new forms and, in secular writing, probably thought only in terms of *tragedia* and *comedia* (unhappy and happy narrative), *satira* (social comment), *elegia* (descriptive writing), and such forms as *planctus* (elegy), and panegyric. Love poetry, as might be expected, is virtually nonexistent. It is clear, however, that on the fringes of scholastic circles new forms were being tried. We are fortunate in possessing a manuscript of the eleventh century, known as the Cambridge Songs. The manuscript, which is now in the Cambridge University library in England, is generally believed to be a collection of poems written in Germany in the late tenth or early eleventh century. A few words of vernacular occur in some of the poems, but they are mostly lyric or short narrative pieces written in Latin verse, largely rhythmic. A number of the pieces are religious; some are panegyric (in praise of the Emperor Otto III); some are versified forms of such well-known stories as that of the merchant who, returning home after an absence of several years, is presented by his wife with a child "conceived of the snow." He says nothing to this, but when the child is grown, he takes it with him to the East, sells it into slavery, and returns home with the sad news that the child has melted away in the hot sun. Such poems are probably those designated with scorn by medieval scholars as *cantilenae* (although the term probably includes vernacular works too). More important for the study of the development of the lyric are two or three poems of a type new in Western literature. One is a description of spring, which in itself would be nothing new if it were not for the fact that the description is the forerunner of innumerable brief descriptions of an ideal spring landscape which were incorporated into love poems and, by the end of the twelfth century, were regarded as virtually indispensable to such poems, whether in Latin or the vernacular. The "paysage idéal de printemps" or "Natureingang" has been the subject of a great deal of rather pointless discussion. There is no doubt that Curtius is right when he derives it not from any one classical author but from an established rhetorical topos. The fact that similar descriptions occur in the liturgy and in Easter hymns does not invalidate this theory. The ideal landscape is always described in the same way—the sky is again blue; the sun has driven away the winter; ice has melted; color has returned; trees are green; flowers bloom; birds sing. The description is almost always extremely formal. The rose and the lily are virtually the only flowers named; the lime and very rarely the pine and elm are the only trees. There is no interest in the sound of winds, in clouds, in brooks. A selection is made of stock epithets and in many cases the natural description is obviously taken from a grab bag of rhetorical terms. Yet often the description uses these same terms with such skill that critics have seen in them a new fresh inspiration in Western literature, a sudden interest in nature, and the spontaneous invention of Latin terms of description unknown to classical antiquity. Miss Helen Waddell writes in her enthusiasm: "For this is the amazing discovery of medieval lyric. Spring comes slowly up that way, but when it comes it is an ecstasy. In the North, far more than in the South, Persephone comes actually from the dead. It is a new thing and their own." [3] The truth, as usual, lies somewhere in between. There is a beautiful description of the return of spring in the fifth ode of Horace's fourth book, but spring in Italy is not quite the event that it is in northern Europe. Anyone who had spent the winter in a cold and drafty medieval dwelling would certainly welcome the spring. The fact that he did so in terms learned in the schools of rhetoric does not prove that he was not sincere, but only

[3] *The Wandering Scholars,* 7th ed. (1952), p. 222.

that he used the terms considered appropriate in literature. Skylarks are symbols of spring in English literature, but many English-speaking people have never heard one sing, nor have they heard the love notes of the nightingale. Medieval poets were perfectly conscious that the spring they described was an idealized and formalized fiction. They were interested only in the way the fiction was used and the skill with which the image was conveyed.

The ideal picture of spring was introduced into love poetry because it showed a relation between nature and man.[4] As the winter was warmed by spring, so the cold heart was warmed by love. The lovely spring landscape was the pleasure park in which love could revel, the earthly paradise into which love carried its devotees. The lovers were thus part of the harmony of nature in spring and fulfilled the purpose of nature in the universe. There is ample evidence of this attitude in the philosophical thinking of the time, but we need not believe that the association of the spring landscape and love in poetry was an intellectual phenomenon. It was often a mechanical device which came alive only in the hands of the best poets, but it is important to remember that it is not merely a formal introduction with no relation to the love poem that follows. Gottfried von Strassburg used it, as we saw, as a background for the love idyll, and we shall see it again in the Latin narrative love poem, *Phyllis and Flora*. Of its use by the troubadours and *Minnesänger* there will be occasion to speak later.

The manuscript of the Cambridge Songs contains another poem of great significance, the "Invitatio Amicae." The poem sets forth in four-lined strophes of irregular rhythmic rhymed verse an invitation, written in the first person, by a man, pre-

[4] Medieval views of nature vary considerably. Sometimes she is a separate goddess, sometimes the handmaid of God. See Curtius, *European Literature,* Chapter VI. In all her aspects, however, she is viewed in her relationship to man. The *Complaint of Nature* of Alan of Lille is a most important work for the connection between man's activities and the natural world.

sumably a student or scholar, to his girl friend. He boasts of providing the best of music and food and adds as many blandishments as he can imagine. The girl's reply, that she is a simple country person who loves the solitude of the woods, is brushed aside, and he ends by asking her not to delay the inevitable surrender. Her reply to this is not recorded. Some critics have seen in the use of the word "soror" when addressing the lady an indication that she is a nun and the writer therefore a cleric. Such evidence is very flimsy and certainly not strong enough to support the theory that the poem falls into the category of cleric and nun poems. Some critics, in particular Brinkmann, have seen a line of development from epistolary (and very spiritual) love declarations from clerics to nuns and vice versa to the exalted love of the *Minnesang*. That there is a direct connection is unlikely but, even if there were, no one could call the "Invitatio Amicae" spiritual. It is an example of the application of verse techniques learned for more formal poetry to occasional verse, and demonstrates the lightness of touch and absence of seriousness which characterizes most Latin, as contrasted with most vernacular, love poetry.

One other type of poem which appears in the Cambridge Songs should be mentioned, not because of its content but because of its form. This type of poem, known as the sequence (*sequentia*), had developed from church music by a process usually described as follows. The Alleluia sung at the end of the Mass was, during the early Middle Ages, prolonged by a melismatic series of notes, often of great complexity. In order to facilitate the memorization of these additional melodies, they were later provided with words (*prosa*), which were not arranged metrically and had no significance as literature. Later still the melodies were separated from the Alleluia and were given accompanying metrical lyrics. The fact that the sequences were sung by two half-choirs in antiphony explains their peculiar form. The strophes are arranged in pairs, the first and last corresponding in metrical structure, and the remainder grouped in pairs in the same way. The pairs of strophes are often completely different from each other in length, rhyme scheme, and metrical form, but the two strophes within each pair correspond exactly. The sequence is a good example of a poetical form directly dependent upon music. It is used not infrequently in secular poetry and it is interesting to note that older editions (e.g., Schmeller's *Carmina Burana*) failed to recognize the sequence form and hence printed the poems wrongly.

Medieval Latin lyric is very largely anonymous. We possess lyrical pieces from such authors as Marbod of Rennes (died 1123), Baudri de Bourgeuil (1046–1130), Hildebert of Lavardin (died 1133), and Serlo of Bayeux (1050–1120), but these works, often of considerable formal beauty, remain generally within the framework of the older genres and are most successful in occasional pieces and in satire. It is quite certain that Abélard wrote secular love poems, for he mentions his embarrassment at hearing them sung in the streets, but no extant poem can be ascribed to him with any certainty. The poems which strike a new note in love poetry and which show the highest skill in comment and satire are almost all anonymous, and when an author is named we usually have very little information about him. The poems are found in manuscripts which are clearly later collections of smaller groups of poems—the Arundel 384 and Harleian 913 and 978 in the British Museum, the Rawlinson G109 at Oxford, St. Omer 351, and, most famous of all, the *Carmina Burana,* Songs of Benediktbeuern, a thirteenth-century manuscript found in the Bavarian Abbey of that name when the monasteries were secularized at the beginning of the nineteenth century. Many poems are found in two or more of the manuscripts and many too are elsewhere ascribed to specific authors such as Gauthier de Châtillon, Primas of Orleans, or the Archipoeta. The existence of such general collections led many scholars to describe them as "Goliard songbooks," collections made up for wandering students and hence to designate the poetry they contained as "Goliard poetry" or "Vagantendichtung." The supposition was supported by the fact that some of the poems were gambling and drinking songs, some were obscene (although they seem mild by modern standards), and almost all were lighthearted and convivial. Some of them were probably written by wandering students, but there is no reason to believe that students had a monopoly on jollity and conviviality. Many were doubtless written for amusement by respectable scholars and clerics, even more by the semiprofessional literary men at wealthy bishops' courts. Of the latter class the person known as Archipoeta is the supreme example. The term Goliadic poetry has significance only as a term covering light occasional poetry on secular life, not as an indication of authorship. It is worth noting that a large proportion of the poetry in the *Carmina Burana* is religious or moral in nature, a fact conveniently overlooked by many commentators.

The satirical poetry found in these manuscripts and that written by Gauthier de Châtillon and the Archipoeta is among the most effective ever written. It makes its attacks principally upon the decay of morals and the conduct of the church. It should be noted that the institution itself is very rarely the object of ridicule, but that the men who operate the church for their own benefit are the sufferers. Simony, great wealth, gluttony, sloth, almost all the deadly sins are ascribed to the officers of the church and in particular to the cardinals and chamberlains of the Holy See. It has been pointed out with justice that in most of the poems we merely have standard attacks on declining virtues, comparisons of an actual prevailing low standard of morals with a theoretical former high standard. The fact does not lessen the effectiveness of the satire, which is dependent on linguistic skill and allusion rather than on the deploying of facts. Parody, particularly of sacred texts, is a favorite method. Such parody does not necessarily indicate irreverence, still less blasphemy. The sacred texts—certain parts of the Bible and the Fathers—were very well known to any educated man, and successful parody is dependent upon instant recognition of the material being parodied. The technique was particularly effective in the Middle Ages, when educated men knew a few books well rather than many superficially. The absence of good literary parody in our own day may perhaps be due to the contrary situation. The use of excerpts from sacred texts in contexts anything but holy in itself produced the desired effect of contrast between the real and ideal, between the state of religious holiness and the state of profane abuse. A fine example of the use of parody is to be found in a poem sometimes attributed to Gautier de Châtillon, *Carmina Burana,* No. 42:

1. Utar contra vitia
   carmine rebelli.
   Mel proponunt alii,
   fel supponunt melli,
   Pectus subest ferreum
   deaurate pelli
   Et leonis spolium
   induunt aselli.

1. I intend to attack vice with a song of disgust. Others serve honey, but honey mixed with gall. Beneath the gilded skin is a heart of iron, and asses dress in lions' skins.

2. Disputat cum animo
   facies rebellis,
   Mel ab ore profluit,
   mens est plena fellis;
   Non est totum melleum,
   quod est instar mellis,
   Facies est alia
   pectoris quam pellis.

2. Appearance and spirit are at odds, they quarrel with one another; honey flows from their mouths, but in their mind is bitterness. All is not sweet which looks like honey, and heart and outward seeming are not the same.

3. Vitium in opere,
   virtus est in ore,
   Tegunt picem animi
   niveo colore,
   Membra dolent singula
   capitis dolore
   Et radici consonat
   ramus in sapore.

3. In their deeds there is wickedness, in their speech virtue; with the color of snow they cover the pitchy blackness of their spirit. When the head is in pain, each limb feels it too, and the branch's taste is that of the root.

4. Roma mundi caput est,
   sed nil capit mundum,
   Quod pendet a capite,
   totum est immundum;
   Trahit enim vitium
   primum in secundum,
   Et de fundo redolet,
   quod est iuxta fundum.

4. Rome is the head of the world, but there is nothing clean in it. That which hangs from the head is totally unclean, for the first sin brings with it the second and that which is near the bottom stinks of it.

5. Roma capit singulos
et res singulorum,
Romanorum curia
non est nisi forum.
Ibi sunt venalia
iura senatorum,
Et solvit contraria
copia nummorum.

5. Rome seizes every man in turn and
in turn his possessions. The Roman
curia is but a market. Here the rights
of the princes of the church are for
sale, and every dispute is solved by
the flow of money.

7. Romani capitulum
habent in decretis,
Ut petentes audiant
manibus repletis.
Dabis, aut non dabitur,
petunt, quando petis,
Qua mensura seminas,
et eadem metis.

7. In their books of law the Romans
have a section that only those with
full pockets may be heard. Give or it
will not be given unto you, they demand when you petition. As you sow,
so shall you reap.

11. Solam avaritiam
Rome nevit Parca:
Parcit danti munera,
parco non est parca,
Nummus est pro numine
et pro Marco marca,
Et est minus celebris
ara quam sit arca.

11. In Rome the Fate spins only greed:
the gift giver she spares, to the sparing she is unsparing. There gold is
god, the mark stands for Marcus, the
altar has less currency than the
money chest.

This poem, written towards the end of the twelfth century, was probably as well known as any of the numerous anti-clerical satires, if we are to judge by the large number of manuscripts in which it is found and by the indignation it caused among churchmen, notably Giraldus of Bari. It is a typical piece of learned poetry, which employs every rhetorical trick to hammer home its main point, the difference between the fair outward seeming of the church, and particularly the Roman Curia, and its inward spirit. The key words are "carmine rebelli"—a song of rebellion, of opposition, of contrast. Throughout the poem contrast is made on several levels. The general use of words and phrases associated with the Scriptures in utterly secular contexts (as in Strophe 7) is clear from the start, implying the perversion of the spiritual to the worldly. But the poet delights in virtuosity, and his verbal arrangements demonstrate great skill. Sound contrasts are extremely common: *fel* (gall) is contrasted with *mel* (honey), *nummus* (coin) with *numine* (godhead, spirit). Lines are set out so that the beginning and end of each clash in meaning, although they are alike in sound:

> Vitium in opere
> virtus est in ore.

The poet delights principally in the use of *annominatio,* the juxtaposition of words very similar in sound but utterly different in meaning. The strophe beginning "Roma mundi caput est" is an excellent example. Another example is the brilliant (and untranslatable) series of puns in the last strophe quoted here. (The poem is actually much longer.) Parca is one of the Fates who recognizes only greed at Rome. But "parca" could also mean "thrifty" and "sparing" in the sense of "pitying." Thus a pitying or careful person would find only avarice awaiting her. Similarly in line 4 "parco non est parca" could mean "not sparing to a pitying man," an ironical perversion of the actual truth. There is a telling resemblance in sound between *nummus* (which is the true god at Rome) and *numine* (which ought to be). The pun on Mark (the saint) and mark (the sum of money) is frequent in this type of satire. *Ara* (the altar) and *arca* (the money chest) differ by only one consonant.

It is worth noting that it is not doctrine which is attacked in this poem, but behavior and in particular the unjust use of the law. The officials of the Curia had often to decide final appeals on legal questions, and the poet, like many other writers of his time and later, was convinced that bribery was an important element in the decision reached.

This poem illustrates as well as any the effectiveness of fully developed Latin rhythmic poetry. The light tripping "Goliardic" line is eminently suitable for satire. Originally, no doubt, a long (thirteen-syllable) line of descending rhythm it is here used in two parts: /x/x/x/ /x/x/x so that the first half has a rising, the second a falling rhythm. The even lines rhyme, often providing effective parallels or contrasts in the rhyming words.

It is obvious that such poetry as this belongs to learned circles. No one not thoroughly trained in rhetoric could appreciate or even understand it, and it may be noted that in certain strophes not quoted here the technical terms of Latin grammar are used as a stick to beat the Roman Curia. The "accusative" brings the victim to court, but the dative ("giver") can secure an "ablative" (annulment of the charge). Such poetry can raise a smile and provoke admiration for its verbal acrobatics, but the satire itself should not be taken too seriously. It is very much like political poetry, an accepted genre for cultured amusement. There is no reason to think that any but the most rigid ecclesiastics resented it, or that it was only "clerici ribaldi" who wrote it. Of its effectiveness we may also be a little sceptical. Such reforms as did take place were usually effected by simpler souls than the writers of Latin satire.

How far mockery of sin, confession, and penitence could be carried may be seen from the following extracts from what is probably the best known of all medieval Latin secular poems (except *Gaudeamus igitur*). The portion of it beginning "Meum est propositum" is still in use as a students' song in Germany.

1. Estuans intrinsecus
ira vehementi
In amaritudine
loquor meae menti:
"Factus de materia
levis elementi
Folio sum similis,
de quo ludunt venti."

1. I seethe within in mighty wrath, in bitterness I thus address my spirit: "I am made of the stuff of the unstable element, I am as a leaf, a plaything of the winds."

2. Cum sit enim proprium
viro sapienti
Supra petram ponere
sedem fundamenti,
Stultus ego comparor
fluvio labenti
Sub eodem tramite
numquam permanenti.

2. The wise man knows that he must set his seat upon the rock, I, a fool, am like unto a flowing river, never staying on the same course.

5. Via lata gradior
more iuventutis;
Implico me vitiis

5. Along the primrose path I go in the way of youth; unmindful of virtue, I entangle myself in vice. Pleasure I

immemor virtutis.
Voluptatis avidus
magis quam salutis
Mortuus in anima
curam gero cutis.

6. Presul discretissime,
veniam te precor:
Morte bona morior,
nece dulci necor:
Meum pectus sauciat
puellarum decor,
Et quas tactu nequeo,
saltem corde mechor.

8. Quis in igne positus
igne non uratur?
Quis Papie demorans
castus habeatur,
Ubi Venus digito
iuvenes venatur,
Oculis illaqueat,
facie predatur?

11. Tertio capitulo
memoro tabernam:
Illam nullo tempore
sprevi neque spernam,
Donec sanctos angelos
venientes cernam
Cantantes pro mortuis,
Requiem eternam.

12. Meum est propositum
in taberna mori,
Ut sit vinum proximum
morientis ori.
Tunc cantabunt letius
angelorum chori,
"Sit Deus propitius
huic potatori!"

15. Iam nunc in presentia
presulis beati
Secundum Dominici
regulam mandati
Mittat in me lapidem
Neque parcat vati,
Cuius non est animus
conscius peccati.

love more than my salvation; I am
dead in soul as I pursue the delights
of the body.

6. Most noble bishop, I beg your forgiveness. I am dying a good death, I
am making a most sweet end. It is
the beauty of girls which wounds my
breast, and with those whom I cannot touch I commit adultery in my
heart.

8. What man, when placed in the fire,
would not burn? What man when
stationed in Pavia can remain chaste,
where Venus chases young men,
crooking her finger, ensnares them
with her eyes, and captures them
with her face.

11. In the third place I may mention the
tavern. I have never scorned it and
never shall until I see the holy angels coming and singing eternal rest
to the dead.

12. It is my intention to die in a tavern,
so that wine may be near me as I die.
Then the chorus of angels will sing
even more cheerfully: "May God be
merciful unto this man—a drinker."

15. And now in the presence of our
blessed bishop, according to the law
laid down by our Lord, let him among
you who is free of guilt throw a stone
at me, nor let him spare the bard.

Although this poem has been so frequently printed and translated, it is doubtful whether its full force has been often appreciated. Almost all manuscripts which give it a title at all include the word "confession." This does not mean a mere informal recital of misdeeds but a formal statement. The declaration is made to a high ecclesiastic, no less a person than Reinhald Dassel, archbishop of Cologne. In outward appearance it follows a strict pattern: a description of the poet's state of mind, his agony of spirit, his feeling of unworthiness, and his realization of his unstable conduct. Then follows a direct appeal to his master and an explanation of the three sins of which he is conscious: wenching, gambling, and drinking. After his attempt at justification he asks for mercy, promises amendment, and remarks that no one should be too stern.

The confession is, however, no confession, but a frank acknowledgment of delight in pleasure and a not too subtly veiled statement that the archbishop enjoys the same things. The effects are obtained in numerous ways, but parody and double meaning are by far the most important. A few examples must suffice. The first lines recall the first verse of the tenth chapter of the Book of Job: "My soul is weary of my life; I will leave my complaint upon myself; I will speak in the bitterness of my soul." The second verse of the same book, not parodied but certainly well known to his hearers is: "I will say unto God, Do not condemn me; show me wherefore thou contendest with me." It is in the third verse, however, that the sting comes: "Is it good unto thee that thou shouldst oppress, that thou shouldst despise the work of thine hands, and shine upon the counsel of the wicked?" There can be little room for doubt. Whatever the poet is, he is so because of his bishop and the attacks on him are made by the wicked, those who throw stones (John 8:7) but are themselves just as guilty.

The word play in strophe 2 is of a different kind. The reference is, of course, to Matthew 7:24, "Therefore whosoever heareth these sayings of mine, and doeth them, I will liken him

unto a wise man, which built his house upon a rock. . . ."
Obviously, the poet is the foolish man who builds on sand—
except that "super petram" had another meaning which could
not escape any medieval audience which constantly heard the
play on *petra* and Petrus in reference to the Curia, and "sedem
fundamenti" also had a meaning fairly adequately conveyed by
the English "seat" or "fundament."

Almost every line of the poem has such neat plays. Most
effective, however, is the device of what might be called "re-
versing the anticipated." In strophe 6, for example, the words
"I am dying a good death, I am making a good end" might be
expected to refer to his imminent departure in a contrite and
repentant state of mind. In fact, as the next two lines show, he
is dying with love of the girls and, with a neat reversal of the
words of Matthew 5:28: "But I say unto you that whosoever
looketh on a woman to lust after her hath committed adultery
with her already in his heart," he says that he will touch them
if he can, but if he cannot, will imagine it.

Mock moralizing, careful argued excuses for his "inability to
fight nature" abound. Most amusing is his virtual threat that
cutting off his supply of wine will dry up the springs of his inspiration—tavern wine, too, not the Bishop's watered stuff. The
crowning act of impertinence is the substitution of the word
potatori [drinker] for *peccatori* [sinner] in the formula "God
have mercy upon him, a sinner."

This poem is a triumph of learning made mellow. It has gone
beyond the virtuosity and obvious cleverness of "Utar contra
vitia" to a use of parody and double meaning which is subtle
and effective without heaviness. Its irony and complete shame-
lessness have delighted generations of readers, for it takes no
cognizance of rank or of pompousness. But again, it is a professional job. Although we know nothing of the "archpoet"
who wrote it, he was clearly a man who made his living by his
pen. We should acknowledge also the culture of a court which
could appreciate such work and laugh with the poet, and which

was willing to patronize poets who had learned to use with such matchless skill the rhymed and rhythmic forms of Latin. We should add briefly that there are other, less witty but not unamusing, parodies of the Mass, the Sacred Offices, and even the Lord's Prayer which, however generously interpreted, can hardly escape the stigma of blasphemy. Such are the *Evangelium secundum marcas argenti* (Gospel according to St. Silver Mark), the *Goliard's Mass,* and others. Such works are the sub-literary efforts of educated men. They had their equivalents in nineteenth-century college songs.

Not a little of the medieval Latin love poetry found in the collections falls into the same category. It is obscene, often telling of a visit to a brothel or a chance encounter with a girl. The story is frequently told very amusingly (as, for example, in the *Carmina Burana* poem No. 76, *Dum caupona verterem*). The girl's resistance is often more apparent than real (*C.B.,* No. 72), and she is often more concerned about discovery by her parents or brother than about the incident itself. Such poems have a good deal in common with the French *pastourelle,* and there are one or two actual examples of a Latin *pastourelle.* In the best-known of these, *Lucis orto sidere* (*C.B.,* No. 157), a man (type unspecified) saves a shepherdess's flock from a wolf—after being promised her favors as reward. The parallel between Biblical sheep and wolves is clear.

Such poems are not, however, typical of Latin love poetry as a genre. It has been correctly pointed out that Latin poetry contrasts sharply with medieval vernacular poetry in concentrating on the social rather than the individual aspects of love. The poet calls upon everyone, cleric and layman, to join with him in greeting the spring and stepping down into the meadow to dance. There is almost invariably a description of the ideal spring landscape and of its effects on the hearts of men. The only individual note in most poems is a statement that the author's beloved is the most beautiful in the dance, without peer among her fellows. Of melancholy yearning, of inferiority, of

despair there is rarely a trace. Such love poetry is formal and
basically of classical inspiration. It is often tinged with irony,
virtually never sublimated or spiritual. Only a few poems of the
Carmina Burana, all apparently written by the same author,
rather rhetorically describe the author's own misery at being in
love and yet despised.

It is typical of medieval Latin love poetry that its finest flower
should not be in lyric form but a debate poem or *altercatio.*
The poem "Phyllis et Flora" appears in several collections and
was still popular in Elizabethan times, when it was translated
as "The Swete and Civile Discourse of Phyllis and Flora."
Sweet and civil it assuredly is, and there is small wonder that
it was one of the few medieval works which appealed to a
Renaissance audience. The subject of the poem is a question
often debated, in various forms, in medieval literature: which
made the better lover, the cleric or the knight? The question
itself, of course, is reminiscent of Andreas Capellanus and
reflects, in my opinion, an actual social phenomenon, for there
were no doubt courts at which clerics, once the only polished
verbalizers of love's language, were feeling the pressure of
educated knights. Phyllis believes that the soldier is the better
lover, Flora the cleric. The reasons advanced by each are ingenious, amusing, and often tinged with irony. The cleric is
represented by his lady as rich, generous, well-fed, a polished
lover and courtier—in other words, all the things a true cleric
should not be. The opposition, on the other hand, mentions such
little drawbacks as his black clothing, tonsured head, and appearance at morning mass with a hang-over. The knight, she
urges, may not be rich, but he is handsome, devoted and brave.
He cries his lady's name as he goes into battle and writes poems
to her in the heat of the fray. This latter point, rather reasonably, is disputed by Flora, who claims for her cleric that he is
the true literary man and any poor knowledge the knight may
have is derived from him. The two ladies—both princesses, needless to say, and of fabulous beauty—now decide to lay their

question before the god of love himself. Here the poem moves, with brilliant imaginative transition, from the real world to the imaginative. The transition is marked by the mounting of two remarkable steeds, presents to the ladies' mothers by divine personages for services not specified. Mounted on these beasts the ladies enter the enchanted wood of love (again the *paysage idéal*). Before long they arrive at the court, are suitably overwhelmed by its magnificence, and explain their problem. The question is debated by this, the highest authority, and the cleric is declared the winner. It is hard to escape the feeling that the verdict is given tongue in cheek. On the other hand the poem is written with a limpidity of style, a mastery of versification, and a wealth of classical allusion which could stem only from a clerically educated person—but not necessarily from a cleric. We should not forget that we found the same characteristics in Gottfried von Strassburg.

In this poem love is an idealized pastime. The question of sensuality or spirituality does not arise, for the discussion is theoretical. Only the social graces are discussed, not the personal relations and, in spite of their protestations, one feels that one can say with Rosalind that Cupid has but clapped them on the shoulder. Many of the characteristics found in the poem are those of the vernacular love lyric—the idealized setting, the deliberate striving for virtuosity in expression, the formalism in describing love's effects, and above all the insistence that the love affair should be conducted according to strict conventions. In spite of these resemblances, however, the gulf between Latin love poetry and that in the vernacular remains so wide that the one can hardly be derived directly from the other.

The earliest vernacular love poetry is that of Provence. The term "Provence" is rather misleading, since few of the poets were actual natives of the area. It is used simply to denote all poetry written in the formal language of southern France, the Langue d'Oc, usually called Provençal. Provençal poetry begins with the works of William IX, count of Poitou and duke of

Aquitaine, but it is clear that he was working within an established tradition. Some of the features of this tradition undoubtedly came from Latin sources—the verse form, the *paysage idéal*—but the real distinguishing marks are not those of Latin poetry. From the very beginning, vernacular poetry displays several remarkable new characteristics, of which by far the most important are the idea of humble and often unrewarded service to the lady, an air of melancholy arising from unrequited love, and the idea of love as an ennobling force, which made a man rise above himself. These qualities are rarely found in Latin poetry. It is untrue to say that vernacular love poetry is spiritual and despises sensuality. The statement is true only of certain poets when they wrote in the *canzon* form. Much of the poetry of, for example, William IX and Marcabru is sensual to the point of obscenity. Yet the characteristic of the highest type of vernacular poetry is that the beloved is beyond the reach of the lover and that his reward consists in the privilege of worshiping her from afar and in being ennobled by his love for her. There can be no doubt that much of this distance between lover and beloved can be accounted for by the difference in social rank between a lady who is a patroness and must be flattered and a professional poet of lower rank—for no other Provençal poet was a duke or count. Even so, it seems necessary to search for some source from which the idea could be derived.

One theory has received wide publicity, but has little substance. There was during the twelfth and thirteenth centuries a heretical sect in southern France and also in Germany, known as the Catharists. Their beliefs were similar to those of the Gnostics so strongly condemned by St. Augustine, that is, they believed in two separate, opposed powers of Good and Evil. The power of evil dwells in the flesh and the only way in which the good can be liberated is by the destruction of the flesh. Thus they were not supposed to eat meat, nor to propagate. In practice these doctrines were confined to the *perfecti,* a very small proportion of the Catharist community. The majority led normal, if somewhat ascetic, lives. It has been argued that the Provençal (and German) poets were in fact deeply imbued with the doctrine of negation of the flesh and that their "spiritual" love poems were in fact inspired by the idea of nonsensual love or indeed were elaborate allegories in which the Catharist "church of love" was represented by the beloved lady. Such theories diligently ignore certain facts. Many of the ladies celebrated are known; few Provençal poets write *only* "spiritual" love poems; there was no persecution of the Catharist heresy before 1210, so why should there be such elaborate concealment? Furthermore, it has yet to be proved that any troubadour was a Catharist. The fact that some of their patrons protected Catharists proves nothing. The whole theory seems farfetched and vulnerable.

Much more important is the proposal that Provençal poetry was deeply influenced by Arabic poetry. The idea has been circulating since the sixteenth century, but recent scholarship has uncovered more and more convincing evidence. Arabic love poetry shows remarkable resemblances in detail to various Provençal lyric genres. The watcher who cries that the dawn is here in the Provençal *alba* has his counterpart (*raquib*), as does the jealous detractor (*wâchi*). The ideas of service, of the misery of love, dream motifs, secret love, and spiritualization of passion are all present. Furthermore, there is a marked correspondence of metrical and strophic forms. All this could be explained away as coincidence if it were not for proven cultural contacts, not with the Arabs in the East, as was formerly believed, but with the rich Arab culture of Spain. Although there is no Spanish poetry of the troubadour type before the thirteenth century, and even this is clearly an imitation of Provençal, we now have clear evidence of Arab songs with refrains written in the vernacular which show that the two cultures were blending. It is hardly surprising that such influences should spread to southern France, for Catalonian and the Langue d'Oc are very similar languages, there was much social contact between the areas, and it is highly probable that Jewish travelers acted as cultural intermediaries. Recent scholarship has added a great deal of indisputable evidence of contacts between the Arab and Romance lyric.[5] No doubt more will be found.

The problem of the origin of the love concepts of the Provençal lyric is by no means solved, but this much we may say. Classical models and medieval Latin lyric provided most of the imagery, the language, the rhetorical ornament, and the metrical structure. The basic themes of certain types, such as the *canzon* and the *alba,* may well have been inspired by Arabic poetry, but owe their development also to a large degree to the social conditions prevailing in the sophisticated courts where educated women were frequently the patronesses of literature. Without this social milieu the medieval vernacular lyric could not have developed.

The poetry of William IX of Aquitaine is simple in form. Some of the ideas of the later troubadours, such as love in absence and the exaltation known as *joi,* are found in his work, but they are undeveloped. Marcabru, writing in the first half of the twelfth century, still thinks of love mainly in sensual terms and chastises the troubadours as fosterers of adultery. He is a brilliant poet, but hardly typical of what is to come later. His contemporary Jaufré Rudel is the first poet in whom appear those characteristics which are regarded as typical. The poem to his distant love has been made famous by numerous imitations, and its theme was expanded by the anonymous author of his *vida* or biography in order to make it appear that he did in fact love a lady in Tripoli in Syria whom he had never seen. He set out for the East to see her, fell sick, and was carried dying into her presence. In the poem there is none of this. "Distant love" may well mean nothing more than unattainable love, that love for a person of such beauty, such virtue, and such fame

[5] See L. Spitzer, "The Mozarabic Lyric," *Comparative Literature,* Vol. IV (1952); P. Zumthor, "Au berceau du lyrisme Européen," *Cahiers du Sud,* Vol. XL, No. 326 (1954).

that the lover is exalted merely by loving her from afar. In this poem love appears as a purely spiritual experience, an act of adoration before a supreme being, and it comes close to religious ecstasy: "Never shall I enjoy love, if I do not enjoy this distant love, for I know of none more noble, or better in any place, whether far or near. So pure is its quality and so perfect that I would have myself taken captive by the Saracens for its sake."

The *canzon* was developed along these lines by subsequent authors. Love is a dominant, often a tyrannical, power. The lady is cruel in not loving the poet, but he cannot leave her, for separation would be worse than cruelty. The idea of service without reward becomes a dominant theme. The love of the poet must be kept secret, for his lady's reputation cannot be allowed to suffer. Hence he either mentions no name at all or uses a *senhal* or pseudonym. Marriage is never the aim of the lover, for marriage destroys love, and in any case the lady is unattainable. Yet we should beware of pinning the label "adulterous" on the love described in the *canzon*. The ladies addressed were indeed married but the love declarations in the *canzon* are homage, not attempted seduction. In the *alba* the situation is different, as we shall see.

For most modern readers, Bernart de Ventador is the most readable of the troubadours. His use of the "spring opening" is effective and simple; he has a freshness and frankness of approach lacking in later authors. It is not hard to believe that Bernart might really have loved the ladies he addressed (although they are probably fictional), and his quiet melancholy strikes a sympathetic chord. Bernart's verse forms are relatively simple, but already there appears the type of strophic arrangement which became virtually standard in later troubadour poetry and which was transmitted to their German and Italian imitators. This strophic form has three parts. The first two have each the same number of lines of the same metrical pattern, although within each part they may vary to any extent. The

third part may be of any length or metrical pattern. A typical
scheme would be

```
8a 8b 8a 8b
8c 8d 8c 8d
8d 6e 6e 8d 8f 8f
```

The first two parts are called in Provençal *pede* [feet], the two
parts together are known as the *fronte*. The third part is the
cauda [tail]. In Italian the names correspond. In German the
parts are called respectively *Stollen* (the two together *Auf-
gesang*) and the third *Abgesang*. The whole was known in
Provençal as a *cobla,* and there were intricate combinations of
these: *coblas doblas,* in which the strophes were in exactly corresponding pairs; *coblas capcaudadas,* in which the end of one
strophe had the same rhyme form as the beginning of the next
(head to tail); and *coblas retrogradas,* where the whole rhyme
scheme is reversed in alternate strophes. In late poets such
formal tricks seem of more importance than matter, and their
preoccupation with metrical virtuosity and curiosities of language and ornament has led to the charge that they had really
nothing to say. Some substance is lent to this opinion by the
statements of contemporaries and later medieval critics, including Dante, who clearly preferred authors of great technical skill,
such as Arnaut Daniel, Folquet de Marseilles, and Raimbaut
d'Orange, to more original spirits such as Peire Vidal. It is clear
that the pursuits of difficult and recherché rhymes must inevitably have limited the author's power of expressing his
theme. Well-established clichés of love poetry were used over
and over again, and only the linguistic form was varied.

The monotony—for a modern reader—is intensified by two
other circumstances. The concentration on the strophe as a unit
led to a marked lack of unity within the poem. Often there
appears to be no connection between two succeeding strophes
and, particularly in the case of *coblas doblas,* it is frequently
difficult to determine, in the absence of consistent manuscript

tradition, what the true order of the pairs of strophes should be. The poem appears as a set of strophic pairs, lacking continuity of sense.

The second difficulty is closely bound up with the various types of rhetorical ornament already discussed—the *ornatus facilis* and the *ornatus difficilis*. The earlier troubadours practiced the *trobar plan* or simple type of writing. Sentiments were expressed in plain language, with simple, conventional imagery. After the middle of the twelfth century, however, increasing professionalism led to the development of two types which became the normal means of expression—the *trobar ric* and the *trobar clus*. The *trobar ric* is a logical rhetorical development. It seeks to use ornament of great complexity, *rimes rares,* much simile, complicated metrical patterns. It does not, however, become difficult to understand. *Trobar clus,* on the other hand, is deliberately obscure. It is part of the allegorizing tradition already discussed, so that the surface meaning is unimportant. Each section has to be carefully reinterpreted to find the hidden meaning. Words are frequently used in senses widely divergent from normal usage, with the result that many passages in the poets who practice the *trobar clus* are today incomprehensible. It may be added that the *trobar clus* is a factor which encourages the critics who urge the Catharist connections of the troubadours. The poems can be interpreted as religious allegories.

Many Provençal poets protested against the *trobar clus* and refused to practice it. Certainly the attitude of the poets themselves indicates that, with few exceptions, their interest lay in the technical problems of poetry rather than in the analysis of the problem of love. Analysis of the poet's own feelings is relatively rare and is usually confined to a few stock images, while the element of homage to the lady remains strong. Jeanroy's criticism, "Even if one has no right to say that all the poems are the products of the same pen, one is really tempted to believe that all the poets loved the same lady," is to a large extent justified.[6] Only occasionally do we catch a glimpse of real feeling. The following analysis of a *canzon* (by Bernart de Ventador) will be of more use than a great deal of general criticism. The reading departs somewhat from conventional interpretations in its insistence on the extension of the initial image. It is easier to point out the succession of attitudes and emotions which the succeeding strophes indicate, and in poems by less gifted authors it is impossible to do more than recognize the appearance and reappearance of stock clichés.

Quan vei la laudeta mover
De joi sas alas contral rai
Que s'oblid'es laissa cazer
Per la doussor qu'al cor li vai,
Ailas! quals enveja m'en ve
De cui qu'eu veja jauzion!
Meravilhas ai, quar desse
Lo cors de dezirier nom fon.

When I see the lark move its wings in joy in the sun's light and then, forgetting self, falling in the sweetness which goes to its heart, alas, the desire that comes upon me for her whom I should see with joy. I marvel that my heart does not burst with desire.

Ailas! tan cujava saber
D'amor e tan petit en sai!
Car eu d'amar nom posc tener
Celleis dont ja pro non aurai.
Tout m'a mon cor et tout m'a se
E mi mezeis et tot lo mon;
E quan sim tolc, nom laisset re
Mas dezirier e cor volon.

Alas, how much I thought I knew of love and how little I do know! For I cannot keep myself from loving her from whom I can expect no return. She has all my heart and all my mind, and me and all my world; and when she has taken all, she leaves nothing but desire and a willing heart.

Ane non agui de mi poder
Ni no fui meus deslor en sai
Quem laisset en sos olhs vezer,
En un miralh que mout me plai,
Miralhs, pos me mirei en te,
M'an mort li sospir de preon;
Qu'aissim perdei cum perdet se
Lo bels Narcissus en la fon.

I have had no power over myself since the hour when she allowed me to look into her eyes, into a mirror which delights me. O mirror, since I saw myself in you, I have died of deep sighs. I am lost as Narcissus was lost in the fountain.

De las domnas mi desesper;
Jamais en lor nom fiarai,
Qu'aissi cum las solh captener
Enaissi las descaptenerai.
Pos vei que nulha pro nom te

I despair of ladies; I shall never trust myself to them; just as I once defended them, henceforth I shall do the opposite. Since I saw that none of them will help me against

*See A. Jeanroy, *La Poésie lyrique des troubadours* (1943), II, 106.

Ves leis quem destrui em cofon,
Totas las dopt e las mescre,
Que ben sai qu'atretals se son.

D'aissos fai ben femna parer
Ma domna, per qu'eu l'o retrai,
Quar vol so qu'om no deu voler
E so qu'om li deveda fai.
Cazutz sui en mala merce
E ai ben fait cum fols en pon;
E no sai per que m'esdeve
Quar cujei pujar contral mon.

Merces es perduda per ver
E eu non o saubi ancmai
Quar cil que plus en degr'aver
Non a ges, et on la querrai?
A quan mal sembla, qui la ve
Que aquest caitiu desiron
Que ja ses leis non aura be
Laisse morir que no l'aon!

Pos ab mi dons nom pot valer
Precs ni merces nil dretz qu'eu ai,
Ni a leis no ven a plazer
Qu'en l'am, jamais no loi dirai.
Aissim part de leis em recrei
Mort m'a e per mort li respon,
E van m'en, pos ilh nom rete
Faiditz en eissilh, no sai on.

Tristans, ges non auretz de me
Qu'eu m'en vau caitius, non sai on,
De chantar me gic em recre.
E de jui e d'amor m'escon.

her who destroys and confounds
me, I doubt them all, I renounce
them all, for they are all alike.

In this my lady makes herself appear a true woman and for this I
reproach her. For she wants what
no one should want, she does what
she is forbidden to do. I have fallen
into poor pity. Like the fool on the
bridge I don't know how this has
happened, for I believed I was
climbing a mountain.

All pity is in truth lost and I have
never known it. For she who should
have most of it has none and where
then shall I search? No one would
believe it who sees her, yet this
poor amorous wretch, who will
never be happy without her, she
leaves to die and does not help him.

Since I can do nothing with my
lady, not with prayers, not with
thanks, nor rights which I should
have, and since it gives her no
pleasure that I love her, I shall
never tell her. Thus I part from her
and renounce her. She has caused
my death and by death I reply and
go, since she will not keep me,
forced into exile, I know not where.

Tristan, you will hear nothing of
me For I go off, poor wretch, I
know not where. I shall cease to
sing and renounce it—I shall keep
away from joy and love.

The poem is written in *coblas unissonans,* that is, strophes of
the same rhyme scheme which use the same rhyming sounds in
the same position in each strophe. The scheme is thus ababcdcd
or, using the sounds, -er, -ai, -er, -ai, -e, -on, -e, -on. This is a
very simple scheme by Provençal standards. Each line is octosyllabic. The poet is not striving after any special effects of rhyme

or meter. Each strophe divides into the *pedes* (*pede*), two groups of two lines, and the *cauda* (*coa*) of four lines. It will be seen that there is a division of sense as well as of structure after the first four lines. The last four lines, which use the *cauda* as formal model, are in fact a *cauda* or *envoi* to the whole poem.

It might be expected that the simple formal structure would be accompanied by simplicity of thought, and the poem has indeed been frequently interpreted as if it were relatively naive and uncomplicated. In fact this is not so. Any attempt to find a logical thought sequence in the poem is doomed to failure, as it almost always is in assessing the Provençal lyric. We must seek for unity another way.

The first strophe is of great importance. It is not a mere conventional tribute to the joy of spring but an important image which, in various ways, dominates the poem. The lark moves upwards towards the light; the light inspires him with love, with upward striving towards the source of light. The sensation he feels is joy, exaltation, the urge to go ever higher in pursuit of the light which inspires him. So great is the joy he feels that he can drop down again, still dazzled, and never notice it in the sweetness of desire—even though he has not attained the light he sought. The image occupies four lines. The *cauda* applies it to the poet. He too is inspired to love his lady in this way, but is prevented.

In assessing the strophe it should not be forgotten that it was the image of the lady transmitted through light which awoke in the poet's heart that ideal picture of beauty which became permanently fixed there as an image of his lady, and with which he fell in love. His soul, like the lark, yearns to reach the source of light.

The second strophe examines the idea of loss and forgetfulness. For the poet too has lost himself in the aspiration towards the light: he has lost his heart—the center of emotions—and his mind—the center of thought—but not in order to attain the sweetness which the lark attained. What he would have given voluntarily has been taken from him. He strives up like the lark, but his fall is different. Nevertheless his desire to strive still remains.

The third strophe examines another aspect: the loss of will. The lark had completely lost all sense of itself. So has Bernart. He has no power to resist since he has looked into his lady's eyes. The light image returns, for in looking her image has fixed itself into his soul. The first four lines merely describe the loss of will. The *cauda,* as so often, is the comment upon them. The story of Narcissus, who fell into the pool which he was using as a mirror for his own beauty, is well known. The Middle Ages extended the idea. In several poems Narcissus is lost because he is contemplating ideal beauty and cannot tear himself from it. So it is here. The poet is lost not because he is in love with his own image in the lady's eyes, but because of the ideal beauty he finds there. Why then does he mention the mirror at all? The answer almost certainly is that the mirror is used as an ideal ("the glass of fashion") and also that the mirror reflects the lady's soul and allows the poet to fall in love with it. The eyes allow the lady's soul to be seen. But they also reflect the lady's image into the poet's soul, where it merges with the concept of the ideal of feminine loveliness already there. Thus within his soul the lady's beauty becomes not a transitory physical impression but an eternal image of perfection.

After this splendid image, it is disappointing to find a typical cliché of troubadour poetry: All women are alike, so I shall stop being their champion. It is a logical enough extension of his theme. The next strophe is mysterious, for the statement about the madman on the bridge must be proverbial. One can only assume that Bernart intends us to believe that there is no way in which one can rely on fickle woman. The point is, of course, that power and sense are lost after gazing into the lady's eyes, but no substitute is to be found which will reveal the way to her heart. This confusion is neatly expressed in the next strophe, which is carefully composed to illustrate it. There is no pity, for pity can be granted only by the lady. She inspires the feeling which calls for pity but will not give it. If she did, of course, the yearning would no longer be there, the love-tension would be destroyed. This is the eternal problem of the troubadour: How can the lady be merciful without destroying the very unattainability which makes her the object of desire? The motif is expressed in a different way in the *cauda*. The lady inflicts a mortal wound, which she alone can cure. If she were to cure it, her function would disappear, for there would be no more yearning. This antithesis/complement-relation abounds in troubadour poetry. The wound of love and the cure of love; the arrow and the salve; love as war and love as deepest attachment.

The poet's solution is in the last strophe. Only by absence can he maintain the relationship. He is dying of love, so he will be dead for her; she will not retain him—which would end the tension but soothe him—so he will go—which will retain the tension but keep his love alive. This idea of separation retaining love is perhaps the true explanation of the *amor de lonh*. The *envoi,* addressed to the lady under her *senhal* or cover name of Tristan [7] (possibly because of the impending separation), repeats the determination—absence and lack of song.

Now it is perfectly clear that the poet wishes to tell the lady that she is cruel in not accepting his love. Yet everyone knew the conventions of this type of poetry: the lady was in fact unattainable. Thus the figure of the lark is particularly apt, for it too is making for an unattainable source of light. The difference is that the lark sinks back without despair because it has filled itself with the sweetness of the light. This the poet cannot do, for the lady, who is its source, denies him the opportunity. Her attitude prevents him from enjoying the light which reaches him from her and, unlike the lark, he must leave it without sweetness. The unity of the poem is by no means complete. But such unity as it has comes from the grouping

[7] "Tristan" may have been the name of the jongleur who sang the song.

of images round that of the original strophe, and it is usually more rewarding in Provençal lyric to seek for unity of this kind rather than a logical development of ideas from strophe to strophe.

The close connection of a particular attitude towards love with a certain lyric form is well illustrated by the differences between the *canzon* and the *alba*. These two forms were often used by the same author (eleven *albas* are extant, the earliest by Giraut de Bornelh), although it is perhaps significant that no *albas* of Bernart de Ventadorn are known to us. The *alba* is highly conventional. The poem invariably describes the parting of a knight from his lady at dawn, and it is made perfectly clear that their love is illicit and must be kept secret. There is no question of spiritual love here. The poem is often in dialogue form and usually is written from the point of view of the lady. The watchman (*gardador*) who cries the coming of dawn may be friendly, hostile, or merely neutral to the lovers. There is great stress on the activities of the lying talebearers (*lauzengers*) and on the difficulties of conducting such a love affair. That the poems may reflect an actual situation is obvious—but the situation itself is so conventionalized as to be almost absurd and is subject to relatively slight variations. The main characters are shadowy, the lover particularly so. The poem centers entirely on the emotions at parting and on reminiscence of the pleasures of the previous night. Its structure is rarely as complex as that of the *canzon,* although it uses the same metrical and strophic forms. A good example of the *alba* is the brilliant poem of Giraut de Bornelh (fl. 1170–1200) "Reis glorios, verais lums e clartatz" ('Glorious King, true bringer of light and clarity') which, after its brilliant opening address to the sun, consists of a dialogue between lovers at parting.

Among the more vigorous products of Provençal poetry are the *sirventès,* or poems of comment, and the *tenzons,* the debate poems. Almost any subject may be discussed and some are purely theoretical, for example, the celebrated debate between

Peire Vidal and the king of Navarre on the topic of whether the king or the knight made the better lover, the point being that the knight did not have to overcome the "handicap" of his rival's rank, for a lover should be judged on his personality alone. The *sirventès* was often vigorous and outspoken comment on the politics of the day, and the poets did not mince their words. Richard the Lionheart comes under the lash of Bertran de Born for failing to support his allies.[8] Such poems owe a great deal to the contemporary Latin satirists, as may easily be seen by comparing them with such collections as those of Wright, *Anglo-Latin Satirical Poems,* but they should also be read as the productions of poets who identified themselves closely with the courtly milieu in which they worked. The love poem and the political poem were, in the last analysis, all manifestations of the professional poet, writing for a small cultivated audience. He sought to please his patron and to produce the best specimens of conventionally accepted types of which he was capable. Some of the *sirventès* demonstrate how he could turn his skill to abusive purposes if a patron proved ungrateful.

Two types of lyric poetry are relatively little represented in Provençal poetry, the crusading song and the *pastourelle.* In the *vida* of Marcabru we have an intriguing statement that he wrote *pastourelles* "in the ancient fashion." It would be interesting to know what this was. It is certain that he wrote one beautiful example of the genre, of an almost fairylike quality, but after him there is no extant example until well into the thirteenth century. The new type abandons the sensuality and coarseness which we find in earlier and contemporary northern French specimens and becomes very similar to classical pastoral poetry. The peasant girl proves a great deal wittier than the knight, and the poems usually consist of a spirited refutation by the girl of the seductive arguments of the knight.

[8] Dante puts him in Hell for his warlike nature and his incitements to battle.

The *pastourelle* was clearly not a popular type during the flowering of Provençal poetry, probably because it was thought to be on too low a plane for a cultivated audience. The crusading song was written by a few Provençal authors, but it will be better to treat it with the poetry of the trouvères of northern France, where it attains its greatest development. As we have said, Provençal lyric is essentially the work of skilled professionals. Few of its greatest exponents were noblemen themselves, but they wrote for noble patrons. Their work has the polished impersonality of the true professional, a concentration on beauty of form and skill of workmanship. Whatever the origin of their deification of women and of their spiritualized love, it fitted well into the social pattern and into the society for which they wrote. Protestation of love is very close to flattery, and the effects of love upon the male are those which might be best calculated to flatter the female ego. The best poets are able to infuse these declarations with a truly white glow of passion and pure exaltation, but such instances are relatively rare. The Provençal love lyric remains detached, occasionally ironical, sometimes almost brutal but, one suspects, rarely sincere. Its great achievements are in form, and here it is superb. It would be hard to find in European literature a period in which such tremendous strides were made in the mastery of imagery, meter, and the expression of beauty through poetic ornament. This mastery of form was the great contribution of the Provençal lyricists to literature. But the attitude to women and to love which they celebrated, sincere or not, also left an indelible mark upon European attitudes. For centuries European love lyric followed their example and treated its ladies as idealized beings, above all sensual and fleshly desire.

In most respects the lyric poetry of the trouvères of northern France is a pallid imitation of Provençal. Even the best writers, such as Blondel de Nesle (fl. 1190), Conon de Bethune (fl. 1180–1220), and Thibaut de Champagne (1201–1253), show considerably less skill in handling lyric themes than their

Provençal contemporaries. Their formal skill is very limited, nor are they as expert in the use of imagery. Only in two genres, the *pastourelle* and the crusading song, are they superior. The *pastourelle* in French literature is so well exemplified (130 as against 25 in Provençal) that there is no difficulty in tracing its development. In its simplest form it is the record of a knight who sees a peasant girl tending her sheep or merely wandering in the woods. His approach is that recommended by Andreas Capellanus. He goes up to her and frankly asks for her love; any refusal he attempts to overcome either with flattery or promises. If these fail he uses bribes and, in the last resort, physical force. At the end of the poem, he rides off laughing and enjoying the girl's discomfiture. There is nothing pretty or refined about the *pastourelle*. It is written from the point of view of the upper class and illustrates only too well the social relationship between noble and peasant. Its attitudes are as much a part of the social scene as those of the *canzon*. Probably it was thought of as a type of comic poem, and it may even have been used as a satire on courtly poetry. Certainly its subsequent development seems to point in this direction, for as the genre develops new elements are introduced. The peasant girl becomes more spirited, more determined in her resistance, and the knight often finds himself confronted with her peasant lover, Robin, and is obliged to take to his heels in the face of threats or actual beatings. The comic battle between knight and peasant thus introduces an element of burlesque, which may be seen not only in the *pastourelle* but in such musical dramas as *Robin et Marion*. The peasant gradually ceases to be an ineffective clod and stands up for himself. The *pastourelle* persisted for many centuries in various forms, but always kept the basic element of conflict between two social orders and always retained its burlesque-comic treatment.

The crusading song was originally a call to abandon all worldly things and to fight God's battle with a pure heart. The earliest in Provençal is that by Marcabru, and some thirty-five are extant, most of them serious calls to arms. The crusading songs of northern France show considerably more variety. They were perhaps influenced by the popular *chanson de toile,* the song of the woman left alone by her lover who has gone to the wars. Often the crusade is used merely as an excuse to debate the question of the effect of separation upon the poet's relations with his lady and to expound the torments of decision between service to God and service to his mistress. The idea of the separation of body and soul becomes, in this connection, almost a cliché, and many of the crusading songs are in the end little more than disguised love poems.

The lyric inspiration of northern France in the twelfth and thirteenth centuries is slight. Its greatest literary achievements were, as we have seen, in the field of romance. Not until the fourteenth century did France produce two great lyric poets, Guillaume de Machaut (c. 1300–c. 1377) and Eustache Deschamps (c. 1346–c. 1406), who developed new strophic forms and musical accompaniments (the motet is largely Machaut's invention, and both did much to standardize forms with refrain such as the virelai and ballade). Yet even these two masters show little inspiration or concern for subject matter. They treat the worn-out themes of the decay of manners and the sorrows of love and old age almost *ad nauseam.* Their principal interest lies in their comments on the contemporary scene and their personal reaction to important historical events. Both were learned men, and their poetry stands in fact closer to the tradition of medieval Latin poetry than to that of the earlier vernacular. Only François Villon can be regarded in any sense as the heir of the tradition of frank comment and real emotion found occasionally in the best of the troubadours.

A superficial glance at the German *Minnesang* reveals its absolute dependence upon French and Provençal models. A more thorough inspection makes this dependence less certain. Some French critics, such as Jeanroy, treat both German and Italian lyric poetry in the twelfth and thirteenth centuries as mere offshoots of the French. The more nationalistic critics in Germany reject any influence. Both positions are untenable, but the relationship between the lyric poetry of the two countries is not easy to determine. The existence of a school of lyric poetry in the Danube area about the middle of the twelfth century complicates matters considerably. A poet known as Der von Kürenberg, from a reference in his own works, wrote a series of lyric strophes whose order and connection is hard to determine, in the same verse form as that of the *Nibelungenlied*. There is little that is "courtly" or "spiritual" in their attitude. Several are "Frauenstrophen," written from the woman's point of view and frankly yearning for her lover. When the man speaks he makes it clear that the lady must accept him as he is or not at all. There are no servile grovelings or protestations of undying love and unrewarded service. The stress is usually on the pain of parting or the difficulty of winning love. Yet some courtly concepts can already be seen, if only in rudimentary form: the exaltation of love (although as yet unanalyzed), the presence of the jealous rival and the spy. In spite of this the man is dominant, and love is still a primitive force. The influence of Romance lyric is negligible in Kürenberg, but in Dietmar von Aist it is already more apparent. His charming *tageliet* (*alba*) has many of the characteristics of the Provençal form.[9]

French influence seems to have been first apparent in the Rhine area, as might be expected. It is marked by the emergence of the lady as an object of worship, a superior being, by the conception of *Minnedienst,* or service of love, and by the idea of the moral exaltation conveyed by love. Contemporaries believed that Heinrich von Veldecke was largely responsible for the change, but they were probably thinking rather

---

[9] The poems of these authors are to be found in *Minnesangs Frühling.* See M. Ittenbach, *Früher deutscher Minnesang* (1939).

of his adoption of Romance verse techniques. Certainly he introduces the "paysage de printemps" (*Natureingang*), but it cannot be said that his ideas of love are as yet those of the *canzon*. True affinity first appears in the works of Friedrich von Hausen, a nobleman of a distinguished family, who was certainly writing for his own amusement and not for a patron. At this point we should note one or two general points about the *Minnesänger*. Of those who are usually regarded as the best of the German lyric poets, Friedrich von Hausen, Heinrich von Morungen, and Albrecht von Johannsdorf were not, so far as we can see, professional writers but men of substance who wrote to please themselves. Reinmar received patronage from the dukes of Austria. Walther von der Vogelweide was definitely a professional. After Walther there is great variation in social circumstances. It is important, however, that the early writers were practicing poetry for its own sake. Secondly, we should note that in an age when writers went out of their way to attach themselves to an earlier authority, no important *Minnesänger* ever mentions a Romance author or acknowledges a debt to him. Moreover, the number of poems where imitation of a Romance model can be proved is insignificant. Music may well have been borrowed, but verbal imitation is very hard to demonstrate.[10]

Yet the structure of the German lyric is undeniably derived from Romance models. There is never the attempted virtuosity of Provençal poetry, although a few later authors make fools of themselves by attempts at exaggerated rhyme patterns, but the tripartite strophic form of the *canzon* is very common in the German *Liebeslied,* and it would be possible to find a Provençal model for almost every strophic form used in the *Minnesang*. The concepts of love, too, are taken from Provençal poetry. All the usual statements can be found—the humility of

[10] Texts and music of poems which show correspondences are to be found in *Trouvères und Minnesänger,* Vol. I (texts), ed. I. Frank (1952), Vol. II (music), ed. W. Müller-Blattau (1956).

the lover, the perfection of the lady, despair at rejection, and fear that to cease hoping would be worse. The ladies celebrated by the German *Minnesänger* seem, if anything, even more cruel than their Provençal counterparts. The same images can be found too—the wound of love and the cure of love, the comparison of the lady with sun and moon, the motif of the bird as messenger. Correspondences can be (and have been) found for all such things in Provençal poetry.

Yet in spite of the clear connection, the German *Minnesang* is not the same as the Provençal *canzon*. The main reason for the difference lies in a shift of emphasis. The Provençal troubadours, for the most part, sang *for* someone. Their love songs were aimed at a person and, even when this was not so, the form of the *canzon* was determined largely by the basic panegyric element. This element is obscured or completely absent in German lyric. The lady is an utterly shadowy personage, and the duty offered to her is largely formal. The poet is concerned not with the lady's feelings but with his own, and it is not too much to say that the best *Minnesang* is entirely poetry of reflexion. Hence the theme "what is *Minne?*" is very widespread in German poetry and is not a mere rhetorical question, for most lyric proceeds, in a fashion more logical than that of Provençal poetry, to analyze the poet's feelings and attitudes. The majority of poets before Walther von der Vogelweide make a distinction between *liebe,* the more natural, often sensual affection, and *Minne* the devoted, spiritualized adoration which, though it yearns for fulfillment, yet fears it, since it would end an ideal conception.[11] In the poems of true *Minne,* there is al-

---

[11] Many critics have tried to distinguish two completely different concepts. See P. Schmid, "Die Entwicklung der Begriffe 'Minne' und 'Liebe' im deutschen Minnesang bis Walther," *Zeitschrift für deutsche Philologie,* Vol. LXVI (1941); A. Moret, "Qu'est-ce que la minne? Contribution à l'étude de la terminologie et de la mentalité courtoises," *Etudes Germaniques,* Vol. IV (1949). Kolb, in *Begriff der Minne,* deals with the problem in some detail. *Niedere Minne,* ascribed to Walther, is better called natural love.

ways tension between the desire of the poet to have the lady
return his love and fear that her recognition of him will lower
her worth and thus shatter his ideal. *Minne* is thus essentially
sorrow, for it has no possible fulfillment if it is to remain
ideal.[12] Three poets and only three can be said to have written
Minnesang in its highest form—Friedrich von Hausen (fl. 1180–
90), Heinrich von Morungen (fl. 1190–1200), and Reinmar
der Alte (fl. 1180–90). The last of these brought the technique
of analysis to its perfection, a fact explicitly recognized by
several contemporaries, among them Gottfried von Strassburg.
He was chiefly renowned, in fact, for his melodies, and his
poems must have depended very largely for their effect upon a
subtle combination of word and music. His theme is always
melancholy love. He writes no *pastourelle,* no *alba,* no song of
political comment. The only variation is a beautiful elegy put
into the mouth of the widow of Duke Leopold. Reinmar worked
out a restricted, specific vocabulary of love, much narrower
than that of the Provençal poets. He played every possible variation upon his theme, with the result that all subsequent *Minnesang,* even by such poets as Ulrich von Lichtenstein and Tann-
häuser, is feeble repetition or imitation. Friedrich von Hausen
and Heinrich von Morungen show more variation. The former,
killed in the East on a crusade, wrote two or three crusading
songs in which the stock image of the separation of heart, body,
and soul takes on new life. The heart wishes to stay with the
lady, the soul to fight for God. His study of this problem is
mystical in its intensity and its language, for he sees his heart
still with his lady, safe in her keeping so that his soul may be
free for higher things. The love for his lady in this poem is
equated with his love for God. Heinrich von Morungen, though
not so subtle as Reinmar, is probably the better poet. He writes
a brilliant *Tagelied* (*alba*), not without humor, and a kind of
"courtly" *pastourelle.* His strength lies in daring images and
intensity of visualization. The *Minnelied* which follows will

---

[12] For a detailed analysis, see Kolb, *Begriff der Minne.*

demonstrate the best qualities both of the *Minnesang* and of Heinrich von Morungen's poetry. The poem makes an interesting comparison with that of Bernart de Ventadorn.

Mirst geschên als eime kindelîne,
daz sîn schônez bilde in eime glase er-
                                    sach
unde greif dar nâch sîn selbes schîne
sô vil biz daz ez den spiegel gar zerbrach.
dô wart al sîn wünne ein leitlich unge-
                                    mach.
alsô dâhte ich iemer frô ze sîne,
do ich gesach die lieben frouwen mîne
von der mir bî liebe leides vil geschach.

Minne, diu der werlde ir fröide mêret.
sêt, diu brâhte in troumes wîs die frou-
                                    wen mîn
dâ mîn lîp an slâfen was gekêret
und ersach sich an der besten wünne sîn.
dô sach ich ir werden tugende, ir liehten
                                    schîn,
schône und für alle wîp gehêret;
niwan daz ein lützel was versêret
ir vil fröiden rîchez rôtez mündelîn.

Grôze angest hân ich des gewunnen,
daz verblîchen süle ir mündelîn sô rôt.
des hân ich nu niuwer klage begunnen,
sît mîn herze sich ze solcher swêre bôt,
daz ich durch mîn ouge schouwe solche
                                    nôt,
sam ein kint daz wîsheit unversunnen
sînen schaten ersach in einem brunnen
und den minnen muose unz an sînen tôt.

Hôer wîp von tugenden und von sinne,
die enkan der himel niender ummevân,
sô die guoten diech vor ungewinne
fremden muoz und immer doch an ir
                                    bestân.

It has happened to me as to a small child which saw its beautiful reflection in a mirror and reached so hard for its own image that it broke the glass. Thus all its joy was turned to bitter sorrow. So did I think that I could be happy forever as I saw my dear lady. In loving her I have suffered great sorrow.

Love, who brings increase of joy to all the world, see, she brought my lady to me in a dream as I lay asleep and I was lost in the contemplation of my greatest joy. I saw her wonderful qualities, her bright image, beautiful beyond those of all other women; only her little red mouth, so rich in joys, was a little disturbed.

Because of this I felt great fear, that her mouth, so small, so red, should be pale. So I began a new complaint. My heart was tortured by such misery that my eyes should make me gaze upon such sadness. I was like a child who has not learned wisdom and who saw his reflection in a pool and must love it till he dies.

The heavens encompass no ladies of greater perfection and of more lofty spirit than the noble one whom I, to my misfortune, must leave and

ôwê leider, jô wând ichs ein ende hân,
ir vil wünneclichen werden minne:
nu bin ich vil kûme an dem beginne.
des ist hin mîn wünne und ouch mîn ge-
                              render wân.

yet be attached to always. Alas for me, I had hoped to have attained my goal, the winning of her sweet and worthy love. Now I find myself scarcely at the beginning, and all my joy and all my yearning thoughts are vain.

The first strophe begins with a striking use of the mirror image already discussed. At first it would appear a simple comparison—a thoughtless child, delighted by the picture it sees, attempts to grasp it and thus shatters irreparably the source of its pleasure. There are, however, deeper implications. The mirror was the symbol of perfection, the image within it ideal and unattainable, so that the poet, in trying to convert his ideal love into reality, shatters the ideal image. Perfect love can exist only in the mirror of perfection. Any attempt to grasp it physically inevitably destroys it forever. When the child sees its image, it believes that some other person is there. It does not know that the beauty is a reflection of itself and depends upon the presence of the mirror to maintain it. So the poet has failed to realize that only in the mirror of love was his joy possible. Many other associations of the mirror-image also come to mind —the deceitfulness of the mirror, its magic power to show the beloved. The intellect, too, is a mirror, for it reflects the sensory image and compares it with an ideal. In the *Abgesang* the poet makes it clear that he had believed that his ideal love could exist forever when he actually saw his lady—but all his love turned to sorrow.

The second strophe pursues the same theme, this time using the dream motif. Again the poet can contemplate the lady's ideal beauty, and admire her many virtues, but again only in imagination. Dreams, too, are unsubstantial and deceiving, and again there is a flaw in the poet's joy, for the lady's red mouth, the very symbol of her perfect beauty, is a little, a very little

disturbed. Exactly what this disturbance is, we can only guess—
pain, longing, or annoyance.

Whatever it is, the poet's joy turns to fear, fear for the loss
of ideal beauty, fear for the loss of love. His eyes again have
brought him misery, for the picture of her sorrow renews in
him all his yearning and desire. The mirror image returns, but
this time in a different form, for the pool in which the child
sees the image is indestructible and his concentration upon his
ideal love will last until death, even though the beauty remain
ever unattainable. The parallel with Narcissus is obvious: he
too died in contemplating ideal beauty, but it need hardly be
said that there is no hint of narcissism here. The stress is on
love of beauty lasting until death—a love which, as the poet
observes, is in defiance of all "wisdom."

The last strophe explains the situation of suspense in simple
terms. There can be no end to this love and no attainment. The
lady must remain forever distant and yet forever near. The beginning is the end and the end the beginning. Love is inextricably mixed with sorrow. Only the lady's high qualities could
make such a tension bearable.

The poem abounds in antitheses, especially those expressing
joy and sorrow, and significant juxtaposition of words (e.g.,
first strophe, "wünne ein leitlich ungemach"). The word *schin,*
with its double significance of "beauty" and "appearance," is
the most characteristic word in the poem, for it contains the
essential elements of the beauty and deceptiveness of light
which pervade the whole imagery. Few poets have ever used
so tellingly the associations of a series of metaphors to convey
a complex emotional state.

It is worth noting that, in the best poets of the *Minnesang,*
the *Natureingang* is the exception rather than the rule. After
Walther von der Vogelweide it becomes a rigid and exasperating
formula. The *Tagelied* is also rare, although Wolfram von
Eschenbach wrote some brilliant specimens. The earlier *Minne-*
sänger use one or two types rare or absent in Provençal litera-

ture. We have already mentioned the *Frauenstrophe* or complaint of the lady. This dies with the rise of true *Minnesang*. Another form, the *Wechsel,* is a series of strophes, where man and woman alternately express their thoughts, although they are not actually talking to one another. A variation of this type is the *Botenlied,* where the lady tells her thoughts to a messenger, thus declaring her love but maintaining the convention of distance. The man, too, can use this form. Obviously both types are connected with the *salut d'amour,* a kind of epistolary declaration of love, found in Latin and Provençal poetry. All these types became very rare in the later *Minnesang*.

It is no accident that the *Minnesang* reached the peak of its development in so short a time. Much of the metrical and poetical material was already available in French models. The peculiarly German contribution, the intensive study of the poet's attitude to pure love, was so restricted in scope that it reached its full development in a few years. The result was that the very numerous later *Minnesänger* had nothing to add. They repeated the same conventionalities and could differ from their models only in slight variations of form or emphasis. For the most part they make dreary reading. The greatest of medieval German lyric poets, perhaps the greatest lyric poet of medieval Europe, found the conventions of the *Minnesang* too irksome for his genius. Walther von der Vogelweide (*ca.* 1170–*ca.* 1228) was a professional poet in the fullest and best sense of the term. Born probably in the Tyrol, he learned the art of the *Minnesang* at the Austrian court under Reinmar. Thereafter his life was a series of sojourns at the courts of patrons until finally, in 1220, he was given a small fief near Würzburg by the Emperor Frederick II. His earliest poems are entirely in the tradition of the *Minnesang*. They are good examples of the genre but do not compare with the best of Reinmar or Heinrich von Morungen. For Walther the genre was too artificial, too narrow in scope, too unnatural. The last term is used deliberately, for

Walther restored the love poem to nature. For him, as for all great lyricists, love was a natural thing, a part of the growing world. He uses the *paysage idéal* not as a mere prologue, but as a frame within which love naturally develops. In his mature love poems the ideas of melancholy brooding, of love unfulfilled, of worship and yearning have been replaced by a frank adoration of feminine beauty, by companionship in love, and by a feeling that nature draws man and woman together into happiness. Woman is to be worshiped not because she is a distant highborn lady but because woman is God's most wonderful creation. The social and panegyric element so often noted disappears almost completely. Among Walther's most beautiful poems is a dream sequence in which he sees a beautiful woman as an integral part of nature. Walther views nature not from the conventional rhetorical viewpoint of the Latin lyric but as God's creation. He devotes many poems to a study of the natural order, sometime viewing it pessimistically as an eternal struggle, but in his love poems it is to the ideally beautiful side that he turns, and its greatest manifestation is woman.

It is for this reason that the purely courtly aspects of love receive scant attention after his youthful period of imitation. Although he praises the women of the courts, it is as women, not as noble ladies, and he is equally ready to praise their less distinguished sisters. Some critics have stated that Walther introduced the "niedere Minne" into the German lyric, by which they mean that in many of his poems he portrayed love for women not of the noble classes, thus departing from the normal practice of courtly lyric. The truth of the matter is that Walther, in his mature work, abandons such distinctions as "hohe" and "niedere" Minne, and thinks in terms of natural love. The poem most often quoted in this regard, the famous "Unter der Linden," is very difficult to interpret. It is placed in the mouth of a girl who muses over a lover's meeting in the woods. In its air of reminiscence it has elements of the dawn song, but it is joyous, not sad. In the fact that the man is obviously of superior social status to the girl there are elements of the *pastourelle*. The poem's greatest charm lies in its brilliant expression of naive trust and love and its association of love with nature. But behind it there is gentle irony. Walther brings humor and good sense back to poetry. He could not accept seriously the exaggerated protestations of courtly love, and what was not sincere he despised. Therefore all his love poems are written with charm, tenderness, and a gently lifted eyebrow. The poem "Muget ir schowen waz dem meien" is a good example. He calls on his audience to contemplate the power of the month of May —not the usual warm sun and green trees, but magic effects on everyone, young and old, layman and even cleric. They all dance and sing—but not vulgarly! Nor do the birds merely sing, they sing their best. The grass gets longer, each stalk playing the game of "I'm king of the castle" with the one next to it. The description is delightful, and a neat parody of some more ponderous efforts. In all this beauty, it is inevitable that love should follow, but there is no prostration before a cruel, distant mistress. He neatly uses the well-worn motif of the overwhelming effect of the lady's beautiful lips, but in a new and ironical way. She should stop smiling, he says, for such an action is too harsh for such a fine morning—its effects are too cruel! In fact, he goes on, her lack of kindness generally is utterly out of keeping with the beautiful day. Surely, just today, a little kindness would be in order.

The whole of this poem is a play upon the stock themes of the *Minnesang*. They are introduced in a way which robs them of all seriousness. Even the contrast between the beauty of the day and the lady's cruelty is treated with humor. The whole poem is a plea for good sense, humor, kindness, and enjoyment of nature, but, as so often in Walther, the language is very largely parodistic, a laughing travesty of more serious themes. In this use of parody, often so skillful as to seem guileless, Walther reveals that he has learned much from the medieval Latin lyric.

He has learned in other respects too. Walther is the greatest of medieval German love lyrists, but as a writer of political and moral poetry he is without a peer. Before his time there existed a type of short poem known as the *Spruch*. This was usually a sententious piece of comment on standard virtues and vices, with little reference to actual contemporary events. It is usually stated that Walther elevated this type to a dignified literary genre, but the connection between the earlier *Sprüche* and Walther's poetry is slight. In fact his political and moral poems owe much more to Latin satire and the Provençal *sirventès* than to any German type. Much of his political comment has the biting irony and verbal astringency of the best Latin poetry, but it has another element which is peculiarly his own, a high seriousness of purpose. Walther's political poetry is almost always positive in nature.[13] He urges action to support a candidate for the imperial crown, he urges the emperor himself to secure his throne. In his day three candidates struggled for power— Philip II, Otto IV, and Frederick II. Walther's support went to each of these in turn (to Otto only after Philip's death) and there is no doubt that hopes of tangible reward played some part in his decisions. But in his poetry at least his motives are beyond reproach. He wished Germany (he thought in terms of a German people) to be free of foreign interference and particularly of interference by the Roman church. Unlike the vague, if witty, accusations of the Latin satirists, his attacks on the pope are personal, savage, and specific. He believed Germany was being despoiled for the benefit of Italians, and said so. Many of his own countrymen thought he went too far. Yet he was deeply religious, and his poetry shows that he thought of the actions of the pope and the political opponents of the emperor as attacks upon an ideal order in which the will of God should be expressed on earth by the religious wisdom of the pope, the secular power of the emperor, and the kindness

[13] Details of the political situation are given in Wilmanns, *Leben und Dichten Walthers von der Vogelweide* (1882), pp. 82 ff.

and generosity of men brought up in the true tradition of courtliness. His best political poems are like trumpet calls to men of good will.

The poems of moral reflection show the same qualities. He seeks that *summum bonum* which is the goal of medieval philosophy and tries to decide how the search for wealth and worldly fame can be reconciled with the pursuit of high ideals. Order, in the best sense, is what he desires for the world, an order which conforms to God's purposes. For Walther the courtly ideal is more than mere formality and outward convention; it is rather the education of a noble man. As a result, the true nobleman should be a superior being, not merely in birth but in character and attainments. In Philip II and the young Frederick II he saw such men. But the years disillusioned him. He saw his ideals polluted, the courts filled with parvenus and men of base motives and baser character. Thus in his last poems he laments the passing of a period of great ideals, the end of courtly song and true religious fervor. He was right. His laments were not merely those of an old man praising the time of his youth, for the great period was over.

Walther is by far the most versatile of medieval lyric poets. He surpasses all his German contemporaries in variety of language, fertility of imagination, feeling for nature, and power of invective. Although he uses the fully developed strophic forms both for his songs and his *Sprüche* (the latter often of only one strophe), he rarely seeks to display virtuosity of technique. On the contrary, his language is deceptively simple and gains great strength from its clarity and firmness. Walther's debt to the Bible, to Latin poetry, and to Provençal is obvious, but his greatness lies in his grasp of man's place in the universe and in his search in poetry for the ideal in love and the ideal in social life. Walther, the professional poet, realizes more clearly than any other writer the motivating forces of the Hohenstaufen courtly ideal. The following poem is a mixture of reflection and politics.

Ich saz ûf eime steine
und dahte bein mit beine:
dar ûf satzt ich den ellenbogen:
ich hete in mîne hant gesmogen
daz kinne und ein mîn wange.
dô dâhte ich mir vil ange,
wie man zer welte solte leben:
deheinen rât kond ich gegeben,
wie man driu dinc erwurbe
der keines niht verdurbe.
diu zwei sint êre und varnde guot,
daz dicke ein ander schaden tuot:
daz dritte ist gotes hulde,
der zweier übergulde.
die wolte ich gerne in einen schrîn.
jâ leider desn mac niht gesîn,
daz guot und weltlich êre
und gotes hulde mêre
zesamene in ein herze komen.
stîg unde wege sint in benomen:
untriuwe ist in der sâze,
gewalt vert ûf der strâze:
fride unde reht sint sêre wunt.
diu driu enhabent geleites niht, diu
          zwei enwerden ê gesunt.

Ich hôrte ein wazzer diezen
und sach die vische fliezen,
ich sach swaz in der welte was,
velt walt loup rôr unde gras.
swaz kriuchet unde fliuget
und bein zer erde biuget,
daz sach ich, unde sage iu daz:
der keinez lebet âne haz:
daz wilt und daz gewürme
die strîtent starke stürme,
sam tuont die vogel under in;
wan daz si habent einen sin:
si dûhten sich ze nihte
si enschüefen starc gerihte.
sie kiesent künege unde reht,
si setzent hêrren unde kneht.
sô wê dir, tiuschiu zunge,
wie stêt dîn ordenunge!
daz nû diu mugge ir künec hât,
und daz dîn êre alsô zergât.

I sat upon a stone and crossed one leg over the other, rested my elbow on it and propped my chin and one cheek on my hand. Then I thought hard about how a man should live in this world. I could find no way of attaining three things without destroying one of them. Two of these are honor and the goods of this world, which are often at odds with one another. The third is the worship of God, which exceeds in worth the other two. All three I would gladly have together in one chest, but this cannot be, for goods and honor in this world cannot be together in one heart with worship of God. There is no path or road for them there. Treachery lies in ambush, violence roams the streets. Peace and justice are gravely wounded. If these two are not sound, the three can never be protected.

I heard the sound of water, I saw the fishes swim. Everything in the world I saw, field, wood, leaves, reeds, and grass. Whatever creeps and flies or bends its legs upon the earth, all this I saw and I say to you: not one of these lives without enmity. Wild beasts and creeping things are engaged in heavy fighting, and so too are the birds among themselves. But in one thing they show good sense. They would think themselves lost if they did not have a definite order. They choose kings and laws, they appoint lords and servants. Alas for you German people, how is it with your order! The flies have their king and your honor dies! Repent, repent. It is the minor nobles who

bekêrâ dich, bekêre.
die cirkel sint ze hêre,
die armen künege dringent dich:
Philippe setze en weisen ûf, und
    heiz si treten hinder sich.

Ich sach mit minen ougen
mann unde wîbe tougen,
daz ich gehôrte und gesach
swaz iemen tet, swaz iemen sprach.
ze Rôme hôrte ich liegen
und zwêne künege triegen.
dâ von huop sich der meiste strît
der ê was oder iemer sît,
dô sich begunden zweien
die pfaffen unde leien.
daz was ein nôt vor aller nôt:
lîp unde sêle lac dâ tôt.
die pfaffen striten sêre:
doch wart der leien mêre.
diu swert diu leiten si dernider
und griffen zuo der stôle wider:
si bienen die si wolten
und niht den si solten.
dô stôrte man diu goteshûs.
ich hôrte verre in einer klûs
vil michel ungebaere:
dâ weinte ein klôsenaere,
er klagete gote sîniu leit,
"owê der bâbest ist ze junc: hilf,
    hêrre, dîner kristenheit."

rule, the petty kings who oppress
you. Philip, put on the imperial
crown and bid them get behind you.

I looked with my eyes into the secrets of men and women, so that I
heard and saw what everyone did
and said. In Rome I heard them
lying and deceiving two kings.
From this arose the greatest strife
that had ever been as the priests
and the laity disagreed. That was a
disaster worse than all disasters.
Body and soul lay there dead. The
priest struggled hard, but the laymen were their masters. Then the
priests laid down their swords and
turned back to the stole. They put
the ban on those whom they dislike, not on those who deserve it.
Thus the house of God was deso-
late. Far off in his cell I heard a
hermit cry out in great misery as
he poured out his sorrows to God:
"Alas, the Pope is too young: help,
Lord, your Christian people."

This poem, one of the most famous and most typical of
Walther's poems of comment on the contemporary social and
political scene, was written almost certainly in two parts, the
first two strophes in 1198, the second in 1201. The dates can
be determined by the references to the support of Otto IV, the
rival of Philip II for the imperial throne, by Pope Innocent III
and to the excommunication of Philip, which, by implication,
affected all his supporters. Richard I of England, one of the
petty kings alluded to in the second strophe and Otto's principal
supporter, had died in 1199, so that the lines must have been
written before then. On the other hand, Innocent III did not

openly espouse Otto's cause until 1201, so that it would hardly be possible for Walther to allude so openly to his deception of "two kings" (Philip and the young Frederick) before that time.

The poem is written deliberately in a metrical form usually reserved for narrative poetry, namely, rhyming couplets, thus giving an air of smoothness and detachment to the whole. But there is more art in this form than meets the eye. The lines are arranged in alternating pairs of which the first pair has three main stresses and one secondary stress on the final syllable, the second four main stresses. The strophe ends with an extra four-stress line, making a total of twenty-five lines and one hundred stresses in each strophe. The additional line of four beats is of great importance as an expression of the poet's own view, and the three taken together show that only under Philip's leadership can there be a restoration of moral stability.

Walther's purpose is clearly to attack the interference by the papacy and by priests in general on what he regards as the internal affairs of Germany. He does this more directly in several other poems; here he is concerned much more with the general principle involved—the disturbance of the social order by unjustified meddling with natural forces. The poem is in this respect very different from the attacks made in Latin poetry on the papacy, by which Walther is otherwise considerably influenced. It is not corruption at the Curia which he is attacking, but something much more fundamental, the claim of the Church to determine political issues and to govern men rather than guide them.

The poet's devices to make his attack effective repay examination. He assumes at the beginning of the first strophe the traditional posture of contemplation and reflection, thus informing the reader that he is writing calmly and judicially. It is in this posture that he is shown in the famous miniature in the "Manessa" manuscript. His thoughts in the first strophe are entirely concerned with abstract questions and in particular with that which most occupied the thoughts of the greatest of those who wrote within the courtly tradition, namely, the balancing of worldly goods and of worldly fame against the full worship of God. There is no need to attempt a neat equation of these three with the classical *utile, honestum,* and *summum bonum,* although there can be little doubt that, whether consciously or not, the connection was felt. Walther is trying to evolve not a philosophical system but a way of living. He sees that a man might well desire all three, and that the fulfillment of such a desire could bring perfect happiness but, under the conditions he is living in, such a reconciliation is impossible. It is important to notice that at the end of the strophe he makes it clear that it is the state of the world that makes the reconciliation impossible. The last two lines point to the lack of "geleit," of protection by the powers that should protect the virtues.

This leads by a neat transition to the second strophe which, as so often happens in Walther's poetry, relates man to nature. Still in his role as contemplative seer, the poet has a vision of nature and sees how each creature has its appointed place and its appointed function. The echoes of the language in which the creation is described are unmistakable. This order of nature is not an idealized state, but one in which the creatures fight as fiercely as men. They do, however, have leaders who can impose order and prevent the chaos into which man is descending. At this point the pose of seer is cast off. In a sudden cry to the German people, Walther abandons impersonal contemplation and utters the cry of the prophet: "Repent before it is too late." It is not of Hell he is thinking, however, but of political extinction. It is the miserable princelings who wish to reign where the emperor alone should rule. From the people Walther turns to Philip and asks him to assume the imperial crown with its single large diamond above the neck. To see this diamond the princelings must be where order demands that they should be, behind the emperor. This strophe must have been written before Philip's coronation took place in September, 1198. It would have formed a fitting conclusion, for Walther has shown that contemplative wisdom and natural order itself call on Philip to assume his role as emperor and hence lawgiver to the German people.

It is worth noting how simple and direct the language in the second strophe is. Line after line has a verb at or near its beginning, as the poet drives home his point about the active elements in nature and their positive steps to ensure order. Walther avoids anything rhetorical. He is appealing for action, not thought.

The third strophe resumed the calm observation of life in a more pessimistic tone. The situation has changed. Philip is emperor, but the order which is so sorely needed has not returned. Walther leaves no doubt about the responsibility. With his seer's ability to penetrate into men's hearts, he knows that the unchristian ambition of the Curia is to blame. Its members use for political ends the weapons of excommunication and interdict which should be reserved for spiritual offenses, and thus destroy the very Church which they should protect. Characteristically it is a simple man of religion who cries out against the abuses—not a priest. The pope was indeed young—forty years of age in 1201—but Walther's opinion of him in other poems makes it clear that he held him responsible for the deeds of the papacy. The hermit is perhaps too simple in heart to perceive it.

Although the third strophe was written three years after the other two, it provides an excellent climax, for Walther moves from abstraction to nature and from nature to personal leadership, and so with devastating effect lashes out at those who reverse nature by undermining leadership in the name of religion. Walther was a religious man, but the political activities of the papacy were contrary to his deeply rooted love for Germany. Opinions may differ about the justice of his attacks.[14] Of their sincerity there can be no doubt. In this poem he gives expression to the finest of political sentiments—the use of leadership to attain for everyone the finest development of his bodily

[14] Walther's attacks are deplored by Thomasin von Zirclaere, ed. H. Rückert (1852), vv. 1163 ff.

and spiritual powers. The simple, sincere, and dignified language raises the treatment to a high level of lyric poetry, for the formal medieval concept of God's established order is made human by the poet's feeling for man within nature and the need for high spiritual values to enable him to fulfill his purpose on earth and prepare his soul for Heaven.

Walther's influence on subsequent writers was enormous but, as might be expected, they imitated only the outward forms. The *Minnesang* degenerated into a repetition of clichés. The more natural attitude to love which Walther had introduced led, even in his own lifetime to "peasant" poetry, in which love making between peasants was portrayed with the trappings usual for courtly love making. Walther deplored this element of crudity, but it was brilliantly used by Neidhart von Reuental and other writers. The poetry they wrote had apparently two objects: to ridicule the elaborate courtly formulas by putting them into the mouths of crude peasants and to satirize peasants by showing them trying to rise above their station. Neidhart's parodies are often brilliant and graphically realistic, but they show how far the notion of courtly ideals had sunk. A courtly audience was apparently quite content to see them unmercifully pilloried. The most lively element in the lyric poetry of the thirteenth century is this peasant parody of the *Minnesang*. The formal lyric became petrified and passed ultimately into the hands of the *Meistersinger* and formal pedantry.

Provençal troubadours visited Italy at a comparatively early date. Raimbaut de Vaqueiras was there about 1180; Peire Vidal was at home in Italian courts. The first Italian imitators wrote in Provençal, for example, Cigala and Sordello, but in the middle of the thirteenth century a school developed at the court of the Emperor Frederick II at Palermo which imitated in Italian the more extreme exaggerations of Provençal style. Their importance lies less in their intrinsic merit than in the service they performed in shaping the Italian language for lyric poetry. Here Giacomo da Lentino wrote the first sonnets. In

THE MEDIEVAL LYRIC

Florence there also arose a school of poets, headed by Guittone d'Arezzo, and it was here that the influence of scholastic philosophy made itself felt in an increasing tendency to write poetry in a philosophical, learned style. This style is the "dolce stil novo," in so far as an accurate definition of the term can be given. The poets themselves refused to clarify their methods or even to explain their deliberate obscurities. Only from Dante's works can their poetry be, at least in part, understood. They were interested in love as a phenomenon, not an emotion. (The *Minnesänger* had preceded them in this, but with far less conscious philosophical background.) Women as persons cease to have much importance. Guido Cavalcanti and his associates were writing for a small group of intimates and were apparently intent upon impressing one another with the subtlety of their analyses and the difficulty of their language. We can be impressed but hardly moved by the result.[15]

English lyric poetry stands largely aloof from Continental developments. The influence of the better-known Latin hymns appears to have been considerable, and there must, of course, have been considerable contact with the French lyric written at the Anglo-Norman court. Yet the earliest vernacular lyric of the thirteenth and fourteenth century is of a simplicity both of theme and form which appears close to folk poetry. A great deal of the lyric material is religious, celebrating the principal Christian feasts and persons. It is generally unsophisticated and lacks, for the most part, the conscious allegorization common in Latin hymns. The secular poetry is often poetry of spring and nature, but the elements are not those of the formal *paysage idéal* but rather of the English countryside. The love poems show little trace of courtly influence or of

[15] See L. di Benedetto, *Rimatori del dolce stil novo* (1939); F. Figurelli, *Il dolce stil novo* (1933), *Poeti del dolce stil novo* (1945); F. A. Ugolini, *La poesia provenzale e l'Italia* (1939); M. Valency, *In Praise of Love* (1958); K. Vossler, *Die philosophischen Grundlagen des süssen neuen Stils* (1904).

the idealization of love, largely, no doubt, because of the separation of the English language from court circles. The English lyric thus has a pleasing naïveté and simple charm, but also a monotony of theme and lack of technical skill. Subsequent English literature drew upon the tradition, but it was without influence outside its homeland.

The twelfth century was one of the great periods of lyric poetry in the history of European literature. The forms and themes which had been slowly developing in Latin literature came to full flower. The vernaculars adopted many of these forms and improved upon them. The lyric was adapted to the needs of a sophisticated, closely knit society, and limited itself to a few highly wrought and specialized types in which excellence of technique and beauty of melody were probably regarded as more important than variety of theme or sincerity of sentiment. A few poets rose above these "requirements" and enlarged the conventional framework to produce great poetry. To them the theme of idealized love was not merely a subject for formal celebration and the embroidery of stylized images, but a matter for emotional speculation and poetic analysis. In the few instances where this search for idealized love is combined with technical excellence, great poetry is the result. The importance of this lyric poetry for European literature can hardly be exaggerated. The vernaculars were shown to be capable of the most refined subtleties of expression and the most complicated verse techniques. The problem of the expression of love in lyric poetry was solved so well that subsequent generations adopted the solution almost as a matter of course, and European manners to this day reflect the attitude to Woman which was exalted in the lyric of Provence.

9

The Drama

To the modern reader it may well seem incredible that the drama, brought to what many would regard as its point of greatest achievement in fifth-century Athens, and continued throughout Hellenistic and Roman times, could disappear from Western Europe for centuries and be revived only in a long slow development from liturgical formulas and religious tropes. Yet there is much evidence that such was, in fact, the case. Isidore of Seville shows in his definitions of comedy and tragedy that he has no idea of the dramatic elements which are their essential constituents; to him all spectacles are alike and all equally reprehensible.[1] Texts of Plautus and even more of Terence were available throughout the Middle Ages, and Terence at least was frequently read, but comment and illustration both appear to indicate that his plays were regarded merely as a type of monologue to be rhetorically declaimed.[2] It is quite certain that classical comedies were never performed in the

---

[1] In his *Etymologiae*, XVIII. xlv, xlvi. See also Tertullian, *De spectaculis*, especially Chapter X, in Migne, *PL.*, I, 702 ff.

[2] For discussion and sources, see Frank, *Medieval French Drama*, pp. 1 ff., and Creizenach, *Geschichte des neueren Dramas*, pp. 1 ff. References to Terence by authors in the early Middle Ages are listed by Manitius, *Geschichte der lateinischen Literatur des Mittelalters*, Vol. I; the transmission is discussed on p. 251.

modern sense. There is virtually no indication that classical tragedy was read at all.

In spite of all this evidence, however, it is hard to accept the complete disappearance of any idea of a dramatic performance. Several writers of the Middle Ages wrote plays deliberately modeled on those of Terence. The most famous of these authors was Hroswitha of Gandersheim, of whom more will be said later, but there were others too—Vitalis of Blois wrote, probably in the eleventh century, a comedy called *Geta,* similar to Plautus' *Amphitryo,* and an *Aulularia.* Both of these were fashioned after works wrongly ascribed to Plautus. There were also numerous "elegiac" comedies, learned nondramatic pieces, but with the appearance of *Babio,* probably written in England in the twelfth century, we are very close to the classical comedy of the miserly old man. Was their imitation merely mechanical, or did they have some idea of performance? The question is unlikely ever to be answered, but there are other aspects of drama which repay examination. We may be quite certain, for example, that the fertility plays of spring, the comedies of the harvest, and the midwinter festivals flourished throughout the Middle Ages. They remained unwritten because they were condemned by the clergy as pagan, which indeed they were. Patient investigation has discovered scores of such plays and many of them are performed to this very day. Such "plays" are not, of course, real drama. They are merely dramatic symbols of primal elements of man's relation to nature. But they were acted, and they kept alive among the unlettered the idea of dramatic representation. Many of them contained genuine elements of comedy—the Feast of Fools and the Boy Bishop, in particular, are examples of one of comedy's stock situations, the undignified reversal of social norms. Contemporary events and religious legend brought new elements to these plays. The Crusades brought the conflict of Saracen and Christian, played with suitable slapstick; legend provided in England the figure of St. George. The evil spirits who figure in so many of the plays provided many of the characteristics of the devils who appear later in the Easter dramas, and their origin accounts for many of their comic characteristics and even for their appearance. The devils' masks are surely pagan in origin.

The existence of these dramatic representations can hardly be disputed, but there have been wide differences of opinion as to the extent to which they affected the growth of genuine drama. It is clear that they affected comedy much more than tragedy and that they affected characterization much more than plot or structure. By themselves they could hardly have produced drama in the true sense of the term, for they lacked the interest and support of educated men and of the Church and state. It was this support which had led to the amazing development of Greek drama.

Even more obscure—and perhaps more important—is the role of the successors of the professional actors of classical antiquity. Actors had never enjoyed a high social status in Rome, although there were witty men among them, such as Publilius Syrus, who enjoyed the friendship of the great. Under the Empire their reputation sank still lower beneath the attacks of the satirists and the detestation of the growing Christian community. The mime was the most popular dramatic performance under the Empire, and it often was closer to the circus or vaudeville than to dramatic art. Yet its exponents were professionals, often of great skill, and it is inconceivable that the demise of the formal theater meant the extinction of professional entertainers as a class. The evidence for their existence is to be found in the frequent attacks of the Church upon them, in the exhortations to the priest who performed a wedding to leave before the "actors" took over, so as to avoid being involved in scandal. The example of the modern circus proves how strong family tradition is in professional entertainment and how certain tricks and acts continue from one generation to another. There is no reason to believe that the situation was otherwise in the Middle Ages. The professional entertainer preserved those roles which were standard in the New Comedy and in the mime for centuries—the foolish and doting father, the truculent boaster, the parasitical hanger-on, the miserly husband, and the loose wife. Such types are not part of the religious drama or of seasonal festivals. Yet they appear with remarkable speed as soon as the drama revives. The boasting soldiers provided broad humor at the sepulcher of Christ; the devil himself is very much like them. The scene in which the three Maries buy unguents from a peddler is developed so that it becomes a separate comedy of the old husband, the loose wife, and the tricky servant. It is hard to escape the feeling that professional actors were bringing to the plays stock characters and scenes which were part of their repertoire and had been so for centuries. The influence of classical comedy on medieval drama is perhaps most strongly felt through the remote successors of the actors who had played their roles, for it is not until the fifteenth century that the literary influence of the classical drama can again be perceived.

It would, of course, be foolish to deny that observations of his own milieu by a gifted author could not be incorporated into a drama. The brilliant tavern scenes in Jean Bodel's *Jeu de St. Nicholas* are in themselves sufficient proof. Yet it must also be realized that such observations could effect at most the realistic depiction of certain scenes. They could not produce drama or shape dramatic form. For the growth of drama some tradition was needed, some framework within which it could grow. For the Middle Ages this framework could and did come from two main sources—the classical tradition already discussed and the ceremonies and traditions of the Christian church. Both were influenced by oral tradition and popular performance but in the last resort only the church could give to the drama sufficient respectability to allow it to develop as a literary form.

The development of "church" drama, which includes liturgical dramatizations, extended Easter and Christmas tropes, Easter and Passion plays, prophet plays and legends, has been frequently described. The casual reader can easily receive a false impression from the somewhat oversimplified accounts of its development. These accounts run somewhat as follows. During the early Middle Ages it became the custom to insert in the celebration of the Mass on Easter Sunday, before the *Introit,* a "trope," or short Latin verse, which was sung by two half-choirs in alternation and which, in its simplest form, involved a question by the angel at the tomb of Christ and a reply by the three Maries who visited the tomb on Easter morning. The angel asked "Quem quaeritis, mulieres?" (Whom do you seek, women?) and they answered "Jesum Nazarenum, crucifixum." The angel then told them that Christ was risen, and they rejoiced. The words are not taken from the Bible, but they are similar to those found in Matthew 27, Mark 16, Luke 24, and John 17. Such tropes were not uncommon in various services of the church. Indeed, numerous attempts were made to stop their excessive proliferation. Nor were they essentially more dramatic than other parts of the mass, which, as Karl Young points out, is itself a type of dramatic symbolism. Originally and for a long period the music was of far more importance than the words or any dramatic gestures. Easter, however, is a dramatic event in the Christian year, and it is a feast at which more people are present in church than at any other time. Ceremonies not directly attached to the liturgy sprang up—the *Adoratio Crucis,* the Deposition of the Cross (or Host) on Good Friday, the Elevation of the Cross (or Host) at Easter. Such ceremonies could be dramatized the more easily because they were not part of the formal service of the church. From the tenth century on there are many manuscripts from all parts of Europe of a dramatized office (usually called *Visitatio Sepulchri*), which incorporated the various Easter tropes and which was performed after Matins on Easter Sunday. Since it was now detached from the Mass, more freedom was possible and more dramatic elements were introduced. A "sepulcher" was constructed near the altar, the angel sat above it or near it, the Maries walked up to it and so on.[3] The tropes were extended, first by the addition of mere words, presumably in order to increase the amount of singing, then by the addition of new scenes: the meeting with Jesus as gardener, the arrival of the apostles and their haste to visit the tomb, and the meeting with Christ on the Emmaus road. Although the texts are never quoted exactly from the Vulgate, the scenes in these early representations are always those described in the New Testament. An important liturgical text which became part of the Visitatio was the *Victimae Paschali,* in which the Maries are questioned about what they had seen. It was retained in the later vernacular Passion plays. That there was some attempt to represent them dramatically we know from stage directions such as the following, from the *Ordo Paschalis* of Klosterneuburg: "Then let the soldiers go around the Sepulchre singing." "And then in silence the angel should draw his sword and chanting 'Alleluia, the Victor is risen from Hell' he should strike one of the soldiers with his sword and they should all fall flat upon the ground." "The soldiers should remain lying on the ground as if dead. Then Mary with the others should come to buy spices and should sing." "The spice-merchant should reply and *do his business.*" "When they have bought the spices, they go to the Sepulchre singing in unison." When Christ goes to Hell, he should "break down the doors with great force." All this implies some properties and some action by the players. At this stage, however, such feeling as there is comes from the nature of the Biblical scenes and their associations rather than from any added element of drama.

An important step forward was taken with the introduction of scenes which are merely mentioned in the Biblical account

---

[3] The word "sepulchrum," so frequently used in stage directions, is hard to define. Sometimes it clearly refers to the altar but it can also be a specially constructed "cave," put up in the choir or a symbolic sepulcher in the transept. Close examination of many rubrics shows how hard it is to obtain accurate information without the context possessed by contemporaries. See N. C. Brooks, *The Sepulchre of Christ in Art and Liturgy* (1921).

or which have to be assumed from it. Of these the best known is the scene in which the three Maries buy unguents from a peddler. Originally the scene is innocent enough, and the peddler says nothing or merely makes a formal remark that he has unguents to sell. But the scene is expanded. Mary Magdalene is shown in her unregenerate state, buying cosmetics to seduce men, and is turned to a holier purpose. The unguent seller bargains with the women; he acquires a wife who abuses him for giving them too favorable a price and (as we shall see), the whole scene gets out of hand and becomes a separate low comedy episode quite out of harmony with the solemnity of the occasion. It is significant that this scene was the first to be played in the vernaculars.

Other scenes were introduced, many of them dependent not upon Biblical accounts but upon the Apocrypha, and in particular upon the enormously popular *Gospel* of *Nicodemus.* Christ's descent into Hell and the releasing of the patriarchs of the Old Testament, already officially sanctified in the Apostles' Creed, became an important scene. Other scenes were added, particularly the attempts of the Jews to persuade Pilate to guard the tomb of Christ, and the failure of the soldiers to do so. Needless to say, this expansion necessitated the removal of the drama from the altar. There is some evidence that side chapels were used for such performances but, as they expanded and developed vernacular additions, they were banished from the church altogether and were performed on temporary staging outside the church door.

This neat account is pleasant to read and sounds very reasonable but a few words of warning are necessary. First it should be noted that only in France and Germany can we produce substantial evidence of the nonliturgical additions. The Winchester book of tropes is one of the earliest pieces of evidence of the existence of Easter tropes, but there is little more evidence of such activity in England. The famous cycle plays, which will be discussed later, seem to have developed independently, although probably under the influence of French models. There is very little evidence of dramatic activity in Spain or Italy (except for a few examples from the north). Even in France and Germany, it is hard to find continuous development in any one place. The manuscripts are often of little help in deciding the date of introduction of a particular feature, for a fifteenth-century codex may often record a tradition dating from the eleventh. All that can be said is that evidence can be produced, mostly from northern France, the Low Countries, and Germany, for each of the stages mentioned in the account. The *Visitatio* is attested in manuscripts from the tenth to the fifteenth century. The apostles' visit first appears in a twelfth-century manuscript, the Mary Magdalene scene in one of the thirteenth. In some churches, no doubt, the dramatization never progressed beyond the original trope. In others, under the direction of some livelier spirit (or secular influences), quick progress was made. Undoubtedly churches must have heard of what others had done and have copied it. Schools and similar institutions copied plays too. It is quite certain that it is in those areas from which we have most evidence of secular dramatic activity that most of the religious manuscripts come.

It is very doubtful whether the Easter tropes, and their counterparts at Christmas, could ever have led to the development of drama in any real sense of the term. The severe restrictions on the characters and their actions prevented any real expansion beyond a few tricks of staging and verbal variation. The real development comes with the introduction of extraneous material from the Apocrypha and the development of the non-Biblical scenes. Why were these scenes introduced? To us it seems obvious that such characters as the *unguentarius* were bound to strike a discordant note in a religious "drama," but there is no evidence that the medieval church believed this. There was more tolerance of such elements than we like to believe. But the introduction of scenes written in the vernacular and deliberately comic in nature is another matter. Such scenes could hardly be played by the priests, monks, nuns, and deacons who, as we know, had sung the original, simpler forms. They were designed to be understood, not merely listened to. It seems highly probable that, in some areas, professional actors were called in to perform the plays and that they used the opportunity to introduce some of their own repertoire in the shape of the swindling merchant, his shrewish wife, and his rascally assistant, Rubin (Robin of the French *pastourelle* tradition).

It is significant that there are very few fully developed Easter plays written entirely in Latin. A thirteenth-century manuscript from Tours and the examples in the Fleury play book are the only surviving French plays; from Germany we have those from Benediktbeuern and Klosterneuburg. The Easter play, in fact, does not become a real dramatic performance until it acquires extraneous elements and is performed largely in the vernacular. The transition may easily be seen in the manuscripts from Origny, where much of the dialogue is in French, and in those from Trier (fourteenth or fifteenth century) and Wolfenbüttel (fifteenth century), where German "translations" are given. Such plays as those from Muri (thirteenth century), Innsbruck (1391), and Vienna (1472), written in German, follow the same general lines as the Latin plays, but with much more vivacity of dialogue and situation.

A short account of the Innsbruck play will best indicate the stage of development reached by the transitional plays. The manuscript is dated 1391; the text indicates that the play was written in the second quarter of the fourteenth century. The original form is much older, and lines of Latin, presumably from an earlier version, are scattered through the text. After a brief introduction Pilate appears with his court and is petitioned by the Jews in an extraordinary mixture of languages to set a watch at the grave of Christ. A messenger is sent to fetch soldiers who, suitably bribed, guard the sepulcher, fall asleep, and later complain bitterly when the grave is found to be empty. The Descent into Hell is at first handled with becoming solemnity, but after the release of the patriarchs the influence of popular plays makes itself felt. A baker, condemned to Hell for short weight, is caught by the Devil as he tries to sneak out, and other butts of popular discontent, a shoemaker, a butcher, and a priest, are made to confess their sins. The mood again becomes serious with the appearance of the three Maries, but the riotous *unguentarius* scene which follows well illustrates the reasons why the Church authorities felt obliged to issue injunctions against the drama. The spice merchant is represented as a seller of quack medicines. He chooses a vagabond, Rubin, as his assistant, who proclaims his master's extraordinary powers of healing with all the tricks usually associated with such performances. He has an assistant, Pusterbalk, with whom a violent fight soon develops, and his old friend, an ugly customer known as Lasterbalk, keeps the fun going with a "love declaration" to Antonia, the spice merchant's wife and, after being refused, by impersonating a member of the medicant orders. Meanwhile Rubin mixes an impossible potion for his master and livens the negotiations between the merchant and the three Maries with his jokes. After their departure there is the usual violent quarrel between the merchant and his wife, and this leads naturally to the final departure of Antonia with Rubin, leaving the merchant to bewail his loss. There follows immediately the scene with the angel at the grave and the serious part of the Easter play.

Throughout the play Latin text is used for the serious parts, immediately followed by a free German adaptation. Serious music accompanies the religious scenes. But it must be clear that for most of the audience the comedy was the most important part of the show, and this comedy clearly incorporates traditional scenes already developed by the strolling actors.

In France, on the other hand, the vernacular Easter play seems to have been uncommon. The closest extant version is that usually called *La Seinte Resurection,* written in England in the twelfth century and surviving in two manuscripts, which is fragmentary and combines numerous liturgical, Biblical, and

Apocryphal elements in describing the negotiations for the burial of the body of Jesus and the watch over the tomb. It is written in Anglo-Norman, and probably for a popular audience, but is far from the vigorous representation found in the (later) German plays. French dramatic genius found a more congenial outlet in other forms.

Easter was not the only season at which dramatized tropes and offices were performed. There is early evidence of such performances at Christmas—the *Officium Stellae* or play of the arrival of the Three Kings at Christ's crib, and the *Officium Pastorum* or Shepherds' play. These two, originally separate, were combined into a Christmas representation. Except in England the former was immeasurably more important. In the separate performances (originally preceding the *Introit* in the Mass on Christmas Day and Epiphany respectively, later transferred to Matins) and in the combined form the action was very simple, consisting merely of the revelation of the infant Christ to the shepherds and the Magi by priests representing midwives. But as early as the eleventh century the figure of Herod appeared, at first as a sober king (as in the texts from Nevers) but soon developing those characteristics of wild anger and cruelty which became traditional. In the Compiègne version (eleventh century) the full Christmas story is told: the Magi visit Herod, are warned to return by another route, and an invented character, the armor-bearer, advises Herod to slaughter the innocents. In a few later plays the slaughter is actually dramatized (the *Ordo Rachelis*). The most elaborate Continental Christmas play is that from Benediktbeuern, which combines the various dramatizations already mentioned with the Prophet play (found separately in France and Germany). Here we find long disputes between Augustine, as chief of the prophets, and the leaders of the Jews about such points as the possibility of a virgin birth. They are followed appropriately by the events of the Christmas season and the wrath of Herod. Numerous comic elements found in this play have caused speculation

that it may show the influence of the numerous burlesque performances, such as the Boy Bishop and the Feast of Fools,
which scandalized sober churchmen during the Christmas season.
Once again we see that the livelier elements of the dramatization proceed from elements imported into the sacred observ-
ances from secular and even pagan sources.

Except for a remarkable development in England, the Christmas plays remain limited in scope and generally lacking in
drama. Nor do the Easter plays progress beyond the limits already described. Ultimately they were merged into the dramatizations of the whole season of Passiontide, which in their turn
were extended backward and forward in time until they often
encompassed events ranging from the fall of man to the Day
of Judgment. Such "Passion plays" naturally incorporated already established dramatic representations—incidents of the
Old Testament, such as the Daniel play to be discussed below,
and plays about the various prophets. The incidents of the
Passion itself must have been the subject of Latin offices, but
little evidence survives. It is likely that such events as the betrayal by Judas, the trial of Jesus, the Crucifixion, the death of
Judas, and the denying of Christ by Peter were added in most
cases to existing Easter Plays. The earliest surviving examples
(the most important of them again from Benediktbeuern) deal
with events immediately before and after the Crucifixion and
Resurrection, and the longer Benediktbeuern play has vernacular passages of some length. The development of the full "Passion play" was gradual, and long before it reached its full flower
in the fourteenth and fifteenth centuries the circumstances of
dramatic performances had vastly changed.

The Easter and Christmas tropes and plays had been performed by clerics and deacons in church. Originally the scene
had, of course, been the altar. The early forms were closer to
oratorio than drama, and were dignified tableaux with little action and much music. Costumes were those of the services, but
as rich and handsome as could be arranged. As the plays de-

veloped and were detached from the services, they were probably moved, sometimes to the nave, sometimes to a side chapel. So long as they retained their religious character, they continued to be performed in the church, but the constant addition of extraneous and comic elements must have rendered the more developed forms totally unsuitable for presentation in a religious building. Moreover, their function had become different. They were felt to be material which aroused interest in religion, but they were not directly connected with the offices and liturgy. In this they had much in common with the feast of Corpus Christi, instituted in 1264, a feast held at a period of the year (May or June) when fine weather might be expected and the pageantry of ritual could be shown in the open air. It soon became customary for short plays to be included in the celebrations, and during the thirteenth and fourteenth centuries the developed Easter plays began to be performed at this season not by clerics, deacons, and other members of religious orders but by groups of laymen. Such groups may well have taken part in plays performed on special stages just inside the west door of the church and later on similar stages outside the church. Exact information on the transitional period is lacking, and doubtless plays were performed inside and outside the church at the same period. We know, for example, of a highly complex performance of the *Presentation of the Virgin* at Avignon in the fourteenth century which was performed on an elaborate stage within the church, but at this time it is quite definite that many dramatic ventures had been moved outside.

It has often been said that the increasing use of the vernacular was the main reason for the "banishment," but it is more likely that the scenes which could be played only in the vernacular were the real cause. For they changed the whole character of the play. Instead of merely listening, the audience could understand, it demanded more, and it expected to be amused. The result of these various factors was the elaboration of the Easter and Passion plays into the long, combined plays involving almost any part of Christian tradition and spoken (not sung) entirely in the vernacular. These plays gradually passed into the hands of various civic organizations, and in England, particularly, into the hands of the guilds. At this point it is probably better to describe the performances as "Mystery plays," an odd but traditionally sanctified term of origin still unexplained. It is doubtful whether there was any real distinction between the terms *mysterium* (confused with *ministerium*), "miracle," and numerous other terms.[4] They are all very broad in scope and include the true Passion plays as well as the longer versions.

Since there is no clear line of development, it will probably be best to describe a few representative plays from several countries which incorporate and dramatize events of Christian history, as distinct from plays about saints' lives, which form a separate category. Of the plays appearing in France one of the earliest and most significant is the *Mystère d'Adam*. Written in Anglo-Norman between 1146 and 1174, this play was probably intended to show how the Old Testament prefigured the salvation of the world by Christ. In its extant form it is incomplete and includes only three sections, the stories of Adam and Eve and of Cain and Abel, and a prophet play in which Old Testament figures foretell the coming of Christ. Of these scenes the first is by far the most successful. The author shows real skill in characterization, particularly in his handling of the temptation scenes, where the serpent and Eve play upon the vanity and weaknesses of Eve and Adam respectively. The stage directions show that the author was much concerned about the actual playing of his drama. There is a careful description of the properties to be used in depicting the Earthly Paradise, and the dress of the various participants and their gestures are

4 The term occurs in the sense of "specialized craft" in late Middle English. Whether there is any connection between this and the fact that the individual plays in the English mystery cycles were put on by separate guilds is doubtful. The derivation from the French name for plays is more likely. "Mystère" in French is virtually synonymous with "jeu." The word is not used for plays in German.

given in detail. The play was to be staged outside the church, against an entrance. God and his prophets could thus enter the stage from the church itself. A higher platform was used for Paradise, a lower one for the earth into which Adam and Eve were driven after the fall, and at the very bottom of the steps was Hell or Limbo into which Adam, Eve, Cain, and Abel were finally led by devils.[5]

There is good reason for thinking that the author of the *Mystère d'Adam* was a highly original dramatist. We have no evidence of earlier works of such elaboration or with such original treatment of Biblical material, nor is it in the least improbable that he was contemplating a play like the later mysteries or cycles, in the course of which the history of salvation was to be represented.

The New Testament portion of this history is represented by several Passions. The *Passion des Jongleurs* is a narrative account of the events of the Passion, important only because it was apparently used by later dramatists. Of the plays which are based on it, by far the most important is the *Passion du Palatinus,* dating in its present form from the fourteenth century, which begins, after a rhymed prologue, with the entry into Jerusalem and carries the story to the Resurrection. Although it takes over almost word for word much of the material of the *Passion des Jongleurs,* the *Palatinus* demonstrates one of the aspects of the Passion play which was to be of increasing importance both in France and Germany, namely, the expansion of certain scenes by the increasing use of realistic dialogue and description of minor characters, often with deliberate local mannerisms and, inevitably, crude humor and even sadism. The

---

[5] This is the conventional reading of the stage directions. It is, however, perfectly possible to interpret them in other ways. It is certain that the actor representing God moved in and out of the church building. The devils go "per populum" and "per plateas," probably at ground level. Fairly elaborate scenery is called for in the representation of Paradise. See the modernized version by G. Cohen (1936) and its notes, and the same author's *Mise en scène.*

scenes of Judas with the Jews, the trial and scourging of Christ, and the Crucifixion itself were particularly suitable for this kind of treatment. In the *Palatinus* the torturers Cayn and Huitacelin flog their victim until they are tired, the nails for the execution are forged on the stage, and the nailing of Christ to the cross, performed by the smith's wife, is made to appear as horrible as possible. The events were no doubt well within the experiences of people accustomed to barbarous forms of public execution, and provided the same kind of excitement that the "Christians to the lions" scenes in modern films furnish for their audiences.

Full use is made in the *Palatinus* of the comic possibilities of the Harrowing of Hell by dialogue between the boastful Satan and the fearful Enfer as to the best means of defense, and of the *unguentarius* scene by making the spice merchant a doctor of Salerno (the great medieval medical center) and representing him as using magic herbs no doubt well known to the audience.

The play, though by no means as great an artistic achievement as the *Mystère d'Adam,* has nevertheless several features which show a real feeling for the dramatic. The text makes it clear that there was a considerable amount of stage "business" which, with the realism already mentioned and the homely, not to say coarse, language, could be calculated to hold the interest of the spectators and retain their attention for the serious scenes which were the *raison d'être* of the performance but were doubtless less appealing to the groundlings. The writer also had a feeling for verse. He varies the verse form from octosyllabic couplets to decasyllables or longer lines, and sometimes uses stanzas of shorter lines with more complicated rhyme schemes. The *Palatinus* Passion is the most successful of the French dramatic efforts of the period. Not until the late fifteenth century do we find more effective productions. These great plays must now be briefly described.

The most important are those known as the *Passion de Semur* (earliest manuscript 1488), the *Passion d'Arras* by

Eustache Mercadé, who died in 1440, and the great *Mystère de la Passion* by Arnoul Greban, written before 1450. Of the first we need only say that it was designed to be played over two days and contained an enormous number of different scenes, beginning with the Creation and ranging through the Old Testament, the Prophets to the birth of Jesus, the story of John the Baptist, and the Temptation. The second day carries the story through the life, death, and Resurrection, and Ascension. Many of the scenes are new and often have no direct connection with the Bible or the Apocrypha. Although the other two plays are longer, their scope is less. The *Passion d'Arras* was over 25,000 lines long and needed four days for its performances. The greater length is accounted for by the careful structure of the play which represents the life of Jesus as a deliberate act of God to save the world upon the plea of such allegorical figures as Mercy and Justice. The play bears the marks of didacticism natural to a teacher of rhetoric.

Arnoul Greban was also a teacher, of choir boys at Notre Dame, but he was of considerable learning and originality of mind. His play is by far the most distinguished of medieval French Passion plays and has been adapted and performed from Greban's day to our own. There exist various versions of the play, of varying lengths, but they agree in presenting the events of the Old Testament and prophets only in a prologue. The play itself follows the general lines of the *Passion d'Arras,* but with far greater skill. Not only is there careful motivation of the act of redemption, but Greban stresses greatly the role of the Virgin as Mother of God and intermediary between the sinners and the justice of God. The author pays great attention to the delineation of particular scenes.[6] He effectively uses lyric

[6] The scenes before Pilate are excellent examples. Even more striking are the appearances of Judas, whose actions are carefully motivated by making avarice the dominant influence on his conduct. He is treasurer of the disciples; in a soliloquy he asks what there is to be gained by his service; he deplores the money wasted by Mary Magdalen in anointing the feet of Christ. It is made clear that avarice—not only in regard to money—is one of the gravest sins.

poetry to heighten the emotional impact of such scenes as that of the shepherds before the birth of Christ. Still more important, however, is his ability to use effective detail in characterization. In this respect he is one of the very few writers of religious plays who clearly possess a genuine feeling for character and the ability to create, within the relatively rigid framework prescribed, persons clearly differentiated who blend harmoniously with the Christian revelation.

Yet his very abilities reveal the weakness of the religious play as a means of developing the drama. The opportunities, even for a gifted poet and dramatist, to create tension and represent conflict by the development and clash of character were so severely limited by his material as to be negligible. Charming though the individual scenes may be, well constructed though the entire drama is, it remains essentially a recital of fixed events, whose interest and motivation derives from the importance of the Christian religion for the audience, not from the story and characters which the author himself creates.[7] Like most playwrights who wrote in the medieval tradition, Greban gives careful attention, both in the selection of incident and in the delineation of particular scenes, to specific theological issues—sin and repentance, Christ's sacrifice and the redemption of humanity—and all his energies are bent on making this clear to his audience. The "realism" of his and other late medieval plays is designed to drive home these points in the most effective manner possible. To understand medieval drama it is essential to consider its theological aspects first. The lack of dramatic sense is clearly illustrated by the amount of attention given to scenes which, while often amusing in themselves, have little or no importance for the action of the play. Such, for example, are the farcical interludes for which a place was found even in the best productions. It is highly doubt-

[7] It should be noted that the sequence of incidents and the details of the scenes in the Gospel of Nicodemus had a profound effect on the structure of the French and German Passion plays. The *mystères* of Mercadé and Greban are carefully worded to bring out specific theological and, in Mercadé's work in particular, legal points.

ful whether the religious drama of the Middle Ages could have produced true secular drama without influence from other sources.

While the Passion play was developing on these lines in France, similar developments were taking place in Germany and England. From the former country we have several groups of plays, all of the fifteenth century, which illustrate the expansion of the original Easter material. The Frankfurt group, which includes plays from Frankfurt and Alsfeld, included originally a dispute between the Prophets and Jews about the coming of Christ, but this later disappeared in favor of expansion of the scenes in the life of Christ itself. The stage directions make it clear that the Alsfeld play was designed to be performed over two days, and it is characteristic of German mysteries in general that most attention should be paid to scenes capable of comic expansion: assemblies of devils, the unregenerate life of Maria Magdalena, the *unguentarius* scene were then, as now, more popular than the more edifying sections. The treatment of such scenes is popular and in both style and versification less elaborate than that of the French Passion plays. The observation of Creizenach is worth repeating here: German humor seems to run in the direction of comic beatings, quarrels between man and wife, and parody of Jewish customs which at times amounts to outright anti-Semitism. The French, on the other hand, while not ignoring the comic possibilities of a good slapstick fight, place more stress on tavern and drunkard scenes. In the French plays too, there is the frequent mockery of the crippled, the blind, and other unfortunates which can be found even in medieval books of strong moral tone.

Of the Heidelberg Passion play we need note only that it deliberately uses Old Testament scenes as prefigurations of events in the life of Christ. The Low German Easter play from Redentin is remarkable for its detailed satirical treatment of various characters in Hell and illustrates probably better than any other play the influence of popular humor and humorists on the original material.[8] The poet shows great skill in inventing suitable, if horrifying, punishments for the various professions. There are numerous other plays from all parts of Germany belonging to this period, but there is nowhere the dramatic skill or structure we have already noted in the great French plays. The play from Donaueschingen is perhaps the best constructed and does show considerable skill in its use of such characters as Mary Magdalene to demonstrate the way from sin to salvation and of realistic treatments of Christ's sufferings to point up the magnitude of his sacrifice.

The plays which have been discussed must have been staged in varying places at different times and in different forms. We know, for example, that the Passion play written by Arnoul Greban was requested for performance in Abbeville in 1482 and was also played in other towns in northern France. Who precisely performed them is harder to determine. They were often financed by civic bodies or by town authorities themselves; priests and other ecclesiastics frequently played the dignified roles; laymen were drawn in for other parts. Yet the amount of improvisation and stage business required, particularly in the comic scenes, makes it virtually certain that professionals were employed for such parts as the *unguentarius,* the devils, and Herod. More important than any actor was the *maître de jeu,*[9] who would now be called a producer. When a town council or group of citizens (and almost all performances during the late Middle Ages were given in towns) decided to put on a play, they called in the services of a man of skill and experience to organize the event. It is very probable that the text of the play ultimately presented depended very much on

[8] The Redentin play follows the Gospel of Nicodemus very closely. But in the second part (the "restocking" of Hell), the material and treatment seem to derive entirely from a popular comic tradition. Considerable use is made of topical allusions in the satire of unpopular professions.

[9] The term "maître de jeu" seems to be the normal one, but again it is hard to find evidence for an exact description of his functions.

which version the *maître de jeu* happened to possess or had access to. In the hands of this producer rested all the arrangements. He had to find actors, who were bound by oath to appear once they committed themselves—an interesting sidelight on the medieval artistic temperament. He had to find a suitable place for performance, arrange the stage, find costumes and, above all, raise money. Sometimes the actors themselves had to contribute, a fact which makes it clear that appearance in such a play was as much sought after as appearance today in a television show—but less lucrative. One can hardly envy the *maître de jeu* his role. Passions tended to express themselves through physical force in the Middle Ages, and the distribution of the desirable roles must have been in many respects a preview of the descent into Hell.

Although there is much uncertainty about the personnel who played the dramas, we are better informed about the general features of the stage itself, once the performances had moved outside the church.[10] Although some exceptions can be shown, most plays were performed on the "simultaneous stage." This means simply that throughout the performance certain parts were designated as "Paradise," "Earth," "Hell," "Pilate's House," the "Grave of Christ," etc. Persons whose parts demanded that they operate only in these locales stayed there throughout the play. The main figures, however, such as Christ, the Apostles, and the Devil, necessarily moved from one to another. It is clear that the fully developed Passion play re-

[10] Most references to the medieval continental stage are to the well-known drawing which accompanies the Valenciennes Passion in a manuscript of 1547. This stage faced the audience on one side only. We should be careful, however, not to assume that such an arrangement was universal. The Redentin play was almost certainly performed on a round stage, and the reconstructions of the Passion plays performed at Lucerne seem to indicate that the audience surrounded the stage. For the Valenciennes stage, see the plate in Cohen, *Mise en scène*. For the Redentin play, see the introduction to the English translation by A. E. Zucker (1941). The latest work on the subject is R. Southern's *Medieval Theatre in the Round*.

quired so many scenes that no stage could have held so many separate stations (*sedes* is the common Latin term in the stage directions). It therefore became customary to have certain fixed positions, Heaven to the spectators' left with appropriate trappings, Hell to the right, with gaping monstrous jaws, fire, smoke, and the clanging of innumerable drums, kettles, and pans. Most of the scenes took place in the general location in the middle of the stage with the scene identified by some obviously recognizable attribute. The form of stage clearly derives from the original staging within the church, but also reflects the intention of the medieval dramatist to represent the universe as existing all together and its parts as interacting upon one another. We should never lose sight of the fact that the plays, in spite of crudeness, low comedy, sadism, and bragadoccio, were still acts of faith, designed to bring home to their audiences the essential unity of the Christian world in both time and space. The simultaneous stage, whether consciously or not, helped to preserve this feeling.

Perhaps the feeling of unity was not so strong in England, or perhaps the guilds were better organized and took over the plays more effectively than on the Continent. Whatever the reason, the method of staging the great English cycle plays, which corresponded generally to the continental Passion plays, differed markedly from that used in France and Germany. The directions in the extant versions make it clear that they were to be organized as processional plays. Such plays were known on the Continent, but they were relatively minor and there is no evidence of any attempt to stage any of the great Passion plays in this manner. A processional play was staged precisely as might be expected. The play was divided into scenes, each of which was presented on a wagon specially fitted out with appropriate scenery and properties. The wagons followed each other in sequence of scenes to designated points on the route of the procession. At each of these points the scene was played, and the wagon then proceeded to the next station. Each scene (and wagon) was assigned to a particular guild (the weavers, the tile makers, the fishmongers), and the guild was then responsible for the provision of all necessities and of actors from its members. Such an arrangement certainly made for competition between guilds in richness of costume and scenery and possibly in the provision of good actors. It also had marked effects on the characters of the plays themselves. Continuity was much more difficult to establish and maintain, for each scene had to be complete in itself, and the author felt compelled to reestablish continuity (and order) at the beginning of each new section by the lavish use of narrators and of prologues delivered in swashbuckling fashion by such sure-fire attractions as Herod and Pilate. There could be no question of an ever-present band of devils down below in Hell, ready to spring out on unsuspecting mortals, punishing sin and providing low comedy, so that new comic devices had to be provided, based, so far as one can tell, on traditions of long standing in English popular spectacles.

Much has been written about the great cycles of English plays, those of York, Wakefield, and Chester, and the fragments of cycles known as the Coventry, Newcastle, and Norwich plays. All have characteristics in common; all have major points of differentiation. None of them is a complete unity, for there is evidence everywhere of the preservation of old traditional material and of the incorporation of new ideas and scenes. All the cycles treat of the whole history of the creation, fall, and salvation of mankind, to the Last Judgment, with the appropriate Old Testament scenes and prophecies and the life, death, and resurrection of Christ, but there are great differences in treatment. It is worth remarking that, in general, the Christmas story is treated at much greater length and much more sympathetically than on the Continent. We shall have occasion to discuss the comic additions to the Christmas story in the Wakefield play, but in all the plays the figures of Mary and particularly of Joseph are portrayed with many human touches. Joseph is concerned to provide for his wife such poor comforts as the stable can afford, comforts Mary in her distress when the growing Jesus is lost, and yet is too humble to enter the hall in which the boy is disputing with the learned men.

The events of the Passion are greatly expanded in all the plays by extended treatment of the scenes between the priests, Judas, and Pilate. In the York plays in particular the constant boasting of the great lords contrasts amusingly with their utter ineffectiveness, and all their power is insufficient to prevent them from being dragged out of bed again and again to perform some trivial act. The waiting time is frequently enlivened with a little refreshment, and more chaos is the result. The agony of Judas at his betrayal of Christ is excellently portrayed.

The events of the Passion are particularly well presented in the York cycle, which is probably the oldest of the three, if the term "oldest" can be used of works which consist of so many layers of material. It is virtually certain that the Wakefield cycle (sometimes called "Towneley Plays" because the manuscript was for a long period in the possession of the Towneley family), drew many whole scenes from the York play. The two towns are geographically very close, and York was and still is the center of an archdiocese. Yet the plays show marked differences of emphasis. The Wakefield play carries comedy to the ultimate extreme in a religious play; the story of Noah, for example, and his quarrel with his wife about who shall go in the ark, is a fine example of the stock comedy, and even such a solemn (and usually terrifying) scene as the Last Judgment is enlivened by the presence of the devil Tutivillus. The scene between Cain and Abel characterizes the former as a grasping peasant who displays all the features ascribed to him in contemporary satire, while Abel is a God-fearing and righteous man.

Here, as elsewhere in the plays, it is impossible to ignore the moral, social, and political overtones. Although the manuscripts date from the late fifteenth and from the sixteenth and seventeenth centuries, the period of greatest development was undoubtedly the fifteenth century, a time of great social and political upheaval in England. The plays, by their very nature, reflect the views of the bourgeoisie, and the portraits of bombastic tyrants (even the Emperor Augustus is so portrayed in the Wakefield play) and grasping peasants undoubtedly reflect the opinions of the townspeople about other classes of society. The clergy did not neglect their opportunities either. Cain is a horrible example of a man who does not pay his full tithes when due, and even the Noah's wife episode is to be interpreted as a moral lesson on the subject of marital duty.

The Wakefield mystery is best known for the shepherds' plays which are included in it. The actual visit to the stable in which lies the infant Christ is preceded by a lively scene in which the shepherds discuss the hardness of their life with a realism born of experience. A typical verbal quarrel follows, and then comes a jolly drinking scene which was traditional not only in England but in France too. After the visit to the cradle there follows a second, independent play, the famous *Secunda pastorum*. A sheep-stealer, Mak, purloins a sheep from the sleeping shepherds and takes it home to his wife. Believing quite rightly that suspicion will fall on him, he dresses the ram as a newborn babe and puts it in a cradle. The shepherds arrive, search the house, and find nothing. Only when one of them decides to give a kiss to the child as he leaves is he struck by the extraordinary length of its nose, and the truth is out. The play is funny in itself, but the desperate efforts of Mak and his wife to hide their deception are in the best tradition of slap-stick comedy. Yet it would be unwise to dismiss the play as nothing more than a comic insertion. The possibility that it is a pagan survival must also be considered, and even the possibility of a sacrilegious parody of the crib scene cannot be completely excluded. Here, as elsewhere, we are faced with a curious mixture of the old and the new, the sacred and the profane.

The Chester play cycle differs more from the York and Wakefield groups than they do from each other. The manuscripts of the Chester play are late, dating from the late sixteenth and early seventeenth centuries, but there is evidence of performance in Chester in 1462. Although there is no lack of comic scenes, the didactic element predominates, and there is much deliberate moralization and explanation of the significance of particular events. There is a special scene devoted to the announcement of the articles of faith to the Twelve Apostles. Occasions such as Adam's vision of the future of mankind and Elias' conflict with Antichrist (a traditional feature of the Last Judgment) are used for long expositions of doctrine.

The same didactic tendency, carried to even greater lengths, is to be observed in the so-called Coventry play. The "expositor" or narrator constantly refers to events which are not dramatized and explains them. Even such undramatic material as the explanation of the allegorical significance of the letters of the names Anna and Maria is incorporated. The general effect is that of a collection of isolated scenes and explanations, and the whole question of the provenance and performance of the play is wrapped in mystery. We know that Coventry was famous for its Corpus Christi processional plays, and a seventeenth-century note on the manuscript of 1468 states that these were the plays performed by Franciscans and known as the *Ludus Coventriae*.[11] Few scholars accept the statement, but there is none of the usual evidence in the manuscript of assignment of scenes to guilds, nor is there any statement about how or when the plays were performed. Mention is made of some forty "pageants," but the text is not so divided, and there are

[11] For a detailed discussion of the question, see Hardin Craig, *English Religious Drama*, pp. 239 ff. The appellation "Hegge plays" is certainly less misleading than *Ludus Coventriae* (the ms. once belonged to the Hegge family), but the town where the plays were performed is still unknown—hence they are occasionally called "N town plays." The dialect is that of the Lincolnshire area. Craig's statement that the plays were performed *at* the Grey Friars and not *by* them is very plausible. There are two plays which actually come from Coventry, the pageants of the Weavers and of the Shearers and Tailors. These have nothing to do with the *Ludus Coventriae*.

notices which seem to indicate that separate sections were played each year. It is likely that we have here a late compilation of material which was not performed in its entirety. Curiously, the format of the manuscript is much closer to the normal manuscript designed for reading than are most of the play books.

We have now seen the development of the religious play in England, France, and Germany. In spite of regional differences and varying emphasis on particular scenes, the general development was similar in all three countries (and apparently also in the Netherlands, although evidence from actual plays is slight). All encompass the whole history of salvation; all stress the events of Christmas, the Passion, and the Resurrection; all develop a large element of comedy. In most the verse forms are popular and, with a few notable exceptions, lack distinction. In spite of considerable dramatic skill in characterization within individual scenes and in the presentation of popular or comic elements, none of the Passion plays or religious cycles can in any real sense be called drama. They were constrained by their subject matter and never developed (and never could develop) beyond the stage of a series of individual scenes bound together only by the consciousness of the continuity of the history of salvation. It is significant that the events of the Renaissance left no mark on the religious plays. They continued to be played, unchanged so far as we can determine, until anti-Catholic sentiment banned them in Protestant countries or until new forms of drama superseded them. Nevertheless, the characters they developed and the presentation which became traditional in them exercised far-reaching effects on later secular drama. The effects were due much less to literary influence than to acting tradition and an established demand among the audience. This is particularly true in the field of comedy. The types we have seen in the religious plays persisted and have been noted in Shakespeare, but the religious plays did not invent them. They merely acted as a respectable vehicle for their presentation.

It may be noted in passing that we can find the beginnings of religious drama in Italy. There was, however, no development such as that which took place north of the Alps, where recitation in the vernacular superseded singing in Latin. The principal dramatic developments were in the hands of the orders, particularly the flagellants, and consisted of little more than recitation in character, known as *Laudes*. Another development originated in the interspersion in sermons of edifying dramatic scenes, known as *Devozioni,* which were designed to increase the effectiveness of preaching. A didactic purpose is also obvious in the *Rappresentazioni,* particularly popular in Florence, which were performed apparently by schoolboys and which covered a wide range of Biblical subjects. Although these performances ultimately developed some of the characteristics of the mystery plays, such as comic figures, particularly figures frequently pilloried in popular humor, they never attained the scope of the French or German plays. Long before they reached their full development the attention of literary men was already focused on the literature of classical antiquity.

The history of the plays on the life of Christ has been described at some length because it was, for the medieval population, the most significant of dramatic representations. It has already been noted that it would not, of itself, have produced what could be called drama in a modern sense. There were, however, other religious subjects which could be treated with a great deal more freedom than the life of Christ. Chief among these subjects were the lives of the saints and prophets. These had already been put into popular form in the *vitae* (saints' lives), widely distributed in both Latin and the vernacular. There were so many dramatic representations of such lives that any attempt to list them would be pointless. It is best to confine our attention to one or two which were works of real distinction. Of these by far the most important are the plays on the life of St. Nicholas, a minor saint of Asia Minor who, for reasons still obscure, became extremely popular in western Europe. Perhaps his very obscurity was a help. In any event, the plays of St. Nicholas, particularly that by Jean Bodel, rank among the greatest dramatic efforts of the Middle Ages.

Before discussing these, however, we should mention one phenomenon which has aroused interest among scholars ever since the Renaissance. The German poet Conrad Celtes discovered in the monastery of St. Emmeram, in Regensburg, a manuscript containing works by Hroswitha, a nun of Gandersheim, among them a series of dramatized miracles of saints. In a preface Hroswitha states that she is horrified by the fact that Christians read the plays of Terence because of the beauty of his language and style, and cannot avoid the contagion of his immoral characters and plots. She therefore proposes to write a counterblast by imitating the form of Terence but using as subject matter the lives of saints and martyrs. Her favorites, not unnaturally, are young ladies who suffered martyrdom rather than give up their faith or their virginity and ladies of easy virtue recalled to a decent way of life by saintly men. Hroswitha's statement that she was imitating Terence has been taken seriously by generations of scholars. The nineteenth century, misinterpreting her name, called her the White Rose of Gandersheim (her name, as she herself says, means "Loud Shout," a much less romantic appellation) and treated her accordingly. In fact, her plays do not imitate Terence at all, either in language or structure. She merely tells the story of her saints in dialogue form, using a minimum number of lines to keep the story moving. It is doubtful whether she knew what true drama was, still more doubtful whether she intended her "plays" to be anything but reading matter. Even so her achievement is remarkable. She did succeed in telling a story in dramatic form and in her best play, *Dulcitius,* she succeeds in making the action vigorous and amusing. One cannot help the feeling, however, that much of the praise which has been bestowed upon her is due to her "quaintness," and that many of the virtues ascribed to her have been read into her material by overenthusiastic critics. As Dr. Johnson said of women preachers and dogs which walk on two legs, it is not the quality of their performance we admire but the fact that it could take place at all. Her works had no influence on the subsequent history of the drama and seem to have been unknown outside a very small circle.

There are a number of Latin dramatizations of the miracles performed by St. Nicholas. Some appear in the famous Fleury play book; some were written by the talented writer Hilarius. They concentrate on four of the saint's miracles: his provision of dowries for three deserving girls, which gave rise to such diverse phenomena of modern life as Santa Claus and the three golden balls (originally bags of gold) of the pawnbroker's sign; his restoration to life of three clerics murdered by their host; his recovery of a prince captured by his father's enemy; and finally the recovery of a barbarian's treasure which the saint was guarding. The last of these produced by far the most important plays and we shall concentrate our attention upon it. In the version of the play found in the Fleury play book, the owner of the treasure is a Jew, who is persuaded to entrust his valuables to a statue of St. Nicholas because of the miraculous powers of the saint. Three thieves remove the treasure; the Jew is furious, and denounces the saint's alleged powers. The three thieves are overtaken by St. Nicholas and forced to return the treasure, so that the Jew is compelled to admit that the saint does possess miraculous powers. The whole point of the play is, of course, to show the contrast between the faithful and the unbelievers and to demonstrate the power of the saint to achieve what he promises. The Jew is characterized with considerable care. When his treasure vanishes, he is skeptical of the saint's powers. We shall see that this type of crude, unrestrained unbeliever is continued throughout the St. Nicholas tradition. The thieves, too, are to some extent differentiated; they each offer a solution for extracting the treasure from the box, for dividing it, etc. This is less characterization than mechanical division of the progress of the action between various characters. In this play it is assisted by musical differentiation and by variety in the verse forms. The play shows that certain traditions in handling the relatively simple story were already developing. The same theme was treated in a Latin play written by the twelfth-century cleric Hilarius, a pupil of Abélard, who also wrote a Lazarus and a Daniel play. His St. Nicholas play is simpler than that in the Fleury play book, for it contains only two speaking parts, the Barbarus and the Saint. The robbers are present but do not speak. The only remarkable feature is the inclusion of French refrains.

There is no extant play, either in Latin or French, on the subject of the *Iconia,* which can be dated between the Fleury and Hilarius versions and that of Jean Bodel. We must therefore assume that Bodel's remarkable work is the result of his own originality, of a brilliant dramatic talent, and of the impetus given to the drama by the literary and civic associations which centered on Arras at the end of the twelfth century and the beginning of the thirteenth. The literary societies, known as *puys,* which flourished at this period, encouraged literary productivity of the most varied kinds. One of the greatest of French trouvères, Conon de Béthune, comes from this area, as does the epic poet, Gautier d'Arras. Of the dramatist Adam le Bossu we shall have occasion to speak later.

Of Jean Bodel himself we know considerably more than we do of most medieval writers, which is little enough. He was a member of the Confrérie de la Ste. Chandelle, an organization devoted to the guardianship of a candle which had miraculously appeared to one of its members, and whose membership seems to have consisted largely of professional trouvères and jongleurs, and from its records we derive most of the external evidence about the poet's life and the fact that he died in 1209–10. From his own works, and in particular from his *Congé,* a poem of leave-taking from the world, we know that he contracted leprosy and was forced to leave some official position he held and ask the mayor and corporation to grant him asylum in a leper colony. This pathetic poem must have been written before 1202, since the poet specifically renounces an intention to go on the Fourth Crusade. Other authors refer with admiration to his *pastourelles* and to his epic poem *Chanson des Saisnes.*

His fame rests, however, on his *Jeu de St. Nicholas,* a vernacular version of the *Iconia* story very probably designed to be played on St. Nicholas Eve (December 5) in 1199, when the sacred candle of his confrérie was moved from the shrine of the saint. There are allusions within the play to performance at night, and the season would require it to take place inside. Jean Bodel greatly expands the play as it seems to have been known to contemporaries, not merely by adding descriptive detail or extra dialogue, but by more elaborate characterization and motivation and by the addition of a completely new milieu within which his thieves could operate. Throughout the play the scene shifts between the Eastern realms of the Saracen king and scenes of tavern life where the local gossip and tales of Arras are bandied around and the drink is the Arras local wine. A brief summary will show how Bodel expanded his scanty material and made out of a miracle story something very close to what we think of as drama.

The play opens with a prologue which briefly describes the action which was to follow. It is announced to the king of Africa that the Christians are marching against him in great force. He hurls insults at his god Tervagan, but later asks him for a sign. The god laughs and cries, a fact interpreted by the king's chamberlain to mean that the pagans will win the battle but will be converted. Auberon, the king's courier, while seeking allies, drinks wine at a tavern, disputes about the price, and plays dice with Cliquet for the price and wins. He then finds a number of formidable allies, tells the king, and appears no more in the play. The pagans, boastful and wealthy, and the Christians, humble and heroic, are seen preparing for battle. An angel tells the Christians they will be defeated, but assures them of Paradise. The Christians, we are informed in a rubric, are all killed. The angel blesses them and comforts a "prudhomme," a noble old man who has been discovered by the pagan "Admiral of Orquenie" kneeling before a statue of St. Nicholas, telling him to hold fast to his faith. He repeats the words of encouragement when the king of Africa, to mock at Christianity, announces publicly that he will entrust his treasures to the statue of St. Nicholas and that the prudhomme will "pay with his life" if they are stolen. The terrified man is roughly hustled off to a dungeon, while the king's crier makes the public announcement and in the course of it finds himself embroiled with a rival crier who has been sent out to advertise the innkeeper's wares. The tavern owner himself has to calm them down and define their functions. Cliquet and a fellow low-life character, Pincedés, discuss the difficulties of a life of crime —and the poor quality of the wine—and then are joined by the third thief, Rasoir, who tells them of the projected robbery (of the treasure). They pass the intervening time by playing dice. The usual accusations of cheating follow, and again the host has to act as peace maker. He also is cut in for a share of the loot, in exchange for providing receptacles to carry it. The theft is carried out and is followed by a boisterous debauch. The king's seneschal, who has dreamed of the loss of the treasure, finds his fears justified and the prudhomme, sentenced to death, barely obtains a delay of one day, much to the annoyance of the executioner who describes in some detail what he proposes to do. The angel again assures the prudhomme that his prayers to the saint will be answered, and in the next scene we see the thieves rudely awakened, told by the saint bluntly what he thinks of them and ordered to return the treasure on pain of death. The landlord, eager to establish his own innocence, drives them out, while his potboy grabs the cloak of

Cliquet to pay the score they have run up. The thieves part with expressions of mutual dislike. The king and the seneschal both dream of the treasure's being returned and confirm the fact. The pagan king sends for the prudhomme and announces the miracles. There is a general conversion to Christianity and devotion to St. Nicholas. Even the Emir [Admiral] of Orquenie makes a formal recantation. The play ends with the destruction of the statue of Tervagan and the singing of the Te Deum.

This summary makes clear how far removed is the *Jeu de St. Nicholas* from the meager miracle play in the Fleury book and from the version of Hilarius, but no summary can do justice to the brilliance of the individual scenes. Jean Bodel has converted the original "Barbarus" into a live, Mohammedan king, the enemy of Christendom, a ruthless but brave and efficient tyrant whose power was only too well known to the Crusaders. He is perfectly willing to abuse his own god if his ends are not properly served, but equally ready to make honorable amends when the saint proves his power and fulfills his promises. Around this figure the author has created a group of clearly differentiated characters who represent various aspects of paganism—the crudely ambitious and stiff-necked Emir of Orquenie, the brutal executioner Durant, the flattering seneschal. Such characters, all original inventions so far as we can tell, are not merely there to advance the plot. They bring home the nature of the enemy against whom the Crusades were fought; they are the people who must be vanquished before Christendom can rest secure. No better method can be imagined to stir up enthusiasm for the Fourth Crusade.

Opposed to them are the Christian heroes. All are lightly sketched, but they are characterized by the greatest of Christian virtues, humility. Bodel's invention of the figure of the prudhomme is a stroke of genius. He makes possible the intervention of the saint not merely in order to prove his power, but to save a helpless but trusting Christian man. The prudhomme is not a hero. He trembles at the threats of torture and death;

he is overawed by the pagan majesty of the king of Africa. Yet his simple faith is more powerful than all their worldly power, as the angel quietly assures him. By this invention Jean Bodel has changed a somewhat mechanical miracle story into a drama, for the interest of the audience inevitably centers upon the very human experiences of the man rather than upon the undoubted power of the saint. The dramatic elements of tension and suspense have once again entered European literature.

The tavern scenes are triumphs of close observation and dramatic characterization. In assessing Bodel's achievement here it should not be forgotten that all that is required for the story is the presence of three thieves. Upon this slight foundation the author has constructed a whole world of low life which is carefully integrated into his story. The thieves are professionals who live by their wits. They are carefully characterized as a group and as individuals. All love gambling, drinking, and boasting. All are prone to fierce quarrels. All speak in thieves' cant, so that much of the meaning of their conversation remains guesswork to this day. Yet Cliquet differs remarkably from Rasoir, as Rasoir does from Pincedés. Cliquet is boastful, eloquent, easygoing, loud in his expressions, but fearful in action. He alone remarks about the possible punishment for theft. Rasoir, on the other hand, is more secretive and more of an organizer. He suggests the exploit and makes the plans to carry it out. He is cool in making the plot and persuading the other two to fall in with his suggestions, equally cool in giving up when he sees the game is lost. Pincedés is a completely different type. The most skillful of the three at dice, he easily loses both his head and his winnings. He revels in physical force, but his anger quickly passes. A simpler soul than the other two, he is more deeply affected by the appearance of the saint, even to the point of repeating a few half-forgotten Latin words to preserve himself. M. Foulon is probably right in calling him the type of "good criminal," who was (and is) popular with audiences.[12]

[12] In *L'Oeuvre de Jehan Bodel,* pp. 670 ff.

The thieves, as we have said, demanded a world in which to move. The invention of the inn provides not only a center for their activities but also a set of characters who are part of their world: the innkeeper, in particular, anticipates many later variations of the type with his sharp practice and greed, coupled with a fervent desire to make money illegally without entangling himself with the law. His potboy Caignet is a worthy apprentice to such a master.

The inn provides a contrast to the palace, the contrast of high life and low life. The life which moves through it is, of course, the life of Arras, and no doubt many of the allusions now difficult to follow were of great interest to contemporary audiences. The tavern also serves as a connecting point between the pagan East and the world of thieves and robbers, for into it come Auberon the courier, and the crier who announces the "availability" of the treasure. It is worth noting that Bodel realizes, as very few medieval playwrights did, how important it is to make his characters enter separately and thus become known to the audience, and to give his work verisimilitude. The thieves, whose very names show their characteristics, come into the inn separately and talk with the innkeeper and others. They make clear their motivations and characteristics.

It has often been noted that the course of the action involves impossible journeys between the pagan East and the tavern world of Arras. In fact, this was not Bodel's intention. Although the tavern scenes are full of local allusions and expressions, of Arras dialect and thieves' cant, the intention is to portray a "universal" world of low life, and the best way to do this was by showing the life with which the audience was acquainted. There is, after all, no such thing as a Moslem tavern. Incongruities and inconsistencies mattered as little to Bodel as they did to the writers of the Passion plays or to Shakespeare —or to any audience at any time.

We could mention many more features of this remarkable play—its crusading spirit, its skillful versification, its careful tripartite structure, each major section being close to 500 lines long. But its greatest feature transcends all these. It is drama. Some critics have remarked that Bodel seems to have been acquainted with the imitations of classical comedy and to have been influenced by them. This may be so. But it was a genius for dramatic arrangement which produced the *Jeu de St. Nicholas*. Its like was not to appear again for centuries.

The remaining saints' plays from France, with a few exceptions, serve only to make us realize how remarkable was the achievement of Jean Bodel. The long, dull *Martyrdom of St. Denis,* full of descriptions of cruelty and torture, comes from the collection of plays from the Bibliothèque Ste. Geneviève. As might be expected, the manuscript also contains a series of miracles attributed to the patroness of the library which, though didactic in tone, do have some realistic scenes. The fourteenth and fifteenth centuries saw a continuous stream of plays of very uneven quality, usually performed by local confréries of a local patron saint. Rarely is there much relief from the gruesome details of martyrdom and often, when present, it is in the form of crude jests to the audience in the middle of scenes of horror. In the five-day play of St. Barbara, the tortures were somehow extended over almost three days.

We have to return to the thirteenth century to find a play even remotely comparable to the *Jeu de St. Nicholas.* The lyric and satirical poet Rutebeuf, a professional writer of great wit and skill and deeply concerned with the problems of his day, wrote about the year 1261 a play about the miracle of Theophilus. The play might more correctly be described as one of the miracles of the Virgin, for it shows her direct and successful intercession with Christ for a man's soul. Theophilus was the administrator of a bishopric in Asia Minor in the sixth century. On the death of the bishop he was offered the succession, refused, and was promptly ejected from his post by the new incumbent. In despair he called on the devil for aid. At this point the play opens. The devil, conjured up by a magician, insists on a written pact and the renunciation of all Christian acts. Theophilus agrees and recovers his position. He becomes arrogant and disliked, and soon repents of his deed. At length he implores the help of the Virgin. After a stern rebuke she wrestles with Satan, recovers the pact, and thus saves his soul.

The resemblance to the Faust theme is obvious, but in the original story, as told by John the Deacon and Gautier de Coincy, the emphasis is on the power of the Virgin, not the weakness of Theophilus. Rutebeuf to some extent changes this because of his personal interest in a person rejected and cast out, as he himself only too often was. His poetic skill makes the play pleasant to read, but the faults so often noted are still present—sparse action, sudden transitions, insufficient motivation. Nevertheless the play, vigorous and colloquial, yet artistic, is far superior to most saints' plays.

We have noted that this work is strictly a "Miracle de Notre Dame." Such miracle plays were particularly popular in France, and forty of them, written during the fourteenth century, are extant. The manuscripts, incidentally, in which they are preserved, are justly famous for their beautiful illustrative miniatures. The stories are drawn from widely differing sources and concern almost all types of sinner, but they have many features in common. All have interspersed *rondeaux* and lyric verses sung in honor of the Virgin; all the dialogue is in octosyllabic couplets. Many of the plays are preceded by prose sermons. The unity of form seems to argue a common source, though probably not a common author, and also a common purpose. The sermons would indicate that they were designed for use in honor of the Virgin on her feast days, quite possibly for performance by a particular *puy* which honored the Virgin. It is certain that the manuscript was a deliberately made official collection.

Direct intervention by the Virgin to save a sinner is always the subject. The interest centers on the sins committed, and it seems sometimes that the choice of the evil deeds of the person to be saved was made to give the audience plenty of excitement. There is plenty of realism here, as in all plays of the period, but little motivation or genuine characterization. The most appalling deeds are committed without scruple. As always, such dramatic talent as the authors possessed was expended on realistic scenes of contemporary life. The many opportunities for real drama are never realized.

Miracle plays must have existed in other countries besides France, but there is a curious lack of extant examples. A play of St. Dorothea from Germany is mentioned, but we have no text. Of the Theophilus play already mentioned there are several versions, the best in Low German (the Trier manuscript), which unfortunately breaks off at the pact with the devil.[13] It portrays the story from the beginning (unlike Rutebeuf's version) and is effectively written with considerable ability in the characterization of both Theophilus and the devil (a minor one—he reports his success to Lucifer).

The only other play on a subject other than the life of Christ is the curious *Spiel von Frau Jutta* of Dietrich Schernberg (*ca.* 1490).[14] This play based on the legend of Johanna, the woman pope, tells the story of the learned young lady who dresses as and passes for a cleric. Such is her learning that she moves up the ecclesiastical ladder and becomes pope. However, she has not been able to resist the temptations of the flesh, and gives birth to a child in public. She dies shortly afterwards, and the devils whisk her away. A lively description of her tortures follows until the Virgin, hearing her genuine contrition, intervenes to save her, much to the disgust of the denizens of Hell. The play has the usual overdone realism and slapstick comedy, but is not without its dramatic appeal.

England too seems to have been less interested in presenting saints' plays. Although there are mentions of plays of St.

---

[13] The German Theophilus plays have been edited by R. Petsch (1908) and Ch. Sarauw (1923). There is a modern German translation by J. Wedde (1888).

[14] Edited by H. Schröder (1911).

George and others—and indeed, to judge by the New Year mummers' plays, they must have been popular—no texts are extant. Only a play of the unregenerate life of Mary Magdalene survives, and this has little dramatic significance. The Middle Ages dramatized almost any incident, whether Biblical or Apocryphal, which could be used for edification. A few of the most important of these may be noted. The incident of the raising of Lazarus enjoyed considerable popularity in view of its interpretation as a parallel to the raising of mankind from spiritual death by the intervention of Christ. The Fleury play book contains a dignified but uninspired version. Hilary wrote a rather more lively drama on the subject, and it was incorporated into several mysteries. Even more popular was the dramatization of the parable of the wise and foolish virgins. The task of dramatization was made easy by the nature of the parable, and "plays" on the subject are among the earliest of which texts are extant. A fine version is to be found in the S. Martial manuscript, written in Limoges during the first half of the twelfth century. As always in the treatments of this theme, the stress is upon the irrevocability of the divine judgment. The parable is expanded so that the virgins are several times warned to be prepared. The foolish fall asleep, allow the oil to run from their lamps, appeal to their wiser companions, then run to buy oil. They fail, and the door is closed against them. No doubt is left in the minds of the audience that the bridegroom is Christ and that the sinners will be punished. Their personal appeals to the Bridegroom are vain, and devils appear to drag them to hell. The theme was particularly suitable for early efforts at drama. It is the earliest known play which contains any considerable amount of French, and the dramatic effect of the increasing terror of the virgins could be heightened by the use of formal lament and of musical accompaniment.

How effective such a play was is demonstrated by an interesting story told about a German version played by clerics and school children in Eisenach before Friedrich, margrave of

Thuringia, in 1321. So profound was the effect upon the nobleman that he is said to have cried out: "Of what use is Christianity if a man cannot obtain grace even by the intercession of the
Virgin and the saints!" He could not free himself of the horror
which filled his mind, and died of a stroke five days later.[15]
This is almost the only reference we possess to the emotional
impact of a play upon a medieval audience, and it acts as a
salutary warning against condemning such representations. The
statement, made several times in this chapter, that most of these
plays are not dramatic in the literary sense is valid, but it does
not mean that they were without effect upon the audience. Quite
the reverse is probably true. The comic scenes were designed
to produce immediate response, and it should not be forgotten
that the religious scenes depended for their impact largely on
the permanent emotional attitude of the audience towards the
subjects which they portrayed.

The play which so moved the margrave was almost certainly
a version of the drama preserved for us in two manuscripts,
one Thuringian of the third quarter of the fourteenth century,
the other of 1428 from Hesse. The earlier of these still preserves in many places the beginnings of lines of the Latin text
from which it was translated and adopted. The later version
has additional material. We can thus be sure that in both France
and Germany there were Latin plays on the subject of the
Sponsus [Marriage feast] from which vernacular versions developed. The most important addition in the German play is
a scene which probably provoked the margrave's outburst. The
virgins appeal to Mary, who in turn uses every effort and argument to persuade Christ to have mercy. He refuses, saying that
even for his mother his word cannot be changed. This inter-

---

[15] Editions of the *Sponsus* (Wise and Foolish Virgins) play are:
W. Cloetta, "Le Mystère de l'époux," *Romania,* Vol. XXII (1893); in
K. Young, *Drama of the Medieval Church,* II, 361 ff.; O. Beckers, *Spiel
von den zehn Jungfrauen* (1905), modern German version by A. Freybe
(1870). The incident of the margrave is recorded in several chronicles.
See Creizenach, *Geschichte des neueren Dramas,* II, 121.

esting variant on the role of Mary as intercessor, so strikingly different from her achievements in the *Miracles* already discussed, seems to have been confined to this particular theme. Obviously tradition demanded that the parable of the foolish virgins should be an example of the fate awaiting those who do not repent in time. A song sung by the foolish virgins emphasizes this—they will enjoy the world for thirty years, then enter a cloister and repent! This is one of the most effective medieval German plays, with relatively well-drawn characters and deep solemnity of tone and dignity of verse. In view of the evidence of its emotional impact, we would be ill-advised to criticize it.

Plays of the Last Judgment, of which a few exist, have the same edifying purpose, but are by no means so effective. Many mystery cycles incorporate such plays. Mention should be made of one more type—the play of Antichrist. This play is frequently coupled with plays of the Last Judgment (the only example from France combines the two), and depends on Apocryphal sources for its plot. The earliest piece is the Tegernsee *Antichrist,* usually dated at the end of the twelfth century. It is in Latin and of complicated structure, considering its relatively early date, but consists rather of a series of musical scenes than of true dramatic representation. First there is a prologue in which Christians, Jews, and heathens set forth their views. In strophic songs in various meters, the mastery of the Roman empire over other kings is shown, and the heathen king of Babylon is defeated. But then arises Antichrist, the compendium of every unchristian quality. With the help of such personified qualities as Hypocrisy and Heresy he wins over all the princes of the world—except the king of Germany! Even he, however, gives his allegiance when Antichrist performs numerous miracles and puts him in charge of the army. The Jews, too, come over to him and not until the prophets, particularly Elias, have called down the wrath of God upon him is Antichrist struck down. This version of the play must have been remarkable for its singing rather than for any dramatic impact.[16] Nevertheless, there are a number of topical allusions in the play, and it is noteworthy that the author makes the king of Germany the last to yield. Many critics have seen in the figure of Hypocrisy an attempt at anticlerical satire.

The French *Jour de Jugement,* which includes the play of Antichrist, has considerably more detail about the connection between him and the devil, about his birth, and about the pomp and circumstance of worldliness. The struggle between Antichrist and Elias ends in the prophet's defeat and execution. Only the direct intervention of God through his angels restores Christianity. The French play belongs to the fourteenth century, and doubtless its chief attraction lay in its processional aspect and the large number of players and scenes involved. Here, after all, was the final contest between good and evil. The spectators were on the side of good, but there was no reason why evil should not put on a good show for its brief period of triumph.

We have seen that Old Testament scenes were freely incorporated into the Passion plays. One incident, however, attained great popularity—the story of Daniel in Babylon. Several plays on the subject are extant, but we need discuss only one, that from Beauvais. This play has recently been given a splendid production in New York and is now probably the best known of medieval plays. It is a good choice. The manuscript contains

[16] It does show considerable structural skill in balancing the world of Christ against that of Antichrist, in producing contrasts by putting Biblical words in the mouths of Antichrist and his followers, and in characterizing the various empires in political and theological terms. The play stands apart from the general tradition and is unique in its use of apocryphal material for the purpose of commenting on the contemporary scene. Even if one discounts the theories which see references to Friedrich Barbarossa in the descriptions of the German emperor, there can be no doubt of the author's opinions about the relative value of the great powers of his day. The material follows fairly closely the account of Antichrist given by Adso, whose text is given in Young, *Drama of the Medieval Church,* II, 496 ff.

musical notation, and although, as always, the exact transcription is open to discussion, the combination of splendid staging, dignified verse, and solemn music upon exotic instruments produces a profound effect even upon a modern audience. The clash of cymbals and sound of horns at the loud revel in Belshazzar's palace is interrupted by the voice of doom. The prophecy is interpreted, and confusion reigns, to be succeeded by the onward march (in procession) of the soldiers of Darius. There is great emotional impact too in the scene with the lions. Hilarius had already written a play on the subject, which dramatized the feast of Belshazzar, the interpretation of the prophecy, the triumph of Darius, Daniel's disgrace, and his escape from the lion's den. The Beauvais play, dating probably from the middle of the twelfth century, seems to have close connections with the Hilarius version in structure and versification, but it is a more finished play. The motivation is better, the characters more consistent. It is clear, however, when the play is performed, how much depends on the impact of the individual scenes, which are designed, by combined aural and visual effects, to impress on the reader such contrasts as pagan splendor and Christian simplicity and steadfastness, the passing of worldly pomp as compared with the eternity of the Lord and, most of all, the inevitable punishment of wickedness. It should not be forgotten that the drama of Daniel was one of the best-known prefigurations of Jesus and that his rescue from the lions was interpreted as the saving of mankind by Christ—and equally that the death of the wicked counselors represented the punishment of the wicked in Hell. Medieval lions made a very fair substitute for devils. It hardly comes as a surprise, therefore, to learn that the play was designed for the Christmas season. The later mystery plays usually included Daniel's story in the part of the play devoted to those prophets who had foretold the coming of Christ.

The Daniel play, like other religious dramas, moved the audience by the pictorial and musical presentation of scenes which illustrated beliefs fundamental to their life—the reality of hell, the punishment of sin, the need for repentance. The justification for dramatic presentation, so far as the Church was concerned, lay in the fact that they intensified such beliefs in a way that a mere sermon could not. It is no accident that the great period of religious drama coincides with such phenomena as the flagellants, mass preaching, and other emotional aspects of religion. The need for greater vividness, for stronger doses of emotion, was apparently in the air.

Nevertheless there was another type of religious play which sought its effects in a different way, one conditioned by a widespread literary fashion which was itself ultimately dependent on theological teaching. It has already been noted in connection with several of the French Passion plays that they introduced allegorical figures, such as Mercy and Justice, to explain and clarify the actions of the play. In doing so they were following a common practice in secular literature. The *Roman de la Rose* had shown how personified characteristics could be made to move as human beings and provide a continuous narrative. Such abstractions had the great advantage of being easily recognizable characters who would act in a predictable way. Their didactic value is obvious, and a combination of them made up a world which agreed well with the medieval view of human character as composed of various combinations of qualities. For the world was, in final analysis, the human soul in which these various qualities sought to obtain the upper hand. The *Psychomachia* of Prudentius had taught the Middle Ages to think in terms of such an allegorical conflict, and it had many readers and successors. The later Middle Ages loved the allegory, with all its possibilities of description, analysis, and didacticism, and used it for the most varied purposes, to represent the pursuit of love and to show a conflict between two ways of life. Some of these uses appeared in drama, for example, the French love allegory, but the principal dramatic use of allegory was to represent the fate of the human soul.

Some preliminary semidramatic attempts in the form had been made in such works as the contest between Fasting and Carnival (examples from Sweden and Italy), and in the Dances of Death, where Death calls on representatives of all social orders to do his bidding. But it is not until the fifteenth century that we find real allegorical drama and then chiefly in England, France, and the Netherlands. These works are usually called moralities, probably after the French term "moralité" or way of life; contemporary England called them "moral plays." The earliest, *Mankind* and *Mind, Will and Understanding,* as well as a fragment, *Pride of Life,* are relatively primitive. The first mingles the struggle for man by the deadly sins and the virtues with crude burlesque by associated devils. The second is strongly didactic and scholastic; the third shows the worldly pride of a great king which is, no doubt, suitably chastised. The first two of these were bound into the same manuscript (from the first half of the sixteenth century) as a fine allegorical play, *The Castle of Perseverance.* The action here is much more complicated than in the others and much better motivated. The World, the Flesh, and the Devil, here called Belial, appear, followed by Humanum Genus, here shown as a newborn child. The good and bad angels make bids for his soul in long arguments and, as so often in these plays, evil triumphs by using the argument that there is plenty of time for repentance. Humanity is led off to the world and put in charge of Foolishness, Pleasure, and Backbiting. Care ensures that he stays there, and the deadly sins soon join him. The good angels persist, however. Penitence finally leads him to Confession, and she cares for him in the Castle of Perseverance. An attack by the sins is beaten off by the virtues, but Humanity, now an old man, is lured out by Avarice. Death approaches and, in spite of the pleas of Mercy, demons seize Humanity's soul. Once again Mercy and Peace plead with God against Justice and Truth, and the soul is rescued.

The Castle of Perseverance is an interesting sample of a type which the late Middle Ages obviously appreciated. We can admire its ingenuity rather than like it. But the play of *Everyman* has excited and moved audiences in every age and has been frequently revised and adapted. The reasons for this are not immediately clear from a summary or even from a reading. The play begins, after the usual preliminary exposition, with a prologue in Heaven in which God expresses his sorrow at Man's disregard of the sacrifice his Son had made and at his way of life. He sends out Death to inform Everyman that he must go to his reckoning at once. Everyman, horrified, begs for time, even a day, to amend his account, but there is no respite. He must go. Now begins a search for a companion on his way. One after another of those he had thought faithful profess their readiness until they hear his destination—Fellowship, Kindred, Cousin, Worldly Goods, all forsake him. Good Deeds would gladly go, but is held down by Everyman's sins. In despair he turns to Knowledge. She is prepared to go and be his guide. She leads him to Confession, who gives him penitence, sorrow, and contrition which free Good Deeds. Then Strength, Discretion, Five Senses, and Beauty join them. Everyman's time draws near, and he is ready to meet his doom, but as Beauty sees the grave, her determination fades; she runs away. Strength, Discretion, and Five Senses too depart. Only Knowledge and Good Deeds make the final journey and see Everyman received by the Angel into Heaven. A "Doctor" provides the final summation.

The play clearly puts into dramatic form the theologically prescribed way to salvation. The stress on knowledge and good deeds, on the necessity for confession, penitence, and absolution, the long disquisition on the seven sacraments, the opposition between the vanities of this world and the joys of the next, all these show a piece written, if not by a cleric, then under strong clerical influence. The printed copies of it (there are no manuscripts) are probably later than the Reformation, but there is no hint in the play of any doubts. The sources on which the work is based are not difficult to see. The well-known story of Balaam and Josaphat (a Christianized version of the Buddha story) contained an episode about a man who searched for his true friends which was "interpreted" in much the same way as in *Everyman*. The later Middle Ages was rich in books on the *Ars Moriendi* (How to die), which follow a very similar pattern to the play. It is even possible that *Everyman* is a translation of the Dutch play *Elckerlijk* by Petrus Dorlandus of Diest, a Carthusian monk, but the reverse is equally possible.[17] Thus the material and the treatment are not original. Yet the play, when performed, is deeply moving. It is easy to account for this by saying that Everyman's experience is one which everyone must face and that we therefore identify ourselves with him. Undoubtedly the medieval audience did so identify itself, but such an explanation does less than justice to the author. He has characterized each of the qualities brilliantly, bringing into their speeches all the little touches to be expected of persons who embody them. Not only is the matter adjusted to their characterization but the language in which it is couched reflects the personality—Fellowship's loud protestations, reinforced by frequent oaths, contrast sharply with the calm quiet of Knowledge, the firm gentleness of Confession, and the modesty and kindness of Good Deeds. The author also brings about the feeling of suspense so necessary to a play of this kind, particularly in the mounting anguish of Everyman at his friends' desertion, the relative calm of the climax where he becomes assured, only to be followed by a second series of desertions before the grave itself. Simple though the matter is, the author has imparted to it dramatic plausibility—a difficult task when the characters are labeled and the end is known. In many ways

[17] Much evidence has been adduced, particularly the rendering of individual words in the two languages, to demonstrate the priority of one play over the other. The article by E. R. Tigg, "Is *Elckerlijk* Prior to *Everyman?*" *Journal of English and Germanic Philology*, Vol. XXXVIII (1939), seems to show that the Dutch play was earlier.

Everyman is the most permanent of the religious plays of the Middle Ages.

There were, of course, morality plays in many countries of Western Europe. Mention is made of several in the Low Countries, in addition to the play of Petrus Dorlandus already noted. Titles are rare in Germany, but in France we find many whose themes can easily be guessed from their names—*Bien-avisé—mal avisé, L'homme Pêcheur, Les Enfants de maintenant,* etc. Not all are concerned with religious themes; we find such titles as *Condamnation de banquet* and the usual allegories of love. None of them bears comparison with *Everyman.*

Our survey of the medieval drama is almost complete. There were numerous plays on secular themes in the late Middle Ages, of which perhaps the best known are the play of Griseldis, whose story is well known from Chaucer's *Clerk's Tale,* and is based on Boccaccio's tale, and the enormous *Mystère de Troie la grant,* a play lasting four days and containing over 30,000 verses. The material is taken from Guido di Colonna's version. Its author, Jacques Milet, wrote the play between 1450 and 1452, obviously intending it for performance, but the lack of information about any presentations, coupled with the large number of extant manuscripts and editions, indicates that its success was more literary than dramatic. Its technique is entirely that of the religious plays, a long series of individual scenes with little or no dramatic unity. The Netherlands produced some interesting plays, called *Abele Spelen* whose subjects are often drawn from the romances, although the treatment of the characters is vastly different.

One type of dramatic production has hardly been mentioned —true comedy. Examples are hard to find before the late fifteenth century, and the French farces and *sotties,* the German *Fastnachtspiele* come too late to be included in medieval drama. Except for a few isolated examples in Latin, we must return to Arras for the only true comedy of the Middle Ages. Adam le Bossu, Adam de la Halle, or Adam d'Arras, as he is variously called, was a professional trouvère, apparently a member of a *puys* and a person of some note in his native town, who spent some time in Paris and died, shortly after 1288, in Italy in the service of Robert d'Artois. He clearly belongs to the same tradition as that of Jean Bodel. His play *Jeu de la Feuillée* is pure entertainment. It opens with the author himself upon the stage, ironically stating that he is tired of his wife and must go away for relief. His praise of her, however, makes it perfectly clear that he is deeply attached to her. His father agrees that he should go to Paris to study, but argues that his own state of health does not allow him to part with any money. A doctor diagnoses his disease as avarice, and there follow descriptions of others who suffer from the same disease, easily recognizable to the audience. A series of scenes follow which make fun of unfaithful wives, corrupt and lecherous clergy, and of many citizens of Arras. Night is now presumed to fall, and a fairy procession enters headed by Fée Morgue [Morgan la Fée], with Harlequin and others. Most of the mortals receive their wishes, but Riquier is to be cursed with a bald head and Adam is to stay at home with his wife. A drinking scene follows, broken off only by bells tolling St. Nicholas' Eve.

There can be no question that this piece is pure comedy. It has no didactic purpose, for the object of its satire is fun at the expense of others, not moral instruction. Yet it owes nothing to classical comedy and little to the comic elements which have been mentioned in connection with the mystery plays. The bringing on to the stage of characters known to the audience, including the author himself, is characteristic of the earliest stages of comedy, yet the play is sophisticated, full of irony and pointed jests. The introduction of the fairy rout associates it with pagan festival plays, but the introduction of Fée Morgue and her companions is really a further opportunity for satiric comment. The play has little form, no plot worth speaking of, but a great deal of liveliness of thought and language. It is what all true comedy should be, enlightened comment on the human scene. It is not surprising, however, that the work had no successors. The mere assembly of characters upon the stage could produce an interesting play only in the hands of a master of observation and wit. In the hands of a lesser man it would be boring or nonsensical. It also depended on such organizations as the *puy* or confrérie for its performance. Without such an organization its chances of performance were small indeed.

Adam's other play, *Robin et Marion,* on the other hand, belongs to a quite different tradition. We have seen how the lyric form known as the *pastourelle* achieved wide popularity in northern France. Such a form was well adapted for dramatic presentation, and it is probably because of his reputation that Adam's version has survived. There may very well have been others. The play, or rather musical comedy, for it contains numerous songs, begins with Marion singing the praises of her lover, Robin. A knight appears, makes love to her, and is rejected. Robin and Marion eat, sing, and dance, but while Robin is fetching their friends, the knight again appears in search of a lost falcon. Again he is rejected, but now Robin appears, with the falcon, and is promptly beaten for mistreating it. The resulting confusion enables the knight to swing Marion on his horse and make off. Robin and his friends make elaborate plans to recover her, but they are not necessary. She has escaped merely by telling the knight she prefers Robin to him and thereby branding herself a complete fool. Robin is full of heroics, which he partly justifies later by rescuing a sheep from a wolf, but the rest of the play passes in singing and feasting.

Here we have something very close to pastoral drama. The shepherd's life is idealized, and even the necessary incident with the knight here is resolved without trouble and to the advantage of the shepherdess. The theme, such as it is, is the sweetness and simplicity of country life, the charm—and the play has great charm—comes from the artless characters, the singing and dancing, and the air of peaceful content. A slight but effective piece of entertainment.

The later Middle Ages offers numerous examples of low comedy—the farce, *sotties,* comic interlude—but few are of great literary value. Their interest lies chiefly in the influence they exerted on the literature of the Renaissance. The "transition" from medieval drama to drama in the modern sense is smoothest in the field of comedy, since the basic elements remained unchanged. Any attentive reader of Shakespeare can easily trace the connection between his comic characters and their medieval counterparts. In tragedy the gulf between the Middle Ages and the great works of the seventeenth century is wide indeed. Here the models from classical antiquity were so important that it is hardly possible to observe any continuity. Only in the characteristics of certain figures is it possible to see the continuation of a medieval theatrical tradition.

Generally speaking the drama is, for modern taste, the least successful of the literary genres practiced in the Middle Ages. Only rarely did it attract an author of real genius, and it is clear, both from its language and style and from the forms in which it has reached us, that it was rather a popular amusement than a literary type. Even in its serious manifestations it wears the marks of the amateur. Nowhere do we find anything like the subtle characterization or deep psychological insight which marks the best of the romances. Nevertheless, the late Middle Ages laid the foundations of a popular theater, of an acting tradition, and of certain basic characters upon which, under the influence of the classics, a great edifice of European drama was to arise.

10

The Beast Epic

It is customary nowadays to think of animal stories in connection with children. The "good" animals, who are in a majority, are usually chubby, have large eyes, and amuse themselves by dancing and singing, often in rather surprising tones. The few bad specimens, mostly dark in color and lean, exist only to be discomfited by the overwhelming innocence of their more favored compatriots. They live in a kind of paradise where storms are rare and the more urgent needs of life take care of themselves. The Middle Ages thought otherwise. They reserved Paradise for the hereafter or, at most, for a small number of very special human beings on earth. The animals they portray are very hard characters, not one of whom is innocent, unless he is too stupid to be anything else, and every one of whom has certain "defects" of character which either make him very successful, like Reynard the Fox himself, or very much the opposite, like the wolf Isengrim. I know of no medieval work in which dog actually eats dog, but the principle is there in all the beast epics, in whatever language they are written and in whatever century they appear. Such a literary form is perfectly adapted to satire, and it was used in this way by virtually every writer who reshaped the material which accumulated about the person of Reynard the Fox.

There are animal stories in all languages in all parts of the earth, and everywhere certain characteristics are attributed to each animal. It is worth noting that these characteristics by no means always correspond to the actual character of the beast in question. The wolf, whose reputation is so low in the European tradition, is, the naturalists tell us, by no means the stupid, greedy, and faithless animal he is represented to be. Nevertheless, once a tradition has been established, it continues and the wolf and others must suffer. Nineteenth-century critics, led by Grimm, went to great lengths to prove that the beast epic was somehow connected with Germanic and Indo-European tradition, that it was part of a very ancient heritage. Wider knowledge has exploded such theories. Voigt, the editor of the Latin beast epic *Ysengrimus* (one of the best edited texts in medieval literature), pointed out that it was very strange that such a deep-seated tradition should at first manifest itself only in obvious translations from the French, and that later works, whether written in Germany or the Netherlands, should change the style and point of view, but not the fundamental material.

There is little doubt that stories about animals circulated orally in all countries of Europe. The characters were to some extent determined by the various versions of the *Physiologus,* a bestiary of serious purpose, but often fantastic in its descriptions of animals.[1] But when we consider the beast epic as it exists in writing, certain facts force themselves on our attention. The first is that almost all extant versions of the Reynard the Fox material stem from the Low Countries, northern France, and western Germany. This remarkable phenomenon surely indicates that the beast epic as we have it is not a haphazard gathering of tales about Reynard the Fox, but a gradual expansion of a story which was popular in one area. An examination of the written versions confirms this supposition. The core

[1] The various versions are more concerned with the alleged "properties" of the animals and their allegorical significance than with accurate description.

of all of the earlier versions is the story of the curing of King Lion's sickness by Reynard. The shortest versions include the incident; it is a high point of the longest. It would thus appear very probable that some form of this incident became very well known either in oral, or in written form, that it attracted the attention of literary men and was worked into epic form, and that subsequent authors invariably used a previous literary form of the story upon which to build longer works in verse or prose. The lion's sickness episode disappears from the later Flemish and Low German stories but its locale—the gathering of animals at the court of King Lion—remains. The possibility that this same "core" could have been used independently by different writers in different times and at different places is remote.

The basic story is found in the collection of fables attributed to Aesop. These fables were not known in the West in their original language during the Middle Ages. The collection in Greek which we now possess was put together in the Eastern Empire during the tenth century. The Middle Ages knew Aesop's *Fables* through the Latin versions of Phaedrus (in verse, first century A.D.), and Avianus (fourth to fifth century A.D.). The fables of Phaedrus, rewritten in Latin prose, were known as the fables of Romulus, and to him numerous collections were ascribed. The "Romulus" fables do little more than tell the bare story, emphasizing the moral. A large number of the episodes in the longer versions of the Reynard story can be traced to the "Romulus" collections, but not—and this is important —the core story of the curing of the lion. The story was known either through oral transmission or from a collection now lost, and since it appears in neither Avianus nor Phaedrus, the likelihood of oral transmission is strong. The text of the Aesop fable is as follows: [2]

The lion had grown old and lay sick in his lair. All the animals came to visit him except the fox. The wolf, seeking favor, accused the fox before the lion, saying that he had no respect for the all-powerful [monarch] and therefore had not come. At this point the fox appeared

[2] *Aesopica*, ed. B. E. Perry (1952), p. 421.

and heard the last words of the wolf. The lion roared at him, and he looked for some way of excusing himself. "Who," he said, "of those here values you as much as I; I have wandered everywhere, seeking a cure for you from the physicians—and I have found one." The lion immediately bade him tell of the cure, and he said: "Flay the wolf alive and wrap his warm hide around you." As the wolf lay dead before him the fox said, laughing: "You should not rouse bad temper in a master but good temper."

The story shows that a person working against another turns the trick against himself. That this story was known as early as the ninth century is certain, for there exists a version of it in sixty-eight Latin verses by Paulus Diaconus (early ninth century). The bear, admittedly, loses his skin instead of the wolf. Many details, not in Aesop, are added, which were later to become an integral part of the tradition, for example, the production by the fox of the shoes he says he has worn out in searching for a cure. We naturally cannot tell whether Paulus added these details himself or whether they were already established as part of the story. It may be noted that no moral is attached.

The next evidence we have of the story is of a very different kind. It is found in a narrative Latin poem of 1,228 lines, usually called *Ecbasis Captivi,* intended as a religious allegory, which was written about 940 by a German monk of the monastery of St. Evre in Toul.[3] A calf, tired of the farmyard, runs away and is captured by a wolf. The wolf, naturally, intends to eat it and begins to feed it up for the next day. Meanwhile the farmyard is aroused, and the dog leads the bull and the rest of the herd towards the wolf's lair. The wolf regales his companions, the otter and the hedgehog, with the story of how the fox proposed to King Lion that he could be cured of his sickness by wrapping himself in the wolf's skin. As the wolf finishes, the herd arrives. The calf escapes in the confusion, the wolf is tossed by the bull into a high tree. The calf returns to his safe farmyard.

[3] *Aesopica,* p. 622. Also in *Monumenta Germaniae Historica,* Poetae aevi carolini, ed. E. Dümmler, I, 62 ff.

The interpretation of the frame story is clear—the inexperienced monk leaves the cloister for the outer world, is snared by the devil, and is saved only by the intervention of his brother monks. The inner story is there only for entertainment, but it is worth noting that the well-known words of Matthew 7:15, "Beware of false prophets which come to you in sheep's clothing but inwardly they are ravening wolves," were constantly applied to erring monks. It is by no means impossible that the wolf of the *Ecbasis* was not Satan, but a worldly monk who led others astray.

The inner story has expanded the sick lion theme a little. The author is very mannered and loves to show off his Latin vocabulary, so that it is hardly surprising that he gives us a full description of the lion's court at which the animals assemble. It may, in fact, be said that the *Ecbasis* is the first work in which the story reaches epic proportions. Although hardly a great work of art (it was probably a school exercise), it shows a conscious effort at elaboration and epic fullness.

The *Ecbasis* had been provided with additional material to increase its length and interest. If, as seems likely, the author was using a vernacular, or at least popular, story as the basis for his composition, it is fair to assume that a narrative version was already in existence in the regions west of the Rhine. Nevertheless, we have no written evidence of its existence until the twelfth century, and it is so much the more surprising to find the story next appearing as the core of one of the most perfectly constructed narrative poems of the Middle Ages. The work was first published in 1832 under the title *Reinardus vulpes,* but the title of the standard edition (1884) by E. Voigt, *Ysengrimus,* is more accurate. For this poem, alone of these which tell of the struggle of Reynard and Isengrim, has the wolf as its hero. It has been said with some justice that the poem might well be entitled "Isengrim's not," the life and death of Isengrim, for, like the *Nibelungenlied,* it tells of the decline and fall and ultimate death of the wolf. It may be remarked at once that *Ysengrimus* is the only one of the very numerous stories in which he appears which tells of his death.

The author is named in one manuscript as Magister Nivardus, a person about whom we have little definite knowledge. He was certainly an extremely learned man; he had certainly traveled considerably in the Low Countries and northern France; he had probably studied in Paris. Although the name is fairly common, there are no extant documents containing it which could possibly refer to him. We must be satisfied to call him Master Nivardus of Ghent. There are numerous references to events in the early twelfth century in the poem, and a careful study of them has made it virtually certain that the work was written about 1150.

Magister Nivardus was a master of Latin and a master of epic form. He writes in the classical quantitative distich, a hexameter followed by a pentameter, and his lines follow very closely the classical rules. The only variations which occur are due to differences in the length of certain vowels which were normal in medieval Latin and to the introduction of alliterative and internal rhyme. These latter features were regarded by most medieval writers as embellishments adding variety to a verse form which, it should be remembered, was for them a matter of formal rules. Nivardus had no more *feeling* for quantity than has a modern imitator of classical Latin verses. It might even be said that Master Nivardus knew his Latin too well. His vocabulary is enormous, and he is so at home in the language that his statements are often elliptical and fraught with double meanings.

It is obvious that a poem of 6,574 lines must contain a great deal more material than the story of the sick lion and, as will be seen from the following summary, the poet has indeed drawn upon numerous sources for other stories which tell of the enmity of Isengrim and Reynard and which may be used, in the best epic tradition, to weave a story pattern of the relation between them and other animals. We find at the beginning of the poem that Reynard is in danger from Isengrim, because of tricks he has played about which we hear later. He succeeds in buying a temporary peace by obtaining a shank of ham for the two of them. Reynard receives the bone. At their next encounter he pays the wolf back by persuading him that he owes it to his position as an ex-monk to eat fish. The wolf lowers his tail through a hole in the ice and is neatly frozen in. Reynard meanwhile steals a rooster and leads the ensuing pursuit past Isengrim, who receives a horrible beating before wrenching himself free. Again there is an interval until Reynard persuades the wolf to act as a judge in a real-estate dispute between four rams, the only result of which is that Isengrim receives the impact of all their four heads at once as they charge at him from opposite corners. He had been naive enough to ask for their fleeces as his payment.

Now comes the sickness of the lion. The version is much expanded, for here the wolf makes himself very unpopular by suggesting that the lion is above the law and might eat, for example, the ox and the ram. The intended victims chase him away, and there is a general call for Reynard. The hare goes to fetch him, but Reynard is officially not at home. When he does appear he has herbs, a mass of worn-out shoes, and a long story of his visit to Salerno, the famous medical center, to find a cure for the lion. The wolf's skin is called for and obtained. The lion is cured, and Reynard loaded with honors. A long poem about his deeds is composed by the bear and recited by the wild boar.

This recapitulation is, of course, a deliberate imitation of the classical epic tradition, and even the silence of the animals is reminiscent of the scene at Dido's court when Aeneas begins his tale. The first exploit is how the fox saved a pilgrimage from attacks by wolves, with the help of Carcophas, the donkey. Reynard's success, however, rather increases the fear Sprotin, the rooster, and Gerard, the goose, feel for him, and the fear is justified when he persuades Sprotin to sing with his eyes shut and grabs him by the neck, only to be tricked in his turn when Sprotin prevails upon him to reply to the insults of pursuing farmers. Another encounter between Reynard and Isengrim follows. Reynard has himself tonsured and tells the wolf that some delicious pies he is eating, which he shares with Isengrim, are normal provender in a monastery. The wolf loses no time in enrolling himself as a novice, but his manners are so crude and his ignorance so crass that the monks almost beat him to death in an alleged ceremony of consecration. When he staggers back home, he finds that Reynard has violated his wife and insulted his children. At this point the story opens and the reasons for Isengrim's anger are clear.

The main story now resumes. Isengrim suffers one misfortune after another. He asks the horse Corvigar to give him his skin to replace the one he gave the lion, and in justification accuses him of stealing rings from the door of the convent where he was a monk. The horse agrees, says he is wearing them on his feet and, when the wolf bends to look, kicks him into insensibility. Reynard now persuades Isengrim to attempt revenge on Joseph, the ram, but the only result is another severe butting.

Reynard now goes to the lion and says that the wolf has expressed a desire to entertain him. The lion with his whole family appears before the surprised Isengrim. He has nothing to offer, but catches a cow and stupidly divides it into equal portions. The incensed lion claws him severely. Reynard, with a more lively appreciation of what is meant by the lion's share and the rights of kings, keeps only a foot for himself.

Now Isengrim is persuaded to claim from Carcophas the skin owed by his father Baudouin. The donkey does not absolutely refuse but, on a suggestion from Reynard, asks for an oath on "relics." The "relics" prove to be a trap, the wolf's paw is caught, and he is forced to bite it off to escape. Weak and unable to defend himself, he meets Salaura the pig and her tribe. His plea for peace is rejected, and he is torn to pieces. Salaura and Reynard say a hypocritical funeral oration over his body and declare that, had he lived, he would have restored the honor of the pope.

This outline does less than justice to Master Nivardus. It does, however, make it clear that the author composed his work by adding to the sick lion episode a series of adventures, most of which involve both Reynard and Isengrim. Voigt shows very clearly that many of these can be traced, in one form or another, to fable collections or similar sources. Almost all of them appear, though never in the same order or in exactly the same form, in later versions of the Reynard the fox story. The great exception is, of course, the death of Isengrim, which appears in no other version and seems to be the poet's own invention. There was apparently a legend that Mohammed had been mutilated by swine. Nivardus very cleverly makes this the fate of the renegade monk Isengrim.

We have already noted how the epic begins with the enmity between fox and wolf already established. It opens with the wolf's only triumph, his obtaining the larger share of ham. From then on his progress is steadily downward to the first major catastrophe, the flaying. Here, with great artistic skill, the author pauses so that he may explain the enmity. The only encounter between fox and wolf is the story of the wolf as monk, a key scene, for it determines the wolf's character throughout and, as we shall see, is the basis upon which the very important satirical elements of the story are built. When the main story resumes, the downward progress continues, with the pattern always the same: the fox acts as *agent provocateur,* inciting the wolf to make demands upon other animals which lead to increasingly severe physical injury, and ultimately to death. The number of actual incidents in the whole story is relatively small, and each is carefully selected to harmonize with the whole. There is not, in Nivardus's work, the proliferation of stories which is so characteristic of most of the Reynard material, the addition of incidents whose only connection with the main theme is that they have Reynard as their "hero." In fact, of course,

Reynard is a subsidiary character. The poem is concerned with the downfall of Isengrim, and Reynard is the instrument by which the downfall is effected.

Few works of medieval literature show such attention to character drawing and motivation as does the *Ysengrimus*. One example must suffice to illustrate this. The scene with the sick lion, told in a few lines by Aesop, in 68 by Paulus Diaconus, is expanded to fill the whole third book, almost 1,200 lines. A very large part of the new material is dialogue. The wolf attempts to curry favor with the king by suggesting that the vegetarian diet advocated by physicians is not necessarily right for a sick lion (Charlemagne is said to have been furious with doctors who deprived him of his favorite roasts!), and recommends that he select some of the assembled company for a meal. Thus the wolf's stupidity, greed, and clumsy attempts to curry favor turn public opinion against him at the start and prepare the way for the enthusiastic reception of the proposition that he shall be flayed. The speeches of the fox and the wolf are masterpieces of character drawing. The fox is cool, reasonable, almost scientific, full of the technical terms of medicine. There is no crude suggestion that the wolf be flayed—merely that a wolf's skin be used. Clearly the wolf should know best where one might be obtained, says the bear. "Well, yes," says the fox "perhaps, but he used not to know much about his relations, unless he has been studying the subject in the monastery." The wolf sees the danger; he eases towards the door, only to be stopped when the fox remarks, "Why, surely, uncle, you're not leaving us. I could have sworn the door moved. And just when we need you." The next moment the fox has made the motion, "Why are we going to look for a wolf when we have such a fine specimen here?" "What do you mean, here? I'm the only wolf here." Even now he writhes, trying to escape: he is too old, his hair is white. But the other animals now see their chance. The fox cunningly asks for testimony about the actual age of the wolf and, since they are sworn, the witnesses have to put themselves in the position of enemies to Isengrim and are thus on the side of the fox. Still the wolf struggles; his pelt is not large enough, he will get another. To this the fox replies that he will gladly add his own if Isengrim's is not big enough, but he is afraid the colors will clash! Even Isengrim's claws are not spared, for the fox cunningly begs the bear to leave Isengrim at least them, only to be accused by other animals of attempting to diminish the worth of the wolf's sacrifice. When the flaying is finally performed, the whole is compared to the divesting of ecclesiastical vestments—very suitable for the wolf as monk.

The whole assembly scene is, of course, in the epic tradition. The lion takes little part. It is the cunning speeches of the fox, the self-interest of the individual members, which are brought to the fore. They are happy to see that the lot has fallen on someone but not on them. The effects are produced almost entirely by speeches. There is little comment by the author, and little is necessary. The dialogue, in spite of the restriction placed on it by the verse form, is not in the least stilted. The cool reasoning of the fox is opposed to the crude, often abrupt conversation of the wolf. The author is well able to reflect character and even mood. A beautiful example occurs in the second book, where Isengrim is caught in the ice. As Reynard approaches, he first merely asks for help. Then he wheedles: "Please, don't leave your old uncle here." But when he sees that he is not going to be helped, he breaks into a torrent of coarse abuse.

We could comment on many new features: the traditional names of animals, many of which survive to this day in popular speech and which are of German, not French, origin; the enormous learning of the work; the highly effective use of proverbs, of local color, and of history; the rhetorical skill of the speeches. Not even the traditional importation of a goddess is omitted, for the third book begins with a discussion of the way Fortune treats poor Isengrim. Yet these are only incidental The purpose of the work was satire, not simply general satire of human foibles but satire of wolfish monks, of men who used their position only for their own selfish ends. Any reader of the *Ysengrimus* notices that the animals are not mere types or caricatures who speak as humans. It is true that each has some definite characteristic which is predominant, but this aspect is stressed far less than in some of the later versions. Each animal is a complex character, who acts like a human being. Their world is not a fairyland or a representation of any particular place. It is a kingdom run by animals by human methods.

To this kingdom Isengrim is the principal menace. He is ever seeking what he may destroy and his conduct is determined, as far as he is able to determine it at all, by his belly and the ever-pressing need to fill it. He admits as much. His is not one of your tiny little stomachs which can easily be filled. His order, he says, calls on him to take more because he needs more. Over and over again the author makes the wolf speak like a member of a religious order. His unsuccessful fishing is caused at least as much by his greed in leaving his tail in for so long as by Reynard's original suggestion. Not only is Isengrim greedy, but he is stupid. This makes him even more of a danger. He claims rights which only an intelligent man could receive. It is right that the fox should vanquish him. But the fox is not treated sympathetically either. He is at least not hypocritical, but he is sharp and unpleasant to a degree. The wolf wished to mingle in the world, and he met the fox and got his deserts. Reynard, however, is not the clever rascal of most of the works that bear his name but a cunning deceiver who has other people do his dirty work. His final sermon over Isengrim is entirely in character.

The *Ysengrimus* is not a charming work. It is cold, often bitter, deadly in the precision of its satire and its laying bare of men's motives. But it is superb in its rhetorical skill, its structure, and its characterization. If ever a poem deserved to be known to a wider audience, it is this.

It might be assumed that a work of such stature as *Ysengri-*

mus would have had a profound influence on the subsequent development of the beast epic, and some critics have indeed claimed to be able to trace such an influence in the various branches of the *Roman de Renart*. The majority of the five manuscripts of the poem date from the fourteenth century, so that the work must still have been known then, but surely if it had been consciously imitated or even well known to later writers of the beast epic we would find other versions with the same incidents in the same order and at least once some mention of Isengrim's death. It is, in fact, much more likely that any resemblances between *Ysengrimus* and later works are due to Nivardus' having borrowed incidents already popular in folk tale (for example, the animals' pilgrimage and the fishing wolf), for which no source or even parallel exists in Aesop or any other fable writer. Such a conclusion would assume that such tales were already circulating, either orally or in writing, in northern France or Flanders.

Except for a shorter version of the *Ysengrimus,* which is very probably nothing more than an abridged version of the longer poem, the next appearance of the story of Reynard is in a poem of Heinrich der Glichezaere, an Alsatian and probably a professional singer. The original poem, written about 1180, survives only in four fragments totaling 685 lines, but an anonymous reworking of it, 2,266 rhyming lines in length, and written about 1240, survives in full. It is no masterpiece. The work divides neatly into three parts, the first of which shows Reynard tricked in turn by Schantekler, the rooster, by a tomtit, by Diezelin, the raven, and by Dieprecht, the cat. These are his only defeats. In the next section he confounds Isengrim on numerous occasions, some of them incidents found in the *Ysengrimus.* The third section is the familiar story of the lion's sickness. Three animals are sent to fetch Reynard from his lair. The bear and the cat suffer in the process. The badger, a relation, is finally successful. Reynard receives great favors for his cure, his friends receive high office—and he ends by poisoning the king.

The element of satire is again strongly marked, but it is generalized. The animals represent human types who live in a rigidly stratified society. The fox is a cunning and utterly amoral person who succeeds in his selfish schemes by using guile, treachery, flattery and, when he can, physical force. The moral seems to be that, in human society, goodness and meekness are no match for cunning and hypocrisy. The poem is crudely constructed. Incidents succeed one another with baffling suddenness; there is little motivation or genuine characterization. Only the figure of Reynard provides any unity.

It is a curious trick of transmission which has left us this unimportant poem and which has deprived us of the earlier versions of the French *Roman de Renart*. The oldest *branches* or sections probably antedate Heinrich's version, and the marked resemblances, but not exact correspondences, between the French and German poems seem to indicate that the German incidents are based on old forms of extant *branches*. It is worth noting that Heinrich uses a mixture of French (Pinte, Schantekler, Hersant) and German (Dieprecht, Diezelin) names.

The numbering and dating of the various *branches* (the term is a medieval one) is a highly complex matter, and understanding of it is not made any easier by the fact that different editors use different systems, often renumbering according to their own hypotheses about the dating of the various *branches*. The reader should be aware that there is no such thing as a *Roman de Renart* in the sense that there is a *Roman de la Rose* or even a "Roman de Tristan." When we use the term "romance" in Arthurian literature we usually can speak of one version of a story, with slight variants, or of several different versions of the same basic story. The *Roman de Renart* is simply an agglomeration of stories most but not all of which have Reynard as a central figure. It is possible to arrange these in a sequence so that we have the "infancy" of Reynard at the beginning and his death at the end, but the extant versions do not follow this sequence. The adventures in between these two terminal events have often only the slimmest connection with one another, although knowledge of the events of one story is often assumed in another. The *Roman de Renart* is really a number of varying collections of stories about Reynard and his associates. The latest editor, Roques, divides the extant manuscripts into three groups which have fundamental similarities, and bases his edition on these. A glance at the edition will show that his order has no logical sequence. His story begins with the judgment at the lion's court upon Reynard for the crimes he has committed against Isengrim; the siege of Mauperties, Reynard's castle, where he has taken refuge; his cunning defense, final capture, and pardoning. This seems very like a story's end—but it is immediately followed by a completely separate adventure about Reynard, disguised by paint. The second *branche* (using Roques' numbering) tells of Isengrim trapped in a well, clearly a separate story, and then of the birth of the fox and the wolf. Obviously there is no sequence. Not until *Branche* VIII do we reach the story which gives the reasons for Isengrim's appeal to the king in *Branche* I.

Other groupings in different manuscripts give the same impression of disorder. All we can hope to do here is to give some idea of the date of composition of the various parts and comment on a few of the more important features. For convenience, the various *branches* will be given Martin's numbering, which has been most widely adopted. The earliest extant *branche* (II) is that written by Pierre de St. Cloud, which is concerned with the defeat of Reynard by the other animals and with the adultery between him and Hersant, the female wolf. These stories are found in the version of Heinrich der Glichezaere. A reasonable guess at the date of composition would be 1174–77. The myth of the creation of fox and wolf is also included. After this came the flight of Reynard from court, a story of the wolf drunk (V), the fishing episode (III), Isengrim in the well (IV), and minor stories about 1178. The dates of the remaining *branches* are usually assigned as between 1179 and 1205. The most important stories are in *Branches* X (cure of the lion), VI (the judicial duel between Reynard and Isengrim), and VIII (the pilgrimage of the animals). Later works such as *Renart le Novel* (1288–92) and *Renard le contrefait* (before 1342) are conscious imitations, not part of the original *Roman.*

The sources of these new stories are in many cases unknown. We can speculate that there is a connection between some of them (e.g., the fox and the crow) and the fables of Aesop. Some are probably popular stories of animals which became attached to the Renard cycle because of its rapidly growing popularity. It is also very probable that many were not originally animal stories at all, but were put into this form so that the satire they contained became generalized and thus allowed the author to escape censure for what might otherwise have been regarded as over-personal references. The later *branches,* indeed, became so full of contemporary allusions that the popularity of the *Roman* began to wane, and by the fifteenth century it had been forgotten in France.

Many of the stories in the French collection are there purely for amusement. Some are clearly reworkings of a story already incorporated in the *Roman;* for example, there are two sieges of Mauperties, two incidents involving the ringing of church bells by animals, Reynard commits adultery with the lioness as well as the female wolf, Reynard enters a monastery as well as Isengrim. An interesting feature of the later *branches* is the introduction of human characters. They are, of course, always in the background, but in some episodes there is conversation between animals and humans and even agreements between them. This element reaches the height of absurdity in a scene in which a hare rides (on a horse!) to the lion's court with a peasant on the end of his lance, tied by the feet. He had been forced to chastise him for insulting his honor! Under such treatment the genre was bound to suffer. It becomes ridiculous rather than amusing.

Many critics have discussed the satirical aspects of the *Roman de Renart,* and the general tendency has been to ascribe to the various parts satirical intentions of great subtlety. The animals are regarded as manifestations of the seven deadly sins: the lion represents pride, the bear gluttony, the lioness avarice, etc. Such clear-cut definitions are out of place. The wolf is a combination of many sins; Reynard himself at one time or another shows all of them. Truly virtuous animals are hard to find. Those who do not sin refrain because they are either too weak or too stupid. Other critics have seen in the *Roman* a comprehensive satire of the medieval social order from the point of view of "little people." They point to the selfish tyranny of the lion, who does not hesitate to kill or maim other animals for his own interest and yet will pervert justice for a real crime when suitably bribed; they mention the misuse of the sanctuary afforded by the church to criminals, for "repentance," which merely affords an interlude during which further crimes can be worked out. The main occupation of the "nobles" who crowd the lion's court is said to be the pillaging and torture of those weaker than themselves. It is, however, very doubtful whether popular writers of the beginning of the thirteenth century would have thought in such comprehensive terms. The satire is on a much smaller scale. It criticizes the foolish acts of men in general, their greed, their gullibility, their sanctimonious behavior, their hypocrisy. Such behavior is found in any society. Reynard succeeds usually because he is utterly realistic and amoral. He pushes to their logical conclusion the use of the antisocial qualities which others use less efficiently. He is as greedy as the bear, as proud as the lion, more lecherous than any of the other animals, and so hypocritical that he sounds sincere. The view that makes him the avenger of the weak upon the strong, and his own rare defeats examples of the triumph of still weaker animals, seems to me to be reading into the work a social awareness which was not present in the minds of the authors.

It is, of course, true that certain *aspects* of medieval society are satirized. Chief among these is the worldliness of the church and particularly of the monasteries, but tyrannous rulers and grasping peasants, vain ladies and cowardly knights are not neglected. They were the objects of satire in many genres. As the *Roman* developed, it was used for specific effects, particularly satire of the romance of chivalry. Each author has his own pet aversion and used the work to attack it. In the end, however, the story of Reynard caters to several very human characteristics, of which the chief is the pleasure most people receive from watching established authority baffled and defeated by the clever and unscrupulous individual. Reynard is, to put it crudely, a successful gangster. He finds the weaknesses of those in authority and uses them for his own ends. He represents the destructive forces usually latent in society, held in check by laws and codes and formally disapproved of by decent citizens. His exploits are therefore a kind of literary safety valve, a realization of these forces with which very many people have a secret, unacknowledged sympathy. His crimes are outrageous, but he baffles the law and remains the perfect example of the successful rogue.

There is a great deal more unity in the *Roman de Renart* than might at first appear. The characters, once established in the earlier versions, remain consistent whoever the author happens to be. The names given to them reflect these characteristics. Only occasionally do we find a burlesque version in which an animal steps completely out of character, as does, for example, the hare Couard in the episode with the peasant mentioned above. This consistency was, of course, a great advantage in the adding of episodes. Each animal could be expected to behave in a certain way, and in the better written episodes the authors were highly successful in adapting the conversation to the animals' characters. There is also a consistency of a different kind. Similar patterns can be traced in a very large number of the incidents. A plot is formed to trick one or the other animal, often by using him as a decoy to steal something. The animal, lured by greed, goes along with the plot, is caught, and suffers a beating from which he barely escapes with his life. Frequently Reynard, the master plotter, obtains the prize which the other animal had sought. The fishing scene already mentioned is a good example of this. Even better is the episode in which the bear comes to summon Reynard to court. The fox regrets that he can offer the bear nothing but honey, poor food for a bear. Needless to say, Brun vigorously denies that honey is distasteful to him and asks to be led to it. With apparent reluctance Reynard leads him to a split oak near a peasant's yard and gets him to thrust in his nose. He is, of course, neatly trapped and soundly thrashed.

The relations between the sexes in this animal world are interesting. The period in which the *Roman de Renart* was for the greater part composed was, it should be remembered, the zenith of the cult of courtly love. The terminology of this cult appears quite often in the various *branches,* but the attitudes are startlingly different. When any episode involves relationship between the sexes, it may be assumed that such relations will be on the lowest possible level. The lion is harassed by his wife, and she is ready to marry the fox at once when her husband is reported killed. Reynard commits adultery with the wife of Isengrim and on another occasion rapes her merely to annoy the wolf. Deceit and unfaithfulness are assumed. The level is, in fact, exactly that found in the *fabliaux, Schwänke,* or *facetiae,* immoral where it is not farcical, and often both together.

The whole story of Reynard is, in fact, on the same literary plane as the prose tales of the Middle Ages and the comedy scenes in the drama. It is unpretentious and popular. The animals live in a world close enough to ours to be credible, far enough away to allow us to approve and be amused at much which would be crude or immoral among humans. In this circumstance lies its greatest charm. Its deep hold on the people is shown by one thing. In the French language the original word for fox (*goupil*) was replaced by "Renard."

The stories of Reynard were popular in other places than France. In Flanders a version was being developed which, unlike the French *Roman*, shows remarkable unity, and which served as the basis for all later German versions. This Flemish version has none of the length and loose form of the French, for it selects its incidents very carefully and attempts with considerable success to make a unified narrative from the various stories. The work, written in Middle Dutch and usually called *Van den vos Reynaerde*, exists in several manuscripts, each containing slightly different versions.

There has been considerable discussion about the authorship of this Middle Dutch version, but it cannot be said that any definite decision has been reached. The Coburg manuscript, written about 1400, has a prologue of forty lines which states that the work was written by a certain Willem. The words following the name have obviously been changed from the original reading, which is found in a Brussels manuscript and reads "Willem die Madok maecte" (Willem who wrote *Madok*). This, while interesting, throws no light on the personality of the author, and a reference in another manuscript to a certain "Arnout," whose work Willem had completed, further complicates the matter.[4] There is little evidence of different styles in the extant version, and we may well assume that the author is Willem, possibly the cleric of that name who is mentioned in a document as living in Hulsterlo in 1269. There are references to Hulsterlo in the poem.

Whoever the author was, his version of the adventures of Reynard formed the basis of all subsequent versions in Dutch, Low German, and High German. Unlike the French *Roman de Renart*, it is a unified story centered around the judgment at

---

[4] It has been suggested, with some justification, that "Arnout" may be nothing more than "Perrot" (i.e., Pierre de St. Cloud, the author of the first *branche* of the Roman de Renard), with the capital omitted. The omission of capitals for later insertion by a specialist illuminator is common practice in medieval manuscripts.

348 THE BEAST EPIC

court. Nevertheless, the basis is *Branche* I of the *Roman,* and the author claims that he has used French sources. Several new features are introduced, of which the most important is Reynard's "hidden treasure." It seems likely that the German-speaking parts of the Low Countries had already modified, at least in oral form, the story of the judgment. The story opens with the claims of the animals about the wrongs inflicted on them by Reynard. Isengrim complains of the abuse of his wife and children; the dog Cortois, speaking French, tells of the theft of a sausage, but is promptly reminded by Tibert the cat that he had originally stolen it himself. Pancer the beaver tells of wrongs done to many animals. Only Reynard's nephew, Grimbart the badger, attempts any defense. He is having some success when a procession approaches. It is Chanticleer, accompanied by a funeral procession bearing the body of his wife, Coppe. His pitiful tale of Reynard's depredations turns the scale. Brun the bear is ordered to fetch the fox. He obeys with alacrity, only to have his greed for honey turned to his own destruction. Reynard leads him to a split oak in which there is said to be a huge store of his favorite food. Brun is trapped and beaten almost to death by the aroused country folk. He arrives back in court with one ear torn off and minus a great deal of skin. Tibert has little more success. This time it is greed for mice that leads him into a trap. He escapes, after mauling a priest who, in his anxiety to catch the animal which has been stealing his chickens, runs to the scene naked. Grimbart now undertakes the mission. He prevails upon Reynard to come with him and on the way listens to his confession—a neat method of introducing many of the other adventures of the fox, including the incidents of his causing Isengrim to be caught in the ice, his adventures in the monastery, and his being trapped when stealing ham. For his misdeeds he receives twenty-four strokes from Grimbart, but his attitude is far from repentant: he has to be restrained from pursuing chickens as they make their way to court.

Reynard's condemnation is little more than a formality. Isengrim, Brun, and Tibert undertake to carry out the hanging. But Reynard has one more confession to make, and on the gallows he tells a long story of how his own father had come into possession of "Ermanrich's treasure" and had used it to win over the support of Tibert, Isengrim, Brun, and Grimbart for his own plans to supplant Nobel the lion and substitute the stupid Brun. Reynard claims to have seen his father bury the treasure and to have moved it so that when his father failed to find it, he hanged himself in rage and the conspiracy failed. The king and queen are interested immediately when they hear the word "treasure." They take Reynard to one side for consultation. He names the hiding place at which the treasure may be found, Kriekenput near Hulsterlo. The king, not unnaturally, is mistrustful of Reynard's statements, even when made as confessions on the gallows, and is not convinced until the hare, Cuvaert, is called in to testify to their truth.

All is again sweetness and light. Reynard is forgiven and placed under the royal protection. He cannot, unfortunately, go with the king to find the treasure because he is under the papal ban and has to make a pilgrimage to Rome. For this he needs a pilgrim's satchel and new shoes, and the queen feels no compunction in ordering the bear to give up a piece of his skin for a satchel and Isengrim and his wife each to sacrifice the skin from two paws. Reynard sets off, accompanied by the sanctimonious Belin, the ram, and Cuvaert, the hare. He turns aside to his castle, lures Cuvaert inside, and eats him. To Belin he gives a "message" in his wallet, to be opened before the king. When Belin does so Cuvaert's head is revealed. Again Reynard is denounced; there is universal sympathy for Reynard's victims. Firapel, the leopard, proposes that the fox be placed under the ban and that Belin, as an accomplice, be handed over, with all his family and descendents, to any beast of prey who can seize him.

The author has used many devices to expand his story—the long descriptions of the hue and cry after Brun and Tibert, and

the introduction of named human beings with definite characteristics and of local topographical allusions. The whole story is
full of popular sayings and realistic description, but the judgment scene sets its tone. There is much use of medieval legal
terminology, and the complaints before the king follow the
contemporary system of pleading. It is therefore hardly surprising that the satirical aspects of the work should also concentrate
on the abuse of judicial powers. Reynard's misdeeds have been
presented to the reader and he has himself confessed to many
more. His utter lack of any scruples has been shown again and
again. But, as soon as there is any mention of money, the judge
begins to take a forgiving attitude to his crimes, and both he
and his queen are ready to show mercy to a repentant sinner
when there is any prospect of gain. Typically, they do not suffer anything worse than disappointment from Reynard's treachery. It is the lesser creatures who suffer, Isengrim, Hersant,
Belin, Cuvaert, who fall victims to the failure of justice. All the
pomp and circumstance of the court are shown to be nothing but
an empty shell. The great king is under the thumb of his wife;
each of the animals is the dupe of his own weaknesses; each
seeks nothing but his own advantage. The cunning fox, as wicked
as the rest, differs from them in that he can play on the weaknesses of the individuals who make up the whole and can rely
on them to form associations to exploit anyone who is weaker
than themselves.

This Middle Dutch version is not obviously didactic. The
story is the most important thing and it is well told, with a great
deal of humor and excellent character drawing. Yet the satire
cannot be missed. The jokes at the expense of the monastic
orders, of married priests, of greedy peasants, are all there. But
the tone differs from the earlier versions in its opposition to the
aristocracy. There can be no mistaking the meaning of the judgment scenes, for they caricature the whole system of medieval
justice.

Willem's work was probably written before 1270; a Latin

translation of it was made before 1280. More than a century later there appeared a lengthened version, composed in West Flanders, which added a large amount of material from various sources, much of which had little connection with the story of Reynard. The structure of the addition follows closely the form of the earlier work. Again Reynard is summoned to court; again he defends himself subtly and this time is supported by the queen's favorite, Rukenowe, the she-ape. This time he mentions a different treasure, a magic ring, comb, and mirror, whose description gives the author an opportunity to display some oddly assorted fragments of learning. Isengrim, however, refuses to be placated, and there is a long description of a "judicial" combat which the fox wins by using every low trick imaginable. His victory makes him the chief of all the animals, and he is made chancellor by the lion.

The satire is more obvious, the didacticism more purposeful in *Reinaert II* than in its predecessor. The judicial combat is clearly a parody of such affairs; there is much moral and theological comment and insertion of moralizing fables. The speeches are often monotonous and dreary. Yet this inferior product is of great significance, for from it stem the important versions of the Reynard story in English, Dutch, and Low German.

In 1479 there was printed in Gouda a prose version of *Reinaert II,* and in 1485 the same work was printed in Delft. From the Gouda version the English translation was made which Caxton printed in 1481 and which served as a basis for the popular English chap book. Still more important was the rhyming poetical version, with modernized language, which was printed in Antwerp in 1487. Of this edition only the so-called Culemann fragment remains, but this is enough to show that the text was not exactly that of the earlier version. Furthermore, we find that the poem was accompanied by a prose "explanation" of the moral of the various episodes. This same gloss is repeated in a reprint of the Delft prose version made in 1564, and gives us the name of the author of the new version,

352 THE BEAST EPIC

Hinrik van Alckmer. It was for a long time believed that this Hinrik was the author of the Low German version, because here again a prologue was taken over from the earlier Antwerp version. Of the personality and history of Hinrik we know only what he tells us—that he was a teacher for the duke of Lorraine. From his version, however, there came the greatest of all works in Low German, *Reinke Vos,* first printed in Lübeck in 1498 and again in Rostock in 1517. This work enjoyed enormous popularity. It was reprinted on many occasions until the seventeenth century, and enjoyed the distinction of being adapted into High German by Goethe himself. The explanations of the various chapters already mentioned were retained in the Lübeck and first Rostock editions, but in that made in Rostock in 1539 they were replaced by others of a definitely Protestant tone. The reformers were very conscious of the opportunity for propaganda which the Reynard story afforded them.

The "second prologue" of Hinrik van Alckmer makes very clear the application of the animal world to human society. It explains how men were divided into the four main classes of society—workers, traders and gatherers, priests, and rulers. To each of these corresponds a group of animals; the beasts of burden are workers; the hares and rodents are gatherers; the lion is the supreme ruler with many subsidiary nobles under him, such as the fox, wolf, and bear. No animal corresponds to the clerics but, says the author, the clergy are satirized often enough. In spite of this prologue and the explanations of each chapter, the Low German version is relatively free from direct moralization within the story itself. A comparison with the prose source shows that the story is better told and the dialogue and verse are both handled well, and there is a pleasing simplicity and straightforwardness in the narration. The judicial language and procedure which were so obvious in the earliest Dutch version have been much modified. Nevertheless, there is much wit and clever allusion in the speeches, for example,

Reynard's description of the linguistic ability of a Jew Abrion who alone understood the words written in the magic ring and spoke "all the languages between Poitrou and Luneburg," a distance of less than twenty miles! The literary defects of the work are obvious—there is too much repetition, both of motifs and events, too much digression and obvious moralizing, but the form suited the taste of the period which delighted in loosely strung compilations and didacticism. The story of Reynard became part of the folklore of the German-speaking peoples, and the names and characters are alive today in popular speech and, as might be expected, children's books.

Conclusion

The medieval works which have been studied in the preceding chapters will have given the reader some idea of the richness and depth of medieval literature. Any such selection must inevitably be arbitrary, and it would be perfectly possible to argue that the Spanish national epic, the *Cantar de Mio Cid* would be a more worthy example of the popular narrative poem than the *Nibelungenlied*. The German work was chosen because it permits a better comparative study than the Spanish. Yet it must be admitted that the omission of certain medieval genres gives a distorted picture of medieval literature. Allegory, for example, became increasingly popular from the thirteenth century on and is by far the most characteristic literary form during the later Middle Ages. Allegory in this sense is something quite different from the "allegorical interpretation" which has been so frequently mentioned. It is a sustained narrative in which all, or almost all, of the characters are personifications of abstract qualities which behave like human beings but are always under the dominant influence of the characteristic they represent. The most famous of such works, the *Roman de la Rose,* begun by Guillaume de Loris (fl. 1235–60) and completed, in a different sense and much greater length, by Jean de Meung (*ca.* 1260–1315), is the best known and probably the most successful. The section written by Guillaume is a consistent allegory, where all the aspects of the pursuit of ideal love are conveyed with great charm. All the qualities involved in such a pursuit—Fair Welcome, Generosity, Fortune, Pity, Sweet Glance, Beauty, Hope, and others—which aid the lover and Jealousy, Shame, Evil Rumor, Faithlessness, Greed, Hypocrisy, Fear, Poverty, and even Reason and Chastity, which hinder him, appear, personified, and their actions produce a narrative which has unity and coherence, provided that the reader is aware of the conventions of the genre. Such a treatment of the love theme is admirably adapted to convey in poetical form a theoretical attitude to the pursuit of love. It can be, and was, expanded by all the devices of rhetorical ornamentation. The Middle Ages, taught, as we have seen, to think of character in terms of abstract qualities, enjoyed allegory and found the analysis of it a fascinating pursuit. Of all genres it most clearly approaches the Horatian dictum that literature should mix the pleasant with the useful.

A modern reader, however, usually find allegory tedious. Even *Piers Plowman* requires considerable effort. The problems it studies have little or no immediate interest for him, and his concept of character and, indeed, his whole literary training lead him to reject the convention of fleshless personification and almost mechanical action and reaction. The first part of the *Roman de la Rose* has poetical virtues which make it attractive in spite of its form, but the forcing of the pursuit of love into such allegorical forms as the hunt (Laber's *Jagd*) and the chess game strike us as a tour de force rather than as true literature. Interest in medieval allegory will probably remain the province of specialists.

No such statement could be made about the *fabliaux,* the broad popular narrative works in verse which told stories almost as old as human speech, tales of love of a quite uncourtly kind, of faithless wives and cuckold husbands, of tricks played on the gullible and, as often as not, of immorality triumphant.

The literary value of the *fabliaux* collections themselves is, however, not very great. They are of importance for the source material they provide for the great masters, in particular for Chaucer and Boccaccio. Many of the finest stories of the *Canterbury Tales* and the *Decamerone* are based upon *fabliau* material, itself undistinguished. The same purpose was served by the numerous collections of *Schwänke* and *Facetiae*. They are popular material awaiting the touch of genius to turn them into literature.

No apology is needed for the omission of works whose connection with true literature is remote—didactic material such as the collections of *exempla* and books on manners and conduct; religious material, such as the lives of saints, sermons, and mystical writings. All of them provided material for literature, but that is the extent of their importance.

A study of medieval literature which has hardly any mention of Dante may very well seem like *Hamlet* without the Prince of Denmark. The reasons for not studying him are the result of his very greatness. He is of and yet above medieval literature. In his work he combines virtually all the attitudes and literary values which have been discussed in this book. His vision of love transcends even that of Gottfried von Strassburg; his sense of the relation of man to God is more profound even than that of Wolfram von Eschenbach. He combines the conventions of allegory with those of the starkest realism, the learning of the classics with that of the medieval philosophers. There is ample material for the study of Dante available to English-speaking readers, but perhaps the discussions of lesser artists in this book may help towards the understanding of the most important literary figure of the Middle Ages.

Like all literature, that of the Middle Ages cannot be understood without some knowledge of the attitudes of the times and of the problems which men thought important. Some of these have been discussed in this book. Let us repeat once again that the Middle Ages was a long period. The evolution of the vernaculars into literary languages was a long slow process. The twelfth and early thirteenth centuries saw those vernaculars in full flower, and a fairly short period of relative prosperity and settled conditions gave an opportunity for leisure, without which no great literature is possible. The flowering period was short, the decline long and painful. Only in England is medieval literature at its greatest in the fourteenth century, and then largely because of impulses from an Italy already moving into the Renaissance. But, during this brief flowering, works were produced which for imaginative sweep, depth of humanity, beauty of form, and striving for an ideal have rarely been surpassed.

Chronology

Important works of literature are listed here in the chronological order of their composition. They have been classified as follows: Nar. poetry (narrative poetry, including epic, romance, verse saga, and longer didactic poems), Lyric (lyric, satirical, and occasional poetry in which the narrative element is either secondary or completely absent), Drama (any works designed for presentation orally by two or more persons, whether religious or secular), Prose (works written in prose whose purpose is literary rather than theological, philosophical, or historical). A few works which are not strictly literary have been included because of their importance for the literary development of the Middle Ages. It should be remembered that very few dates in the history of medieval literature are definite and some are the subject of marked disagreement among scholars. In this list an attempt has been made to give the dates most generally accepted. The following conventions have been used:

1116–65	Birth and death dates of an author, both definitely known
ca.1116–1165	Birth date of an author uncertain, date of death known
ca.1116–ca.1165	Both birth and death dates uncertain
1116	Date of composition of a work definitely known
ca.1116	Approximate date of composition of a work
ca.1116/20	Date of composition of a work probably falling between the two dates given
fl.1116–30	Period of an author's activity

Languages are designated as follows: Eng.-English; Fr.-French; Ger.-German; It.-Italian; Lat.-Latin; Prov.-Provençal; M.Dutch-Medieval Dutch; M.Eng.-Middle English; M.H.Ger.-Middle High German; O.Eng.-

Old English; O.Fr.-Old French; O.H.Ger.-Old High German; O.N.-Old Norse; O.Saxon-Old Saxon.

ca.480–524	PROSE: Boethius, *De consolatione philosophiae;* trans. of Aristotelian works on astronomy, music, geometry, etc. (Lat.)
ca.480–ca.570	PROSE: Cassiodorus, *Institutiones, Variae, De orthographia* (Lat.)
ca.535–ca.600	LYRIC: Venantius Fortunatus (Lat.)
ca.570–635	PROSE: Isidore of Seville, *Origines* or *Etymologiae* (Lat.)
fl.660–80	LYRIC: Caedmon, hymns, etc. (O.Eng.)
ca.670–739	PROSE: Bede, *De orthographia, De arte metrica,* etc. (Lat.)
8th–12th cent.	NAR. POETRY: Poems of the Older *Edda* or verse *Edda* (O.N.)
ca.720	NAR. POETRY: *Beowulf* (O.Eng.)
ca.770–840	PROSE: Einhard, *Vita Caroli* (Lat.)
ca.780–856	PROSE: Hrabanus Maurus, *De universo,* etc. (Lat.)
fl.790	LYRIC: Anghilbert; Paulus Diaconus; Theodulf; Walafrid Strabo (Lat.)
Early 9th cent.	NAR. POETRY: *Hildebrandslied; Muspilli* (O.H. Ger.)
	HYMNS: Cynewulf (O.Eng.)
ca.810–869	HYMNS: Gottschalk (Lat.)
ca.830	NAR. POETRY: *Heliand* (O.Saxon)
ca.840–912	LYRIC: Notker Balbulus (Lat.)
fl.850	LYRIC: Sedulius (Lat.)
ca.870	NAR. POETRY: Otfried von Weissenburg, *Evangelienbuch* (O.H.Ger.)
881	NAR. POETRY: *Ludwigslied* (O.H.Ger.)
ca.910–ca.990	NAR. POETRY: Egill Skalla-Grimsson, *Sonatorrek,* etc. (O.N.)
ca.940	NAR. POETRY: Eckehard I (?), *Waltharius, Ecbasis captivi* (Lat.)
fl.970	DRAMA: Hroswitha of Gandersheim, *Dulcitius, Pafnutius, Abraham, Gallicanus, Sapientia* (Lat.)
ca.970–1028	LYRIC: Fulbert of Chartres (Lat.)
After 991	NAR. POETRY: Maldon (O.Eng.)
ca.1000	NAR. POETRY: *Hague Fragment* (of deeds of Charlemagne) (Lat.)
11th cent. to 13th cent.	DRAMA: Easter and Christmas tropes with some dramatic expansion from Limoges, Beauvais, Soissons, Nevers, Vienna, Klosterneuburg, Cividale, etc. (Lat.)
ca.1030	NAR. POETRY: *Ruodlieb* (Lat.)

11th/12th cent.	DRAMA: Limoges *Sponsus* (Lat.)
1035–1123	LYRIC: Marbod of Rennes, *Liber lapidum,* and short poems (Lat.)
*ca.*1040	NAR. POETRY: *Chanson de St. Alexis; Chanson de St. Foy* (O.Fr.)
1056–1133	LYRIC: Hildebert of Lavardin (Lat.)
*ca.*1060	NAR. POETRY: *Barlaam and Josaphat* (Lat.)
1079–1142	PROSE: Abélard, *Historia calamitatum;* letters to Héloïse (Lat.)
*ca.*1095–1143	PROSE: William of Malmesbury, *Liber de antiquitate Glastoniensis ecclesiae, De gestis regum Anglorum* (Lat.)
*fl.*1100	LYRIC: Serlo of Wilton (Lat.)
*ca.*1100	NAR. POETRY: *Chanson de Roland; Gormand et Isembart* (O.Fr.); *Kulhwch and Olwen* (Welsh)
*ca.*1100/50	NAR. POETRY: *Pèlerinage de Charlemagne* (O.Fr.)
Early 12th cent.	NAR. POETRY: *Chançun de Willame* (Norman-Fr.)
*ca.*1100–1154	PROSE: Geoffrey of Monmouth, *Historia regum Britanniae* (Lat.)
*ca.*1110–1180	PROSE: John of Salisbury, *Policraticus, Metalogicon,* etc. (Lat.)
*ca.*1120	NAR. POETRY: Albéric de Briançon, *Alexandre* (O.Fr.)
*ca.*1125	DRAMA: Hilarius, *Daniel, St. Nicholas, Lazarus,* etc. (Lat.)
*ca.*1130	NAR. POETRY: Pfaffe Lamprecht, *Alexanderlied* (M.H.Ger.)
	DRAMA: Beauvais *Daniel* (Lat.)
*fl.*1130–50	LYRIC: Guillaume IX of Aquitaine, Cerçamon, Marcabru (Prov.)
*ca.*1130/50	NAR. POETRY: *Couronnement de Louis* (O.Fr.)
1131 (or *ca.*1170)	NAR. POETRY: Pfaffe Kuonrat, *Rolandslied* (M.H. Ger.)
*ca.*1135	NAR. POETRY: Philippe de Thaon, *Bestiaire* (O.Fr.)
*ca.*1137–*ca.*1209	PROSE: Walter Map, *De nugis curialium* (Lat.)
*ca.*1140	PROSE: *Liber Sancti Jacobi* (Pseudo-Turpin) (Lat.)
*fl.*1145–80	LYRIC: Bernart de Ventadorn (Prov.)
*ca.*1150	NAR. POETRY: *König Rother* (M.H.Ger.); *Roman de Thèbes* (O.Fr.); *Ysengrimus* (Lat.)
*ca.*1150/60	NAR. POETRY: *Charroi de Nîmes; Prise d'Orange* (O.Fr.)
*fl.*1150–70	LYRIC: Der von Kurenberc; Dietmar von Aist (M.H.Ger.)
*ca.*1150/70	LYRIC: *Altercatio Phyllidis et Florae; Concilium in monte Romarici* (love debates) (Lat.)

*ca.*1150/70	DRAMA: *Jeu d'Adam* (O.Fr. with Lat. stage directions)
*fl.*1150–80	LYRIC: Archipoeta; Gautier de Châtillon; Primas of Orléans (Lat.)
*ca.*1150/1200	LYRIC: Poems in Arundel, Orléans, Harleian, and *Carmina Burana* collections (Lat.)
Second half 12th cent.	LYRIC: Bernard of Morlais (Cluny), *De contemptu mundi* (Lat.)
	DRAMA: *La Seinte Resurreccion* (Anglo-Norman)
	NAR. POETRY: *Cid* (Spanish)
1155	Wace, *Brut* (Norman-Fr.)
*ca.*1160	LYRIC: Jaufré Rudel (Prov.)
	DRAMA: Tegernsee *Antichrist* (Lat.)
*ca.*1160/70	NAR. POETRY: Béroul, *Tristan* (O.Fr.)
*ca.*1160/75	NAR. POETRY: *Flore et Blancheflor* (O.Fr.)
*fl.*1160–1200	NAR. POETRY: Chrétien de Troyes, *Erec* (1165/70), *Cligès* (*ca.*1170/71), *Lancelot* (*ca.*1172/75), *Yvain* (*ca.* 1172), *Perceval* (*ca.*1177/90) (O.Fr.)
*ca.*1165	NAR. POETRY: Benoît de Ste. Maure, *Roman de Troie* (O.Fr.)
After 1165	NAR. POETRY: Gautier d'Arras, *Eracle* (O.Fr.)
*ca.*1170	NAR. POETRY: *Graf Rudolf; Herzog Ernst* (M.H. Ger.); Marie de France, *Lais, Fables,* etc. (Norman-Fr.)
	DRAMA: *Babio* (Lat.)
*ca.*1170/80	NAR. POETRY: Thomas of Britain, *Tristan et Yseult* (Norman-Fr.)
*ca.*1170–*ca.*1230	LYRIC: Walther von der Vogelweide (M.H.Ger.)
1175–1220	LYRIC: Peire Vidal (Prov.)
*fl.*1175–1220	LYRIC: Giraut de Bornelh; Arnaut de Mareuil; Peirol; Arnaut Daniel (Prov.)
After 1175	NAR. POETRY: Earliest branches of *Roman de Renard* (O.Fr.)
*ca.*1180	NAR. POETRY: Bertrande Bar-sur-Aube, *Girard de Vienne* (O.Fr.); Eilhart von Oberge, *Tristram und Isalde;* Heinrich der Glichezaere, *Reinhart Fuchs;* Heinrich von Veldecke, *Eneide* (M.H. Ger.); Bernardus Silvestris, *De mundi universitate* (Lat.)
	PROSE: Andreas Capellanus, *De arte honeste amandi* (Lat.)
*fl.*1180–90	LYRIC: Friedrich von Husen (M.H.Ger.)
*fl.*1180–1200	LYRIC: Albrecht von Johannsdorf; Heinrich von Morungen; Heinrich von Veldecke; Reinmar der Alte; Rudolf von Fenis (M.H.Ger.)

*fl.*1180–1220	LYRIC: Conon de Béthune; Blondel de Nesles (O.Fr.)
*ca.*1180–1236	LYRIC: Philippe de Grèves (Lat.)
*ca.*1180–1245	PROSE: Caesarius of Heisterbach, *Dialogus miraculorum* (Lat.)
*fl.*1189–1215	NAR. POETRY: Hartmann von Aue, *Büchlein* (1189), *Erek* (*ca.*1190), *Gregorius* (*ca.*1195), *Der arme Heinrich* (after 1197), *Iwein* (*ca.*1204) (M.H.Ger.)
*ca.*1190	NAR. POETRY: Joseph of Exeter, *De excidio Troiae* (Lat.)
1194	NAR. POETRY: Ulrich von Zatzikhoven, *Lanzelet* (M.H.Ger.)
*fl.*1197–1218	NAR. POETRY: Wolfram von Eschenbach, *Parzival* (*ca.*1200/10), *Willehalm* (*ca.*1215), *Titurel* (*ca.* 1217) (M.H.Ger.)
End 12th cent.	NAR. POETRY: *Aimeri de Narbonne; Aliscans; Aspremont; Chevalerie Vivien; Raoul de Cambrai* (O.Fr.)
	DRAMA: Christmas and Easter plays of Benediktbeuern (Lat.)
Before 1200	PROSE: *Ancren Riwle* (M.Eng.)
	NAR. POETRY: Nigel Wireker, *Speculum stultorum* (Lat.)
*ca.*1200	NAR. POETRY: Layamon, *Brut; The Owl and the Nightingale* (M.Eng.); *Barlaam et Josaphat;* Guillaume de Dole, *Lai de l'ombre;* Raoul de Houdenc, *Ailes de prouesse, Songe d'enfer, Voie de Paradis;* numerous *fabliaux* (O.Fr.)
	DRAMA: *Aucassin et Nicolette* (O.Fr.); First dramatized versions of *Ordo prophetarum* (Lat.)
*fl.*1200–30	LYRIC: Folquet de Marseille; Guilhem de Cabestanh; Raimbaut de Vaqueyras (Prov.)
*ca.*1200/1210	NAR. POETRY: *Carmen de proditione Guenonis* (Lat.); *Doon de la Roche* (O.Fr.)
*ca.*1200/50	NAR. POETRY: *Gui de Warewic; Boeve de Haumtone; Parténopeus de Blois* (O.Fr.)
First half 13th cent.	NAR. POETRY: Development of Dietrich epics, *Ortnit, Wolfdietrich, Biterolf und Dietlieb,* etc. (M.H.Ger.)
*ca.*1201	NAR. POETRY: Robert de Boron, *Roman de l'histoire dou Sant Graal* (O.Fr.)
1201–53	LYRIC: Thiebaut de Champagne (Thiebaut de Navarre) (O.Fr.)
Before 1202	NAR. POETRY: Alain de Lille (Alanus de Insulis), *Anticlaudianus, De planctu naturae* (Lat.)

*ca.*1202/5	NAR. POETRY: Wirnt von Grafenberg, *Wigalois* (M.H.Ger.)
After 1202	PROSE: Prose version of Grail romance of Robert de Boron, sometimes called *Didot Perceval* (O. Fr.)
*ca.*1203	NAR. POETRY: *Nibelungenlied* (M.H.Ger.)
*ca.*1205	NAR. POETRY: *Enfances Vivien* (O.Fr.)
*ca.*1205/10	NAR. POETRY: Gottfried von Strassburg, *Tristan und Iseult* (M.H.Ger.)
Before 1210	LYRIC: Bertran de Born (Prov.)
	DRAMA: Jehan Bodel, *Le Jeu de St. Nicolas* (O. Fr.)
*ca.*1210	NAR. POETRY: *Gudrun* (M.H.Ger.)
*ca.*1210/23	PROSE: *Historia septem sapientium* ("Dolopathos") (Lat. and O.Fr.)
13th cent.	DRAMA: Fleury Playbook (Lat.); Easter plays from Hildesheim, Muri, Trier, Wolfenbüttel (Lat. and M.H.Ger.)
*ca.*1212	NAR. POETRY: *Perlesevaus* (O.Fr.)
1212–94	NAR. POETRY: Brunetto Latini, *Tesoretto*, etc. (It.)
*ca.*1215	PROSE: Der Stricker; *Pfaff Amis* (M.H.Ger.)
	NAR. POETRY: *Daniel vom blühenden Tal* (M.H. Ger.)
*ca.*1215/20	NAR. POETRY: Heinrich von dem Türlin, *Lanzelet, Der Aventiure Krone* (M.H.Ger.)
After 1215	NAR. POETRY: Thomasin von Circlaere, *Der waelsche Gast* (M.H.Ger.)
*ca.*1220	NAR. POETRY: Konrad Fleck, *Flore und Blanscheflur* (M.H.Ger.)
	PROSE: Brother Robert, *Tristanssaga ok Isonda* (O.N.)
*fl.ca.*1220	LYRIC: Guy d'Ussel (Prov.)
*fl.*1220–50	LYRIC: Neidhart von Reuental (M.H.Ger.)
*fl.*1220–54	NAR. POETRY: Rudolf von Ems, *Alexander, Barlaam und Josaphat, Der gute Gerhard, Weltkronik* (M.H.Ger.)
*ca.*1220–87	NAR. POETRY: Konrad von Würzburg, *Herzmaere, Schwanritter, Partenopier, Silvester, Trojanerkrieg, Weltlohn*, etc. (M.H.Ger.)
*ca.*1225–1274	LYRIC: Peire Cardenal (Prov.)
*ca.*1225–*ca.*1300	LYRIC: Guido Cavalcanti (It.)
*ca.*1225/30	NAR. POETRY: *Bevis of Hamtoun* (M.Eng.); Gerbert de Montreuil, *Violette*, Continuation of Chrétien's *Perceval* (O.Fr.)
*ca.*1227	NAR. POETRY: Guillaume le Clerc, *Bestiaire* (O. Fr.)

ca.1230	NAR. POETRY: Freidank, *Von der Bescheidenheit* (M.H.Ger.)
	NAR. POETRY: Guillaume de Tudèle, *Chanson de la croisade contre les Albigeois* (O.Fr.)
ca.1230/40	PROSE: Snorri Sturluson, *Heimskringla;* Younger (prose) *Edda* (O.N.)
fl.1230–60	NAR. POETRY: Ulrich von Türheim, Continuations of Wolfram's *Willehalm* and Gottfried's *Tristan* (M.H.Ger.)
fl.1230–70	LYRIC: Der Marner; Der Tannhäuser (M.H.Ger.)
1230–1306	LYRIC: Jacopone da Todi (It.)
1235	NAR. POETRY: Huon de Meril, *Le Tournoi d'Antéchrist* (O.Fr.)
ca.1235	PROSE: *Laxdaela Saga* (O.N.)
1237	NAR. POETRY: Guillaume de Loris, *Le Roman de la Rose* (O.Fr.)
fl.ca.1240	LYRIC: Gottfried von Neifen (M.H.Ger.)
fl.1245–80	LYRIC: Rutebeuf (O.Fr.)
	DRAMA: Rutebeuf, *Miracle de Théophile* (*ca*. 1261) (O.Fr.)
Before 1250	NAR. POETRY: *Enfances Guillaume* (O.Fr.)
ca.1250	NAR. POETRY: *La belle Helène* (O.Fr.); *King Horn* (M.Eng.); *Laurin, Rosengarten* (M.H.Ger.)
	PROSE: *Karlamagnussaga* (O.N.)
fl.1250–75	LYRIC: Ulrich von Lichtenstein (M.H.Ger.)
ca.1250/80	NAR. POETRY: Willem, *Van den Vos Reynaerde* (M.Dutch)
fl.1250–1300	LYRIC: Steinmar von Klingenau (M.H.Ger.)
ca.1260/71	DRAMA: Adam de la Halle (Adam le bossu), *Jeu de la Feuillée, Robin et Marion* (O.Fr.)
ca.1263/88	PROSE: Jacobus de Voragine, *Legenda aurea* (Lat.)
Before 1264	PROSE: Vincent of Beauvais, *Speculum maius* (Lat.); Brandr Jonnson, *Trojummanasaga, Alexandersaga* (O.N.)
Before 1270	PROSE: *Tristan en prose* (O.Fr.)
1270–1337	LYRIC: Cino da Pistoia (It.)
ca.1270/85	PROSE: Guido de Columnis, *Historia destructionis Troiae* (Lat.)
fl.1270	LYRIC: Guido Guinicelli (It.)
1272	NAR. POETRY: Albrecht von Scharpfenberg, *Der jüngere Titurel* (M.H.Ger.)
Before 1282	NAR. POETRY: Wernher der Gartenaere, *Meier Helmbrecht* (M.H.Ger.)
1286	NAR. POETRY: Jean de Meun, *Le Roman de la Rose* (second part) (O.Fr.)

1288	NAR. POETRY: Jacquemart Gielée, *Renard le nouvel* (O.Fr.)
*ca.*1290	NAR. POETRY: Heinrich von Freyberg, Continuation of Gottfried's *Tristan* (M.H.Ger.)
After 1293	LYRIC: Dante, *Rime* (It.)
*ca.*1300	NAR. POETRY: *Havelock the Dane* (M.Eng.); Hugo von Trimberg, *Der Renner* (M.H.Ger.)
	PROSE: *Njals Saga; Grettla; Gunnlaug* (O.N.)
*ca.*1300–*ca.*1340	LYRIC: Hadlaub; Heinrich von Meissen (M.H. Ger.)
*ca.*1300–*ca.*1365	NAR. POETRY: Guillaume de Machaut, *Prise d'Alexandrie* (O.Fr.)
	LYRIC: Guillaume de Machaut, *Jugement du Roi de Navarre*, *Voir dit* (O.Fr.)
Early 14th cent.	NAR. POETRY: *Sir Tristram* (M.Eng.); Hadamar von Laber, *Die Jagd* (M.H.Ger.)
*ca.*1306/9	PROSE: Dante, *De vulgari eloquentia* (Lat.), *Il Convivio* (It.)
	LYRIC: *Vita nuova* (It.)
*ca.*1307/21	NAR. POETRY: Dante, *Divina commedia* (It.)
*ca.*1310/14	NAR. POETRY: Gervais du Bus, *Fauvel* (O.Fr.)
1312	NAR. POETRY: Jacques de Longuyon, *Voeux du paon; Renart de Montauban* (O.Fr.)
	PROSE: Dante, *De monarchia* (Lat.)
1321	DRAMA: *Spiel von den weisen und törichten Jungfrauen* (M.H.Ger.)
*ca.*1325(?)	DRAMA: Beginnings of the Chester cycle of Mystery plays
Before 1325	NAR. POETRY: *Guy of Warwick* (M.Eng.)
1340	LYRIC: Ulrich Boner, *Der Edelstein* (M.H.Ger.)
*ca.*1340–1400	NAR. POETRY: Chaucer, *Booke of the Duchesse* (*ca.* 1370/80), *Parlement of Fowles* (*ca.*1382), *Troilus and Criseyde* (*ca.*1383), *House of Fame* (*ca.* 1384), *Legend of Good Women* (*ca.*1385), *Canterbury Tales* (1387/95)
1341	NAR. POETRY: Boccaccio, *Teseide* (It.)
1342	NAR. POETRY: Petrarch, *Africa* (Lat.)
1344	NAR. POETRY: Boccaccio, *L'amorosa visione, Fiammetta, Ninfale fiesolana* (It.)
*ca.*1345–*ca.*1405	LYRIC: Eustache Deschamps, *L'art de Dictier, Miroir de mariage*, lyric cycles, etc. (O.Fr.)
1348–53	PROSE: Boccaccio, *Decamerone* (It.)
*ca.*1350	DRAMA: *Frankfurter Dirigierrolle* (M.H.Ger.)
	PROSE: *Gesta Romanorum* (Lat.)
Mid-14th cent.	DRAMA: *Miracles de Notre Dame* (O.Fr.)

*ca.*1363–*ca.*1430	DIDACTIC POETRY: Christine de Pisan (O.Fr.)
1366	LYRIC: Petrarch, *Canzoniere* (It.)
Before 1370	LYRIC: Heinrich von Mügeln (M.H.Ger.)
1375	NAR. POETRY: Barbour, *The Brouce* (Scots)
Late 14th cent.	NAR. POETRY: "Langland," *Piers Plowman* (M. Eng.)
	DRAMA: Trier Easter play (M.H.Ger.)
*ca.*1380	NAR. POETRY: Gower, *Confessio amantis* (M. Eng.)
1385–1433	LYRIC: Alain Chartier, *Livre des quatre dames, La belle dame sans merci,* etc. (O.Fr.)
1387	DRAMA: Earliest mention of York Mystery cycle (M.Eng.)
1391	DRAMA: Manuscript of Innsbruck trans. of Passion Play (M.H.Ger.)
1391–1468	LYRIC: Charles d'Orléans (Fr. and Eng.)
*ca.*1400	NAR. POETRY: *Gawain and the Green Knight* (M. Eng.)
	LYRIC: *The Pearl* (M.Eng.)
	DRAMA: Erlauer Passion Play (M.H.Ger.)
	PROSE: Johannes Saaz, *Der Ackermann aus Böhmen* (Ger.)
Early 15th cent.	LYRIC: Hans Rosenplüt (M.H.Ger.)
15th cent.	DRAMA: Moralities *(Bien avisé-mal avisé,* etc.) (Fr.)
*ca.*1412/20	NAR. POETRY: John Lydgate, *Histoire, Siege and Destruction of Troy; Story of Thebes* (M.Eng.)
1425	DRAMA: Manuscript of *Castle of Perseverance; Mankind; Mind, Will, and Understanding* ("Macro Plays") (M.Eng.)
After 1425(?)	DRAMA: Developed form of Chester cycle (M. Eng.)
*ca.*1426	NAR. POETRY: Wittenweiler, *Der Ring* (M.H.Ger.)
*ca.*1430–*ca.*1465	LYRIC: François Villon, *Le petit Testament* (1456), *Le grand Testament* (1461) (Fr.)
Before 1440	DRAMA: Eustache Mercadé, *Passion d'Arras* (Fr.)
*ca.*1440/60	PROSE: Antoine de la Salle, *Cents nouvelles nouvelles, Les quinze joies de mariage, La salade* (Fr.)
Before 1445	LYRIC: *Oswald von Wolkestein* (Ger.)
*ca.*1452	DRAMA: Arnoul Greban, *Mystère de la Passion;* Jacques Milet, *Mystère de Troie la grant* (Fr.)
After 1450	LYRIC: Robert Henryson, *Moral Fabillis of Esope* (Scots)
1465	DRAMA: Redentiner Easter play (Low Ger.)

1470	DRAMA: *Maître Pierre Pathelin* (Fr.)
	PROSE: Malory, *Morte d'Arthur* (Eng.)
ca.1476	DRAMA: Bozen, Lucerne Passion Plays (Ger.)
1479	PROSE: Gouda prose version of *Reinaert II* (Dutch)
1481	PROSE: Caxton's trans. of the Gouda version, *The History of Reynard the Fox*
Before 1485	DRAMA: Wakefield Mystery cycle
1485	PROSE: Delft version of *Reynaerde* (Dutch)
1488	DRAMA: Manuscript of *Passion de Sémur* (Fr.)
ca.1490	DRAMA: Arnoul and Simon Greban, *Actes des Apôtres* (Fr.)
1490	DRAMA: Dietrich Schernberg, *Spiel von Frau Jutta* (Ger.)
1493	DRAMA: *Frankfurt Passion Play* (Ger.)
1498	NAR. POETRY: *Reinke de Vos* (Low Ger.)
End 15th cent.	NAR. POETRY: Ulrich Füetrer, *Buch der Abenteuer* (Ger.)
Before 1500	DRAMA: *Everyman* (Eng.); Alsfeld, Donaueschingen Passion Plays (Ger.)

Bibliography

GUIDE TO ADDITIONAL READING

The bibliographical material which follows is arranged to facilitate the further study of medieval literature. Many of the lists, e.g., "Cultural Background and History," are self-explanatory. They provide titles of standard works on various aspects of medieval civilization. For further study of the literature itself, it is usually best to begin with the appropriate literary history, which provides a continuous account of the development of literature within a particular country. The amount of detail and the method of treatment vary considerably from one work to another. The best book to begin with in each list of national literary histories is indicated by an asterisk. The bibliographies provided for the chapters on the individual genres list the standard editions and, where possible, translations of the major works, important specialized bibliographies, books which discuss the genre in general and specialized aspects of it, often with reference to one country only, and works on major authors. These works, and those listed in the bibliographies they themselves contain, will usually be sufficient for anything but the most specialized study of a subject.

To find all the literature on a given topic, it will be necessary to use the bibliographical reference works given in the lists at the beginning of the guide. Occasionally there will be a specialized bibliography on the topic, but the dates should be noted carefully. The next step is to search for the topic and books on it in the lists of works which are available for all the countries of Western Europe and for America, again noting the years which they cover.

Further search should then be made in the cumulative book indexes which have been appearing in most countries for many years and which list material by subject as well as by author and title. Finally, the topic should be looked up in the indexes to periodicals, either general ones or those specializing in literature. These too have a subject list as well as one for authors and titles. The method of procedure is outlined in several of the works on the technical aspects of bibliography which are listed below. Fortunately, there exists for each of the national literatures a good and reasonably up-to-date bibliography—Bossuat for French literature, Körner for German, and the *Cambridge Bibliography of English Literature*. These should be the starting point for any detailed study.

GENERAL BIBLIOGRAPHY

BIBLIOGRAPHICAL REFERENCE WORKS

Baethgen, Fr. *Die internationale Bibliographie der Geschichtswissenschaft* (Forschungen und Fortschritte, Vol. XXVI).

Barrow, J. G. *A Bibliography of Bibliographies in Religion*. 1955.

Bestermann, Th. *A World Bibliography of Bibliographies*. 3 vols. and index, 3d ed., 1955.

Bibliographia philosophica, 1934–45, ed. G. A. de Brie. 2 vols., 1950–54.

Bibliographie der versteckten Bibliographien aus deutschsprachigen Büchern und Zeitschriften, 1930–35. 1956.

Bibliotheca celtica: A Bibliography of Works Relating to Wales and the Celtic Peoples, 1909–33. 10 vols., 1910–39.

Bibliotheca hagiographica latina antiquae et mediae aetatis, ed. Socii Bollandiani. 2 vols., 1898–1901. Supplement, 1911.

Bonser, W. *An Anglo-Saxon and Celtic Bibliography (450–1087)*. 2 vols., 1957.

Brunet, J. C. *Manuel du libraire et de l'amateur de livres*. 5th ed., 6 vols., 1860–65. Supplements, 3 vols., 1870–80.

Carmody, F. J. *Arabic Astronomical and Astrological Sciences in Latin Translation: A Critical Bibliography*. 1956.

Collinson, R. L. *Bibliographies, Subject and National*. 1951.

Esdaile, A. *A Student's Manual of Bibliography*. 3d ed., 1954.

Gesamtkatalog der Wiegendrucke. 1925–32. Numerous supplements.

Graesse, J. G. Th. *Trésor des livres rares et précieux ou nouveau dictionnaire bibliographique*. 8 vols., 1859–69.

Gross, C. *The Sources and Literature of English History . . . to about 1485*. 2d ed., 1915.

Hain, L. F. T. *Repertorium bibliographicum ad annum MD*. 2 vols. in 4, 1826–38, repr. 1948. Supplements by W. A. Copinger, 3 vols. and index, 1949; by D. Reichling, 2 vols., 1952.

Halphen, L., and Y. Renouard. *Initiation aux études d'histoire du moyen-âge*. 1952.

Hassall, W. O. *A Select Bibliography of Italy*. 1946.

Lehmann, P. *Mittelalterliche Büchertitel*. 1949.

McKerrow, R. B. *An Introduction to Bibliography for Literary Students*. 1928.

Milkau, F., and G. Leyb. *Handbuch der Bibliothekswissenschaft*. 2d ed., 3 vols., 1950.

Paetow, L. J. *A Guide to the Study of Medieval History*. Rev. ed., 1931.

Potthast, A. *Bibliotheca historica medii aevi: Wegweiser durch die Geschichtswerke des europäischen Mittelalters bis 1500*. 2 vols., 2d ed., 1954.

Roberts, A. D. *Introduction to Reference Books*. 3d ed., 1956.

Stein, H. *Manuel de bibliographie générale*. 1897.

Totok, W. *Bibliographischer Wegweiser der philosophischen Literatur*. 1959.

———, and W. R. Weitzel. *Handbuch der bibliographischen Nachschlagewerke*. 2d ed., 1959.

Wattenbach, W. *Deutschlands Geschichtsquellen*. 6th ed., 2 vols., 1893–94.

———, and R. Holtzmann. *Deutschlands Geschichtsquellen im Mittelalter: Deutsche Kaiserzeit*. 1948–.

———, and W. Levison. *Deutschlands Geschichtsquellen im Mittelalter: Vorzeit und Karolinger*. 3 vols., 1952. See additions by L. Wallach, in *Speculum*, Vol. XXIX (1954).

Williams, H. F. *An Index of Medieval Studies Published in Festschriften, 1865–1946*. 1951.

Winchell, Constance M. *Guide to Reference Books*. 7th ed., 1951. Supplements, 1950–52, 1953–54.

See also the catalogues of the great national libraries, Library of Congress, British Museum, Bibliothèque Nationale, Bodleian, etc., many of which have subject indexes for the later publications. Especially important for English literature is R. Proctor, *Index to the Early Printed Books in the British Museum* . . . *to 1500, with Notes of Those in the Bodleian Library* (1898–99, with later supplements).

CURRENT BIBLIOGRAPHY

Bibliographie de la France. 1811–. Supplemented by *Biblio* (monthly).

Bibliographie der deutschen Zeitschriftenliteratur. 1897–. Supplementary volumes go back to 1861. There is a gap for the years 1944–48.

Bibliographie der fremdsprachigen Literatur. 1911–. There is a gap for the years 1944–48.

Bibliotheca nazionale centrale di Firenze. *Bolletino delle pubblicazione italiane ricevute per diretto di stampa.* 1866–.

British National Bibliography. 1950–. Arranged according to the Dewey decimal system.

Cumulative Book Index. 1898–. After 1929 lists all books in English wherever printed. Before 1929 the entries are mostly books printed in U.S.A. Continues *U.S. Catalog.*

Deutsche Nationalbibliographie. 1931–. But note that this is a new name for *Wöchentliches Verzeichnis der erschienenen und der vorbereiteten Neuigkeiten,* 1840–1930.

English Catalogue of Books. 1835–63. Supplemented by retrospective volumes for 1801–36 and by subsequent cumulative volumes. Draws material from *The Publisher's Circular* (1857–) and *Whitaker's Cumulative Book List* (1924–).

Heyl, L. *Current National Bibliographies: a List of Sources of Information concerning Current Books of All Countries.* 1942.

Hinrichs Halbjahrskatalog. 1797–1916. Continued as *Halbjahrsverzeichnis der Neuerscheinungen des deutschen Buchhandels* to 1944.

International Index to Periodicals. 1907–.

Kayser, C. G. *Index locupletissimus: vollständiges Bücherlexikon.* 1750–1910.

New York Public Library. *A Check List of Cumulative Indexes to Individual Periodicals in the New York Public Library.* 1942.

Österreichische Monatsbibliographie. April, 1946–.

Peddie, R. A. *National Bibliographies: a Descriptive Catalogue of the Works Which Register the Books Published in Each Country.* 1912.

Poole's Index to Periodical Literature. 1802–81. Supplements to 1906.
Quarterly Checklist of Medievalia, A. 1958–.
Reader's Guide to Periodical Literature. 1900–.
Scheda cumulativa italiana. 1932–. Lists works printed in Italy.
Schweizer Buchhandel. 1943–. Lists works appearing in Switzerland.
Subject Index to Periodicals. 1915–, except 1923–25.
Union Catalogue of Periodical Publications in the University Libraries of the British Isles. 1937.
Union List of Serials in the Libraries of the United States and Canada. 2d ed., 1943. Supplements at intervals. Lists the libraries in which runs of periodicals may be found.
United States Catalog. Lists books in print on January 1, 1899 (1st ed.); 1902 (2d ed.); 1912 (3d ed.); 1928 (4th ed.).

BIBLIOGRAPHIES OF LITERATURE

Anderson, H. P. "Bibliography of Scandinavian Philology," *Acta philologica scandinavica,* XIX (1945/46), 229–351.
Année philologique, L': bibliographie critique et analytique de l'antiquité gréco-latine. 1924–.
"Annual Bibliography of the Modern Language Association of America." Originally consisted of material written by Americans or published in American journals. Since 1956 covers all publications in the English, Romance, and Germanic languages. Appears in the *Publications of the Modern Language Association of America.*
Archiv für das Studium der neueren Sprachen. Prints current bibliographical information in each issue, in the form of tables of contents of individual journals.
Arnold, R. F. *Allgemeine Bücherkunde zur neueren deutschen Literaturgeschichte.* 3d ed., 1931. Contains much valuable information for older literature.
Baldensperger, F., and W. Friedrich. *Bibliography of Comparative Literature.* 1950.
Bateson, F. W. *Cambridge Bibliography of English Literature.* 5 vols., 1941–57.
Baxter, J. H., C. Johnson, and J. F. Willard. *Index of British and Latin Writers, 400–1250 (Bulletin Du Cange,* Vol. III [1932]).
Bibliographie linguistique des années 1939–47. 1948. Various supplements.

Bossuat, R. *Manuel bibliographique de la littérature française du moyen âge.* 1951. Supplement, 1953. The most valuable bibliography for medieval French literature.

Caplan, H. *Medieval "artes praedicandi": a Handlist.* 1934. Supplements in *Cornell Studies in Classical Philology,* Vols. XXIV (1934) and XXV (1936).

Cousin, J. *Bibliographie de la langue latine, 1880–1948.* 1951.

Critical Bibliography of French Literature, A. Vol. I, The Medieval Period, ed. U. T. Holmes. 2d ed., 1952.

Cross, T. P. *Bibliographical Guide to English Studies.* 10th ed., 1951.

Engelmann, W. *Bibliotheca scriptorum classicorum.* 8th ed., 1880–82.

Eppelsheimer, H. W. *Bibliographie der deutschen Literaturwissenschaft, 1945–53.* 1956.

—— *Deutsche Bücher, 1939–45.* 1947.

Esdaile, A. *The Sources of English Literature.* 1928.

Fabricius, J. A. *Bibliotheca latina mediae et infimae aetatis.* 3 vols., 1858–59.

Faider, P. *Répertoire des éditions de scolies et commentaires d'auteurs latins.* 1931.

—— *Répertoire des index et lexiques d'auteurs latins.* 1926.

Farrar, C. P., and A. P. Evans. *Bibliography of English Translations from Medieval Sources.* 1948.

Frauwallner, E. H., H. Giebisch, and E. Heinzel. *Die Weltliteratur: biographisches, literar-historisches und bibliographisches Lexikon in Übersichten und Stichwörtern.* 3 vols., 1951–54.

Hansel, J. *Bücherkunde für Germanisten. Wie sammelt man das Schrifttum nach dem neuesten Forschungsstand?* 1959.

Herescu, N. *Bibliographie de la littérature latine.* 1943.

Hubner, E. *Bibliographical Clue to Latin Literature,* with additions by J. E. B. Mayor. 1875.

Jahresberichte über die Erscheinungen auf dem Gebiete der germanischen Philologie. Appeared 1877 to 1939, resumed 1954. New issue has now (1960) reached the year 1945. Most valuable single bibliographical work for the literature of the Germanic peoples in the Middle Ages.

Körner, J. *Bibliographisches Handbuch des deutschen Schrifttums.* 3d ed. 1949.

Literaturblatt für germanische und romanische Philologie. 1880–1943. Monthly bibliographies.

Lowndes, W. T. *Bibliographer's Manual of English Literature.* 6 vols. in 11, 1858–64.

Moebius, T. *Catalogus librorum Islandicorum Norvegicorum aetatis mediae.* 1856.

Moll, O. E. *Sprichwörterbibliographie.* 1957.

Palfrey, T. R., and others. *A Bibliographical Guide to the Romance Languages and Literatures.* 4th ed., 1951. An extremely useful compilation.

Pollard, A. W., and G. R. Redgrave. *A Short-title Catalogue of Books Printed in England, Scotland, and Ireland, and of English Books Printed Abroad, 1475–1640.* 1926.

Prezzolini, G. *Repertorio bibliografico della storia e della critica della litteratura italiana dal 1902 al 1932.* 4 vols., 1937–48.

Sattler, P., and G. von Selle. *Bibliographie zur Geschichte der Schrift bis in das Jahr 1930.* 1935.

Seris, H. *Manual de bibliografia de la literatura española.* 1948–.

Simon-Diaz, J. *Bibliografia de la literatura hispanica.* 2 vols. published, 1950–.

Stemplinger, E. *Griechisch-lateinischer Literaturführer von Justinian (527) bis heute.* 1934.

Strecker, K. *Introduction to Medieval Latin*, trans. R. B. Palmer. 1957. The enormously increased bibliographical information makes the original German edition obsolete. This is the handiest single bibliographical guide for students of medieval Latin literature and of its associations with other literatures. Note especially the lists of important text series.

Wells, J. E. *A Manual of the Writings in Middle English, 1050–1400.* 1916–. 9 supplements to 1945. In course of revision.

Year's Work in English Studies, The. 1919–. Appears annually. Arranged by periods. Critical.

Year's Work in Modern Languages, The. 1930–. Appears annually. Arranged under each language and by periods within the language. Vol. XI covers material published between 1940 and 1949. Critical.

Zeitschrift für romanische Philologie: Bibliographische Supplementhefte. 1875–1937. There are occasional gaps.

DICTIONARIES AND BOOKS ON LANGUAGE

These books are aids to reading the various languages rather than to the study of linguistics.

Anglade, J. *Grammaire élémentaire de l'ancien français.* 1918.

Bachmann, A. *Mittelhochdeutsches Lesebuch.* 6th ed., 1944. Contains outline of grammar.

Bartsch, K. *Chrestomathie de l'ancien français.* 12th ed., 1958. Has grammar summary.

Baxter, J. H., and C. Johnson. *A Medieval Latin Word List from British and Irish Sources.* 2d ed., 1935.

Beeson, A. *Primer of Medieval Latin.* 1925.

Blaise, A. *Dictionnaire latin-français des auteurs chrétiens.* 1955.

—— *Manuel du latin chrétien.* 1955.

Braune, W. *Althochdeutsche Grammatik.* 9th ed., 1959.

—— *Althochdeutsches Lesebuch.* 13th ed., 1958.

Browne, R. A. *British Latin Selections* AD 500–1400. 1954.

Campbell, A. *Old English Grammar.* 1959.

Cleasby, R., and G. Vigfusson. *An Icelandic-English Dictionary,* with supplement by W. A. Craigie. 1957.

De Boor, H., and R. Wisniewski. *Mittelhochdeutsche Grammatik.* 1956.

Ducange, C. *Glossarium mediae et infimae Latinitatis.* 5 vols., latest ed., 1883–87, repr. 1954–55.

Gordan, E. V. *An Introduction to Old Norse.* 1938.

Grandgent, C. H. *An Introduction to Vulgar Latin.* 1907.

Habel, E. *Mittellateinisches Glossar.* 1931.

Hakamies, Reino. *Glossarium Latinitatis medii aevi Finlandicae.* 1958.

Hall, J. R. C. *A Concise Anglo-Saxon Dictionary.* 3d ed., 1931.

Koerting, G. *Lateinisch-Romanisches Wörterbuch: Etymologisches Wörterbuch der romanischen Hauptsprachen.* 3d ed., 1923.

Kurath, H. *Middle English Dictionary.* 1959–. Had reached letter C in 1959.

Levy, E. *Petit Dictionnaire Provençal-Français.* 2d ed., 1925.

Lewis, C. T., and C. Short. *A New Latin Dictionary* (Harpers Latin Dictionary). 1878.

Lexicon mediae et infimae Latinitatis Polonorum. 1953–. Definitions are in Polish and Latin.

Lexer, M. *Mittelhochdeutsches Handwörterbuch.* 1872–78.

—— *Mittelhochdeutsches Taschenwörterbuch.* 24th ed., 1944.

Mayhew, A. L. *A Concise Dictionary of Middle English from 1150–1580.* 1888.

Mittellateinisches Wörterbuch bis zum ausgehenden 13. Jahrhun-

dert. 1959–. Publ. Bayerische Akademie der Wissenschaften. In progress.

Mossé, F. *Handbook of Middle English,* trans. J. A. Walker. 1952.

Niermayer, J. F., ed. *Mediae latinitatis lexicon minus.* 1954–. In progress, A–L complete in 1960.

Nunn, H. P. V. *An Introduction to the Study of Ecclesiastical Latin.* 3d ed., 1951.

Quirk, R., and C. L. Wrenn. *An Old English Grammar.* 1955.

Schulz-Gora, O. *Altprovenzalisches Elementarbuch.* 1906.

Tobler, A., and E. Lommatzsch. *Altfranzösisches Wörterbuch.* 1925–. Had reached "joindre" in January, 1960.

Urwin, K. *A Short Old French Dictionary for Students.* 1946.

Wardale, Edith E. *An Introduction to Middle English.* 1937.

MANUSCRIPTS AND PALAEOGRAPHY

Although critical editions usually give the location of the manuscripts of the author or work being edited, the only way to find manuscripts of unpublished authors or anonymous works is to search the manuscript catalogues of individual libraries. These may vary from the elaborate descriptive catalogues of such institutions as the British Museum to handwritten lists of small libraries available only at the library itself. Descriptions of any manuscript may be inaccurate. Not infrequently only the first few sheets have been examined and the presence of important material in later sheets has not been noted. Lists of manuscripts on a particular subject, e.g., M. Bloomfield, "A Preliminary List of Incipits of Latin Works on the Virtues and Vices," *Traditio,* Vol. IX (1955), are often given in the form of "Incipits" (the first few words) and "Excipits" (the last few words) of the manuscript.

Arndt, W. *Schrifttafeln zur Erlernung der lateinischen Paläographie.* 4th ed., 3 parts, 1904–7.

Battelli, G. *Lezioni di paleografia.* 1949.

Bischoff, B., G. I. Lieftinck, and G. Battelli. *Nomenclature des écritures du IXe au XVIe siècle.* 1954.

Cappelli, A. *Dizionario di abbreviatura.* 4th ed., 1939; repr., 1954.

Cencetti, G. *Lineamenti di storia della scrittura latina.* 1954.

Chrous, E., and J. Kirchner. *Die gotischen Schriftarten.* 1928.

Dearing, V. A. *A Manual of Textual Analysis.* 1959.

Denholm-Young, N. *Handwriting in England and Wales.* 1954.
Jenkinson, H. *The Later Court Hands in England from the Fifteenth to the Seventeenth Century.* 2 vols., 1927.
Johnson, C., and H. Jenkinson. *English Court Hand 1066–1500.* 2 parts, 1915.
Kenyon, F. G. *Books and Readers in Ancient Greece and Rome.* 1932.
Ker, N. R. *Catalogue of Manuscripts Containing Anglo-Saxon.* 1957.
Kirchner, J. *Scriptura latina libraria.* 1955. Facsimiles.
Lindsay, W. M. *Early Welsh Script.* 1912.
—— *Notae latinae (minuscule abbreviations 700–850.* 1915. Supplement, 850–1050, by D. Bains. 1936.
Loew, E. A. *The Beneventan Script.* 1914.
Maas, P. *Textual Criticism,* trans. from German. 1958.
Steffens, F. *Lateinische Paläographie.* 1903; supplement, 1909; 2d ed., 1929; French ed., incl. supplement, 1912.
Thompson, E. M. *Handbook of Greek and Latin Palaeography.* 3d ed., 1906.
Weitzmann, K. *Illustrations in Roll and Codex. A Study of the Origin and Method of Text Illustration.* 1947.
Wright, C. E. *English Vernacular Hands from the Twelfth to the Fifteenth Centuries.* 1960.

HISTORY AND CULTURAL BACKGROUND

Agazzi, A. *Educare: Profilo storico della filosofia e della pedagogia dai greci alla scolastica.* 2 vols., 1951–52. 3d vol. to follow.
Anderson, G. K. *The History of the Anglo-Saxons.* 1949.
Artz, F. B. *The Mind of the Middle Ages.* 2d ed. 1953.
Bark, W. C. *Origins of the Medieval World.* 1958.
Barraclough, G., ed. *Medieval Germany, 911–1250.* 2 vols., 1948.
Bernards, M. *"Speculum virginum": Geistigkeit und Seelenleben der Frau im Hochmittelalter.* 1955.
Blume, F., ed. *Die Musik in Geschichte und Gegenwart: Allgemeine Enzyclopedie der Musik.* 6 vols., 1949–.
Bongert, Y. *Recherches sur les cours laïques du Xme au XIIIme siècle.* 1948.
Brehier, L. *Le Monde byzantin.* 3 vols., 1947–50.
Bruyne, E. de. *Etudes d'esthétique médiévale.* 1946.

Buecher, K. *Die Frauenfrage im Mittelalter.* 1910.

Bühler, J. *Die Kultur des Mittelalters.* 3d ed., 1943.

Bursian, C. *Geschichte der classischen Philologie in Deutschland von den Anfängen bis zur Gegenwart.* 2 vols., 1883.

Cambridge Medieval History, ed. J. R. Tanner, C. W. Previté-Orton, and Z. N. Brooke. 8 vols. and 1 vol. maps, 1911–36.

Carlyle, R. W., and A. J. Carlyle. *A History of Medieval Political Theory in the West.* 6 vols., 1903–36.

Chassant, A. L. A. *Dictionnaire des abbréviations latines et françaises.* 5th ed., 1884

Chevalier, U. *Répertoire des sources historiques du moyen-âge.* Topo-bibliography, 2 vols., 1894–1903; bio-bibliography, 2 vols., 2d ed., 1905–07.

Clark, D. L. *Rhetoric in Greco-Roman Education.* 1957.

Clephan, R. C. *The Tournament.* 1919.

Collins, R. A. *A History of Medieval Civilization in Europe.* 1936.

Coulton, G. G. *Europe's Apprenticeship.* 1940.

—— *Medieval Panorama.* 1944.

Crump, C. G., and E. F. Jacob. *The Legacy of the Middle Ages.* 1923.

Davis, R. H. C. *A History of Medieval Europe from Constantine to St. Louis.* 1957.

Deanesly, M. *A History of Early Medieval Europe, 476–911.* 1956.

Delten, G. *Über die Dom- und Klosterschulen des Mittelalters.* 1893.

D'Entreves, A. P. *The Medieval Contribution to Political Thought.* 1939.

Diehl, C. *Byzantium: Greatness and Decline.* 1957. French original, 1919.

Dornseiff, W. *Das Alphabet in Mystik und Magie.* 1925.

Encyclopedia of Islam, ed. J. H. Kramers, H. A. R. Gibb, and E. Lévi-Provençal. 2d ed., 1954–.

Erich, O., and R. Beitel. *Handwörterbuch der deutschen Volkskunde.* 1955.

Evans, Joan. *Life in Medieval France.* 1957.

Falke, J. von. *Geschichte des Geschmacks im Mittelalter.* 1892.

Fontaine, J. *Isidore de Séville et la culture classique dans l'Espagne wisigothique.* 2 vols., 1959.

Ganshof, F. L. *Feudalism.* 1952. French original, 2d ed., 1954.

Gottlieb, Th. *Über mittelalterliche Bibliotheken.* 1890.

Graesse, J. G. Th., and Fr. Benedict. *Orbis latinus.* 2d ed., 1909.

Graf, A. *Mitti, leggende e superstizioni del medio evo.* 1893.

Grupp, G. *Kulturgeschichte des Mittelalters.* 4 vols., 1906–24.

Hampe, K. *Das Hochmittelalter.* 1932; repr. 1953.

Hashagen, J. *Kulturgeschichte des Mittelalters.* 1950.

Haskins, C. H. *Renaissance of the Twelfth Century.* 1927.

—— *Studies in Medieval Culture.* 1929.

Hayes, C. *An Introduction to the Sources Relating to the Germanic Invasions.* 1909.

Hess, L. *Die deutschen Frauenberufe des Mittelalters.* 1940.

History of the Crusades, ed. K. Setton. Vol. I, *The First Hundred Years,* ed. M. W. Baldwin, 1955.

Hodgkin, R. H. *History of the Anglo-Saxons.* 1952.

Hofstaetter, W., and U. Peters. *Sachwörterbuch der Deutschkunde.* 2 vols., 1930.

Hoops, J. *Reallexikon der germanischen Altertumskunde.* 4 vols., 1911–19.

Hopper, V. F. *Medieval Number Symbolism.* 1938.

Hughes, A. *Early Medieval Music.* 1954.

Huizinga, J. *The Waning of the Middle Ages.* 1924. 1st Dutch ed., 1919.

Hull, E. *Folklore of the British Isles.* 1928.

Irsay, S. d'. *Histoire des universités françaises et étrangères* . . . 2 vols., 1933–35.

Jackson, K. H. *Language and History in Early Britain.* 1954.

Kantorowicz, E. H. *Laudes regiae: a Study in Liturgical Acclamations and Medieval Ruler Worship.* 1958.

Koch, Jos. *Artes liberales: von der antiken Bildung zur Wissenschaft des Mittelalters.* 1959.

—— *Humanismus, Mystik und Kunst in der Welt des Mittelalters.* 1953.

Lagarde, Georges de. *La Naissance de l'esprit laïque au declin du moyen-âge.* 1958.

Laistner, M. L. W. *Thought and Letters in Western Europe, A.D. 500–900.* 2d ed., 1957.

—— *Christianity and Pagan Culture in the Later Roman Empire.* 1951.

Lévi-Provençal, E. *La Civilization arabe en Espagne.* 2d ed., 1948.

Lewis, E. *Medieval Political Ideas.* 2 vols., 1954.

Lindsay, J. *Byzantium into Europe.* 1952.

Lloyd, J. E. *History of Wales.* 3d ed., 1939.

Loeffler, K., and J. Kirchner. *Lexikon des gesamten Buchwesens.* 3 vols., 1935–37. There is also a shorter version (1952–53).

Lüthi, M. *Das europäische Volksmärchen.* 1947.

MacCulloch, J. A. *Medieval Faith and Fable.* 1932.

Marrou, H. I. *History of Education in Antiquity.* 1956. 2d French ed., 1955.

—— *St. Augustin et la fin de la culture antique.* 3d ed., 1949.

Menendez-Pidal, R. *Historia de España.* Vol. IV, *España musulmana 711–1031,* by E. Lévi-Provençal. 1950.

Mitteis, H. *Der Staat des hohen Mittelalters.* 1940.

Naumann, H., and G. Müller. *Höfische Kultur.* 1929.

O'Rahilly, T. S. *Early Irish History and Mythology.* 1946.

Painter, S. *French Chivalry.* 1940.

Patch, H. *The Other World According to Descriptions in Medieval Literature.* 1950.

Paulsen, F. *Geschichte des gelehrten Unterrichts in Deutschland.* 1896.

Pauly, A. F., and G. Wissowa. *Realencyclopedie der classischen Altertumswissenschaft.* First series, Vols. I–XXIII^2; second series, Vols. I–VIII^2; 8 supplements, 1894–1959.

Pepin, J. *Mythe et allegorie: les origines grecques et les contestations judéo-chrétiennes.* 1954.

Pfister, K. *Die Welt des Mittelalters.* 1952.

Pirenne, H. *Economic and Social History of Medieval Europe.* 1936.

—— *History of Europe from the Invasions to the Sixteenth Century.* 1956. French original, 1936.

——, and others. *La Civilisation occidentale au moyen-âge du XIme au milieu du XVme siècle.* 1933.

Poole, A. L. ed. *Medieval England.* 2d ed. 1958.

Powicke, F. M. *The Thirteenth Century, 1216–1307.* 1953.

Previté-Orton, C. W. *History of Europe, 1198–1378.* 1951.

—— *The Shorter Cambridge Medieval History.* 2 vols., 1952.

Rand, E. K. *Founders of the Middle Ages.* 1928.

Rashdall, H. *The Universities of Europe in the Middle Ages.* 3 vols., 1936.

Reese, G. *Music in the Middle Ages.* 1940.

Rice, D. T. *The Great Palace of the Byzantine Emperors.* 1958.

Rougemont, D. de. *Love in the Western World.* 1940. Trans. of *L'Amour et l'occident,* 1939.

Runciman, S. *Byzantine Civilization.* 1954.
—— *A History of the Crusades.* 3 vols., 1951–54.
Sandys, J. E. *A History of Classical Scholarship.* 3 vols., 3d ed., 1921.
Sayles, G. O. *The Medieval Foundations of England.* 1948.
Schultz, A. *Das höfische Leben zur Zeit der Minnesänger.* 2 vols., 2d ed., 1889. Uses mostly literary sources.
Smith, E. B. *Architectural Symbolism in Imperial Rome and the Middle Ages.* 1956.
Southern, R. W. *The Making of the Middle Ages.* 1953.
Steinen, W. von den. *Der Kosmos des Mittelalters: Von Karl dem Grossen zu Bernhard von Clairvaux.* 1959.
Stenton, Doris M. *English Society in the Early Middle Ages, 1066–1307.* 1951.
Stephenson, C. *Medieval Feudalism.* 1956.
Strayer, J. R. *Western Europe in the Middle Ages.* 1955.
Taylor, H. O. *The Classical Heritage of the Middle Ages.* 4th ed., 1957.
—— *The Medieval Mind.* 2 vols., 4th ed., 1925; repr. 1959.
Thalhofer, F. X. *Unterricht und Bildung im Mittelalter.* 1928.
Thompson, J. W. *The Medieval Library.* 1939.
Thorndike, L. *A History of Magic and Experimental Science.* Vols. I–VI, 1923–41.
Vossler, K. *Medieval Culture* (trans. from *Die göttliche Komödie* [1925]). 2 vols., 1958.
Whitelock, Dorothy. *The Beginnings of English Society: A History of the Anglo Saxons.* 1952; repr. 1956.
Widmann, H. *Geschichte des Buchhandels vom Altertum bis zur Gegenwart.* 1952.
Williams, A. H. *Introduction to the History of Wales.* Vol. I (to 1063), 1941; Vol. II (to 1284), 1948.

RELIGION AND PHILOSOPHY

Acta sanctorum, publ. Société des Bollandistes. 1643–. Still appearing. Arranged by saints' days.
Aigrain, René. *L'hagiographie: ses sources, ses méthodes, son histoire.* 1953.
Allemann, F. *Das Mysterium der Dreifaltigkeit in der deutschen Literatur bis zum 13. Jahrhundert.* 1959.

Aurenhammer, H. *Lexikon der christlichen Ikonographie.* 1959–. In progress.

Baldwin, M. W. *The Medieval Church.* 1953.

Baron, S. W. *A Social and Religious History of the Jews.* 8 vols., 2d ed., 1952–57. Vols. III–V are on the Middle Ages.

Bauerreiss, R. *Arbor vitae. Der Lebensbaum und seine Verwendung in Liturgie, Kunst und Brauchtum des Abendlandes.* 1938.

Bertholet, A. *Wörterbuch der Religion.* 1952.

Bloomfield, M. *The Seven Deadly Sins.* 1954.

Blume, C., and G. M. Dreves. *Analecta hymnica medii aevi.* 55 vols., 1886–1922.

Boehner, P. *Medieval Logic. An Outline of its Development from 1250 to c. 1400.* 1952.

Borst, A. *Die Catharer.* 1953.

Bradley, Ritamary. "Backgrounds of the Title *Speculum* in Medieval Literature," *Speculum,* Vol. XXIX (1954).

Caplan, H. "The Four Senses of Scriptural Interpretation and the Medieval Theory of Preaching," *Speculum,* Vol. IV (1929).

Catholic Encyclopedia. 15 vols., 1907–14. The Italian *Enciclopedia Cattolica* has fuller articles and is more up to date.

Cayré, F. *Manual of Patrology and History of Theology.* 2 vols., 1936–40. Trans. of 1st French ed., 1927–30.

Copleston, F., *Medieval Philosophy.* 1952.

Cross, F. L., ed. *The Oxford Dictionary of the Christian Church.* 1957.

Cumont, F. *After-life in Roman Paganism.* 1923; repr. 1959.

Deanesley, Margaret. *History of the Medieval Church, 590–1500.* 3rd ed., 1934.

Deckers, E., and A. Gaar. *Clavis patrum latinorum.* 1951.

Deferrari, R. J., and Sister Mary Barry. *A Lexicon of St. Thomas Aquinas.* 1948.

Delehaye, H. *The Legends of the Saints . . .* 1907. Trans. of 1st French ed.

Delhaye, P. *La Philosophie chrétienne au moyen âge.* 1959.

Denifle, H., and F. Ehrle. *Archiv für Literatur und Kirchengeschichte des Mittelalters.* 7 vols., 1885–86; 1888–1900; repr. 1955–.

DeWulf, M. *History of Medieval Philosophy* (abbreviated trans. of *Histoire de la philosophie médiévale*). 3 vols., 6th ed., 1934–47.

Dictionnaire de l'archéologie chrétienne et de liturgie, ed. F. Cabrol and others. 10 vols., 1907–32.

Droulers, E. *Dictionnaire des attributs, allégories, emblèmes et symboles.* 1950.

Ferguson, G. *Signs and Symbols in Christian Art.* 1954.

Fliche, A., and V. Martin. *Histoire de l'Eglise depuis les origines jusqu'à nos jours.* In progress, 1938–. Vols. I to XVII are on the Middle Ages.

Gilson, E. *L'Esprit de la philosophie médiévale.* 2d ed., 1944. Trans. as *The Spirit of Medieval Philosophy,* 1950.

—— *History of Christian Philosophy in the Middle Ages.* 1955.

—— *Introduction à l'étude de St. Augustin.* 1931.

Goodspeed, E. J. *A History of Early Christian Literature.* 1942.

Grabmann, M. *Mittelalterliches Geistesleben.* 3 vols., 1926–56.

Graf, G. *Geschichte der christlichen arabischen Literatur.* 4 vols., 1944–53.

Hagendahl, H. *Latin Fathers and the Classics.* 1898–1920.

Hauck, A. *Kirchengeschichte Deutschlands.* 6 vols., 1952–53.

Jewish Encyclopedia. 12 vols., 1901–.

Katzenellenbogen, A. *Allegory of the Virtues and Vices in Medieval Art.* 1939.

Kelly, J. N. D. *Early Christian Doctrines.* 1958.

Klibansky, R. *The Continuity of the Platonic Tradition during the Middle Ages.* 1939.

Labriolle, P. de. *History and Literature of Christianity from Tertullian to Boethius.* 1924. Trans. of 1st French ed., 1920.

Lexikon für Theologie und Kirche, ed. M. Buchberger. 2d ed., 10 vols., 1930–38; 3d ed., Vol. I, 1959.

McNally, R. E. *The Bible in the Early Middle Ages.* 1959.

Mellone, S. H. *Western Christian Thought in the Middle Ages.* 1935.

Menasce, P. J. de. *Arabische Philosophie.* 1948.

Milburn, R. L. P. *Early Christian Interpretations of History.* 1954.

Molsdorf, W. *Führer durch den symbolischen und typologischen Bilderkreis der christlichen Kunst des Mittelalters.* 1920.

Nirschl, J. *Lehrbuch der Patrologie und Patristik.* 3 vols., 1881–85.

Owst, G. R. *Preaching in Medieval England.* 1926.

Reallexikon für Antike and Christentum, ed. T. Klauser. In progress. Vols. I–III (Dogma) available in 1959.

Sauer, J. *Symbolik des Kirchengebäudes.* . . . 1902.

Schaller, H. *Die Weltanschauung des Mittelalters.* 1934.

Schmidt, H. *Philosophisches Wörterbuch.* 12th ed., 1951.

Schnurer, G. *Church and Culture in the Middle Ages.* Vol. I, *A.D. 350–814,* 1956.

Schutz, L. *Thomas-Lexikon: Sammlung, Übersetzungen und Erklärungen.* 2d ed., 1895.

Smalley, B. *The Study of the Bible in the Middle Ages.* 2d ed., 1952.

Spicq, P. C. *Esquisse d'une histoire de l'exégèse latine au moyen-âge.* 1944.

Steinschneider, M. *Die europäischen Übersetzungen aus dem Arabischen.* Sitzungsberichte der Kaiserlichen Akademie der Wissenschaften in Wien, philosophisch-historische Klasse, Vols. CXLIX and CLI (1904, 1906); repr. 1956.

—— *Die hebräischen Übersetzungen des Mittelalters und die Juden als Dolmetscher.* 1893; repr., 1956.

Ueberweg, Fr. *Grundriss der Geschichte der Philosophie.* Vols. I–III, rev. B. Geyer, 1924–28; repr., 1958.

Ziegenfuss, W. *Philosophen-Lexikon. Handwörterbuch der Philosophie nach Personen.* 2 vols., 1949–50.

LITERATURE

GENERAL

Auerbach, E. *Literatursprache und Publikum in der lateinischen Spätantike und im Mittelalter.* 1958.

—— *Mimesis.* 1946, trans., 1953.

—— *Typologische Motive in der mittelalterlichen Literatur.* 1953.

Bolgar, R. R. *The Classical Heritage and Its Beneficiaries.* 1954.

Chadwick, N. K. *Poetry and Letters in Early Christian Gaul.* 1955.

Charland, Th. M. *Artes praedicandi.* 1939.

Chaytor, H. J. *From Script to Print.* 1945.

Comparetti, D. *Virgilio nel medio evo.* 2d ed., rev. G. Pasquali, 2 vols., 1943–46. Trans. of 1st Italian ed., 1908.

Curtius, E. R. *European Literature and the Latin Middle Ages.* 1953. German original, 1948.

Faral, E. *Les Arts poétiques du XIIme et du XIIIme siècles.* 1923.

Franklin, A. *Dictionnaire des noms, surnoms et pseudonymes latins de l'histoire littéraire du moyen-âge (1100–1530).* 1875, repr. 1959.

Geissler, Fr., *Brautwerbung in der Weltliteratur.* 1955.

Guyer, F. E. *Romance in the Making.* 1954.

Hatzfeld, H. "Esthetic Criticism Applied to Medieval Literature," *Romanic Review,* Vol. XXXIX (1948–49).

Highet, G. *The Classical Tradition.* 1949.

Hunt, R. W. "Introduction to the *Artes* in the Twelfth Century," *Studia Medievalia in honorem Josephi Martini.* 1948.

Lausberg, H. *Elemente der literarischen Rhetorik.* 1949.

Lewis, C. S. *The Allegory of Love.* 1936.

Misch, G. *Geschichte der Autobiographie.* 3d ed., 3 vols., 1949–59. Vols. II and III: *Das Mittelalter.*

Singer, S. *Sprichwörter des Mittelalters.* 3 vols., 1944–47.

Spargo, J. W. *Virgil the Necromancer. Studies in Virgilian Legends.* 1934.

Spemann, A. *Vergleichende Zeittafel der Weltliteratur vom Mittelalter bis zur Neuzeit 1150–1939.* 1951.

Taylor, A. *The Proverb.* 1931.

Van Tieghem, P. *La Littérature comparée.* 1931.

Walsh, W. S. *A Handy Book of Literary Curiosities.* 1892, repr. 1925.

MEDIEVAL LATIN LITERATURE

See also the histories of vernacular literature, which usually contain accounts of the Latin literature written in the countries they discuss.

Du Méril, M. *Poésies populaires latines du moyen-âge.* 1847.

Ghellinck, J. de. *L'Essor de la littérature latine au XIIme siècle.* 2 vols., 1946, repr. 1954. Excellent bibliographical notes.

—— *Littérature latine au moyen âge.* 2 vols., 1939. From the beginnings to St. Anselm.

*Hélin, M. *A History of Medieval Latin Literature.* 1949. Trans. of French ed. of 1943.

Kusch, H. *Einführung in das lateinische Mittelalter,* Vol. I. 1957. A large selection of poetry with German translation. A second volume, consisting of commentary, is proposed.

Lehmann, P. *Die Parodie im Mittelalter.* 1922.

—— *Pseudo-antike Literatur des Mittelalters.* 1927.

Manitius, M. *Geschichte der lateinischen Literatur des Mittelalters.* 3 vols., 1911–31. Vol. I rep. 1959. Vol. I: Justinian to mid-tenth century; Vol. II: Mid-tenth century to investiture struggle; Vol. III: Investiture struggle to end of twelfth century. Superb, highly detailed account of all writings of the period. Excellent bibliography. Locations of MSS of unpublished works.

Raby, F. J. E. *A History of Christian Latin Poetry.* 2d ed., 1953.
—— *A History of Secular Latin Poetry.* 2d ed., 1957.
Wright, F., and T. Sinclair. *A History of Later Latin Literature.*
. . . 1931.

FRENCH AND PROVENÇAL LITERATURE

Anglade, J. *Histoire sommaire de la littérature méridionale au moyen âge.* 1921.
Bédier, J., and P. Hazard. *Histoire de la littérature française illustrée.* 2 vols., 2d ed., 1948–49.
Bossuat, R. *Le Moyen âge.* 1931. Vol. I of *Histoire de la littérature française,* ed. J. Calvet.
Cohen, G. *Littérature française du moyen âge.* 1951.
—— *La Poésie en France au moyen âge.* 1952.
—— *Tableau de la littérature française médiévale, idées et sensibilité.* 1950.
—— *La Vie littéraire en France au moyen âge.* 1953.
Crosland, Jessie. *Medieval French Literature.* 1956.
Gröber, G. *Grundriss der romanischen Philologie.* Vol. I, 2d ed., 1906; Vol. II, 1893–1902.
Histoire littéraire de la France, publ. by the Congrégation de St. Maur, continued by members of the Institute. 1733–63; 1874. Useful for primary sources.
*Holmes, U. T. *A History of Old French Literature.* 1948.
Jeanroy, A. *La Poésie occitane des origines à la fin du XVIIIme siècle.* 1955.
Kukenheim, L., and H. Roussel. *Guide de la littérature française du moyen âge.* 1957. A very brief summary.
Levy, R. *Chronologie approximative de la littérature française du moyen âge* (Zeitschrift für romanische Philologie, Beiheft, Vol. XCVIII). 1957.
Lote, G. *Le Vers français.* 2 vols., 1949–52.
Paris, G. *La Littérature française au moyen âge.* Rev. ed., 1914.
—— *Mélanges de littérature française au moyen âge.* 1912.
Patterson, W. F. *Three Centuries of French Poetic Theory.* 1935.
Petit de Julleville, L. *Histoire de la langue et de la littérature française des origines à 1900.* Vol. I, Parts 1 and 2, for Middle Ages, 1896.
Voretzsch, K. *Introduction to the Study of Old French Literature.* 1931. Trans. of 3d German ed.
Zumthor, P. *Histoire littéraire de la France, VIme–XIVme siècles.*

1954. Good for ideas and movements. Very brief study of individual works.

ITALIAN LITERATURE

De Sanctis, F. *Storia della litteratura italiana.* 2 vols., 1870–72. Also later editions. Trans. by Joan Redfern under title *History of Italian Literature,* 2 vols., 1931.

Storia letteraria d'Italia: Le Origini, by A. Viscardi, 3d ed., 1957; *Il Duecento,* by G. Bertoni, 2d ed., 1954; *Dante,* by M. Apollonio, 2d ed., 1954; *Il Trecento,* by N. Sapegno, 2d ed., 1955; *Il Quattrocento,* by V. Rossi, 5th ed., 1953.

Vossler, K. *Italienische Literaturgeschichte.* 4th ed., 1948.

*Wilkins, E. H. *A History of Italian Literature.* 1954.

GERMANIC LITERATURE

Baesecke, G. *Vor- und Frühgeschichte des deutschen Schrifttums.* Vols. I and II, 1940–53.

Beyschlag, S. *Die Metrik der mittelhochdeutschen Blütezeit in Grundzügen.* 3d ed., 1959.

Becker, H. *Die ältere deutsche Literatur.* 1956.

Bostock, J. K. *A Handbook on Old High German Literature.* 1955.

Courcelle, P. *Histoire littéraire des grandes invasions germaniques.* 1948.

*De Boor, H. *Geschichte der deutschen Literatur.* Vol. I (to 1100), Vol. II (to 1250), 1953. The best introduction. Very useful bibliography.

Ehrismann, G. *Geschichte der deutschen Literatur bis zum Ausgang des Mittelalters.* 4 vols., 1932–35. The standard reference work. Bibliography virtually complete up to time of writing.

Einarsson, S. *A History of Icelandic Literature.* 1957.

Frenzel, H. A. *Daten deutscher Dichtung.* 1952.

Goedeke, K. *Grundriss zur Geschichte der deutschen Dichtung.* Vol. I, 1859; 2d ed., 1881. Now virtually useless except for bibliographical data.

Heusler, A. *Die altgermanische Dichtung.* 2d ed., 1941.

—— *Deutsche Versgeschichte.* 3 vols., 1925–29.

—— *Deutsche Verskunst.* 1951. Shorter version of *Deutsche Versgeschichte.*

Hübner, A. *Die mittelhochdeutsche Ironie.* 1930.

Klein, K. K. *Die Anfänge der deutschen Literatur.* 1954.

Kosch, W. *Deutsches Literaturlexikon.* 2d ed., 1956–. Lists by authors.

Martini, F. *Das Bauerntum im deutschen Schrifttum von den Anfängen bis zum 16. Jahrhundert.* 1944.

Merker, P., and W. Stammler. *Reallexikon der deutschen Literaturgeschichte.* 1925–31. 2d ed. by W. Kohlschmidt and W. Mohr in progress, 1955–.

Neufforge, F. von. *Über den Versuch einer deutschen Bibliothek als Spiegel deutscher Kulturentwicklung.* 1942.

Ranke, F. *Gott, Welt und Humanität in der deutschen Dichtung des Mittelalters.* 1953.

Schmitt, F. A. *Stoff- und Motivgeschichte der deutschen Literatur.* 1959. A bibliography.

Schneider, H. *Heldendichtung, Geistlichendichtung, Ritterdichtung.* 2d ed., 1943.

Schroeder, F. R. *Germanische Heldendichtung.* 1935.

Schwietering, J. *Deutsche Dichtung des Mittelalters.* 1938, repr. 1957.

Singer, S. *Literaturgeschichte der Schweiz im Mittelalter.* 1915.

Stammler, W. *Die deutsche Literatur des Mittelalters. Verfasserlexikon.* 5 vols., 1933–55. A superb work, which gives all known information on German medieval authors and accounts of anonymous works.

—— *Deutsche Philologie im Aufriss.* 1952–57. 2d ed. in progress.

—— *Von der Mystik zum Barock.* 2d ed., 1950. Excellent for later Middle Ages. Detailed bibliographical notes.

Turville-Petre, G. *Origins of Icelandic Literature.* 1953.

Unwert, W. von, and Th. Siebs. *Geschichte der deutschen Literatur bis zur Mitte des elften Jahrhunderts.* 1920.

Vries, J. de. *Altnordische Literaturgeschichte.* 2 vols., 1941–42.

Wehrli, M. *Allgemeine Literaturwissenschaft.* 1951.

Winterfeld, P. von. *Deutsche Dichter des lateinischen Mittelalters.* 1913.

ENGLISH LITERATURE

Anderson, G. K. *The Literature of the Anglo-Saxons.* 1949.

Atkins, J. W. R. *English Literary Criticism—the Medieval Phase.* 1943.

*Baugh, A. C., ed. *A Literary History of England.* 1950.

Cambridge History of English Literature, ed. A. W. Ward and A. R. Waller. Vols. I and II, 1907–30.

Oxford History of English Literature, ed. F. P. Wilson and B. Dobree. Vol. II, Parts 1 and 2, 1954–57.

Sisam, K. *Studies in the History of Old English Literature.* 1952.

Wilson, R. M. *The Lost Literature of Medieval England.* 1952.

SPANISH LITERATURE

*Brenan, G. F. *The Literature of the Spanish People.* 2d ed., 1953.

Diaz-Plaja, G. *Historia general de las literaturas hispanicas* 1949–55. Vol. I covers the medieval period to 1400.

ARABIC LITERATURE

Brockelmann, C. *Geschichte der arabischen Literatur.* 2 vols., 2d ed., 1943–49.

*Gibb, H. A. R. *Arabic Literature: an Introduction.* 1926.

Gonzalez-Palencia, A. *Historia de la literatura arábigo-española.* 2d ed., 1945.

Graf, G. *Geschichte der christlichen arabischen Literatur.* 5 vols., 1944–53. Vols. I, II, and V are on Middle Ages.

Recommended Reading

THE ROMANCE

GENERAL

Note that some of the most important discussions are in the histories of literature previously listed.

Bezzola, R. R. *Les Origines et la formation de la littérature courtoise en Occident 500–1200.* 1944.

Eggers, H. *Symmetrie und Proportionen epischen Erzählens.* 1956.

Faral, E. *Recherches sur les sources latines des contes et romans courtois.* 1913.

Fierz-Monnier, Antoinette. *Initiation und Wandlung. Zur Geschichte des altfranzösischen Romans im 12. Jahrhundert.* 1951.

French, W. H., and M. E. Hale. *Middle English Metrical Romances.* 1930.

Guyer, F. E. *Romance in the Making: Chrétien de Troyes and the Earliest French Romances.* 1954.

Hibbard, Laura. *Medieval Romance in England.* 1924. Reprint with expanded bibliography, 1960.

Ker, W. P. *Epic and Romance.* 1897.

Kohn, Anna. *Das weibliche Schönheitsideal in der ritterlichen Dichtung* (Dissertation, Greifswald). 1930.

Lot-Borodine, Myrrha. *Le Roman idyllique au moyen âge.* 1913.

Maurer, F. *Leid.* 1951.

Naumann, E. "Der Streit um das ritterliche Tugendsystem," in *Festschrift für K. Helm.* 1951.

Taylor, A. B. *Introduction to Medieval Romance.* 1930.

Wilmotte, W. M. *Origines du roman en France, l'évolution du sentiment romanesque jusqu'en 1340.* 1940.

Béroul, *Tristan,* ed. A. Ewert, 1939; ed. E. Muret, 1947.
Chrétien de Troyes. *Werke,* ed. W. Foerster. 4 vols., 1884–99. Still regarded as the standard edition but has numerous inaccuracies; does not include *Perceval. Perceval le Gallois,* ed. C. Potvin, 6 vols., 1866–71, contains the *Perceval* of Chrétien and the two prologues, as well as three of the four continuations. The edition is based on one manuscript only. *Der Percevalroman (Li Contes del Graal),* ed. A. Hilka, 1932, is the standard edition of *Perceval. Erec, Cligès, Yvain, Guillaume d'Angleterre,* Modern French trans. by A. Mary, 2d ed., 1924; English trans. by W. W. Comfort, 1913. *Perceval,* modern French trans. by L. Foulet, 1947; English trans. by R. S. and Laura H. Loomis in *Medieval Romances,* 1957.
"Culhwch and Olwen" and "Rhonabwy's Dream" in *Mabinogion,* trans. G. and T. Jones. 1949.
Didot Perceval, ed. W. Roach. 1941. This is the prose version of the work of Robert de Boron.
Continuations of the Old French "Perceval" of Chrétien de Troyes, ed. W. Roach. Vol. I, 1949; Vol. II, 1950; Vol. III, pt. 1, 1952.
Eilhart von Oberge, *Tristant,* ed. F. Lichtenstein. 1877.
Gawain and the Green Knight, ed. I. Gollancz. Rev. ed., 1940. With bibliography. Modernizations by K. Hare, 1946; M. R. Ridley, 1950; and R. S. and Laura H. Loomis in *Medieval Romances,* 1957.
Geoffrey of Monmouth. *Historia regum Britanniae,* ed. A. Griscom, 1929; ed. E. Faral, in *La Légende arthurienne,* III, 63 ff. Geoffrey's work, as well as that of other historians whose works contain references to Arthurian material, can be found, in English translation, in J. A. Giles, *Six Old English Chronicles,* 1848.
Gerbert de Montreuil. *La Continuation de Perceval,* ed. Mary Williams. 1922.
Gottfried von Strassburg. *Tristan und Isolt,* ed. F. Ranke, 1930; ed. A. Bechstein, 5th ed., 1930. Useful selection with notes, etc., by A. Closs, 1947. Trans., with Thomas version, prose by A. T.

Hatto, 1960; partial, verse, by E. Zeydel, 1948; modern German trans., partial, verse, by W. Hertz, 1907.

Hartmann von Aue, *Der arme Heinrich*, ed. H. Paul, 9th ed., rev. A. Leitzmann, 1949; *Erec*, ed. A. Leitzmann, 1939; *Gregorius*, ed. Fr. Neumann, 1958; *Iwein*, ed. K. Lachmann, 6th ed., rev. L. Wolff, 1959. German trans. of complete works by R. Fink, 1939.

Layamon, *Brut*, ed. and modernized by F. Madden. 1847.

Libeaus desconus, ed. M. Kaluza. 1890.

Mabinogion, trans. J. Loth. 1913.

Malory, Sir Thomas. *Works*, ed. E. Vinaver. 3 vols., 1954. Important introduction and bibliography.

Marie de France, *Lais*, ed. E. Hoepffner, 1921; ed. K. Warnke, 1925; ed. A. Ewert, 1944.

Queste del St. Graal, ed. A. Pauphilet. 1949.

Robert de Boron. *Roman de l'Estoire du Graal*, ed. W. Nitze. 1927.

Suite du Merlin (Huth Merlin), ed. G. Paris and J. Ulrich. 1886. This is a continuation of the prose version of Robert de Boron's work.

Thomas of Britain. *Tristan*, ed. J. Bédier, 2 vols., 1902–5; *Fragments du Tristan de Thomas*, ed. Bartina H. Wind, 1950. English trans. by R. S. Loomis, *Romance of Tristan and Ysolt*, 3d ed., 1951. This is actually a translation of the Icelandic prose version of Thomas, supplemented by Thomas and Gottfried where their texts are extant. J. Bédier, *Le Roman de Tristan et Iseut* (1900) is a compilation of material from almost all the extant Tristan stories, not a translation from any one author; English trans. by H. Belloc and P. Rosenfeld, 1945.

Tristramssaga ok Isondar, ed. E. Kölbing, with German trans. and the Middle English *Sir Tristrem*. 1878.

Ulrich von Zatzikhoven. *Lanzelet*, ed. K. A. Hahn. 1845. English trans. by K. G. T. Webster and R. S. Loomis, 1951. Excellent notes.

Wace. *Brut*, ed. I. Arnold. 2 vols., 1938–40.

Wolfram von Eschenbach. *Parzival*, ed. K. Lachmann, 7th ed., rev. E. Hartl, 1952 (also contains *Titurel* fragments); ed. A. Leitzmann, 3 vols., 1953–55; ed. E. Martin, with commentary, 2 vols., 1900–3. Complete English trans. by Jessie Weston, 1894; partial prose by Margaret Richey, 1935; partial verse by E. Zeydel, 1951. Modern German trans., partial, verse, by W. Hertz, 1898; complete, prose, by W. Stapel, 4th ed., 1950.

Secondary Works

Arthurian Literature in the Middle Ages: a Collaborative History,
ed. R. S. Loomis. 1959. This is by far the most important single
work on Arthurian literature. The chapters are written by specialists in each field. The footnotes provide the essential bibliography for each subject or work. It supersedes J. D. Bruce,
The Evolution of Arthurian Romance (1923), except for the
bibliographical data. Up to 1921, Bruce is virtually complete.
For publications after that date, see: *Bibliography of Critical
Arthurian Literature for 1922–29,* ed. J. J. Parry (1931), and
Bibliography of Critical Arthurian Literature for 1930–35, ed. J.
J. Parry and Margaret Schlauch (1936). Since 1940 a bibli-
ography of Arthurian literature has appeared annually in the
June issue of *Modern Language Quarterly,* covering the literature
since 1936. Since 1949 there has appeared annually the *Bulletin
bibliographique de la Société internationale arthurienne.*
Bindschedler, Maria. "Der heutige Stand der Forschung über
Gottfried von Strassburg," *Deutschunterricht* (1953), No. 2.
Borodine, M. *La Femme et l'amour au XIIe siècle d'après les
poèmes de Chrétien de Troyes.* 1909.
Brown, A. C. L. *The Origin of the Grail Legend.* 1943.
Carman, J. N. *The Relationship of the "Perlesvaus" and the "Queste
del Sant Graal."* 1936.
Chambers, E. K. *Arthur of Britain.* 1927.
Cohen, G. *Un Grand Romancier d'amour et d'aventure au XIIe
siècle.* 2d ed., 1948. Superficial.
Crocetti, C. G. *La leggenda di Tristano.* 1950.
Cross, T. P. *Motif Index of Early Irish Literature.* 1952.
——, and W. A. Nitze. *Lancelot and Guenevere.* 1930.
——, and C. Slover. *Ancient Irish Tales.* 1936.
Entwistle, W. J. *Arthurian Legend in the History of the Spanish
Peninsula.* 1929.
Faral, E. *La Légende arthurienne.* 3 vols., 1929. Strongly critical
of the theory of Celtic origins.
Fourquet, J. *Wolfram von Eschenbach et le "Conte del Graal."*
1938. Basic for the study of the relationship between the texts
of Wolfram and Chrétien.
Frappier, J. *Chrétien de Troyes: l'homme et l'oeuvre.* 1957. The
best single work; objective and precise.

—— *Perceval ou le Conte del Graal.* 1953.

Gardner, E. G. *Arthurian Legend in Italian Literature.* 1930.

Golther, W. *Tristan und Isolde.* 1907.

Gombert, J. *Eilhart von Oberg und Gottfried von Strassburg.* 1927.

Hofer, S. *Chrétien de Troyes, Leben und Werke.* 1954. Strongly supports the theory of the French origin of Chrétien's work.

Hull, Eleanor. *Textbook of Irish Literature.* 2 vols., 1906–8.

Kittredge, G. L. *A Study of "Gawain and the Green Knight."* 1916.

Koppitz, H. J. *Wolframs Religiosität: Beobachtung über das Verhältnis Wolframs von Eschenbach zur religiösen Tradition des Mittelalters.* 1959.

Küpper, H. *Bibliographie zur Tristansage.* 1941. Attempts a complete listing of the literature to 1939.

Leahy, A. H. *Heroic Romances of Ireland.* 1906.

Le Gentil, P. "La Légende de Tristan vue par Béroul et Thomas," *Romance Philology,* Vol. VII (1953).

Lewis, C. B. *Classical Mythology and Arthurian Romance.* 1932.

Loomis, R. S. *Arthurian Tradition and Chrétien de Troyes.* 1948. The best exposition of the evidence for the persistence of Celtic motifs and names.

—— *Wales and the Arthurian Tradition.* 1956.

——, and Laura Hibbard Loomis. *Arthurian Legends in Medieval Art.* 1938.

Marx, J. *La Légende arthurienne et le Graal.* 1952.

—— *Les Littératures celtiques.* 1959.

Meissburger, G. *Tristan und Isold mit den weissen Händen.* 1954.

Mergell, B. *Tristan und Isolde.* 1949.

—— *Wolfram von Eschenbach und seine französischen Quellen.* 2 vols., 1936–43.

Meyer, J. J. *Isoldes Gottesurteil in seiner erotischen Bedeutung.* 1914.

Meyer, R. *Der Graal und seine Hüter.* 1956. A fantastic account of the ultimate origins of the Grail.

Mockenhaupt, B. *Die Frömmigkeit im Parzival Wolframs von Eschenbach.* 1942.

Mohr, W. "*Tristan und Isold* als Künstlerroman," *Euphorion,* Vol. LIII (1959). A good treatment, but probably does not go far enough.

Newstead, Helaine. *Bran the Blessed in Arthurian Romance.* 1939.

Nickel, E. *Studien zum Liebesproblem bei Gottfried von Strassburg.* In *Königsberger deutsche Forschungen,* Vol. I, 1927.

Paton, Lucy A. *Fairy Mythology of Arthurian Romance.* 1903.

Pauphilet, A. *Le Legs du moyen âge.* 1950.

Piquet, F. *L'Originalité de Gottfried de Strasbourg.* 1905.

Ranke, F. *Die Allegorie der Minnegrotte in Gottfrieds Tristan.* Schriften der Königsberger Gelehrten Gesellschaft, geisteswissenschaftliche Klasse, Vol. II, No. 2, 1925. Still the basic work on the subject.

—— *Tristan und Isold.* 1925.

Rhys, J. *Celtic Folklore.* 1901.

Richter, W. *Der "Lanzelet" des Ulrich von Zatzikhoven.* 1934.

Romans du Graal dans la littérature des XIIe et XIIIe siècles, Les, by various scholars. 1956.

Schirmer, W. F. *Die frühen Darstellungen des Arthurstoffes.* 1958.

Schoepperle, Gertrude. *Tristan and Isolt: a Study of the Sources of the Romance.* 2 vols., 1913.

Schröder, W. J. *Der Ritter zwischen Welt und Gott.* 1952.

Schwietering, J. *Parzivals Schuld: Zur Religiosität Wolframs in ihrer Beziehung zur Mystik.* 1944.

—— *Der Tristan Gottfrieds von Strassburg und die Bernhardsche Mystik.* Abhandlungen der preussischen Akademie der Wissenschaften, philosophisch-historische Klasse, 1943, No. 5.

Tatlock, J. S. P. *The Legendary History of Britain.* 1950.

Thurneysen, R. *Die irische Helden- und Königssage.* 1921.

Wapnewski, P. *Wolframs "Parzival": Studien zur Religiosität und Form.* 1955.

Weber, G. *Gottfrieds von Strassburg "Tristan" und die Krise des hochmittelalterlichen Weltbildes um 1200.* 2 vols., 1953.

—— *Wolfram von Eschenbach, seine dichterische und geistesgeschichtliche Bedeutung.* 1928.

Webster, K. G. T. *Guinevere: a Study of her Abductions.* 1951.

Weston, Jessie. *The Legends of Sir Perceval and the Grail.* 1906.

—— *From Ritual to Romance.* 1920.

Witte, A. "Hartmann von Aue und Kristian von Troyes," *PBB,* Vol. LIII (1929).

Zumthor, P. *Merlin le prophète.* 1943.

THE ROMANCES OF ANTIQUITY

Texts

Alexander Romance. *The Medieval French Roman d'Alexandre,* in Elliot Monographs in the Romance Languages and Literatures, ed. E. C. Armstrong and others. 1937–. For other versions, see Bossuat, *Manuel bibliographique;* Pfaffe Lamprecht, *Alexander-lied,* ed. F. Maurer, 1940; *The Gests of King Alexander of Macedon,* ed. F. P. Magoun, 1929; *Kyng Alisaunder,* ed. G. V. Smithers, 2 vols., EETS, 1952–57.

Benoît de Ste. Maure. *Roman de Troie,* ed. L. Constans. 6 vols., SATF, 1904–12.

Chaucer. *Troilus and Criseyde,* ed. R. J. Root. 1926.

Dares Phrygius. *De excidio Troiae historia,* ed. F. Meister. 1873.

De excidio Troiae, ed. E. B. Attwood and V. K. Whittaker. 1944.

Dictys Cretensis. *Ephemeridos belli Troiani libri,* ed. W. Eisenhut. 1958.

Guido de Columnis. *Historia destructionis Troiae,* ed. N. E. Griffin. 1936.

Joseph of Exeter. *De bello Troiano,* with texts of Dares and Dictys. 1825.

Lydgate. *Troy Book,* ed. H. Bergen. EETS, 4 vols., 1906–35.

The Recuyell of the Historyes of Troy. . . . , trans. W. Caxton, ed. O. Sommer. 2 vols., 1894.

Seege and Batayle of Troye, ed. Mary E. Barnicle. EETS, 1927.

Testi inediti di storia Troiana, ed. E. Gorra. 1887.

Thebes. *Roman de Thèbes,* ed. L. Constans. SATF, 2 vols., 1890.

Secondary Works

Cary, G. *The Medieval Alexander.* 1956.

De Grave, S. "Les Sources du Roman de Thèbes," in *Mélanges Wilmotte.* 1910.

Greif, W. *Die mittelalterlichen Bearbeitungen der Trojanersage.* 1886.

Griffin, N. E. *Dares and Dictys.* 1907.

Hübner, A. *Alexander der Grosse in der deutschen Dichtung des Mittelalters.* 1940.

Klippel, Maria. *Darstellung der fränkischen Trojanersage.* 1936.

Merkelbach, R. *Die Quellen des griechischen Alexanderromans.* 1954.

Meyer, P. *Alexandre le Grand dans la littérature française du moyen âge.* 2 vols., 1886.

Pearson, L. *The Lost Histories of Alexander.* 1959.

Schmidbauer, F. *Die Troilusepisode in Benoits Roman de Troie.* 1914.

Warren, F. M. "On the Latin Sources of the *Roman de Thèbes*," *PMLA*, Vol. XVI (1901).

Woledge, B. *Bibliographie des romans et nouvelles en prose française antérieurs à 1500.* 1954.

THE CHANSON DE GESTE

Texts

Aliscans, ed. E. Wienbeck *et al.* 1903.

Chançun de Willame, ed. Nancy V. Iseley. 1952.

Chanson de Guillaume, ed. E. S. Eyler, 1919; ed. D. MacMillan, SATF, 2 vols., 1949–51.

Chanson de Roland, ed. J. Bédier, 1927. This is the standard edition of the Oxford (Digby) manuscript text. There is also a smaller edition with a modern French version by Bédier facing the original text (1947). English translations are numerous: Luquiens (1952); Moncrieff (1919); Sherwood (1938). The other texts of the *Chanson de Roland* have been published by the SATF in ten fascicles, ed. R. Mortier, 1940–49. For details on the research concerning the *Chanson de Roland,* see Bossuat, *Manuel bibliographique,* and A. Junker, "Stand der Forschung zum Rolandslied," *Germanisch-Romanische Monatsschrift,* Vol. VI (1956).

Couronnement de Louis, ed. P. Langlois. SATF, 1888.

Enfances Guillaume, Les, ed. Patrice Henry. SATF, 1935.

Moniage Guillaume, Le, ed. W. Coletta. SATF, 2 vols., 1906–11.

Pfaffe Kuonrat. *Rolandslied,* ed. F. Maurer. 1940.

Wolfram von Eschenbach. *Willehalm,* ed. K. Lachmann, 5th ed., K. Weinhold, 1891.

Secondary Works

Bédier, J. *Les Légendes épiques.* 4 vols., 1908–21.

Bumke, J. *Wolframs Willehalm.* 1959. Notes contain references to virtually all the relevant literature.

Coulet, J. *Etudes sur l'ancien poème du voyage de Charlemagne en Orient.* 1907.

Crosland, Jessie. *The Old French Epic.* 1951.

Faral, E. *Chanson de Roland, étude et analyse.* 1948.

Frappier, J. *Les Chansons de geste du cycle de Guillaume d'Orange.* . . . 1955.

Gay, L. M. *La Chanson de Roland et la Chanson de Willame.* 1924.

Hoepffner, E. "Les Rapports littéraires entre les premières chansons de geste," in *Studi medievali,* N.S., Vols IV (1931) and VI (1933).

Le Gentil, P. *La Chanson de Roland.* 1955. A most useful and objective study of the principal problems.

Paris, G. *Histoire poétique de Charlemagne.* 1865. Still the most detailed study of the materials of the *chansons de geste.*

Rickard, P. *Britain in Medieval French Literature, 1100–1500.* 1956. Some interesting background material for the *chansons de geste* and the romance.

Rychner, J. *La Chanson de Geste.* 1955. Structural studies.

Siciliano, I. *Les Origines des chansons de geste, théories et discussions.* 1951. Original edition in Italian, 1942.

Wilmotte, M. *L'Epopée française, origine et élaboration.* 1939.

THE GERMANIC EPIC

Texts

Beowulf, ed. F. Klaeber, 3d ed., 1936; ed. E. V. K. Dobbie, 1953; ed. C. L. Wrenn, 1953. Numerous English trans., e.g., by J. R. Clarke-Hall, rev. ed., 1950; by D. Wright, 1957.

Deutsches Heldenbuch, ed. O. Jänicke and others. 5 vols., 1866–73. Contains Dietrich legends etc.

Eddas. Verse Edda (Older Edda), ed. G. Neckel, 1914; ed. R. C. De Boer, 1922. English trans. by H. A. Bellows, 1923; French trans. (with other material) by F. Wagner, as *Les Poèmes mythologiques de l'Edda,* 1929; German trans. by F. Genzmer, 1933; *Prose Edda (Younger Edda),* ed. F. Jonnson, 2d ed., 1926; English trans. by Arthur Brodeur, 1916; by Jean I. Young, 1954.

Gudrun, ed. E. Martin, with commentary. 2 vols., 1872, 1902; smaller ed., 1911. Numerous modern German versions, e.g., by K. Simrock, 1843.

Hildebrandslied, ed. G. Baesecke, 1945; and in W. Braune, *Althochdeutsches Lesebuch,* 9th ed., 1959. Modern German trans. in C. Thomas, *Anthology of German Literature,* 1909.

Nibelungenlied, ed. K. Bartsch. 2 vols., 1866, 1880. Outdated, but still the fullest critical edition. C text ed. F. Zarncke, 6th ed.,

1887; A text ed. K. Lachmann, 14th ed., 1927; B text ed. H. De Boor, 1959. English trans. by Margaret Armour, 1913. *Diu Klage,* ed. A. Edzardi, 1875.

Thidriks saga af Bern, ed. Henrik Bertelsen. 2 vols., 1905–11. Modern German trans. by Fine Erichsen. 1924.

Secondary Works

Batchelor, C. C. "The Style of *Beowulf,* a Study of the Composition of the Poem," *Speculum,* Vol. XII (1937).

Bliss, A. J. *The Metre of Beowulf.* 1958. Mainly statistical.

Braune, W. "Die Handschriftenverhältnisse des Nibelungenliedes," *PBB,* Vol. XXV (1900).

Brodeur, A. G. *The Art of Beowulf.* 1959.

Chadwick, H. M. *The Heroic Age.* 1912.

Chambers, R. W. *Beowulf: an Introduction to the Study of the Poem.* 3d ed., 1959.

Craigie, W. A. *The Icelandic Saga.* 1937.

De Boor, H. *Das Attilabild in Geschichte, Legende und heroischer Dichtung.* 1932.

Droege, K. "Thidrekssaga," *Zeitschrift für deutsches Altertum,* Vol. LXVI (1929).

Grimm, W. K. *Die deutsche Heldensage.* 3d ed., 1899.

Hermannsson, H. *Bibliography of the Eddas.* 1920.

—— *Bibliography of the Sagas.* 1938.

—— *The Sagas of the Icelanders.* 1935.

Heusler, A. *Nibelungensage und Nibelungenlied.* 1922. The most important single work on the origins of the poem.

Lawrence, W. W. *Beowulf and the Epic Tradition.* 1930.

Moeller, E. *Poetic Style and Technique in the Heroic Lays of the Edda* (doctoral dissertation, University of California). 1942.

Mudrok, E. *Die nordische Heldensage.* 1943.

Naumann, H. "Stand der Nibelungenforschungen," *Zeitschrift für Deutschkunde,* Vol. XLI (1927).

Panzer, H. *Das Nibelungenlied.* 1955.

Pope, J. C. *The Rhythm of Beowulf.* 1942.

Schneider, H. *Die deutschen Lieder von Siegfrieds Tod.* 1947.

—— *Die Götter der Germanen.* 1938.

—— "Der heutige Stand der Nibelungenforschung," *Forschungen und Fortschritte,* Vol. XVIII (1942).

Thorp, Mary. *The Study of the Nibelungenlied from 1755 to 1937.*

1940. An excellent survey of the immense literature on the subject.

Tonnelat, E. *La Chanson des Nibelungen: Etude sur la composition et la formation du poème épique.* 1926.

THE MEDIEVAL LYRIC

Texts

Latin

A large amount of the medieval Latin lyric poetry remains unpublished. For details of the works written, so far as can be determined, before 1180, see M. Manitius, *Geschichte der lateinischen Literatur des Mittelalters.*

Archipoeta. *Die Gedichte,* ed. H. Watenpuhl and H. Krefeld. 1958. *Die Gedichte des Archipoeta,* ed. B. Schmeidler, with German trans. and notes. 1911.

Cambridge Songs, ed. K. Breul, 1915; ed. K. Strecker, 1927.

Carmina Burana, ed. A. Hilka and O. Schumann, Vol. I, Parts 1 and 2, Vol. II, Part 1. 1931–41. This is by far the best edition but is incomplete. The only complete text is still the antiquated edition of Schmeller, 4th ed., 1907. There is an English translation of some of the poems by J. A. Symonds under the title *Wine, Women and Song,* 1884; frequently repr. See also the work by Whicher noted below. Selected poems have been translated into modern German by L. Laistner, 1954.

Carmina medii aevi posterioris latina, ed. H. Walther. Vol. I (1959) contains the first lines, bibliography, etc. Subsequent volumes will contain the texts.

Gautier de Châtillon. *Die Gedichte Walthers von Châtillon,* ed. K. Strecker, 1925; *Die moralisch-satirischen Gedichte Walthers von Châtillon,* ed. K. Strecker, 1929.

Langosch, K. *Hymnen und Vagantenlieder,* with German trans. 1954. Poems from sources other than the *Carmina Burana.* Useful notes.

Lehmann, P. *Parodistiche Texte.* 1923.

Waddell, Helen. *Medieval Latin Lyrics.* 1930. Includes good translations; frequently repr.

Whicher, G. *The Goliard Poets.* Text and English verse trans. 1949.

French and Provençal

Appel, C. *Provenzalische Chrestomathie.* 6th ed., 1932.
Bernart de Ventadorn. *Werke,* ed. C. Appel. 1915.
Blondel de Nesles. *Die Lieder,* ed. L. von Wiese. 1904.
Cardenal, Peire. *Les Poésies,* ed. with trans. by R. Lavaud. 1957.
Cerçamon. *Les Poésies,* ed. A. Jeanroy. 1922.
Charles d'Orléans. *Poésies,* ed. P. Champion. 2 vols., 1923–27.
Conon de Béthune. *Les Chansons,* ed. A. Wallensköld. 1921.
Deschamps, Eustache. *Oeuvres complètes,* ed. Q. de Saint-Hilaire. SATF. 11 vols., 1878–1903.
Guillaume IX d'Aquitaine. *Chansons,* ed. A. Jeanroy. 1927.
Hill, R. T., and T. G. Bergin. *Anthology of the Provençal Troubadours.* 1941.
Las Leys d'amors, ed. J. Anglade. 1920.
Lommatzsch, E. *Leben und Lieder der provenzalischen Troubadours.* Vol. I, Love songs. 1957. Vol. II, Various types. 1959.
Machaut, Guillaume de. *Oeuvres,* ed. E. Hoepffner. SATF., 3 vols., 1908–21.
Marcabru. *Poésies complètes,* ed. with trans., notes, etc. by J.-M.-L. Dejeanne. 1909.
Risala (The Dove's Neck-ring), trans. A. R. Nykl. 1931.
Rudel, Jaufré. *Chansons,* ed. A. Jeanroy. 2d ed., 1924.
Rutebeuf. *Oeuvres complètes,* ed. A. Jubinal. New ed., 3 vols., 1874–75; ed. E. Faral and J. Bastin. Vol. I, 1959.
Thiebaut de Champagne (de Navarre). *Les Chansons,* ed. A. Wallensköld. 1925.
Trouvères belges du XIIe au XIVe siècle, ed. A. Scheler. 1876.
Trouvères et Minnesänger: recueil de textes pour servir à l'étude des rapports entre la poésie lyrique romane et le Minnesang au XIIe siècle. Vol. I (texts), ed. I. Franck, 1952; Vol. II (melodies), ed. W. Müller-Blattau, 1956.
Vidal, Peire, *Les Poésies,* ed. J. Anglade. 2d ed., 1923.

German

Bithell, J. *The Minnesingers.* 1909. Translations from various German love poets.
Heinrich von Morungen. *Gedichte,* ed. with modern German trans., by C. von Kraus. 1925.
Des Minnesangs Frühling, ed. K. Lachmann. 30th ed., C. von Kraus,

1950. Contains all German lyric which, in Lachmann's opinion, antedated the work of Walther von der Vogelweide.

Deutsche Liederdichter des 13. Jahrhunderts, ed. C. von Kraus and H. Kuhn. 2 vols., 1952–58.

Neidhart von Reuental, *Lieder,* ed. M. Haupt, rev. E. Wiessner, 1923; selection with musical notation, ed. A. T. Hatto and R. J. Taylor, 1958; E. Wiessner, *Kommentar zu Neidharts Liedern,* 1954; —— *Vollständiges Wörterbuch zu Neidharts Liedern,* 1954.

Pfaff, F. *Die grosse Heidelberger Liederhandschrift in getreuem Textabdruck.* 1909. Prints exactly what is in the manuscript. Occasional inaccuracies.

Richey, Margaret, *Medieval German Lyrics.* 1958.

Scheunemann, E. *Texte zur Geschichte des deutschen Tageliedes.* 1947.

Walther von der Vogelweide. *Gedichte,* ed. K. Lachmann, 11th ed., C. von Kraus, 1950; ed. W. Wilmanns, 4th ed., V. Michels, 1924: ed. F. Maurer, as *Die Lieder Walthers von der Vogelweide,* 2 vols., 1955–56. The poems are arranged within each volume in Maurer's chronological order and have modern transcriptions of music where it exists.

Wehrli, M. *Deutsche Lyrik des Mittelalters.* 1955. Best anthology; colored reproductions of miniatures; modern German facing original text.

English

Adamson, M. R. *A Treasury of Middle English Verse.* 1930. Modernized anthology.

Brown, C. *Religious Lyrics of the Fifteenth Century.* 1952.

—— *English Lyrics of the Fourteenth Century.* 2d ed., rev. G. V. Smithers, 1952.

—— *English Lyrics of the Thirteenth Century.* 1932.

Robbins, R. H. *Secular Lyrics of the Fourteenth and Fifteenth Centuries.* 1952.

Secondary Works

Allen, P. S. *Medieval Latin Lyric.* 1931.

—— *The Romanesque Lyric. . . .* 1928.

Anglade, J. *Anthologie des troubadours.* 1927.

Audiau, J. *La Pastourelle dans la poésie occitane du moyen âge.* 1923.

Beare, W. *Latin Verse and European Song.* 1957.

Beck, J. *Melodien der Troubadours.* 1908. Now of purely historical interest.

Becker, A. "Vom christlichen Hymnus zum Minnesang," *Historisches Jahrbuch der Goerres-Gesellschaft,* Vol. LII, Parts 1 and 2, 1932.

Belperron, P. *La Joie d'amour.* 1928.

Brinkmann, H. *Entstehungsgeschichte des Minnesangs.* 1926. Derives Minnesang from clerical epistolary literature.

—— *Geschichte der lateinischen Liebesdichtung im Mittelalter.* 1925.

Brittain, F. *The Medieval Latin and Romance Lyric to 1300.* 1951.

Bucheler, W. *Französische Einflüsse auf den Strophenbau und die Strophenbindungen bei den deutschen Minnesängern* (doctoral dissertation, Bonn). 1930.

Burdach, K. *Reinmar der alte und Walther von der Vogelweide.* 2d ed., 1928.

Denomy, A. "Concerning the Accessibility of Arabic Influence to the Earliest Provençal Troubadours," *Medieval Studies* (Toronto), Vol. XV (1953).

—— "An Inquiry into the Origins of Courtly Love," *Medieval Studies* (Toronto), Vol. VI (1944).

Diez, F. *Die Poesie der Troubadours.* 2d ed., 1883.

Dobiache-Rojdestvensky, Olga. *Les Poésies des Goliards.* 1931. A very useful summary, with some texts, and list of manuscripts.

Erckmann, R. *Der Einfluss der arabisch-spanischen Kultur auf die Entwicklung des Minnesangs.* 1936.

Franck, I. *Répertoire métrique des troubadours.* 1953.

Gennrich, F. "Der deutsche Minnesang und sein Verhältnis zur Troubadour- und Trouvèrekunst," *Zeitschrift für deutsche Bildung,* Vol. II (1926).

—— "Das Formproblem des Minnesangs," *DVLG,* Vol. IX (1931).

—— "Zur Ursprungsfrage des Minnesangs," *DVLG,* Vol. VII (1929).

Gunther, J. *Die Minneparodie bei Neidhart* (doctoral dissertation, Jena). 1931.

Hoepffner, E. *Les Troubadours dans leur vie et dans leurs oeuvres.* 1955.

Huisman, J. A. *Neue Wege zur dichterischen und musikalischen Technik Walthers von der Vogelweide.* 1950.

Ittenbach, M. *Der frühe deutsche Minnesang.* 1939.

Jeanroy, A. *Bibliographie sommaire des chansonniers français.* 1918.
—— *Bibliographie sommaire des chansonniers provençaux.* 1916.
—— *Les Origines de la poésie lyrique en France au moyen âge.* 3d ed., 1925.
—— *La Poésie lyrique des troubadours.* 2 vols., 1934.
Jones, D. J. *La Tenson provençale.* 1934.
Kolb, H. *Der Begriff der Minne und das Entstehen der höfischen Lyrik.* 1958. With bibliography. The latest and most detailed treatment.
Kuhn, H. *Minnesangs Wende.* 1952.
Maurer, F. *Die politischen Lieder Walthers von der Vogelweide.* 1954.
Menendez-Pidal, R. "Poesia arabe y poesia europea," *Bulletin hispanique,* Vol. XL (1938).
Meyer, W. *Gesammelte Abhandlungen zur mittellateinischen Rhythmik.* 3 vols., 1905–36. Thorough study, but now dated in its approach.
Moll, W. H. *Über den Einfluss der lateinischen Vagantendichtung auf die Lyrik Walthers von der Vogelweide und die seiner Epigonen.* 1925.
Mone, F. J. *Lateinische Hymnen des Mittelalters.* 1853.
Moore, A. K. *The Secular Lyric in Middle English.* 1951.
Moret, A. *Les Débuts du lyrisme en Allemagne.* 1951. Probably the best comprehensive study of the subject.
—— "Le Problème des origines du Minnesang," *Etudes germaniques,* Vol. II (1947).
Norberg, D. *Introduction à l'étude de la versification latine médiévale.* 1958.
Nykl, A. R. *Hispano-Arabic Poetry and Its Relation with the Old Provençal Troubadours.* 1946.
Oulmont, C. *Les Débats du clerc et du chevalier dans la littérature poétique du moyen âge.* 1911.
Paris, G. *La Poésie au moyen âge.* 1885.
Piguet, E. *L'Evolution de la pastourelle du XIIe siècle à nos jours.* 1927.
Pillet, A., and H. Carstens. *Bibliographie der Troubadours.* 1933.
Raynaud, G. *Bibliographie des altfranzösischen Liedes.* 2d ed., rev. H. Spanke, Part I, 1955. Part II will be a short history of the Old French lyric.
Richey, Margaret, *Essays on the Medieval German Love Lyric.* 1943.

Scheludko, D. "Beiträge zur Entstehungsgeschichte der altprovenzalischen Lyrik," *Archivum romanicum,* Vols. XI (1927) and XV (1931).

Schirmer, K.-H. *Die Strophik Walthers von der Vogelweide.* 1956.

Singer, S. *Die religiöse Lyrik des Mittelalters.* 1933.

Spitzer, L. *L'Amour lointain de Jaufré Rudel et le sens de la poésie des troubadours.* 1944.

Süssmilch, H. *Die lateinische Vagantenpoesie des 12. und 13. Jahrhunderts als Kulturerscheinung.* 1917.

Valency, M. *In Praise of Love.* 1958. Good select bibliography: excellent for connections between Provençal and Italian lyric.

Waddell, Helen. *The Wandering Scholars.* 1929. A popular but over-romanticized work. Useful for texts referring to the relations between the wandering scholars and the Church.

Walther, H. *Das Streitgedicht in der lateinischen Literatur des Mittelalters.* 1920.

Wechssler, E. *Das Kulturproblem des Minnesangs.* 1909.

Wilmanns, W. *Leben und Dichten Walthers von der Vogelweide,* 1882; 2d ed., rev. V. Michels, 1916. Basic.

Zumthor, P. "Au Berceau du lyrisme européen," *Cahiers du Sud,* Vol. XL (1954).

THE DRAMA

Texts

Latin

Beauvais Daniel. The Play of Daniel: a 13th Century Musical Drama, ed. N. Greenberg, transcription of music by Rev. R. Weakland. 1959. This is the text and score used for the performance and recording of the play. The text may also be found in Young, *Drama of the Medieval Church.*

Cohen, G. *Anthologie du drame liturgique en France,* with French trans. 1955.

Hartl, E. *Drama des Mittelalters.* 3 vols., 1937–42. In *Deutsche Literatur in Entwicklungsreihen.* Contains several Latin plays from the German area.

Hilarius. *Versus et Ludi,* ed. J. B. Fuller. 1929.

Hroswitha. *Werke,* ed. K. Strecker, 1930; plays, trans. C. St. John, 1923, trans. H. J. W. Tillyard, 1923.

Jones, C. W. *Medieval Literature in Translation.* 1950. Contains translations of several Latin and vernacular plays.

Langosch, K. *Geistliche Spiele des Mittelalters.* 1957. With facing German trans. and notes.

St. Nicholas. *Four Latin Plays of St. Nicholas from the Twelfth-Century Fleury Play-book,* ed. O. E. Albrecht. 1935.

Wright, T., ed. *Early Mysteries and Other Latin Poems of the Twelfth and Thirteenth Centuries.* 1838.

Young, K. *Drama of the Medieval Church.* 2 vols., 1933. Contains nearly all the texts of the Latin dramas of Easter, Christmas, Passion, and the Saints. The work is of inestimable value.

English

Adams, J. Q., ed. *Chief Pre-Shakespearean Dramas.* 1924.

Chester Plays, ed. H. Deinling. EETS, 2 vols., 1896–1916.

Coventry Plays, ed. H. Craig. EETS, 1902.

Everyman, ed. F. Sidgwick. 6th ed., 1902. There are innumerable modernizations and adaptations for acting, of which the most recent is that by A. C. Cawley (1959). That by M. J. Moses (1903) is still useful. The Dutch *Elckerlijc,* ed. K. H. de Raaf, 1897, may be an adaptation or the original of *Everyman.*

Loomis, R. S., and H. W. Wells, eds. *Representative Medieval and Tudor Plays.* 1942.

"Macro Plays." (*Mankind, Wisdom, Castle of Perseverance*), ed. F. J. Furnivall and A. W. Pollard. EETS, 1904.

Pollard, A. W., ed. *English Miracle Plays, Moralities and Interludes.* Rev. ed., 1927.

Towneley (Wakefield) Plays, ed. G. England and A. W. Pollard. EETS, 1897.

York Plays, ed. Lucy T. Smith, 1885. Complete trans. by J. S. Purvis, as *The York Cycle of Mystery Plays,* 1957.

Italian

Ancona, A. d', ed., *Sacre rappresentazioni dei secoli XIV e XVI.* 3 vols., 1872.

Bartholomaeis, V. de, ed. *Laude drammatiche e rappresentazioni sacre.* 3 vols., 1943.

French

Adam de la Halle. *Jeu de la Feuillée,* ed. E. Langlois. 1911.

—— *Robin et Marion,* ed. E. Langlois, in *Adam le Bossu: Trouvère artésien du XIIIe siècle,* 1924; ed. G. Cohen, 1935. Modern French trans. of the plays by E. Langlois, 1923.

Aucassin et Nicolette, ed. M. L. Roques. 2d ed., 1929. English trans. by A. Lang, 1902; by L. Housman, 1902. Both frequently repr.

Bodel, Jean. *Jeu de St. Nicholas,* ed. A. Jeanroy, 1925; ed. F. J. Warne, 1951.

Cohen, G., ed. *La Comédie latine en France au XIIe siècle.* 2 vols., 1931.

——, ed. *Mystères et moralités du manuscrit 617 de Chantilly.* 1920.

——, ed. *Recueil de farces françaises inédites du XVe siècle.* 1949.

——, ed. *Le Théâtre en France au moyen âge.* Vol. I: *Le Théâtre religieux,* 1928; Vol. II: *Le Théâtre profane,* 1931.

Faral, E., ed. *Mimes français du XIIe siècle.* 1910.

Frappier, J., and A.-M. Gossart, eds. and trans. *Le Théâtre réligieux au moyen âge.* 1935.

Gassies, G., trans. *Anthologie du théâtre français au moyen âge.* 2d ed., 1934.

Gréban, Arnoul. *Mystère de la Passion,* ed. G. Paris and G. Raynaud, 1878; modern adaptation by Ch. Gailly and L. de la Tourrasse, 1935.

Jeanroy, A. *Le Théâtre réligieux en France du XIe au XIIIe siècle.* 1937. Translation of selected religious plays into modern French.

Jeu d'Adam, ed. P. Studer, 1918; ed. with trans. by H. Chamard, 1924; Modern French trans., with musical notation (of first part only), by G. Cohen, 1936.

Jubinal, A. *Mystères inédits du quinzième siècle.* 1837.

Milet, Jacques. *L'istoire de la destruction de Troye la grant,* ed. E. Stengel. 1843.

Miracles de Notre Dame par personnages, ed. G. Paris and A. Raynaud. SATF, 8 vols., 1876–93.

Miracles de Ste. Genéviève, ed. Clotilde Sennewaldt. 1937.

Monmerqué, L. J. N., and F. Michel, eds. *Théâtre français au moyen âge.* 1842.

Passion d'Autun, ed. Grace Frank. SATF, 1934.

Passion du Palatinus, ed. Grace Frank. 1922.

Pauphilet, A. *Jeu et sapience du moyen âge.* 1951. A good selection of plays in the original texts, including *Courtois d'Arras, Jeu d'Adam, Jeu de St. Nicholas, Passion du Palatinus, Pathelin, Povre Jehan, Robin et Marion, and Théophile.*

Rutebeuf, *Le Miracle de Théophile,* ed. Grace Frank. 2d ed., 1949;
    Modern French trans., G. Cohen, 1934.
Seinte Resurrection, La, ed. Mildred K. Pope and Jean G. Wright.
    1943.

German

Dietrich Schernberg. *Das Spiel von Frau Jutta,* ed. E. Schröder.
    1911.
Froning, R., ed. *Das Drama des Mittelalters.* 3 vols., 1891–92.
Hartl, E. *Drama des Mittelalters,* 3 vols., in *Deutsche Literatur in
    Entwicklungsreihen.* 1937–42. The first volume is a long intro-
    duction. The remaining two contain religious drama including
    (Vol. IV) the Donaueschinger Passion Play.
Keller, A. von. *Fastnachtspiele aus dem 15. Jahrhundert.* 3 vols.,
    1853.
Kürschner, J. *Deutsche Nationalliteratur.* 164 vols., 1882–97. Vols.
    XII and XIV contain plays.
Theophilus, ed. R. Petsch, 1908; ed. C. Sarauw, 1923; modern
    German trans. by J. Wedde, 1888.
Redentiner Osterspiel, ed. C. Schröder, 1893; English trans. by A.
    E. Zucker, 1941.

Secondary Works

There is a very large literature on the medieval drama, particularly
on the drama in England. A great deal of it is trivial and unoriginal.
Only major works are mentioned in the following list. For others
and for texts of plays, see Stratman, *Bibliography of Medieval
Drama.*

Ancona, A. d'. *Origini del teatro in Italia.* 2 vols., 2d ed., 1891.
Anz, H. *Die lateinischen Magierspiele.* 1905.
Bab, J. *Das deutsche Drama.* 1925.
Baeschlin, H. H. *Die altdeutschen Salbenkrämerspiele.* 1929.
Bahlmann, P. *Die Erneurer des antiken Dramas und ihre ersten
    dramatischen Versuche, 1314–1478.* 1896.
Bartholomaeis, V. de. *Origini della poesia drammatica in Italia.*
    2d ed., 1952.
Boas, F. S. *An Introduction to Tudor Drama.* 1933.
Böhme, M. *Das lateinische Weihnachtsspiel.* 1917.
Borcherdt, H. H. *Das europäische Theater im Mittelalter und in
    der Renaissance.* 1935.

Brinkmann, H. *Zum Ursprung des liturgischen Spieles.* 1929.

Brooks, N. C. *The Sepulcher of Christ in Art and Liturgy.* 1921.

Cargill, O. *Drama and Liturgy.* 1930.

Chambers, E. K. *The Medieval Stage.* 2 vols., 1903.

Clédat, L. *Rutebeuf.* 3d ed., 1909.

Cohen, G. "La Comédie latine en France au XIIe siècle," in *Mélanges offerts à M. Jeanroy.* . . . 1928.

—— *Histoire de la mise-en-scène dans le théâtre réligieux français du moyen âge.* New ed., 1951.

Craig, H. *English Religious Drama of the Middle Ages.* 1955.

Creizenach, W. *Geschichte des neueren Dramas.* 5 vols., 1893–1916. By far the best history of the drama ever written for the period covered. Most others lean considerably on the facts provided by Creizenach even when they do not share his opinions. Vols. I and II cover the Middle Ages.

Du Méril, E. *Origines latins du théâtre moderne.* 1849.

Duriez, G. *La Théologie dans le drame réligieux en Allemagne au moyen âge.* 1914.

Dürre, K. *Die Mercatorszene im lateinliturgischen, altdeutschen und altfranzösischen religiösen Drama.* 1915.

Farnham, W. *The Medieval Heritage of Elizabethan Tragedy.* 1936.

Foulon, C. *L'Oeuvre de Jehan Bodel.* 1958.

Frank, Grace. *The Medieval French Drama.* 1954.

Gering-Rook, E. *Das Theater des 15. -16. Jahrhunderts.* 1932.

Gregor, J. *Der Schauspielführer.* 5 vols., 1952–57.

Harbage, A. *Annals of English Drama, 975–1700.* 1940.

Henshaw, M. "The Attitude of the Church towards the Stage at the End of the Middle Ages," *Medievalia et Humanistica,* Vol. VII (1952).

—— "A Survey of Studies in Medieval Drama 1933–1950," *Progress of Medieval and Renaisssance Studies,* Bulletin No. 21.

Kennard, J. S. *Italian Theatre: a History.* . . . 2 vols., 1932.

Kindermann, H. *Theatergeschichte Europas.* 2 vols. published, 1957–59. Vol. I, *Das Theater der Antike und des Mittelalters.*

Mackenzie, W. R. *The English Moralities from the Point of View of Allegory.* 1914.

Mauermann, S. *Die Bühnenanweisungen im deutschen Drama bis 1700.* 1911.

Meyer, Helene. "Die Predigten in den Miracles de Nostre Dame par personnages," *Romanische Forschungen,* Vol. XXXI (1912).

Michael, W. "Das deutsche Drama und Theater vor der Reformation. Ein Forschungsbericht," *DVLG*, Vol. XXXI (1957).
—— *Die geistlichen Prozessionsspiele in Deutschland.* 1947.
Moore, J. B. *The Comic and the Realistic in British Drama.* 1925.
Mortensen, J. *Le Théâtre français au moyen âge*, trans. from the Swedish by E. Philipot. 1903.
Nicoll, A. *British Drama.* 1927.
—— *The Development of the Theatre.* 1937.
—— *The English Theatre.* 1936.
—— *Masks, Mimes and Miracles.* 1931.
Oliver, T. E. *Jacques Milet's Drama "La Destruction de Troie la grant"; Its Principal Sources, Its Dramatic Structure* (doctoral dissertation, Heidelberg). 1899.
Owst, G. R. *Literature and Pulpit in Medieval England.* 1933.
Reich, H. *Der Mimus.* 1903.
Reuschel, K. T. *Die deutschen Weltgerichtsspiele des Mittelalters und der Reformationszeit.* 1906.
Rolland, J. *Théâtre comique en France avant le XVe siècle.* 1926.
Rudwin, M. J. *Der Teufel in den deutschen geistlichen Spielen des Mittelalters und der Reformationszeit.* 1915.
Schmidt, K. W. C. *Die Darstellung von Christi Höllenfahrt in den deutschen und den ihnen verwandten Spielen des Mittelalters.* 1915.
Seefeldt, P. *Studien über die verschiedenen mittelalterlichen dramatischen Fassungen der Barbara-Legende . . .* (doctoral dissertation, Greifswald). 1908.
Southern, R. *The Medieval Theatre in the Round.* 1958.
Stammler, W. *Das religiöse Drama im deutschen Mittelalter.* 1925.
Stoephasurs, Renata von. *Die Gestalt des Pilatus in den mittelalterlichen Passionsspielen.* 1938.
Stratman, C. J. *Bibliography of Medieval Drama.* 1954. Useful for English drama in particular. Considerable omissions of material in other literatures.
Stuart, D. C. *Stage Directions in France in the Middle Ages.* 1910.
Stumpfl, R. *Kultspiele der Germanen als Ursprung des mittelalterlichen Dramas.* 1936. Extremely biased presentation of the hypothesis that drama is derived from popular rituals.
Tigg, E. R. "Is *Elckerlijc* Prior to *Everyman?*" *Journal of English and Germanic Philology*, Vol. XXXVIII (1939).
Tomlinson, W. E. *Der Herodescharakter im englischen Drama.* 1934.

Torraca, F. *Il teatro italiano dei secoli XIII, XIV, e XV.* 1885.
Vocht, H. de. *Everyman: a Comparative Study of Texts and Sources.* 1947.
Ward, A. W. *A History of English Dramatic Literature to the Death of Queen Anne.* 3 vols., rev. ed., 1899.
Wickham, G. *Early English Stages.* Vol. I, 1959.

THE BEAST EPIC

Texts

Aesopica, ed. B. E. Perry. Volume I (1952) contains the Greek and Latin texts of the fables, with commentary. No more published to date.
Baldwinus. *Reinardus vulpes,* ed. W. Knorr. 1860. This is the Latin translation of Willem's poem.
Cambridge Reinaert Fragments (Culemann Fragments), ed. K. Breul. 1927. An edition of the rhyming poetical version printed in Antwerp in 1487, of which only fragments are extant.
Ecbasis captivi per tropologiam, ed. K. Strecker. 1935. Allegorical poem using some of the incidents from the beast epic.
Guillaume le clerc. *Le Bestiaire,* ed. R. Reinsch, 1892; trans. D. C. Druce, 1936. One of the numerous vernacular versions of the bestiary, with allegorical interpretations.
Heinrich von Alckmar. *Reinke de Vos,* ed. F. Prien. 1887. This is the Low German version printed at Lübeck in 1498 as "Reyneke de Vos" and at Rostock in 1517 as "Vom Reyneken dem Vosse." The poem was frequently reprinted thereafter. Prien's edition also contains a 222-line fragment of Reinaert II from the Antwerp edition. Rev. ed. by A. Leitzmann and K. Voretzsch, 1925.
Heinrich der Glichezaere, *Reinhart Fuchs,* ed. G. Baesecke, with introduction by K. Voretzsch, 1925; ed. Ingeborg Schröbler, 1952; modern German trans. by G. Baesecke, under title "Das älteste Tierepos aus der Sprache des 12. Jahrhunderts in unsere Übertragung," 1926.
Hervieux, L. *Les Fabulistes latins depuis le siècle d'Auguste jusqu'à la fin du moyen âge.* 5 vols., 1893–99.
Die Historie van Reynaert de Vos, nach der Delfter Ausgabe von 1485, ed. L. Suhl. 1783.
The History of Reynard the Fox, ed. W. J. Thoms, 1844. First

reprint of the Caxton translation.

The History of Reynard the Fox, ed. D. B. Sands. 1960. This is the original text of the Caxton version with modernized spelling. Very useful introduction. Better than any of the very numerous modernizations.

Die Hystorie van Reynaert die Vos naar den druk van 1479 vergeleken met William Caxton Engelesche vertaling, ed. J. W. Muller and H. Logeman. 1892. This is the Gouda prose version, originally printed by Gheraert Leeu in 1479, reprinted by J. Jacobszoon van der Meer at Delft in 1485.

Jacquemars Gielée. *Renard le nouvel,* ed. J. Houdoy. 1874.

Nivardus of Ghent. *Ysengrimus,* ed. E. Voigt, 1884; modern German trans. by A. Schönfelder, 1955.

Physiologus latinus, ed. F. J. Carmody. Versio B, 1939; versio y, 1941.

Reinaert: Willems Gedicht van den Vos Reinaerde und die Umarbeitung und Fortsetzung Reinaerts Historie, ed. E. Martin, 1874. Contains *Reinaert I* and *II.*

Reinaerts Historie, ed. P. de Keyser. 1938. Facsimile of the Brussels MS of *Reinaert II.*

Reinke de Vos, English trans. by T. J. Arnold, 1954; modern German trans. by K. Simrock, 2d ed., 1877: by D. W. Soltau, 1803, frequently repr.

Le Roman de Renard, ed. E. Martin, 3 vols., 1882–87; ed. M. Roques, 1948–; modern French trans. by L. Robert-Busquet, 1935.

Le Roman de Renard le contrefait, ed. G. Raynaud and H. Lemaitre. 1914.

Rose, W. *The Epic of the Beasts.* 1924. Contains *Reynard the Fox* and the *Physiologus* in translation.

Van den Vos Reinaerde, ed. J. W. Muller. 2 vols., 1939–42. Contains *Reinaert I* only.

Van den Vos Reinaerde. Modern German trans. by E. Poll. 1914. A German version of *Reinaert I.*

Van den Vos Reynaerde, ed. according to the Comburg and Darmstadt MSS by F. B. Hellema, according to the Dyck MS by H. Degering. 1921.

Van den Vos Reynaerde: Diplomatisch uitgegeven naar de bronnen voor het jaar 1500, ed. W. G. Hellinga. 1952. Contains all the Middle Dutch prose and verse versions and the Latin version of Willem's poem in parallel columns.

White, T. H. *The Book of Beasts.* 1954. This is an adaptation of a twelfth-century Latin version.

Secondary Works

Blaser, R. H. *Ulrich Boner, un fabuliste suisse du XIVe siècle.* 1949. This contains a history of the use of various Aesop fables.

Bossuat, R. *Le Roman de Renard.* 1957.

Foulet, L. *Le Roman de Renard.* 1914.

Graf, A. *Die Grundlagen des Reineke Fuchs,* eine vergleichende Studie. 1920.

Keidel, G. C. *A Manual of Aesopic Fable Literature* . . . *to 1500.* 1896.

Muller, J. W. *Critische commentar op Van de Vos Reinaerde.* 1917.

Sisam, K. Introduction to *Chaucer's Nun's Priest's Tale.* 1927.

Sudre, L. *Les Sources du Roman de Renart.* 1893.

Vercouillie, J. *Diersage en Reinaert de Vos.* 1925.

Index

England (*Continued*)
mas plays in, 285-87; guilds in, 289; influence of classical culture in, 12-13; lyric poetry in, 274-75, 403; saints' plays in, 314-15; translation of Reynard story in, 351
Entertainers, professional, 278-79; *see also* Troubadours
Ephesian Tale, The, 25
Epic, 6, 31-32, 53; division of into two sections, 56-57; oral, 191; structure of vernacular, 32; theories of formation of, 176; *see also* Beast epic; Germanic epic; National epic
Epithets, periphrastic (*kennings*), 179, 188-89
Epopée, 68
Erec (Hartmann von Aue), 110-12; conflict of values in, 108, 109-10; character of hero, 86, 96, 120; earliest extant Arthurian romance, 101; King Arthur in, 85; problem of moderation in, 92
Erziehungsroman, 134-35
Esclados li Ros, 102
Estampie, 60
Ethical principles, 13, 29; in *Chanson de Roland,* 167-68; of Germanic epic, 177-78; *see also* Values
Ethiopica, 25
Etienne de Bourbon, 73
Eulogies, 51
Europe, influence of classical culture in, 12-13; *see also specific countries*
Evangelium Nicodemi, 114
Evangelium secundum marcas argenti, 18, 237
Everyman, 322-24, 407
Evil, *see* Good and Evil
Exempla, 21, 25, 72-73, 356

Fables, 66, 78; *see also* Aesop's fables
Fabliaux, 72, 74-75, 346, 355-56
Fabulae Milesianae, 25
Facetiae, 346, 356
Fairy stories, 30
Fairy tale motif, 177, 205
Family ties, importance of, 174, 177, 178, 183-84; in *Beowulf,* 189-90; Wolfram on, 133-34
Farce, 327, 408
Fasting and Carnival, contest between, 321
Fate, acceptance of, 36, 177, 183, 214
Feast of Fools, 287
Feirefiz, 118, 129-30
Fertility king, 113, 115
Fertility plays, 277
Festivals, seasonal, 277, 279
Feudalism, 48-49, 57, 61; *see also* Chivalry
Fiction, romance as, 69-70
Figure poems, 219
Finn, King, 186
Finn cycle, 81
Fisher King, 124-25; *see also* Anfortas
Flagellants, 303
Flanders, Reynard stories in, 347-51
Fleury play book, 284, 305, 315
Folklore, 24; effects of, 30-32; motif of, 81-82, 145, 177, 189-90
Folk lyric, 222
Folquet de Marseilles, 244
Foulon, M., 310
Fox, rivalry between wolf and, 78, 79; *see also* Reynard
France: allegorical drama in, 321, 407-8; Arthurian romances in, 82-83, 88; Easter and Christmas plays in, 285-87; influence of classical culture in, 12-13; life in twelfth century in, 57-59;

Ornatus difficilis, 9-10, 245
Ornatus facilis, 9-10, 245
Otfried of Weissenburg, 49, 50, 223
Otto IV, 266, 269
Ovid, 3, 4; influence of, 219; works of, 6
Owain, 105, 106, 112; *see also Yvain*

Paganism: fear of reversion to, 3, 10, 36; justification for study of works of, 20; origin of Grail story in, 114-16; rejection of values of, 13
Palindromes, 219
Panegyric poetry, 224
Panzer, F., 202
Paris, Gaston, 31, 94
Parody, 18, 65; use of, 229-37, by Horace, 63; by Neidhart von Reuental, 273; by Walther von der Vogelweide, 265
Parzival, 116-35, 393; Arab influence on, 27; as one of Arthurian romances, 88; conflict of values in, 108, 109-10; as Grail story, 100, 113-14; love element in, 96; sins of hero, 132; story summary, 117-22; structure of, 130-33; Trevrezent and Parzival, 124, 125-28
Passion d'Arras, 291-92; *see also* Arras
Passion des Jongleurs, 290
Passion du Palatinus, 290-91
Passion de Semur, 291-92
Passion plays, 279, 287-303 *passim,* 408, 409; incorporation of Old Testament scenes in, 318; in vernacular, 281, 282
Pastoral drama, 326-27
Pastourelle (pastorela), 217, 218, 237, 252-54, 255, 307
Patronage and patrons, 2, 35, 36,

60; desire for, 38-40; women as, 58, 96
Paulinus of Nola, 36
Paulus Diaconus, 331
"Paysage idéal de printemps," 224-26; *see also* Spring motif
"Peasant" poetry, 273
Pede [feet], 244-48
Pèlerinage de Charlemagne, 85, 173
Perceval stories, 85, 87, 101; *see also Parzival*
Percy, Thomas, 30
Performers, 295, 296; clerics and deacons in church as, 284, 287-88; *see also* Actors, professional
Persia, influence of, 24
Persius, 4
Petrus Alfonsi, 25
Petrus Dorlandus, 323
Pfaffe Amis, 74
Pfaffe Kuonrat, *see* Konrad, Pfaffe
Pfaffe Lamprecht, 158, 397
Phaedrus, 330
Philip II, 266-67, 269, 272
Philo or Philo Judaeus, 19
Philosophy, 11-12, 29, 79; courtly code of behavior and, 93; Walther von der Vogelweide and, 271
Phyllis and Flora, 226, 238-39
Physiologus, versions of, 329, 413
Pierre de St. Cloud, 342, 347n
Piers Plowman, 37, 355
Planh, see Laments
Planctus (elegy), 224
Plato, 11, 24, 99
Plautus, 66, 276, 277
Plays, 277; *see also* Drama
Poetry, 6, 8-10, 216-18; *see also* specific forms of, e.g., Lyric
Poetry of reflection, 258
Poets, training of, 41-43
Political poetry, 233, 252; in English cycle plays, 299-300; of

ommended readings in, 391-98; structure of vernacular, 32; treatment of women in, 94-100 *passim; see also Chanson de Geste*

Roman de la Rose, 15, 69, 354-55

Roman de Renart: branches and groupings of, 341-43, 413; characters in, 345-46; relations between the sexes in, 346; satire in, 343-45

Romantics, The, xii, 30-31

Rome: *matière de,* 80; medieval scholars' knowledge of, 5

"Romulus," fables of, 330

Rondeau, 60

Roques, M., 342

Rosengarten, 215

Rudel, Jaufré, 242, 402

Rutebeuf, 312-13, 314, 402, 409

Sacred writings, influence of, 18-22; *see also* Bible; New Testament; Old Testament

Saints, lives of, 22, 73, 356; plays based on, 52, 289, 303-12

Salmon and Marcolf, 108

Salut d'amour, 263

Santa Claus, *see* Nicholas, Saint

Sapphic strophe, 220

Satira (social comment), 224

Satire, 14, 18, 37, 38, 65; antifeminine, 95; in beast epics, 52-53, 328, 338-44 *passim,* 350-51; history of, 63-64; Juvenal's, 63, 64; in lyric poetry, 217, 218, 229-32; in *pastourelle,* 254; in poems of Walther von der Vogelweide, 266-67; in pure comedy, 325-26; Rutebeuf's, 312; social, 63-64; of the twelfth century, 54

Scandinavia: native sagas in, 75; poems, 179-80; *see also Edda* songs

Scheherazade, 56

Schoepperle, Gertrude, 138

Scholasticism, influence of, 60

Schwänke, 346, 356

Schwietering, J., 50, 146

Scyld, 185

Sea-monster, *see* Grendel

Sedes, 297

Seege and Batayle of Troye, 157

Seinte Resurrection, La, 409

Self-restraint, 91-92

Seneca, 4, 66

Seneca, the elder, 20

"Sepulchrum," 281n

Sequence (*sequentia*), 227-28

Serlo of Bayeux, 228

Serlo of Wilton, 228

Sermons, 21, 37, 73, 356

Servius, 19

Shakespeare, William, 157

Shepherds' play, 286, 300, 326

"Shrine of Love," 149-50

Sicily: Greek civilization of parts of, 26; Moslem communities in, 26-27

Siegfried: character of, 210-11, 213; Dietrich and, 207-8, 215; stories of, 75, 85, 194, 204-8; *see also* Brünhilde; *Nibelungenlied*

Sievers, E., 180-81

Sigmund, 186, 191, 195

Sigune, 119-33 *passim*

Sigurd, 193, 195-97 *passim*

Simon or Chèvre d'or, 156

Singers, professional, 32, 35, 47-48; *see also* Troubadours

Sins, 3, 14-17; from Christian point of view, 63-64; Parzival's, 132

Sirventès (social or political comment poems), 217, 218, 251-52, 266

Snorri Sturluson, 192

Social comment (*satira*), 224